American Grand Strategy in the Mediterranean during World War II

This book offers a thorough reinterpretation of U.S. engagement with the Mediterranean during World War II. Andrew Buchanan argues that the United States, far from being a reluctant participant in a "peripheral" theater, had substantial grand-strategic interests in the region. By the end of the war, the Mediterranean was effectively an American lake, with the United States enjoying a predominant position resting on military, political, and economic interests and assets extending from North Africa, via Italy, Spain, France, and the Balkans, to the Middle East. This book examines the multilayered processes by which this hegemonic position was assembled and consolidated. It discusses the changing character of the Anglo-American alliance, the establishment of postwar spheres of influence, the nature of presidential leadership, and the common interest of all the leaders of the "Grand Alliance" in blocking the development of social revolutions emerging from the chaos of war, occupation, and economic breakdown.

Andrew Buchanan is a Lecturer in the Department of History at the University of Vermont. He received his PhD and MA in History from Rutgers University, and earned his BA in Modern History from Oxford University. Buchanan teaches American history, global history, and military history. He has published articles on the diplomatic, military, and cultural history of World War II in the *Journal of Contemporary History*, *Diplomacy and Statecraft*, *Journal of Transatlantic Studies*, and *Global War Studies*.

American Grand Strategy in the Mediterranean during World War II

ANDREW BUCHANAN

University of Vermont

CAMBRIDGE
UNIVERSITY PRESS

CAMBRIDGE
UNIVERSITY PRESS

University Printing House, Cambridge CB2 8BS, United Kingdom

Cambridge University Press is part of the University of Cambridge.

It furthers the University's mission by disseminating knowledge in the pursuit of education, learning and research at the highest international levels of excellence.

www.cambridge.org
Information on this title: www.cambridge.org/9781107620384

© Andrew Buchanan 2014

First published 2014
First paperback edition 2016

A catalogue record for this publication is available from the British Library

Library of Congress Cataloguing in Publication data
Buchanan, Andrew, 1958–
American grand strategy in the Mediterranean during World War II / Andrew Buchanan, University of Vermont.
    pages   cm
Includes bibliographical references and index.
ISBN 978-1-107-04414-2 (hardback)
1. World War, 1939–1945 – Mediterranean Region   2. World War, 1939–1945 – Campaigns – Mediterranean Region.   3. World War, 1939–1945 – Diplomatic history.   4. Mediterranean Region – Strategic aspects.   5. Strategy – History – 20th century.   6. United States – Military policy.   I. Title.
D766.B83   2013
940.53′73091822–dc23   2013023412

ISBN 978-1-107-04414-2 Hardback
ISBN 978-1-107-62038-4 Paperback

To Angus and Brenda Buchanan

Contents

Figures
(with original captions)

Acknowledgments

I would like to thank all those who have collaborated with me on this project. At the head of that list are my friends – and doctoral committee members – Michael Adas, Susan Carruthers, David Foglesong, and Warren Kimball at Rutgers University, and Mark Stoler at the University of Vermont. Their encouragement and intellectual stimulation were indispensible. Their support was complemented by that of my friends and colleagues in the History Department at the University of Vermont; among them, Charlie Briggs and Nicole Phelps were particularly helpful in navigating the rapids of publication.

I am indebted to the staff at numerous archives and libraries for their unfailingly generous help, especially those at the Franklin D. Roosevelt Library in Hyde Park, New York; U.S. National Archives in College Park, Maryland; British National Archives in Kew, London; Sterling Memorial Library at Yale; Seely G. Mudd Library at Princeton; Hoover Institution at Stanford; Special Collections department of Columbia University Library; New York Public Library; Imperial War Museum, London; Alexander Library at Rutgers, New Brunswick; and Bailey-Howe Library at the University of Vermont. I am especially grateful to Amy Schmidt at the National Archives for sharing her insights into the secrets of the Shepherd Project and to Amanda Weimar for her help with documents on OSS operations in Morocco.

Bob Clark and audiovisual archivist Matt Hanson at the FDR Library were invaluable in tracking down photos, as were Don Smith of the 57th Fighter Group Association; J. C. Hare; and his father, pilot and photographer James "Rabbit" Hare. Together, they have given the book an additional visual dimension.

I owe a great deal to Lewis Bateman, senior editor at Cambridge University Press, who saw some merit in this project, and to his editorial assistant Shaun Vigil, who kept things moving along. Thanks also go to my copy editor, Andrea Wright of PETT Fox, Inc., as well as to project manager Bindu Vinod and the production team at Newgen Knowledge Works who made the production process as quick, efficient, and painless as possible.

Special thanks are due to Mark and Judy Nord, who provided accommodation (and climbing trips!) in Washington, DC, and to Phil and Cecilia Lowndes, who housed me during my visit to Kew. Thanks also go to my friends and coworkers at Jarvik Heart in New York City, who helped me juggle work and research. Without their support, this book could not have been written.

It helps to be part of a family of historians. My parents, Angus and Brenda, and my brother Tom provided constant encouragement and sound advice. I also have benefited enormously from the interest shown in this project by many members of the vibrant community in my adopted hometown of Essex, New York. In particular I thank Bryan Burke, Mac MacDevitt, Richard Robbins, and Sharp Swan for their interest, information, and ideas. Sometimes, it turns out, it really does take a village. And last – but by no means least – I am forever grateful to my companion and mapmaker extraordinaire, Mary Nell Bockman, without whom none of this would have been possible.

As I was wrapping up this project in the fall of 2012, I learned with great sadness of the death of my old Oxford tutor, Maurice Keen. Although we rarely saw eye to eye on things in the modern world, Maurice was unfailingly supportive both during my time as an undergraduate at Balliol and later when I returned to academia in 2002. It would, I think, have made him immensely happy to see this book in print.

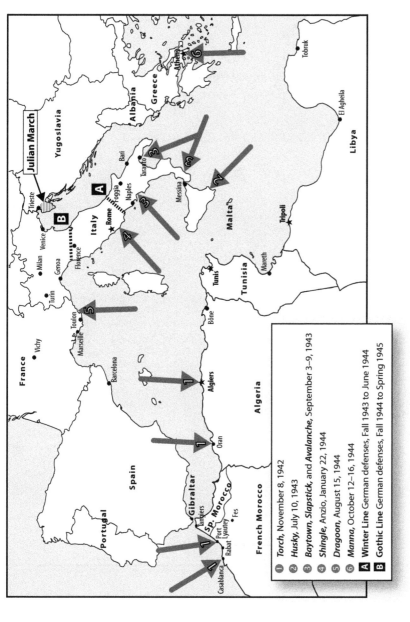

MAP 1. Map of the Mediterranean showing major Allied landings, 1942–1945

Source: Editable map by Map Resources. Design work by Mary Nell Bockman. Finished map used by permission of Mary Nell Bockman. © Map Resources.

Julian March

France
Vichy
Turin
Milan
Venice
Trieste
Genoa
Florence
Marseille
Toulon
Rome
Foggia
Naples
Bari
Taranto
Italy
Messina
Malta
Tunis
Tunisia
Mareth
Bône
Algiers
Oran
Algeria
Barcelona
Spain
Gibraltar
Tangiers
Port Lyautey
Rabat
Casablanca
Fes
Sp. Morocco
French Morocco
Portugal
Yugoslavia
Albania
Greece
Athens
Libya
Tripoli
El Agheila
Tobruk

1 *Torch,* November 8, 1942
2 *Husky,* July 10, 1943
3 *Baytown, Slapstick,* and *Avalanche,* September 3–9, 1943
4 *Shingle,* Anzio, January 22, 1944
5 *Dragoon,* August 15, 1944
6 *Manna,* October 12–16, 1944
A Winter Line German defenses, Fall 1943 to June 1944
B Gothic Line German defenses, Fall 1944 to Spring 1945

MAP 2. Map of the Mediterranean

Source: Editable map by Map Resources. Design work by Mary Nell Bockman. Finished map used by permission of Mary Nell Bockman. © Map Resources.

Introduction

For midshipmen at the United States Naval Academy at Annapolis, the social highlight of their second year is the Ring Dance.[1] It is an event replete with tradition and symbolism during which the midshipman's class ring is ceremonially dipped in a brass binnacle filled with water from world's oceans; the ceremony makes it clear that the young officer can expect to see service in all of them. It is surely, as *Life* magazine described it in 1939, an "odd custom," but it is one that could only be practiced – and taken seriously – by the navy of a world-dominant power.[2] It was not always thus. When the Ring Dance was first held in 1925, the binnacle was filled only with water from the "three U.S. seas" – the Atlantic, Pacific, and Caribbean – representing the waters in which the bulk of an officer's service might be performed and reflecting the essentially defensive posture of U.S. strategy.[3] Water from the rest of the world's great waterways – the Mediterranean Sea and the Indian and Arctic Oceans – was added in 1944 as U.S. military might overspread the globe. The meaning was clear; as one French official noted warily, the "change symbolized that the United States had assumed the role of world power."[4]

By the end of World War II, the Mediterranean had become, as writer on geopolitical affairs Joseph Roucek bluntly described it in 1953, an "American lake."[5] As the fighting ended, Washington moved quickly to consolidate its newly won regional dominance, utilizing the necessity of returning the body

---

[1] My thanks to Bryan Burke, USNA class of 1966, who explained the significance of the Ring Dance.

[2] *Life*, June 12, 1939.

[3] Ibid.

[4] Wasson to State Department, July 6, 1945, *Foreign Relations of the United States* (henceforth FRUS) *1945, The Conference of Berlin (The Potsdam Conference)*, 1:997.

[5] Joseph S. Roucek, "The Geopolitics of the Mediterranean," *American Journal of Economics and Sociology* 13, no. 1 (October 1953), 82.

of the recently deceased Turkish ambassador to his homeland to dispatch the fast battleship *Missouri* to the Mediterranean in early 1946. The ensuing "battleship cruise" furnished, in U.S. ambassador to Greece Lincoln MacVeagh's ponderous phrase, an "ocular demonstration of America's naval strength" in and around the landlocked sea.[6] The *Missouri*'s demonstrative voyage was widely interpreted as a symbol of Washington's undisputed control over the Mediterranean and as a token of its willingness to confront the perceived extension of Russian influence into the so-called northern-tier countries of Greece, Turkey, and Iran. It also signified that the mantle of senior partner in the region was passing from Britain, the prewar hegemon, to the United States.

In October 1946, Washington further strengthened its naval presence, deploying the new aircraft carrier *Franklin D. Roosevelt* to the Mediterranean and using it to project dramatic displays of air power over actual or potential trouble spots from Athens to Algiers. From then on at least one aircraft carrier battle group – the basic unit of modern naval power projection – would be permanently on station in the Mediterranean. In 1948, the U.S. Navy recognized the region's strategic importance by establishing the Sixth Fleet, headquartered in Naples and drawing on numerous wartime base and port facilities established in the Mediterranean. Throughout the Cold War, the Sixth Fleet operated an average of forty major warships in the Mediterranean.[7] In the immediate postwar period, the Air Force followed suit, reactivating wartime airbases from Casablanca to Wheelus Field, Libya, and securing air transit rights through a corridor linking Morocco to the Philippines.[8] In 1954, the first nuclear weapons to be based outside of the United States were sent to U.S. forces in Morocco, and the same year American-led exercises rehearsed a coordinated naval, air, and nuclear response to a projected Russian incursion into the Mediterranean.[9]

These moves consolidated U.S. military predominance in the Mediterranean, strengthened the "southern flank" of the newly formed North Atlantic Treaty Organization (NATO), and provided Washington with a strategic "ace in the hole" with which to project power into Europe.[10] This military force structure rested not only on the successful and large-scale deployment of armed forces in the Mediterranean during World War II, but also on the broad-fronted advance of U.S. political and economic interests with which it was inevitably intertwined. This presence was evident throughout the Mediterranean basin, from

---

[6] Lincoln MacVeagh, quoted in Edward J. Sheehy, *The U.S. Navy, the Mediterranean, and the Cold War, 1945–1947* (Westport, CT: Greenwood Press, 1992), 29.

[7] See C. T. Sandars, *America's Overseas Garrisons: The Leasehold Empire*, (New York: Oxford University Press, 2000), 242.

[8] See Melvyn P. Leffler, *A Preponderance of Power: National Security, the Truman Administration, and the Cold War* (Stanford, CA: Stanford University Press, 1992), 56–59.

[9] See Simon Ball, *Bitter Sea: The Brutal World War II Fight for the Mediterranean* (New York: Harper, 2009), 327.

[10] Roucek, "The Geopolitics of the Mediterranean," 86.

the sprawling U.S. military bases in Morocco to burgeoning commercial investment in Egypt, and from accelerating intervention in Italian politics to blunt the electoral challenge of the Communist Party to the discrete contacts with Franco's Spain that by 1953 would result in Madrid's de facto membership in NATO.

Without substantial wartime preparation, this postwar deployment of U.S. power into the Mediterranean would have been an act of baseless bravado; with it, Washington was able to step confidently into the Greek civil war in 1947 and to strengthen its hand in the Middle East by underwriting the founding of the state of Israel the following year. On top of all this, American business interests pushed eagerly through the doors "blown open," as historian Lloyd Gardner put it, by the "gales of war," taking advantage of the establishment of regimes of U.S.-sponsored "free trade" to drive deep into the economy of the entire region.[11]

While these advances were impressive, the full measure of Washington's political accomplishment in the wartime Mediterranean can only be judged by weighing what did *not* happen as well as what did. In contrast to the years following World War I, when war-generated devastation and economic breakdown gave rise to revolutionary explosions across Europe, the second world war in a generation culminated in Western Europe and the Mediterranean in a relatively smooth transition to a stable new capitalist order under U.S. hegemony.[12] This outcome was by no means inevitable. Throughout the war, U.S. policy makers were haunted by the specter of revolution, whether in the form of workers' insurrections in Italy, France, and Spain, "native" uprisings in French North Africa, or popular resistance to the Axis occupation of the Balkans spilling over into social revolution. These fears were not misplaced, as the "autoliberation" of Naples in October 1943, the outpouring of Algerian nationalism at Sétif in May 1945, and the victory of Tito's Partisans in Yugoslavia demonstrate. Yet by a combination of armed force, adept – if often domestically unpopular – political maneuver, and the forging of a common front with Moscow, Washington and its new allies among regional elites succeeded in containing popular anticapitalist and anticolonial upsurges.

The establishment of U.S. hegemony in the Mediterranean is all the more striking given that the region had not loomed large in American diplomatic and strategic thinking since the wars against the so-called Barbary Pirates in the

---

[11] See Lloyd Gardner, *Economic Aspects of New Deal Diplomacy* (Madison: University of Wisconsin Press, 1964), especially 220–226.

[12] Throughout I use the term "hegemony" in the Gramscian sense of implying leadership of a system of states, and not simply as a synonym for "dominance." Hegemony can include both military coercion and the ideological and political leadership that convinces the elites of subordinate states that the hegemon is acting in their general interest. See David Forgacs (ed.), *The Antonio Gramsci Reader* (New York: NYU Press, 2000), especially 249–251, and discussion in Giovanni Arrighi, *The Long Twentieth Century: Money, Power, and the Origins of Our Times* (New York: Verso, 2010), 28–37.

early nineteenth century. The Barbary Wars (1801–1805, 1815) prompted the development of a blue-water navy and signaled the emergence of the United States as an important but junior power in the Atlantic world.[13] In their aftermath – and not surprisingly in a seaway policed by the British Royal Navy – U.S. commercial interests in the Mediterranean required the support of only a modest naval squadron operating from the British base at Port Mahon, Minorca.[14] In the early twentieth century, the Mediterranean offered a stage on which to show off the rising power of the United States rather than a base for sustained power projection. President Theodore Roosevelt dispatched a battle fleet to the region in 1905 in a demonstration of support for France during the First Moroccan Crisis.[15] Four years later, the "Great White Fleet" transited the Suez Canal and the Mediterranean on its round-the-world cruise, detaching units to garner good publicity by assisting earthquake victims in Naples.

During World War I, U.S. naval units operating from the British base at Gibraltar conducted anti-submarine patrols in the western Mediterranean, but after the war, Washington's interest again declined. During the interwar years, the U.S. Navy maintained a sporadic presence in the Mediterranean, policing the eastern coast of the Adriatic prior to the consolidation of Yugoslavia, evacuating Greek refugees during the Greco-Turkish war, and "showing the flag" in support of U.S. business interests in Syria, Lebanon, and Spain.[16] While this naval activity helped reinforce Washington's diplomatic presence in Europe, its modest scale – and the equally modest significance of the region to the overall development of U.S. overseas trade – reflected the lack of any overarching interest in the Mediterranean. Washington viewed it primarily as a region of British influence, recognizing London's desire to protect both its "imperial highway" from Britain to India via Gibraltar and Suez and its oil interests in the eastern Mediterranean and the Middle East.[17]

American policy makers remained largely indifferent to the looming conflict between Britain and Italy in the mid-1930s, a stance reinforced by Italian dictator Benito Mussolini's positive standing in U.S. ruling circles.[18] In response to the Italian invasion of Ethiopia in 1935, Washington established nonbinding "moral" sanctions against Rome – measures that actually allowed U.S. oil

---

[13] See Frank Lambert, *The Barbary Wars: American Independence in the Atlantic World* (New York: Hill and Wang, 2007), 201.
[14] See Sheehy, *The U.S. Navy*, 10.
[15] See Seward W. Livermore, "The American Navy as a Factor in World Politics, 1903–1913," *The American Historical Review* 63, no. 4 (1958).
[16] See Herbert Maza, "Turkish-Arab Economic Relations with the United States," *World Affairs* 143, no. 3 (1979).
[17] See Hector C. Bywater, "The Changing Balance of Forces in the Mediterranean," *International Affairs* 16, no. 3 (1937); Michael Simpson, "Superhighway to World Wide Web: The Mediterranean in British Imperial Strategy, 1900–1945," in John Hattendorf (ed.), *Naval Strategy and Policy in the Mediterranean* (London: Routledge, 2000).
[18] See John P. Diggins, *Mussolini and Fascism: The View from America* (Princeton, NJ: Princeton University Press, 1972).

exports to Italy to expand – and for much of the Spanish Civil War it joined London and Paris in imposing an arms embargo that effectively undermined the warmaking capacity of the Republican government.[19] None of these policies amounted to a consistent approach to the Mediterranean as a region.

Viewed in the light of America's modest and often inconsistent prewar aspirations in the region, its emergence barely five years later as *the* predominant power in the Mediterranean stands out in sharp relief. By the end of World War II, the United States had replaced Britain as the major power in the region, with its influence resting on its wartime operational experience, on the continuing presence of American arms, and on its residual network of airbases, ports, and military depots. Behind this lay the largely invisible but always critical networks of contacts forged by American diplomats, businessmen, aid workers, technical advisers, intelligence operatives, and military officers with their counterparts in other countries, which make international relations – and great power hegemony – work. A generation of U.S. leaders and officials had, in a few short years, come to know the Mediterranean world and to be known in it.

This book is a study of this dramatic transformation. It is a study necessitated by the fact that, despite the substantial accomplishments of U.S. military, political, and economic engagement, the idea that the United States had *any* strategic approach to the Mediterranean during World War II remains heretical. In both academic and popular histories the Mediterranean is almost invariably described in as a "diversionary theater," at worst a place where U.S. armies squandered many lives and wasted a great deal of time for little gain, at best a useful adjunct to the main story that would unfold in northern Europe after D-Day. In all its many versions this regnant master narrative draws strength from the bitter and protracted opposition of U.S. military leaders to any substantial U.S. involvement in the wartime Mediterranean. Some recent studies have argued that this opposition may not have been quite as protracted as has often been assumed, but the myth of unbending opposition to any Mediterranean front persists.[20] This version of events is grounded in the outlook of senior U.S. planners like General Albert Wedemeyer who, from the time of the first Allied discussions of an invasion of North Africa, viewed Mediterranean operations as the regrettable product of civilian intervention in military affairs and as the consequence of British Prime Minister Winston Churchill's "baneful influence" over President Roosevelt.[21]

---

[19] See Robert Dallek, *Franklin D. Roosevelt and American Foreign Policy, 1932–1945* (New York: Oxford University Press, 1979), 110–121; Dominic Tierney, *FDR and the Spanish Civil War: Neutrality and Commitment in the Struggle that Divided America* (Durham, NC: Duke University Press, 2007).

[20] See James Lacey, "Towards a Strategy: Creating an American Strategy for Global War, 1940–1943," in Williamson Murray, Richard Hart Sinnreich, and James Lacey (eds.), *The Shaping of Grand Strategy: Policy, Diplomacy, and War*, (Cambridge: Cambridge University Press, 2011), especially 204.

[21] Albert C. Wedemeyer, *Wedemeyer Reports!* (New York: Henry Holt, 1958), 330.

In the early 1950s, official U.S. Army histories by Maurice Matloff and Edwin Snell echoed this judgment, as did influential memoirs by General Dwight D. Eisenhower, Secretary of State Cordell Hull, and Secretary of War Henry Stimson.[22] As the Cold War deepened, some authors reworked the old trope of conflict between Washington's advocacy of a cross-Channel assault and London's pursuit of a self-interested "peripheral strategy" to highlight the alleged prescience of Churchill's "Mediterranean Strategy" as a vehicle for confronting Russian expansionism in the Balkans. In this version, expounded in Churchill's own influential history of the war as well as in works by Chester Wilmot and others, U.S. strategy is presented as a naïve, simplistic, and apolitical obstacle to canny and sophisticated British stratagems.[23] But while the poles of the debate shifted, the issues were still framed in narrowly *military* terms. Even as the "historians war" subsided and calmer voices insisted that both Britain and the United States had pursued strategies driven by pragmatic considerations rather than overarching "national ways of war," the idea that, for better or worse, the Mediterranean had been primarily a British concern remained fundamentally in place.[24]

Recent writers have challenged this master narrative, with Douglas Porch reimagining the Mediterranean as the "pivotal theater" without which the final assault on Germany would not have been possible.[25] However, even Porch's revisionist challenge to the view of the Mediterranean as a "cul-de-sac" remains fundamentally trapped within the framework of an argument over *military* strategy.[26] His approach, even as it draws substantially different conclusions, retains the bipolar Mediterranean-versus-cross-Channel framework of the argument first advanced by the Joint Chiefs of Staff in opposition to President Roosevelt's demands for action in North Africa. The problem, as Roosevelt well understood, was that the United States' orientation toward the countries

[22] See Maurice Matloff and Edwin M. Snell, *Strategic Planning for Coalition Warfare, 1941–1942* (Washington, DC: U.S. Government Printing Office, 1953); Maurice Matloff, *Strategic Planning for Coalition Warfare, 1943–1944* (Washington, DC: U.S. Government Printing Office, 1959); Dwight D. Eisenhower, *Crusade in Europe* (Garden City, NY: Doubleday, 1948); Cordell Hull, *The Memoirs of Cordell Hull* (New York: Macmillan, 1948); McGeorge Bundy and Henry L. Stimson, *On Active Service in Peace and War* (New York: Harper & Bros., 1948).

[23] Winston S. Churchill, *The Second World War*, 6 vols. (Boston: Houghton Mifflin, 1948–1954); also see Hanson Weightman Baldwin, *Great Mistakes of the War* (New York: Harper, 1950); Chester Wilmot, *The Struggle for Europe* (New York: Harper, 1952); Sir Arthur Bryant, *Triumph in the West; a History of the War Years Based on the Diaries of Field-Marshal Lord Alanbrooke, Chief of the Imperial General Staff* (New York: Doubleday, 1959).

[24] Trumbull Higgins, "The Anglo-American Historians' War in the Mediterranean, 1942–1945," *Military Affairs* 34, no. 3 (1970); Richard M. Leighton, "Overlord Revisited: An Interpretation of American Strategy in the European War, 1942–1944," *The American Historical Review* 68, no. 4 (1963); Michael Howard, *The Mediterranean Strategy in the Second World War* (New York: Frederick A. Praeger, 1968), 1–2.

[25] Douglas Porch, *The Path to Victory: The Mediterranean Theater in World War II* (New York: Farrar, Straus and Giroux, 2004), especially Conclusion; see also Ball, *Bitter Sea*.

[26] Porch, *Path to Victory*, 675.

of the Mediterranean – or any other part of the world, for that matter – could never be an exclusively military question. On the contrary, it always and inevitably involved the intertwining of the military with broader economic, diplomatic, and political concerns.

America's wartime engagement with the Mediterranean was not driven simply by the requirements of *military* strategy, but rather was the product of a broader *grand* strategy. Paul Kennedy offers a useful working definition of grand strategy, describing it as a "complex and multilayered thing" in which the "nonmilitary dimensions" are as important as the military, and in which the "longer-term and *political* purposes of [a] belligerent state" are primary.[27] War, as British military theorist Sir Basil Liddell Hart argued, must be waged with a "constant regard for the peace you desire:" war is always pregnant with the postwar, and must be conducted with that end in mind.[28] The potentially shocking corollary to this approach is that, contrary to popular belief – and to the early-war thinking of the Joint Chiefs – grand strategic wisdom does not necessarily lie in finding the shortest path to victory. With the postwar always in mind, Roosevelt understood that a U.S. victory required defeating the Axis powers while *simultaneously* preparing a new world order of capitalist nations and free markets structured under the hegemony of the United States. From this point of view, a premature cross-Channel invasion would not only be a highly risky military undertaking but would also short-circuit critical opportunities to shape the emerging postwar configuration of southern Europe and the Mediterranean. Developing such a grand strategy was not optional; the experience of World War I taught that if the foundations of postwar capitalist stability were not firmly established while fighting was still going on, war was likely to be followed by revolution.

The development of grand strategy inevitably puts a great deal of emphasis, as Williamson Murray points out, on national leaderships capable of "acting beyond the demands of the present," transcending the pressures simply to respond to contingent events in order to advance an overarching vision of both the war and the desired postwar.[29] By 1947, the difficult task of securing America's war-won hegemony required the complex coordination of a full spectrum of diplomatic, political, military, economic, and covert elements, leading to the establishment of the National Security Council, an executive council charged with grand strategic planning. As the United States rose to global hegemony during World War II, however, no such body existed. In the interwar years, military and military/political coordination had been improved

---

[27] Paul M. Kennedy, "Grand Strategy in War and Peace: Towards a Broader Definition," in Paul M. Kennedy, ed., *Grand Strategies in War and Peace* (New Haven, CT: Yale University Press 1991), 4, 2.
[28] Basil Liddell Hart, quoted in Kennedy, "Grand Strategy," 2.
[29] Williamson Murray, "Thoughts on Grand Strategy," in Murray et al. (eds.), *The Shaping of Grand Strategy*, 2.

by the establishment of the Joint Army-Navy Board in 1919 and by the organization, after 1935, of episodic contact between it and the State Department.[30]
But these arrangements were incapable of meeting the grand strategic challenge of world war. Even when the establishment of the Joint Chiefs of Staff in
early 1942 further strengthened Washington's capacity for strategic planning,
the initial desire of its members to eschew "politics" ensured that its focus, at
least for its critical first eighteen months or so, remained steadfastly and narrowly military.

In this context, presidential leadership assumed considerable importance.
Franklin D. Roosevelt might seem an unlikely grand strategist; widely recognized as a "master opportunist who disliked rigid planning," he led an administration notorious for its plethora of competing agencies and for its lack of
clear lines of decision making and accountability.[31] Yet beyond all the approxi-
mations, compromises, and short-term expedients, Roosevelt's actions were
informed by a set of ideas – assumptions rather than a clear and coherent ide-
ology – described by Warren Kimball as "Americanism."[32] In part a Wilsonian
vision of liberal American world leadership and in part a straightforward drive
to advance the U.S. military, economic, and political dominance, these ideas are
critical to understanding the overall grand strategic character of U.S. involvement in World War II. It was through war, as publisher Henry Luce argued
in his influential February 1941 *Life* editorial "The American Century," that
the United States could redeem the opportunities for world leadership squandered in 1919, neatly uniting self-interest and idealism in a "truly *American*
internationalism."[33]

Henry Luce's "American Century" reflected the sense of many ruling-class
figures that the time had come to "assert America's wealth and power on an
international stage."[34] In July 1940, Luce joined the Century Group, a secret-
ive bipartisan organization that included presidential speechwriter Robert
Sherwood as well as businessmen, academics, and theologians.[35] Lobbying for
a more aggressively interventionist foreign policy, members shared journalist
Walter Lippmann's exhortation to "make ready" to fulfill America's "destiny"
as leader of the "world of tomorrow."[36] These notions furnished Roosevelt

---

[30] See Mark Stoler, *Allies and Adversaries: The Joint Chiefs of Staff, the Grand Alliance, and U.S. Strategy in World War II* (Chapel Hill: University of North Carolina Press, 2000), 1–3.

[31] Ibid., 36.

[32] See especially Warren F. Kimball, *The Juggler: Franklin Roosevelt as Wartime Statesman* (Princeton, NJ: Princeton University Press, 1991), especially chapter IX.

[33] Henry Luce, "The American Century," *Life*, February 17 1941, reprinted in *Diplomatic History* 23, no. 2 (1999), 166.

[34] Kimball, *The Juggler*, 192; David Reynolds, *Munich to Pearl Harbor: Roosevelt's America and the Origins of the Second World War* (Chicago: Ivan R. Dee, 2001), 122.

[35] See Alan Brinkley, *The Publisher: Henry Luce and His American Century* (New York: Alfred A. Knopff, 2010), 267.

[36] Lippmann, quoted in Brinkley, *The Publisher*, 266.

FIGURE I.I. Roosevelt the navalist: the president under the guns of the USS *Indianapolis*, December 1, 1936. (Courtesy of Franklin D. Roosevelt Library.)

with a world-political framework that reached far beyond short-term opportunism – his typical "quick fixes, fire-fighting, and political balms and soothing oils" – and stimulated the broader vistas of his grand strategic impulses.[37]

Roosevelt's grand strategic notions were underpinned by the insights gleaned from seven years as Assistant Secretary of the Navy (1913–1920), by his admiration for the muscular nationalism of his uncle, Theodore Roosevelt, and by his long-standing respect for the writings of Alfred Thayer Mahan.[38] These formative influences and experiences, including intimate involvement in the global deployment of U.S. naval force, led Roosevelt to approach grand strategy with a navalist's appreciation for global position and regional command rather than with a simple urge to "get there fastest with the mostest." And, as Colin Gray points out, in the looming war for global hegemony, sea power would be the "engine of strategic possibilities."[39]

---

[37] Kimball, *The Juggler*, 192.

[38] See James Tertius de Kay, *Roosevelt's Navy: The Educations of a Warrior President, 1882–1920* (New York: Pegasus Books, 2012).

[39] Colin S. Gray, *The Leverage of Sea Power: The Strategic Advantage of Navies in War* (New York: The Free Press, 1992), 238.

In his feeling for grand strategy Roosevelt shared the approach of leading figures in the new field of security studies.[40] Emerging in response to the deep world crisis of the 1930s, nurtured in well-funded institutions including the Princeton-based Institute for Advanced Study (IAS) and the Yale Institute of International Studies, the new field was ecumenical and interdisciplinary in its approach.[41] Practitioners advocated the integration of academic study and state-level policy making, situating security studies within the context of the close ties between university and government typical of the emerging military-academic complex. Writing in 1937, IAS leader Edward Mead Earle "doubted whether the United States has any officially recognized policy" and argued, as David Ekbladh points out, for a "fully-fledged grand strategy that would ... coordinate the diplomatic, military, and executive branches in the effort."[42] This integration of grand strategic planning and policy making would not attain organizational maturity until the formation of the NSC, but in the late 1930s, the impulse in this direction was already evident.

Much of the geopolitical foundation for the burgeoning field of security studies was furnished by the ideas of British geographer Halford J. Mackinder. As developed by American strategist Nicholas Spykman, this vision centered on maintaining a world balance of power – and America's leading role within it – aimed at controlling the "pivot area" of the Eurasian "heartland" by means of power projected from the chain of maritime "rimlands" stretching from Western Europe, through the Middle East, to India and China.[43] Edward Earle regarded Spykman's "realism" as being too "restrictive and reductive," but the broad outline of his geostrategic vision, his insistence on the necessity of an interventionist foreign policy, and his recognition that this would inevitably involve the use of military force in the "rimlands" were highly influential.[44] What is not so clear is the precise influence of such ideas in shaping President Roosevelt's own grand strategic thinking, either in general terms or in the Mediterranean. Roosevelt certainly had a number of books by Earle's IAS colleagues in his extensive personal library, and while the grand strategic ideas they advocated did not sit well with an army leadership still largely committed to "continental defense," their contents certainly conformed to the president's increasingly interventionist vision.[45] Roosevelt's decision-making process was

---

[40] See Colin S. Gray, "Harry S. Truman and the forming of American grand strategy in the Cold War, 1945–1953," in Murray et al. (eds.), *The Shaping of Grand Strategy*, 238, n. 54.

[41] See David Ekbladh, "Present at the Creation: Edward Mead Earle and the Depression-Era Origins of Security Studies," *International Security* 36, no. 3 (Winter 2011/12).

[42] Ibid., 117.

[43] See Nicholas John Spykman, *The Geography of the Peace* (New York: Harcourt Brace, 1944), especially. chapter V.

[44] See Stoler, *Allies and Adversaries*, 144–145.

[45] The card index to Roosevelt's Hyde Park library shows that it included Spykman's *American Strategy in World Politics*, Bernard Brodie's *Sea Power in the Machine Age*, and *The Rise of American Naval Power* by Harold and Margaret Sprout; on "continental defense," see Michael

notoriously opaque, with numerous and often conflicting lines of command concentrated in his own well-concealed hands.[46] While frustrating to subordinates and historians alike, his modus operandi was remarkably well suited to the task at hand. In the rising arc of a great power's drive to hegemony – before the more prosaic tasks of consolidation become necessary – and as both resources and opportunities expand, national leaderships may be faced with numerous possible lines of advance. Deciding between them in order to shape specific strategies is not, as Williamson Murray stresses, simply a matter of applying a "recipe"; rather, it is an "idiosyncratic process" that flows largely through the informal and hence inherently unrecoverable channels.[47] As William Maltby shows in relation to Britain in the eighteenth century, literally "thousands of discussions in saloons, taverns, dinner parties, balls, and random encounters" went into the making of critical foreign policy decisions.[48] Analogous circles of informal discussion functioned in wartime Washington, centered on Roosevelt and his unofficial national security adviser Harry Hopkins and, via confidants within the upper echelons of the administration and the military, encompassing business figures, financiers, and journalists.

Tracing the development of Washington's grand strategy toward the Mediterranean, therefore, involves "walking back the cat": evaluating results and outcomes in an effort to deduce goals and intentions. Grand strategy, it seems, is often easier to recognize after the fact.[49] Because they involve the movement of hundreds of thousands of men and machines, the specifically military elements of strategy necessarily leave a thicker paper trail and thus can provide a critical framework for understanding the whole. But they can also tend to occlude the ultimately weightier, but often poorly delineated and imprecisely recorded, political, diplomatic, and economic aspects of grand strategy. This is particularly true in the wartime Mediterranean, where fierce fights over military strategy between Washington and London and among the U.S. leaders themselves have dominated the historiography, allowing the broader – and more significant – advance of U.S. economic and political power in the entire region to slip by largely unnoticed.

This book aims to rebalance this picture of U.S. engagement with the Mediterranean world during World War II, placing military strategy in its proper grand strategic context. From this viewpoint it becomes clear that, far from being a diversionary theater or a cul-de-sac, Washington's intervention in the Mediterranean was an indispensible element in the overall process by which America's postwar hegemony in Europe and beyond was established.

McAllister Linn, *The Echo of Battle: The Army's Way of War* (Cambridge, MA: Harvard University Press, 2007), 140–141.

[46] See Kimball, *The Juggler*, chapter 1 and 203; Stoler, *Allies and Adversaries*, 108.

[47] Murray, "Thoughts on Grand Strategy," 9.

[48] Ibid., 3.

[49] Ibid., 10.

I

The President's Personal Policy

The chain of events that would draw the United States into the wartime Mediterranean was set in motion by the unexpected and complete collapse of France in the summer of 1940. The collapse shattered the Roosevelt administration's comfortable assumption that the Franco-German war would be a protracted affair, giving plenty of time for them to prepare the American people for war and to equip the military to fight it.[1] The shocking wreck of the Third Republic left the United States confronting the prospect of a German-dominated Europe, with all of its dire consequences for U.S. economic and geopolitical interests in Europe and Latin America. With the French navy likely to come under German control and the Royal Navy in danger of being lost in a British defeat, the "free security" long accorded to the United States by the Atlantic Ocean was about to vanish.[2] As the influential geopolitical analyst Nicholas Spykman reflected, the defeat of France and the accelerating German-Japanese convergence rendered isolationist hopes that "oceanic distances" would secure "hemispheric defense" increasingly moot.[3]

The fear of a German-dominated Europe was intertwined with another that tended to grip policy makers in moments of acute crisis – the fear of social revolution. To the American elite of this generation, witnesses to the revolutionary upheavals that had followed the Great War in Russia, Germany, and Central Europe, it seemed entirely possible that the economic and social dislocations produced by another modern total war might engender popular insurrections capable of threatening the existence of capitalism. During the interwar years,

[1] On the fall of France and U.S. strategy, see David Reynolds, "1940: Fulcrum of the Twentieth Century?," *International Affairs* 66, no. 2 (April 1990), especially 333–336.
[2] See Waldo Heinrichs, *Threshold of War: Franklin D. Roosevelt and American Entry into World War II* (New York: Oxford University Press, 1988), especially 9–10.
[3] Nicholas John Spykman, *America's Strategy in World Politics: the United States and the Balance of Power* (New York: Harcourt Brace, 1942), especially 450–455.

fear of socialist revolution spreading west from Russia had led some elite figures in the United States to regard Hitler and Mussolini as useful bulwarks
against communism, despite their rhetorical bombast and parvenu manners.
Even as U.S. policy makers came to a consensus on the need to fight against
a German-dominated Europe in the summer and fall of 1940, they never lost
sight of the potential social consequences of the war or of the problematic
nature of the postwar regimes that might emerge from the wreckage.

As German troops approached Paris in late May, William Bullitt, U.S.
ambassador to France and a Roosevelt confidant, demanded that Washington
rush 10,000 Thompson submachine guns and 1 million rounds of ammunition
to France. These weapons were to be used not, as one might have imagined,
to resist the onrushing Germans, but to enable the suppression of potential
"Communist uprisings and butcheries."[4] These concerns were very much in
line with Bullitt's prewar efforts to urge Franco-German reconciliation to
avoid a war from which, he believed, only communists would benefit.[5] Bullitt
was hardly alone in his fear that a new Paris Commune might arise from the
ashes of the Third Republic. General Maxime Weygand, appointed to lead the
French army as German tanks raced toward the English Channel, diverted critical reserves from the front to secure Paris from its own citizens.[6] In the eyes
of many in the French elite, even at this moment of supreme national calamity,
the threat of revolution loomed larger than defeat at the hands of the Germans.
Nor were they alone, with the *New York Times* editorializing on the danger
that a "fury of recrimination" might "rage unchecked," replicating the "horrors of the Paris Commune."[7]

As U.S. commentators and opinion-formers attempted to explain the defeat,
initial expressions of admiration for the "unflinching" spirit of the French people quickly dissolved into a search for agents of corruption within the Third
Republic, with the *New York Times* identifying popular "apathy," government
"incapacity," and political "dry rot" as primary culprits.[8] An analysis prepared
for Roosevelt by former ambassador to Poland Anthony Biddle offered a similar diagnosis, pointing to "moral" factors to explain how a great nation had
"gone soft."[9] The responsibility for this moral degeneration was laid variously
at the feet of Communist-inspired pacifism, "fifth columnists," greedy businessmen, and a paralyzed political system. The emerging consensus was that the

---

[4] Bullitt to Hull, May 28, 1940, *FRUS 1940*, 2: 453.
[5] See David Mayers, *FDR's Ambassadors and the Diplomacy of Crisis: From the Rise of Hitler to
the End of World War II* (Cambridge: Cambridge University Press, 2013), 50.
[6] Alistair Horne, *To Lose a Battle: France 1940* (London: Penguin, 1969), 544; see also Maxime
Weygand, *Recalled to Service: The Memoirs of General Maxime Weygand,* trans. E. W. Dickes,
(Garden City, NY: Doubleday and Company, 1952), 161–162.
[7] Editorial, *New York Times*, June 24, 1940.
[8] Editorials, *New York Times*, June 18 and July 26, 1940.
[9] Memorandum, Biddle to Roosevelt, July 1, 1940, Box 29, President's Secretary's File (henceforth
PSF), FDRL.

damage to the Third Republic had been self-inflicted and that the Germans had simply toppled an edifice whose foundations had already crumbled.[10]

A number of themes that would inform the reshaping of U.S. policy quickly emerged. If, as *New York Times* columnist Anne O'Hare McCormick put it, a "lack of moral courage" had led to military collapse, then perhaps France had forfeited the right to be considered a great power.[11] This certainly was Roosevelt's view. The postwar French government, he concluded, should have no significant voice in world affairs, and on occasion he even floated the idea that the country should be dismembered and a new state of "Wallonia" created out of northern France, Luxembourg, and Belgium.[12] This view naturally questioned the continuation of the French Empire and, until the final months of the war, Roosevelt maintained that Paris should not retain its colonies in Indochina. This approach also meant that policy makers viewed France as a critically weakened state and one whose need for economic assistance would open it to U.S. influence and guidance even as it adapted to life under German domination.

Washington quickly recognized the new French government of Marshal Henri-Philippe Pétain in Vichy as the legitimate continuator of the Third Republic, viewing it both as a bulwark against dangerous radicalism – the "Communist uprisings and butcheries" feared by Bullitt – and as an arena in which Washington could contend for influence. U.S. policy makers claimed to have identified a schism within Vichy between the patriotic Pétain and the pro-Nazi Pierre Laval, and they aimed to strengthen their influence over the former while countering Berlin's control of the latter. But no such divide existed; despite their Byzantine factional struggles, *all* the central figures in Vichy favored collaboration with Berlin.[13] Only in French-ruled North Africa would some high-ranking Vichy officials enjoy the relative freedom from direct German influence necessary to advocate an alternative policy based on an alliance with the United States.

Despite their acceptance of German hegemony in Europe, the legitimacy accorded the Vichy regime by U.S. diplomatic recognition and the prospect of American aid for the ailing French economy made French leaders understandably eager to cultivate good relations with the United States.[14] To this end Vichy policy makers emphasized the autonomy of "unoccupied France"

---

[10] On American attitudes to the fall of France, see Julian G. Hurstfield, *America and the French Nation, 1939–1945* (Chapel Hill: University of North Carolina Press, 1986), chapter 1.

[11] McCormick, "Europe," *New York Times*, July 24, 1940; See also Irwin Wall, *The United States and the Making of Postwar France* (Cambridge: Cambridge University Press, 1991), 21.

[12] See Charles L. Robertson, *When Roosevelt Planned to Govern France* (Amherst, MA: University of Massachusetts Press, 2011), 14–15.

[13] See Robert O. Paxton, *Vichy France: Old Guard and New Order, 1940–1944* (New York: Columbia University Press, 1972); Julian Jackson, *France: The Dark Years, 1940–1944* (Oxford: Oxford University Press, 2001), 10.

[14] Paxton, *Vichy France*, 90.

and their refusal to allow Germany control of the French fleet. This stance encouraged President Roosevelt to strengthen U.S. representation in Vichy by appointing his friend, Admiral William Leahy, as ambassador in November 1940.[15] With his typically personal approach to diplomacy, Roosevelt urged Leahy to counteract German pressure on Vichy by cultivating a "close relationship" with Pétain; the appointment of a senior naval officer to this key post was also designed to underscore Washington's interest in the disposition of the French fleet.[16]

The new ambassador was instructed to support French efforts to "maintain its authority in its North African possessions" by making American food and fuel available to ameliorate increasingly harsh conditions there.[17] Here, policy makers saw the possibility of exercising leverage over developments in France while insuring Vichy against the dangers of social upheaval. Ideological considerations took a backseat; in fact, the conservative domestic politics of the Vichy regime were hardly uncongenial either to policy makers or to broader sections of the American elite. Ambassador Leahy viewed Pétain as an honest and amiable patriot deeply "devoted to the welfare of his people," and embassy secretary H. Freeman Matthews went further, concurring with the marshal's view that the Third Republic had been undermined by Communists and that a deep-going conservative-nationalist regeneration of France was necessary.[18] Both Leahy and Matthews also went to some lengths to disrupt the work of the New York-based Emergency Rescue Committee and other U.S. relief organizations, whose work in aiding the flight of Jewish and other refugees they feared would jeopardize good relations with Vichy.[19]

The necessary reciprocal of Washington's opening to Vichy was a policy of studied hostility toward the "Free French" movement of General Charles de Gaulle. De Gaulle had arrived in London in the summer of 1940 a relatively unknown figure, lacking the backing of any significant section of the French ruling class and with few resources beyond his own imperious drive to see France reborn as a great power. His movement was almost entirely dependent on British support. None of this endeared him to a U.S. administration keen on cultivating ties with Vichy. Ambassador Leahy reinforced Washington's negative appreciation of the Free French, forwarding dismissive estimates of domestic support for de Gaulle and endorsing Vichy's claim to be the target of "Gaullist and Communist" efforts to "stir up trouble [by] inciting revolution."[20] Freeman

---

[15] Roosevelt to Leahy, November 16, 1940, telegram, Box 29, PSF, FDRL.

[16] Roosevelt to Leahy, December 20, 1940, *FRUS 1940*, 2: 426; see Mayers, *FDR's Ambassadors*, 144.

[17] Roosevelt to Leahy, December 20, 1940, *FRUS 1940*, 2: 428.

[18] Admiral William D. Leahy, *I Was There: The Personal Story of the Chief of Staff to Presidents Roosevelt and Truman Based on His Notes and Diaries Made at the Time* (New York: McGraw Hill, 1950), 33; on Matthews, see Mayers, *FDR's Ambassadors*, 145–146.

[19] See Mayers, *FDR's Ambassadors*, 149–153.

[20] See Hurstfield, *America and the French Nation*, 76–77; Leahy to State Department, September 12, 1941, *FRUS 1941*, 2:431.

Matthews was even more blunt, denouncing de Gaulle's followers in London as a gang of "Jews, emigrés, and crooks."[21] The presentation of de Gaulle as a dangerous revolutionary and an ally of Communism played effectively on Washington's fears, making the conservative and increasingly anti-Semitic Vichy regime seem preferable to the dangerous radicalism of the Free French. The failure of the Anglo-Gaullist attack on Vichy-held Dakar, West Africa in September 1940 reinforced Washington's skepticism of the Free French and buttressed confidence in its orientation toward Pétain.

Washington's policy toward Vichy was one element in a broad strategic reorientation undertaken in the aftermath of the fall of France. This now unfolded in a new strategic context, as the British attack on the French fleet at Mers-el-Kébir on July 3, 1940 to prevent it from falling into German hands, and the defeat of the *Luftwaffe* in the Battle of Britain in September, both demonstrated Britain's ability to carry on the fight. As it became clear that the war would go on, U.S. policy makers overcame an initial lurch toward greater isolationism and coalesced around an interventionist (or "internationalist") approach to the war.[22] This consensus within the American ruling class did not necessarily imply support for direct military action, particularly as public opinion remained strongly opposed to participation in the war. But it did point toward deepening U.S. engagement, with Congress authorizing a massive rearmament program – including the first peacetime draft – and stepping up the supply of war matériel to Britain. Broad bipartisan support for this course was reflected in the selection of the interventionist corporate lawyer Wendell Willkie as the Republican presidential candidate in 1940 and in Roosevelt's appointment of Republicans Henry Stimson and Frank Knox to the War and Navy departments, giving the administration something of a "national" character.[23]

A far-reaching revision of U.S. military strategy proceeded alongside this political reorientation. In October 1940, Chief of Naval Operations Admiral Stark outlined the implications of the crisis for U.S. strategy in a memorandum known colloquially as *Plan Dog*. Stark argued that following the fall of France, America's security interests centered on ensuring the survival of Britain. Moreover, while Britain could weather the German onslaught without direct U.S. intervention, it could not go on to win the war alone. Stark concluded that the United States should concentrate its initial military effort in Europe, securing the British Isles and then fighting to overthrow Germany. This "Germany first" approach implied adopting a defensive posture in the Pacific to avoid provoking a premature war with Japan. Stark also argued explicitly that the

---

[21] Matthews to Caffery, July 4, 1941, quoted in Mayers, *FDR's Ambassadors*, 146.

[22] See David G. Haglund, "George C. Marshall and the Question of Military Aid to England, May–June 1940," *Journal of Contemporary History* 15, no. 4 (October 1980), especially 757.

[23] See David Reynolds, *From Munich to Pearl Harbor: Roosevelt's America and the Origins of the Second World War* (Chicago, IL: Ivan R. Dee, 2001), especially 97–101; Marvin R. Zahniser, "Rethinking the Significance of Disaster: The United States and the Fall of France in 1940," *The International History Review* 14, no. 2, (1992).

United States should underwrite the defense of Britain's imperial positions in Egypt, Gibraltar, and West Africa, pointing out that they might provide suitable jumping off points for the "ultimate offensive" into continental Europe.[24] Stark offered no detailed prescription for this great counteroffensive, but it was clear that preparations for it would involve building up a substantial U.S. presence in the Mediterranean.

President Roosevelt quickly approved *Plan Dog*, which set the framework for staff discussions with senior British officials at the ABC-1 talks in March 1941.[25] By the time Anglo-American planners met, the president's own enthusiasm for Mediterranean operations had been further reinforced by reports reaching Washington from Colonel William Donovan, the future head of the Office of Strategic Services. Working closely with British authorities and traveling as an observer for the secretary of the navy – and as Roosevelt's personal emissary – Donovan made a swing through the Mediterranean, visiting Spain, Yugoslavia, Bulgaria, and Egypt, between December 1940 and March 1941.[26] Donovan's experience on the Western Front in World War I naturally inclined him toward strategies of "indirect approach," and his observations in the region, combined with discussions with British leaders, reinforced this perception.[27] In particular, Donovan grasped the importance of viewing the Mediterranean not only as an east-west corridor, but also as a north-south battle line binding together North Africa and southern Europe.[28] It is impossible to judge the effect of Donovan's enthusiastic reports on Roosevelt's thinking, but it is clear that, arriving as *Plan Dog* and the ABC-1 talks were clarifying U.S. strategy and at the same time that the president was pushing for a rapid expansion of diplomatic and economic activity in North Africa, they contributed to top-level interest in Mediterranean strategies.

The ABC-1 talks registered Anglo-American agreement on the critical question of "Germany first." The draft plan adopted at the meeting, also known as ABC-1, sketched out a multifaceted series of offensive operations against German-dominated Europe that included a naval blockade, an escalating bombing campaign, and a campaign to effect the "early elimination" of Italy.[29] These actions, supplemented by a series of "raids and minor offensives" to sap Axis strength, would prepare an "eventual offensive" against Germany itself. These common conclusions were incorporated into America's own strategic

---

[24] *Plan Dog*, November 12, 1940, Stephen T. Ross, ed. *U. S. War Plans: 1938–1945* (Boulder, CO: Lynne Rienner Publishers, 2002), 56.

[25] See James Lacey, "World War II's Real Victory Program," *Journal of Military History* 75, no. 3 (July 2011), especially 825.

[26] See Douglas Waller, *Wild Bill Donovan: The Spymaster Who Created the OSS and Modern American Espionage* (New York: Free Press, 2011), 63–67.

[27] See Peter Ewer, "The British Campaign in Greece 1941: Assumptions about the Operational Art and Their Influence on Strategy," *Journal of Military History* 76, no. 3 (July 2012), 730–731, 735.

[28] Ibid., 735.

[29] ABC-1, March 27, 1941, Ross, *U. S. War Plans: 1938–1945*, 70.

planning with the adoption of *Rainbow 5*, approved in outline by the Joint Board – the forerunner of the Joint Chiefs of Staff – on November 19, 1941. *Rainbow 5* reiterated the "Germany first" approach, setting it in a broader European context by emphasizing operations to force Italy out of the war and underscoring U.S. interest in supporting the "British and Allied military position in and near the Mediterranean basin."[30]

What is striking about this succession of plans is their permissiveness. In contrast to the rigid focus on a cross-Channel assault that came to dominate U.S. military thinking in the early months of 1942, these plans offered a variety of operational alternatives. Clearly, U.S. strategic thinking was in flux, and the "peripheral" approach evident in *Rainbow 5* was, to some extent, already contradicted by the American proposals presented to the Allied summit meeting in Newfoundland in August 1941, which emphasized launching a massive Allied army into Germany.[31] Despite the turmoil, however, as U.S. planners grappled with the question of defending Britain and its key imperial outposts they explicitly recognized the strategic importance of the Mediterranean. Moreover, the idea of securing the "early elimination" of Italy *prior* to invading Germany necessarily implied the commitment of substantial U.S. forces to the Mediterranean. *Plan Dog*, ABC-1, and *Rainbow 5* all allowed for the possibility of a sustained U.S. commitment there.

In the political and strategic reorientation that unfolded following the fall of France, these two developments – the articulation of a policy toward Vichy, and the evolution of a military strategy centered on "Germany first" that included operations in the Mediterranean – coalesced in an impulse toward an U.S. invasion of French North Africa. The "capture of positions" in North Africa would help prepare the "eventual offensive against Germany," while at the same time the appearance of U.S. forces in French-ruled territory, particularly if they arrived at the invitation of local French authorities, might strengthen the fondly imagined anti-collaborationist wing of the Vichy government.[32] Both of these elements appealed to President Roosevelt, who developed a clear and unwavering interest in the region over the late summer and fall of 1940. By the end of the year, French North Africa was well on the way to becoming what Secretary of War Henry Stimson would scathingly describe as the president's "great secret baby," and historian Arthur Funk called his "magnet whose attraction never failed."[33]

As French North Africa emerged as an area of special interest, the State Department pressed its officers in the region for information on the relationship

[30] *Rainbow 5*, November 19, 1941, Stephen T. Ross (ed.), *U. S. War Plans: 1938–1945* (Boulder, CO: Lynne Rienner Publishers, 2002), 138–139.

[31] "The Victory Program," Ross, *U. S. War Plans: 1938–1945*, 104.

[32] Ross, *War Plans*, 70, 138.

[33] Stimson quoted in editorial note, *FRUS 1942*, Washington Conference, 434; Arthur Layton Funk, *The Politics of Torch: The Allied Landings and the Algiers Putsch 1942*. (Lawrence: University Press of Kansas, 1974), 72.

between French colonial officials and the Vichy government.[34] Their initial reports were not encouraging. From Casablanca, consul Herbert Goold reported that French officials were "pure conventionalists" who would neither challenge the Vichy regime nor resist a German occupation.[35] But more encouraging assessments were soon forthcoming, with future CIA head Roscoe Hillenkoetter reporting the existence in Morocco of a "strong movement" rooted in the armed forces and prepared to defend the French protectorate "against all comers."[36] These forces, he added, would welcome an U.S.-led invasion of North Africa with open arms. Hillenkoetter's breathless assessment would turn out to be the first of a long series of exaggerated intelligence estimates driven, if not by pure wish-fulfillment, then by mistaken extrapolation from meetings with officials adept at feeding U.S. agents what they wanted to hear.

Hillenkoetter's optimistic assessment was supported by a meeting between embassy officials in Vichy and Emmanuel Monick, recently appointed Secretary General of Morocco, in which Monick asserted that he had been given a "free hand" to pursue "closer economic relations" with the United States.[37] Sounding the note of gleeful economic opportunism that would form the subtext of U.S. relations with French North Africa, embassy officials concluded that they now had an opportunity to break France's longstanding "monopolization" of trade with the region. Developing this idea, State Department officials responded enthusiastically to the potential benefits of expanded U.S. trade with the Maghreb. Meeting in Washington with the head of Socony Vacuum's Moroccan operations, J. Rives Childs concluded that expanded economic ties to North Africa would strengthen the willingness of French officials to resist Axis domination while simultaneously loosening the region's economic dependence on metropolitan France.[38] In early November, the embassy in Vichy underscored this point, reporting that Monick had again emphasized the importance of U.S. trade for the preservation of North African "independence." This time, officials added, Monick had warned that if U.S. aid were not forthcoming he might be "compelled" to turn to Germany instead.[39]

U.S. diplomats in the region were initially divided over the promotion of closer economic ties with French North Africa. From Casablanca, consul Herbert Goold argued for backing the British naval blockade designed to keep foreign consumer goods out on the grounds that shortages would stimulate "native pressure" for Morocco to follow Chad and Equatorial Africa into the ranks of the Free French.[40] In Tangier, J. C. White took the opposite view,

---

[34] Murray to Goold, July 18, 1940, *FRUS 1940*, 2: 575.
[35] Goold to State Dept., June 26 and August 12, 1940, *FRUS 1940*, 2: 571, 577.
[36] Weddell to Hull, July 26, 1940, *FRUS 1940*, 2: 575–576.
[37] Matthews to State Dept., August 26, 1940, *FRUS 1940*, 2: 579.
[38] Childs, memorandum, October 25, 1940, *FRUS 1940*, 2: 602.
[39] Matthews to State Dept., November 6, 1940, *FRUS 1940*, 2: 613–614.
[40] Goold to State Dept., September 7, 1940, *FRUS 1940*, 2: 585.

proposing that Moroccan government funds in U.S. banks should be unfrozen so that the French authorities could purchase consumer goods in the United States.[41] Consul Charles Heisler concurred, arguing that shortages of fuel and other basic commodities might provoke dangerous "Arab disturbances." While Goold saw "native pressure" turning the Maghreb against the Axis, Heisler, like most U.S. officials, viewed outbreaks of anticolonial protest by the Arab majority as damaging to both French and U.S. interests.[42] Secretary of State Cordell Hull soon made it clear where the administration stood, pressing to develop trade with North Africa and rejecting the view of the department's own Office of the Economic Advisor that U.S. goods would inevitably find their way into Axis hands.

In September 1940, U.S. officials favoring the use of economic incentives to promote closer political relations with North Africa were strengthened by Pétain's appointment of General Maxime Weygand as Delegate-General in North Africa. Weygand, leader of the French Army in the last desperate stages of the Battle of France, was viewed by both London and Washington as a staunch opponent of the pro-German faction in Vichy. Cordell Hull was particularly enthusiastic, describing Weygand as the "cornerstone" on which French opposition to Germany could be rebuilt, and North Africa as the place to do it.[43] U.S. diplomats in Vichy reinforced this appreciation, reporting that the "free air" of North Africa had revived Weygand's "spirit of resistance."[44] American hopes in Weygand were not entirely misplaced. Alone among senior Vichy figures, the old general emphasized the importance of a long-term relationship with the United States, arguing in a letter to Vichy leader Admiral François Darlan that, irrespective of how the fighting in Europe ended, close ties to America would be critical to staving off postwar "economic and social chaos."[45] Not unimportantly from Washington's point of view, Weygand was also clear that France would be the junior partner in this relationship.

U.S. officials hoped that Weygand's desire to keep French North Africa out of German hands would either precipitate a break between officials in the region and the Vichy government or, better still, bring succor to the allegedly anti-collaborationist forces around Pétain. This approach was built on a false understanding of Vichy. While Weygand favored closer ties with the United States, he was no dissident. Vichy was kept fully informed of his discussions with U.S. envoys and his efforts to promote economic ties were sanctioned by Pétain himself. Pétain viewed North Africa as France's "final trump," a card which, if played skillfully, might buttress what was left of French independence by using ties with the United States to strengthen Vichy against Charles de

[41] White to State Dept., September 23, 1940, *FRUS 1940*, 2: 588.
[42] Heisler to State Dept., September 26, 1940, *FRUS 1940*, 2: 593.
[43] Cordell Hull, *The Memoirs of Cordell Hull* (New York: Macmillan, 1948), 1: 853.
[44] Matthews to State Dept., November 8, 1940, *FRUS 1940*, 2: 614–615.
[45] Weygand to Darlan, October 1941, quoted in Weygand, *Recalled to Service*, 375.

Gaulle and his British backers on the one hand and against Germany on the other.[46] Washington's difficulty in judging the internal dynamics of the Vichy government were compounded by the regime's factionalized functioning, culminating in Pétain's sudden removal of Laval from office on December 13, 1940.[47]

At the beginning of November 1940, Washington instructed its embassy in Vichy to negotiate an "arrangement" for closer economic ties; and in Algiers, Weygand was assured that America would provide the economic assistance necessary to maintain the independence of French North Africa.[48] With these discussions proceeding apace, State Department official Robert Murphy arrived in Algiers in mid-December as Roosevelt's personal representative to North Africa. A career diplomat and former protégé of William Bullitt in the Paris embassy, Murphy was recalled from Vichy in September to be briefed on his new assignment. According to Murphy – and there is no reason to doubt his account – Roosevelt explained that he was trying to provide "help" for French officials operating in the "relatively independent" conditions of French North Africa, and he asked Murphy to undertake a tour of the region to evaluate the viability of this project.[49] In particular, Roosevelt instructed Murphy to cultivate a personal relationship with Weygand, a task for which his Catholicism was considered most helpful. "You might," the president quipped, "go to church with him."[50] Roosevelt insisted that Murphy report directly to him, circumventing State Department channels. The briefing left Murphy in no doubt that Washington's emerging orientation toward French North Africa was very much the "President's personal policy."[51]

Robert Murphy finally caught up with Weygand in Dakar, capital of French West Africa, at the end of December 1940. Weygand was in French West Africa to assess the situation in the pro-Vichy colony following the failed Anglo-Free French raid on Dakar in September. While professing support for Britain, both Weygand and Governor-General of West Africa Pierre Boisson favored responding to the attack on Dakar by invading pro-Free French Equatorial Africa to bring it back into the Vichy fold.[52] Their combative response was typical of the reaction of Vichy officials – including both Laval's collaborationist faction and his allegedly pro-Allied opponents – to Anglo-Gaullist encroachments on

[46] See James J. Dougherty, *The Politics of Wartime Aid: American Economic Assistance to France and French Northwest Africa, 1940–1946* (Westport, CT: Greenwood Press, 1978), especially 24; for "trump card" see Robert Murphy to State Dept., January 14, 1941, *FRUS 1941*, 2: 207.

[47] On the removal of Laval, see Paxton, *Vichy France*, 92–101.

[48] State Dept. to Matthews, November 9 1940, *FRUS 1940*, 2: 615; see Welles to Cole, November 14, 1940, *FRUS 1940*, 2: 616.

[49] Robert Murphy, *Diplomat among Warriors* (Garden City, NY: Doubleday & Co, 1964), 68.

[50] Ibid.

[51] Ibid.

[52] Murphy, *Diplomat among Warriors*, 76–77.

the French empire.[53] The deep hostility toward de Gaulle expressed by Vichy officials throughout Africa made it clear to Murphy that continued U.S. opposition to de Gaulle's Free French would be a prerequisite for the development of good relations with French leaders in the Maghreb. In fact, gazing on the "beautiful" battleship *Richelieu* damaged in Dakar harbor by British gunfire, Murphy professed himself well able to understand the "patriotic sense of outrage" expressed by Weygand and Boisson.[54]

As Roosevelt intended, such sentiments enabled Robert Murphy to establish a personal rapport with Weygand, with the general recalling that the president's emissary made an "excellent impression" on him at their first meeting.[55] The fact that Weygand told Murphy exactly what both he and Roosevelt wanted to hear undoubtedly facilitated this burgeoning relationship. The Americans quickly formed an optimistic appreciation of the situation in North Africa, concluding that French forces there were ready for "substantial military action against Germany and Italy."[56] Military preparations, Murphy noted, were being carried out with Pétain's approval and with the idea that North Africa could provide the "springboard" for a rapid "military rebound" if Germany moved into unoccupied France. To prepare this, French officials were keen to strengthen their links with the United States, and Murphy argued that their efforts merited support in the form of substantial shipments of gasoline, kerosene, and heating oil.

Vichy officials supplemented their promises of resistance to any Axis incursion into North Africa with threats that, without infusions of U.S. aid, Arab unrest might make their colonies and protectorates in the Maghreb ungovernable. Warming to this theme, Secretary General Monick explained to Murphy that in Morocco 150,000 French settlers lived among more than 6 million Arabs and Berbers, making the "reasonable contentment" of the native population a necessary precondition for any French action against the Germans.[57] Monick warned that the Germans were "sow[ing] dissention" among the natives to "destroy their faith" in the French and cautioned that if U.S. aid were not forthcoming, Berlin would soon find the "ground fully prepared for fifth column activity." By raising the prospect of "Arab disturbances," French officials were prodding the Americans on the big issue of French colonial rule in North Africa. Did the "anti-imperialism" within which U.S. policy was customarily wrapped imply that Washington favored the decolonization of North Africa? Did the Americans, like the British, seek the "decomposition of French Africa"?[58] Following guidelines from Roosevelt, Murphy assuaged French fears by explaining that America's interest in North Africa was purely

---

[53] See Paxton, *Vichy France*, 97.
[54] Murphy, *Diplomat among Warriors*, 76–77.
[55] Weygand, *Recalled to Service*, 369.
[56] Murphy to State Dept., January 14, 1941, *FRUS 1941*, 2: 207.
[57] Ibid., 208.
[58] Ibid.

"strategic" – i.e. temporary and military – and that relations between France and the "native peoples" were entirely an "affair between them."[59] U.S. economic aid, Murphy concluded, would act as an "incentive" to continued "Arab cooperation."[60]

Despite presidential enthusiasm for a Franco-American trade accord, there remained one major obstacle to an agreement. This lay not in difficulties between Washington and Vichy, but in tensions between Washington and London. Washington's mounting interest in French North Africa presented British policy makers with a dilemma. London desperately needed U.S. assistance in its struggle with Germany and the Churchill government's entire strategic outlook was premised on securing it. From this point of view, Washington's interest in North Africa and the Western Mediterranean was to be welcomed and encouraged. At the same time, however, British officials feared that if the United States established itself in North Africa, it might be there permanently, inevitably posing a challenge to Britain's own plans to strengthen its economic and political interests in the region. In essence, this dilemma highlighted the fact that London both needed and feared U.S. involvement in the war, and it encapsulated the contradiction at the heart of the "special relationship."

Like Washington, London had initially viewed Weygand's assignment to North Africa as a sign that French forces there might be persuaded to reenter the war, and early discussions with him conducted by the Ministry of Economic Warfare (MEW) appeared promising.[61] But by early 1941, London had concluded that Weygand was offering nothing beyond vague promises and when British military leaders suggested that French North Africa should be supplied with oil, Churchill shot back that "something better" than mere verbal assurances were required before "lavishing" scarce British resources on the region.[62] By February, Churchill's patience – always a somewhat limited commodity – was exhausted. Noting Weygand's obvious lack of enthusiasm for the "great offers" made to him by London, the prime minister concluded that the failure of French officials in North Africa to exhibit the slightest "scrap of nobility or courage" meant that they should be put on "short commons" by a tightened British naval blockade until they "came to their senses."[63]

Weygand's failure to respond to British blandishments was in stark contrast to his obvious interest in developing a relationship with Washington, to U.S. officials' obvious glee. The Ministry of Economic Warfare sounded an alarm, with minister Sir Hugh Dalton expressing anger at Robert Murphy's

---

[59] Murphy, *Diplomat among Warriors*, 64.
[60] Ibid., 83.
[61] See Desmond Dinan, *The Politics of Persuasion: British Policy and French African Neutrality, 1940–42* (Lanham, MD: University Press of America, 1988).
[62] Churchill to Chiefs of Staff (COS), January 27, 1941, Prime Minister's Operational Papers, (henceforth PREM 3), PREM 3/187.
[63] Churchill to COS, February 12, 1941, PREM 3/187.

"impetuous" pursuit of a trade agreement.[64] From Algiers, MEW official David Eccles highlighted the danger of growing U.S. influence in the region, citing reports of U.S. officials talking about Morocco as if it were "as much within their orbit as South America."[65] In early 1941, London acted on these concerns, informing the State Department that while Britain would not "discriminate" against U.S. trade, it planned to enforce a tight naval blockade of North Africa.[66] Despite this bold claim, however, London's resolve soon began to crumble as British planners faced the shocking realization that the over-stretched Royal Navy was incapable of actually enforcing a close blockade. Meeting in early February with the State Department's Ray Atherton, British officers grudgingly "welcomed" the "exercise of American influence" in North Africa and acquiesced to a trade deal with the French.[67]

The realization that U.S. intervention in North Africa would not favor Britain's long-term economic interests represented a significant political set-back for the old imperial power. Initially confident that it would make all the critical decisions in the Mediterranean – an area it had long considered vital to its interests – London was now forced to give ground to its noncombatant ally. This was an early and unmistakable intimation that the mantle of junior part-ner would no longer sit easily on American shoulders, and a bellwether of the deep-going shift in Anglo-American relations that would unfold in the coming years. The British government, particularly the Foreign Office and the Ministry of Economic Warfare, did not take their defeat lightly, and Washington was forced to deal with a series of rearguard efforts to derail the dispatch of U.S. economic aid to French North Africa. Not for the last time, Churchill, the con-summate Atlanticist with his eyes fixed on the necessity of an alliance with the United States, had to rein in the more European-minded Foreign Office, issuing a blunt injunction that the British government had to "fall in" with the "pres-ident's wishes."[68]

Having finally secured British approval for the shipment of oil and consumer goods to French North Africa, Washington quickly concluded negotiations in Algiers; on February 26, 1941 Murphy and Weygand initialed a draft trade accord. The agreement was conditional on American goods being consumed within North Africa and it provided for twelve U.S. vice-consuls to be sta-tioned at ports across the Maghreb to ensure that nothing got into Axis hands. Weygand returned to Vichy for the signing of the Franco-American trade agree-ment by the Minister of Foreign Affairs, Admiral François Darlan, on March 10, 1941. A list of urgent requirements – headed by sugar, gasoline, diesel fuel

[64] Hugh Dalton, *The Fateful Years* (London: Frederick Muller, 1957).
[65] Quoted in Dinan, *Politics of Persuasion*, 146.
[66] Memorandum, British Embassy Washington to Dept. of State, January 28, 1941, *FRUS 1941*, 2: 242.
[67] Ray Atherton, memorandum of conversation, February 5, 1941, *FRUS 1941*, 2: 252.
[68] Churchill to Eden, February 20, 1941, PREM 3/187.

and lubricating oil – was appended to the accord. Despite the constant repetition of the argument that the passivity of millions of Arabs and Berbers rested on the supply of U.S. oil and consumer goods, the great bulk of the supplies requested by French officials were clearly destined for French military use.

As Washington had intended, the ratification of the Murphy-Weygand accord and the development of closer economic ties opened the door to a rapid expansion of U.S. diplomatic and political activity in French North Africa. In April, Robert Murphy returned to Algiers as a "sort of ... High Commissioner for French Africa," and the vice-consuls began arriving in June.[69] Officially assigned to monitor the distribution of American goods, their actual responsibilities included gathering the military intelligence and political contacts necessary to support a U.S. military landing. As Murphy noted approvingly, Weygand accepted the vice-consuls' dual roles, and was "playing ball with us in all important respects."[70] Chosen from the ranks of reserve officers, the vice-consuls were a motley collection of French-speaking businessmen, engineers, and lawyers.[71] None of them had any familiarity with North Africa and there was little accumulated diplomatic experience to guide them as the embassy in prewar Paris had paid scant attention to France's African empire.[72] The use of military personnel for a "State Department enterprise" raised bureaucratic hackles, and officials struggled to secure Army and Navy approval for the assignment of its officers. Opposition finally melted when Roosevelt himself insisted on the rapid deployment of the officers, financing the operation from the "President's defense fund."[73]

As the Murphy-Weygand accord was being negotiated in early 1941, Britain's strategic position in the Mediterranean deteriorated rapidly. In January, German aircraft based in Sicily challenged British control of the narrow seas of the central Mediterranean, and in March a renewed Axis offensive under General Erwin Rommel quickly threatened the British position in Egypt. German troops surged into the Balkans in April, reviving the stalled Italian invasion of Greece, expelling a British expeditionary force and launching an airborne assault on Crete. The launch of the German invasion of the Soviet Union in June rekindled Madrid's enthusiasm for the Axis cause and renewed fears that Spain would close the Straits of Gibraltar. This cascading series of reverses heightened Anglo-American fears that the seemingly unstoppable German advance would allow Berlin to pressure Vichy into aligning itself more closely with the Axis, again raising the threat of the French fleet coming under enemy control.

[69] Murphy, *Diplomat among Warriors*, 88.
[70] Murphy to Murray, October 13, 1941, *FRUS1941*, 2: 317–320.
[71] See Hal Vaughan, *FDR's 12 Apostles: The Spies Who Paved the Way for the Invasion of North Africa* (Guilford, CT: The Lyons Press, 2006).
[72] Ibid., 66.
[73] Murray, memorandum, April 19, 1941, *FRUS 1941*, 2: 313–314.

Fears of increased German influence in Vichy seemed to have been realized in May 1941 when, following a meeting with Hitler, Prime Minister Darlan negotiated a new Franco-German agreement. Under these "Paris Protocols," Vichy would grant Berlin the use of bases in Syria from which to succor Rashid Ali's anti-British rebellion in Iraq, along with access to the Tunisian port of Bizerte as a supply center for Rommel's *Afrika Korps* and the establishment of a U-boat base in Dakar. In exchange, Berlin agreed to a modest reduction in occupation costs, permitted a limited release of French prisoners of war and eased restrictions on movement between occupied and unoccupied France. Even more worrying for the Allies was the fact that although Berlin stood to gain the most from the Paris Protocols, the initiative for the new agreement came primarily from Vichy's prime minister. Like his predecessor Laval, Darlan's policy was grounded in acceptance of a German-dominated Europe and aimed primarily at securing a degree of French autonomy within that context.[74]

These developments weighed particularly heavily on British leaders already inclined to see Vichy as becoming more pro-Axis in its actions. From this point of view, sending economic aid to French North Africa was tantamount to supplying the enemy, and the Foreign Office and the Ministry of Economic Warfare stepped up their rearguard campaign against the trade accord, authorizing the detention of the Morocco-bound oil tanker *Scheherazade*.[75] But London's options were narrowing. Even if its naval blockade could be tightened – and that would be virtually impossible in the face of German air power – to do so would be to risk an armed clash with the French *and* a damaging rupture in relations with Washington. The crisis in the Mediterranean, therefore, strengthened the hand of those in Whitehall, headed by Churchill himself, who saw U.S. engagement in the Mediterranean as an indispensable step toward its broader involvement in the war. Consequently, the Murphy-Weygand deal had to proceed, and – at a critical May 26 cabinet meeting – Churchill secured renewed British approval for the accord.[76]

Churchill's confidence in the ability of U.S. diplomacy to wring concessions from Vichy had been strengthened earlier in the spring by a diplomatic coup. When reports reached London in March 1941 that the French planned to move the damaged battleship *Dunkerque* from Mers-el-Kébir to Toulon, Churchill urged Roosevelt to warn Pétain that such an action would result in France "finally forfeiting American sympathy."[77] Roosevelt, who shared Churchill's concern that the ship might fall into German hands, put pressure on Vichy, and he was soon able to report that the French had decided against the move. Churchill responded enthusiastically, hailing Vichy's "remarkable" retreat

[74] See Paxton, *Vichy France*, 118.
[75] On the *Scheherazade* incident, see Dinan, *Politics of Persuasion*, 185–187.
[76] Ibid., 184.
[77] Churchill to Roosevelt, April 2, 1941, in Warren Kimball (ed.), *Churchill and Roosevelt: The Complete Correspondence* (London: Collins, 1984) 1: 158 (henceforth *Correspondence*).

in response to U.S. "representations."[78] As a result of this success, Churchill informed Roosevelt that he was "more than willing" to see Washington "take the lead" in relations with Vichy, using both "favors" – the trade accord – and threats to "get the best" from them.[79] Recognizing that London had "no means of action on that caitiff government," Churchill concluded that U.S. diplomacy offered the "only hope" of deterring closer Vichy collaboration with Germany.[80]

The diplomatic usefulness of the trade accord seemed to be further underscored in June when the Vichy government refused to ratify the newly negotiated Paris Protocols. The defeat of Darlan's "new policy" followed a sustained U.S. diplomatic campaign that included a sharply worded message from President Roosevelt warning that the trade accord would be terminated if there were any sign of French "collaboration" with Axis forces in North Africa.[81] As a token of U.S. intent, the accord was suspended pending clarification of the situation. Buoyed by U.S. support and perhaps chastened by American threats, Weygand's senior officials from West Africa and Tunisia traveled to Vichy to attend the special cabinet meeting called to ratify the Paris Protocols. Weygand and other opponents of the new deal prevailed, perhaps aided by Darlan's own disappointment at the limited scope of German concessions, and the Protocols were shelved. In the meantime, Washington secured British approval for a resumption of the accord, with Undersecretary of State and key Roosevelt ally Sumner Welles convincing British ambassador Lord Halifax that there was "much to lose" by not proceeding.[82]

American officials were convinced that the Murphy-Weygand accord had secured the defeat of the Paris Protocols, with J. Rives Childs reporting from Tangier that U.S. backing had given Weygand the "psychological support" necessary to stand up to Darlan.[83] U.S. opinion-makers were markedly less sanguine, with *Time* magazine arguing that the differences within Darlan's cabinet were divisions over the "degree and method" of collaboration, not the substance.[84] In his influential and widely syndicated "Washington Merry-Go-Round" column, Drew Pearson suggested that by continuing to "appease" Weygand the United States was providing backdoor assistance to the Axis. Arguing along similar lines, the *Nation* editorialized bluntly that Vichy was simply "Berlin in disguise."[85] Historians have likewise tended to downplay the role of U.S.

---

[78] Churchill to Roosevelt, April 13, 1941, Ibid., 1: 169.

[79] Churchill to Roosevelt, May 4, 1941, Ibid., 1: 182.

[80] Churchill to Roosevelt, May 14, 1941, Ibid., 1: 186.

[81] Hull to Leahy (Vichy), May 15, 1941, *FRUS 1941*, 2: 171; Hull to Childs, May 16, 1941, *FRUS 1941*, 2: 335.

[82] Welles, memorandum, May 23, 1941, *FRUS 1941*, 2: 349.

[83] See Hull, *Memoirs*, 2: 963; Childs to State Dept., June 14, 1941, *FRUS, 1941*, 2: 378.

[84] Editorial, *Time*, June 16, 1941.

[85] Pearson, "Washington Merry-Go-Round," July 21, 1941; Editorial, *The Nation*, August 2, 1941.

diplomacy in the rejection of the Paris Protocols, noting that British successes against the Iraqi rebellion rendered concessions in Syria moot, that French officials in North Africa were already inclined to resist any German presence there, and that Berlin was becoming markedly less interested in the Mediterranean as its invasion of the Soviet Union got underway in late June.[86] These judgments are overly dismissive. Whatever the evaluation of the moral character of U.S. policy – and Pearson's charge of appeasement does not seem misplaced – the threat of the withdrawal of U.S. economic support weighed heavily on a government struggling to assert the limited independence open to it.

For its part, Vichy expressed satisfaction with the trade accord and pressed Washington to extend it to West Africa.[87] French leaders were also pleased with the expressions of U.S. support for French rule in North Africa that accompanied its warnings about the dangers of collaboration with Germany. In June, Cordell Hull publicly recognized France's colonies and protectorates in the Maghreb as an "integral part of the French Empire," and in August President Roosevelt assured Pétain that the continuation of French rule in North Africa was a matter of the "utmost importance" to the United States.[88] These statements of U.S. support for ongoing French colonial rule in North Africa – which implied that the right of national self-determination trumpeted in the Atlantic Charter would not apply there – may well have been intended to reward Vichy for its rejection of the Paris Protocols. They also undoubtedly summarized Washington's fundamental stance toward the governance of the region.

In the summer of 1941, Britain's position in the Mediterranean began to stabilize after the disasters in Greece, Crete, and the Western Desert. Imperial troops continued to hold the port of Tobruk despite being cut off by Axis forces, and in early May, with British air and naval attacks taking a heavy toll of Axis supply convoys, Rommel's advance ground to a halt on the Egyptian border. In July, London reorganized its forces in North Africa into the Eighth Army and began reequipping them with Lend-Lease tanks and equipment arriving direct from the United States along routes opened by Roosevelt's decision to permit American merchant shipping to operate in the Red Sea. Under constant pressure from Churchill, the Eighth Army prepared Operation *Crusader,* a counteroffensive against Rommel that was finally launched on November 18. At the same time, the German offensive in Russia began to run into difficulties and, as Berlin's interest in North Africa waned, so did the provision of supplies and reinforcements for Rommel's hard-pressed forces.

Berlin tried to ease its supply problems in North Africa by requesting that Vichy allow it the use of supply routes operated by French military transports

---

[86] See, for example, Paxton, *Vichy France,* 120–121; Julian Jackson, *France: The Dark Years,* 180–181; Dinan, *Politics of Persuasion,* 188; Hurstfield, *America and the French Nation,* 73.

[87] Welles, memorandum, July 1, 1941, *FRUS 1941,* 2: 387.

[88] Hull, press statement, *Department of State Bulletin,* June 7, 1941, 4: 681–682; Roosevelt to Pétain, August 21, 1941, *FRUS 1941,* 2: 417.

running through the Maghreb. As the Paris Protocols had indicated, Darlan was keen to oblige, but Weygand continued to refuse to countenance any Axis presence in French North Africa. In July, Vichy moved against Weygand, appointing him Governor General of Algeria under Darlan's direct supervision and recalling his key ally General Emmanuel Monick to France. Not surprisingly, these developments worried U.S. officials who saw a renewed threat to their cherished vision of what historian Arthur Funk described as a "quasi-independent North Africa nurtured by the United States."[89] Even the normally ebullient Murphy noted Berlin's growing influence in Vichy, endorsing Weygand's view that the French government was increasingly "under German domination and control" and led by men promised "brilliant careers" in the new European order.[90] To avoid upsetting earlier American illusions in Pétain, the old general's health was now said to be "waning" rapidly. With Weygand's influence curbed, signs of collaboration were soon evident in North Africa, with Ambassador Leahy reporting that U.S.-supplied goods were "leaking" into German hands and that French military vehicles were being made available to Rommel's forces.[91]

The crisis came to a head on November 18, 1941 when, on the same day that the Eighth Army launched Operation *Crusader*, Vichy removed General Weygand from office. Leahy surmised that the sacking resulted from a German "diktat" issued in direct response to the British attack and concluded that it threatened not only the trade agreement but also the viability of Washington's entire Vichy policy.[92] But while Leahy recommended that both he and Murphy be recalled for consultations, Washington had a more sanguine reaction.[93] Cordell Hull issued a brief statement blaming Germany for Weygand's removal and announcing another suspension of the trade accord, but he carefully avoided any suggestion of a more profound breach.[94] The American press was less easily mollified, with many editorial writers seeing in Weygand's removal further evidence of a failed policy and a reason finally to break relations with Vichy. The *New York Times,* usually supportive of administration policy, argued that Vichy had become a German "partner," while the *Nation* suggested that Weygand's ouster was a "heavy defeat" for the State Department.[95] All "clear-headed people," the liberal weekly concluded, now favored the breaking of diplomatic relations. *Time* concurred, arguing that Washington was "out of a

[89] Arthur Funk, "Negotiating the 'Deal with Darlan,'" *Journal of Contemporary History* 8, no. 2 (1973), 23.

[90] Murphy to Hull, August 2, 1941, *FRUS 1941*, 2: 406.

[91] Leahy to Hull, September 25, 1941, *FRUS 1941*, 2: 437.

[92] Admiral William D. Leahy, *I Was There: The Personal Story of the Chief of Staff to Presidents Roosevelt and Truman Based on His Notes and Diaries Made at the Time* (New York: McGraw Hill, 1950), 59.

[93] Leahy to Hull, November 19, 1941, *FRUS 1941*, 2: 464–465.

[94] *Department of State Bulletin*, November 22, 1941, 5: 407.

[95] Editorial, *New York Times*, November 21, 1941; *The Nation*, November 29, 1941.

policy."[96] The well-connected and acerbic Drew Pearson blamed opportunistic State Department "career boys" – and the "charming Mr. Robert Murphy" in particular – for pursuing relations with Vichy heedless of the "fascist" character of the Pétain regime.[97]

Despite this intense public criticism and the apparent vindication of those who had opposed "appeasing" Vichy, Washington did not change its approach to the French government. From Algiers, Robert Murphy reported reassuringly that Weygand himself wanted the trade accord to continue, concluding "it would be folly for the United States to abandon the field at a moment when its influence is demonstrated and when it can become indispensable."[98] Ambassador Leahy dropped the proposal for his own recall, arguing instead that he should remain in Vichy to exercise a "restraining influence" on Pétain.[99] From Tangier, Childs offered loyal support, claiming that all U.S. officials in the protectorate agreed that the trade agreement should continue.[100] As the immediate crisis passed, Murphy lobbied enthusiastically for a new "Mediterranean policy," arguing that the trade accord, together with the diplomatic and espionage activities facilitated by it, continued to be critical to the cultivation of "well disposed" French officials throughout North Africa.[101] To prove his point, Murphy soon claimed to have found a group of colonial officials favorable to the establishment of a "provisional government" in North Africa.[102]

Over the following months Murphy's new "Mediterranean policy" led to a far-reaching search for potential French collaborators in North Africa. This effort, conducted under President Roosevelt's personal oversight, overlapped with America's formal entry into the war following the Japanese attack on Pearl Harbor on December 7. Even as it went to war with Germany, Washington reaffirmed its orientation toward Vichy. In mid-December, having secured a renewed French promise that its fleet would not fall into German hands and with public attention fixed on the Pacific, Washington quietly resumed operation of the trade accord.[103] With the exception of oil, which remained temporarily embargoed, U.S. supplies were soon flowing into French North Africa again. London signaled its support, with Churchill assuring Roosevelt that the Allies had no other "worthwhile connections" with the French government.[104] Despite all the blows leveled against it by the press, by opponents in London,

---

[96] Editorial, *Time*, December 1, 1941.
[97] Pearson, "Washington Merry-Go-Round," November 21, 1941.
[98] Murphy to Hull, November 21, 1941, *FRUS 1941*, 2: 472–473. See also Weygand, *Recalled to Service*, 378.
[99] Leahy to Hull, November 22, 1941, *FRUS 1941*, 2: 474.
[100] Childs to State, November 25, 1941, *FRUS 1941*, 2: 476.
[101] Murphy to Hull, November 25, *FRUS 1941*, 2: 479–480.
[102] Murphy to Welles, November 27, 1941, *FRUS 1941*, 2: 483.
[103] Leahy to Hull, December 19, 1941, *FRUS 1941*, 2: 500–501.
[104] Churchill to Roosevelt, December 11, 1941, *Correspondence*, 1: 287.

and by skeptics within the administration led by Treasury Secretary Henry Morgenthau, the trade accord staggered on.

The accord's remarkable longevity is in large part attributable to President Roosevelt's personal support. As ever, it is hard to determine exactly what Roosevelt was thinking, but circumstantial evidence suggests that his general interest in French North Africa, evident since the fall of 1940, coalesced into active pursuit of a U.S.-led invasion at precisely this time. Trusted advisers had been encouraging him to move in this direction for some time. Returning from a mission to review the development of Lend-Lease operations in the Mediterranean and Middle East, Averell Harriman reported on the existence of a "strong anti-Vichy organization" in North Africa that was ready to "cooperate with any [Allied] force coming in."[105] Harriman concluded that U.S. intervention was necessary to "nurse" the French along and to protect them from a much-feared "native uprising." These reports confirmed those generated by Murphy and his network of vice-consuls and channeled directly to the White House.

Perhaps to corroborate these intelligence estimates, Roosevelt dispatched William Bullitt to the "Near Eastern area" in December 1941 as his personal representative.[106] Bullitt was charged with preparing a report on conditions in the region that would enable the president to feel "as though he had been there himself."[107] In Cairo, Bullitt discussed detailed plans for an Allied campaign in North Africa with Colonel Astier de Villatte, head of the Free French Air Force in the Middle East. The authorship of the plan forwarded to Roosevelt as a result of this meeting is unclear, and the roving ambassador's willingness to meet with senior Gaullists must have raised eyebrows in Washington. But the plan itself was sophisticated and prescient, urging U.S.-led attacks on Morocco, Algeria and Tunisia aimed at securing "control of the Mediterranean," followed by an "attack on Italy." Given what we know of Roosevelt's interest in North Africa, this plan must have stimulated – or perhaps confirmed – his enthusiasm for an invasion.[108]

While in Cairo, Bullitt also met with senior British leaders in the region, coauthoring a report to Roosevelt and Churchill with Oliver Lyttelton, the British Minister of State to the Middle East. Their joint telegram was drafted hurriedly and dispatched to Washington in time to arrive during the *Arcadia* conference, the first wartime summit meeting between British and American leaders, that convened on December 22. In it, the two men argued that the

---

[105] Harriman memorandum, July 11–14, 1941, Bullitt papers, Box 120, Folder 561, Yale University Library.

[106] Orville H. Bullitt, ed., *For the President Personal and Secret: Correspondence Between Franklin D. Roosevelt and William C. Bullitt* (Boston, MA: Houghton Mifflin, 1972), 529; also see Will Brownell and Richard N. Billings, *So Close to Greatness: A Biography of William C. Bullitt* (New York: Macmillan, 1987).

[107] Ibid., 528.

[108] Bullitt, memorandum, "Problem of North Africa," n.d., Bullitt papers, Box 120, Folder 565.

unpredictable reaction of French forces in Tunisia to the arrival of British troops advancing from Egypt necessitated making an "immediate start" on plans for a "Casablancan expedition."[109] The presence of U.S. troops in North Africa, they concluded, would secure local French support for the Allied cause, particularly if prepared beforehand by "propaganda and subversive activities" throughout the region.

By the time Allied leaders assembled in Washington for the *Arcadia* conference, several considerations were pointing toward a U.S. invasion of French North Africa. A U.S. invasion, carried out at the invitation of French authorities, was seen by President Roosevelt and his immediate circle as the logical conclusion of the broad strategic reorientation undertaken following the fall of France eighteen months earlier. In particular, by bringing U.S. forces into action in the European theater for the first time, it could be presented as a vindication of the administration's dogged cultivation of good relations with Vichy. Pushed forward in the face of domestic criticism and of opposition from London, the Murphy-Weygand accord was already tying the United States into the unfolding politics of French North Africa while simultaneously facilitating the expansion of diplomatic and undercover activity necessary to generate the actionable intelligence that would justify an invasion. In military-strategic terms, a U.S. invasion of North Africa would also conform to the "Germany first" approach adopted in the light of the French defeat and codified in *Plan Dog*, ABC-1, and *Rainbow 5*, all of which envisaged the possibility of operations in the Mediterranean aimed at establishing positions from which to launch an invasion of southern Europe.

[109] Bullitt and Lyttelton to Roosevelt and Churchill, December 31, 1941, Bullitt, *For the President*, 544.

2

The Decision for *Torch*

Meeting in Washington less than three weeks after Pearl Harbor, Franklin Roosevelt, Winston Churchill, and their senior advisors faced the task of shaping Allied strategy in the new period opened by America's formal entry into the war. Resisting pressure from the U.S. Navy to focus on the Pacific, participants in the *Arcadia* conference reaffirmed the "Germany first" approach that had guided Anglo-American strategy since early 1941, agreeing to expand shipments of war matériel to the Soviet Union to ensure that the Russians stayed in the fight. They also discussed launching their own counteroffensive, adopting a plan drafted by British leaders en route to Washington. This plan, code-named Operation *Gymnast*, featured a U.S.-led invasion of French North Africa. According to Churchill's outline, the invasion would be preceded by a campaign designed to "win over" French colonial officials and their "loyal Moors" by a combination of "inducement" and "pressure." To mollify French Anglophobia, the landings themselves would be spearheaded by a U.S. task-force that would be ready to sail as soon as an agreement with French officials was concluded.[1]

In the chaotic weeks after Pearl Harbor, it was inevitable that the plans adopted at *Arcadia* were to some extent, as historian Mark Stoler emphasizes, "more formal than real."[2] Moreover, when British planners formulated *Gymnast* they were confronting a renewed crisis in the Mediterranean, with the loss of three Royal Navy battleships and mounting air attacks on Malta that posed a challenge to London's strategic position. Now, despite their misgivings

---

[1] Churchill to Roosevelt, December 16, 1941 (presented to Roosevelt between December 22 and 25), Warren F. Kimball (ed.), *Churchill and Roosevelt: The Complete Correspondence* (London: Collins, 1984), 1: 295–296.

[2] Mark Stoler, *Allies and Adversaries: The Joint Chiefs of Staff, the Grand Alliance, and U.S. Strategy in World War II* (Chapel Hill: University of North Carolina Press, 2000), 67.

about Washington's long-term interests in the region, the British wanted the Americans in.

Despite Churchill's early advocacy, *Gymnast* was by no means an exclusively British concept. Conforming closely to President Roosevelt's own developing interest in North Africa, the plan was discussed and decided on by all the assembled Allied leaders. Commenting later on this convergence of British and American strategic thinking, Churchill noted "the President was thinking along very much the same lines as I was about action in French North-West Africa," adding, according to the official British record of the proceedings, that he "set great store on organizing a *Super-Gymnast.*"[3]

The Allied decision to move toward an invasion of North Africa was reinforced by the urgency of the Bullitt/Lyttelton proposal for an American landing in Morocco, and it appeared to be justified by the intelligence reports generated by Murphy and his vice-consuls in the Maghreb. The decision for *Gymnast* was, therefore, neither an aberration nor a British imposition, but was a product of a genuine convergence between British notions of "closing the ring" around Germany and a specifically *American* orientation toward North Africa that had been taking shape since the fall of France.

One potential obstacle to this strategic convergence was the Allies' diametrically opposed attitudes toward de Gaulle's Free French. Churchill alluded to this difficulty in his outline for *Arcadia*, suggesting that the question of Allied, as opposed to British or American, relations with de Gaulle needed to be carefully "reviewed."[4] Noting that de Gaulle had yet to be "any important help to us," Churchill proposed that Allied relations with Vichy and with the Free French should be based on performance. If the French government cooperated in North Africa, they would take precedence; but, if they deepened their collaboration with Berlin, the Free French would be of more "value" and would be "aided and used to the full."[5] This simple solution, allowing London and Washington to continue pursuing their own policies toward Vichy and de Gaulle, was almost upended during the course of the *Arcadia* conference by the actions of the Free French in the Gulf of St. Lawrence.

On December 24, 1941, a Free French flotilla seized the French-ruled islands of St. Pierre and Miquelon at the mouth of the St. Lawrence in Canada, overthrowing the Vichy administrations there and quickly legitimizing their coup by plebiscite. Recognizing that any display of sympathy for the Gaullist coup would undermine the entire framework of Washington's Vichy policy, Secretary of State Cordell Hull quickly issued a statement sharply critical of the "arbitrary action" of the "so-called Free French" and demanding that the islands

---

[3] Winston S. Churchill, *The Second World War* 6 vols. (Boston: Houghton Mifflin, 1948–1954), 3: 574, 624.

[4] Churchill to Roosevelt, December 16, 1941 (presented to Roosevelt between December 22 and 25), *Correspondence*, 1: 297.

[5] Ibid., 298.

be handed back to Vichy.[6] Hull's unfortunate turn of phrase – many liberal opinion-formers were already convinced that de Gaulle represented the real France – provoked a new wave of criticism of Washington's Vichy policy and a flood of protest messages addressed to the "so-called Secretary of State."[7] Hull's intemperate criticism of what many saw as the liberation of St. Pierre and Miquelon from a collaborationist regime seemed particularly incongruous in the light of the ringing declaration of democratic principles, including support for national self-determination, adopted by the "United Nations" at the close of the *Arcadia* conference.

Cordell Hull's outspoken comments made him the focus of public criticism of appeasement, allowing President Roosevelt to feign indifference by, as Churchill put it, "shrug[ging] his shoulders over the whole affair."[8] But although Roosevelt was able to distance himself from an unpopular policy, Hull's stance clearly reflected the president's own pledge to Vichy that the United States would support the "maintenance of the *status quo* in the French colonies of the Western Hemisphere."[9] For his part, Churchill chastised de Gaulle over the timing of the coup and proposed to place St. Pierre and Miquelon under a U.S./Canadian consultative council in the hope that the "two tiny islands" might "relapse into obscurity."[10] In the end, because neither ally was prepared to evict the Free French and Vichy was unable to do so, the Gaullists remained in control. The fact that there was no rupture in U.S.-Vichy relations, despite Hull's warning to the president that the affair might lead to "serious deteriorations … in relation to the French Navy, Mediterranean bases, North Africa etc.," demonstrates Vichy's understanding of the complex position that Washington found itself in and, perhaps more importantly, it underscores the diplomatic efficacy of U.S. trade.[11]

In January 1942, even as the *Arcadia* conference was recommitting the United States to a "Germany first" strategy, the day-to-day attention of U.S. military leaders was riveted on the Pacific. The rapid and sweeping success of Japan's "centrifugal offensive," spiraling outward into Malaya, the Philippines, and Indonesia, presented planners with the disturbing prospect of further Japanese advances toward India, Australia, and the Central Pacific. Above all, it raised the specter that China, cut off from U.S. support, might finally succumb to Japanese arms. Not surprisingly, the fight to stem the Japanese tide dominated the work of the War Department's War Plans Division, including that of its newly appointed deputy chief, General Dwight D. Eisenhower.

[6] Hull, statement December 25, 1941, *FRUS 1941*, 2: 551.
[7] Julian G. Hurstfield, *America and the French Nation, 1939–1945* (Chapel Hill: University of North Carolina Press, 1986), 121.
[8] Churchill, *Second World War*, 3: 591.
[9] Leahy to State Dept., December 19, 1941, *FRUS 1941*, 2: 500.
[10] Churchill to Roosevelt, January 23, 1942, *Correspondence*, 326.
[11] Hull to Roosevelt, February 2, 1942, quoted in Hurstfield, *America and the French Nation*, 137.

Confiding in his desk diary, Eisenhower dismissed *Gymnast* as a "sideshow" and a diversion from the urgent task of reinforcing Australia.[12] Even worse, in his view, the ill-advised operation in French North Africa seemed to demonstrate that strategic planning was in the hands of "amateur strategists" and "prima donnas," with politicians rather than professional soldiers determining critical military priorities.[13]

Eisenhower's critique was that of an archetypal military manager focused on the mobilization and deployment of military resources and skeptical of attempts to extend civilian control over questions best left to professionals.[14] He was not alone either in his dismissal of *Gymnast* or in his opposition to the schemes of civilian leaders. General Joseph Stilwell, the officer initially slated to command *Gymnast*, noted that Army Chief of Staff George Marshall was strongly opposed to the operation, arguing that if German forces captured Gibraltar they would close the western entrance of the Mediterranean, cutting off any U.S. troops in North Africa.[15] In typically acerbic fashion, "Vinegar Joe" added that American troops would then find themselves trapped in a "rathole … under the guns, sure of punishment, and hard to supply."[16] Like Eisenhower, Stilwell blamed politicians, particularly the "rank amateur" in the White House, for designing such an unsound plan. Stilwell also voiced a new complaint, suggesting that Roosevelt had fallen under Churchill's influence, becoming "completely hypnotized" by the "Limeys."[17] *Gymnast*, Stilwell concluded, would simply commit U.S. forces to a British imperial project. It was an accusation that would enjoy a long life.

On January 9, George Marshall presented his opposition to *Gymnast* to the president. In measured language, he delivered a verdict scarcely less damning than the complaints voiced by Eisenhower and Stilwell. Marshall conceded that U.S. control of North Africa might help to "protect the South Atlantic" by blocking any "extension of Axis influence to the West and South," but stressed that U.S. forces would be under constant threat of an Axis advance closing the Straits of Gibraltar.[18] The only "feasible" plan for an invasion of North Africa, Marshall concluded, required a landing in Morocco – *outside* the Mediterranean – launched after securing a definitive "invitation" from French

---

[12] Eisenhower, personal memorandum, January 1, 1942, in Alfred D. Chandler (ed.), *The Papers of Dwight David Eisenhower: The War Years* (Baltimore, MD: Johns Hopkins, 1970) (henceforth *Eisenhower Papers*), 1: 34.

[13] Eisenhower, personal memorandum, January 4, 1942, *Eisenhower Papers*, 1: 39.

[14] Brian McAllister Linn, *The Echo of Battle: The Army's Way of War* (Cambridge, MA: Harvard University Press, 2007), 142–144.

[15] See Barbara W. Tuchman, *Stilwell and the American Experience in China, 1911–45* (New York: Grove Press, 1970), 232.

[16] Stilwell memorandum, January 4, 1942, in Theodore H. White, *The Stilwell Papers* (New York: William Sloane 1948), 21.

[17] Ibid., 15–16.

[18] Memorandum, Marshall to FDR, January 9, 1942, PSF, North Africa folder, FDRL.

officials. Even this modest proposal was "problematical" because it was unrealistic to expect substantial assistance from either the "opportunist French" or their restless "native" subjects.

These statements by Eisenhower, Marshall, and Stilwell make clear the rapid hardening of Army opinion against an invasion of North Africa that took place in the early weeks of 1942. What is less clear is *why* this occurred, particularly in light of the privileged place accorded to French North Africa and to the Mediterranean more broadly in Anglo-American strategic planning from ABC-1 to *Arcadia*. It is as if Army leaders had not expected to have to act on the agreements registered in ABC-1, and only awoke to the realization of what this might involve after the *Arcadia* conference had turned Allied planning in that direction. Once the reaction against *Gymnast* set in, however, it was quickly justified by the simple notions of mass and concentration that had long dominated U.S. military thinking. These principles, ostensibly derived from the Civil War campaigns of William T. Sherman and Ulysses S. Grant, called for the concentration of all available resources for a single, decisive blow; they were increasingly taken as emblematic of an "American way of war."[19]

Initial Army opposition to the perceived squandering of forces in North Africa was based on the necessity of marshaling resources to check the Japanese offensive, and it was reflected in Eisenhower's plea to "drop everything" to "scrape up" all possible reinforcements for Indonesia and Burma.[20] Within a few days, however, the premise on which Army opposition to *Gymnast* was based changed completely, with Eisenhower now arguing against "wasting resources all over the world," and for launching a "land attack" into Europe "as soon *as possible*."[21] Eisenhower would later claim that that the cross-Channel invasion of France had its origins in this laconic personal memorandum; whether or not this is strictly true, it is clear that by late January Army opinion was coming down in favor of an early cross-Channel assault and against the invasion of North Africa advocated by the "amateur" in the White House. Once formulated, this simple military nostrum – defined by senior planner General Albert Wedemeyer as "going for the enemy's jugular vein" – proved remarkably resilient.[22] Justified on the grounds that it would open the shortest road to Berlin, succor the hard-pressed Russians, and achieve a rapid victory by avoiding the wasteful "periphery picking" championed by London, it was the lodestar of U.S. military thought until finally realized in Normandy in June 1944.[23]

Attracted by a strategy that appeared to conform to elementary military principles, Army leaders also displayed a strain of pungent Anglophobia in their

[19] See Russell Weigley, *The American Way of War* (Bloomington: Indiana University Press, 1977).
[20] Personal memorandum, Eisenhower, January 17, 1942, *Eisenhower Papers*, 1: 61.
[21] Personal memorandum, Eisenhower, January 22, 1942, *Eisenhower Papers*, 1: 66.
[22] Albert C. Wedemeyer, *Wedemeyer Reports!* (New York: Henry Holt, 1958), 132.
[23] Ibid.

aversion to Mediterranean operations.[24] This was expressed in the view that Roosevelt's insistence on action in the Mediterranean reflected his susceptibility to British manipulation, with Stilwell arguing that *Gymnast* demonstrated the "tremendous hold the Limeys have on Our Boy."[25] Wedemeyer was similarly acidic, and his deep Anglophobia would lead him to tape meetings with British officers to demonstrate their "unreasonable demands" to Marshall.[26] To many senior officers, London's interest in the Mediterranean seemed to stem from an imperial desire to extend British influence and not from the pursuit of a rapid defeat of Germany. As Eisenhower put it, "Britishers instinctively approach every military problem from the viewpoint of the Empire."[27] Schooled in the separation of military and political power, American officers reacted against a British strategy that they perceived as driven by overtly "political" imperatives.

Attracted by the classical simplicity of a single knockout blow and repelled by the apparently devious "political" machinations of British imperial policy, U.S. strategists adopted the cross-Channel assault as an unshakeable *idée fixe*. The fact that a successful landing in France was beyond the capacity of inexperienced and under-equipped Allied forces in 1942 or even 1943 is beside the point. By early 1942, a uniquely American combination of naiveté, confidence, and strategic simplification had coalesced into a view that the cross-Channel invasion offered the only acceptable operational concretization of the "Germany first" approach. *Gymnast,* with its deep dive into the Mediterranean, would have to go. On March 3, the Americans took their opposition to *Gymnast* to the newly formed Combined Chiefs of Staff (CCS), the top-level committee charged with integrating Allied planning established at the *Arcadia* conference. With the British chiefs of staff focused on the deepening crisis in Burma following of the fall of Singapore and on the continuing battle with Rommel's *Afrika Korps*, the CCS agreed to postpone *Gymnast* indefinitely.

Writing to Churchill on March 7, Roosevelt pointed out that the sidelining of *Gymnast* was the necessary consequence of the decision to allocate substantial U.S. resources to the Pacific, particularly in aircraft and shipping.[28] The unspoken implication was that the main U.S. effort might now be shifted to the Pacific – a reversal in strategic priorities that, as Roosevelt well knew, was unacceptable both to the British, and to the U.S. Army, which viewed the Pacific as a Navy bailiwick. Under Marshall's guidance, the Army's Operations Division (OPD) quickly furnished a European alternative, offering several options for cross-Channel assaults including the build-up of U.S. forces in Britain (*Bolero*); an emergency attack on the Cherbourg peninsula in Normandy to be launched

---

[24] See, for example, Andrew Roberts, *Masters and Commanders: How Four Titans Won the War in the West, 1941–1945,* (New York: Harper, 2009), 148.
[25] Theodore H. White (ed.), *The Stilwell Papers* (New York: William Sloane, 1948), 22.
[26] Wedemeyer, *Wedemeyer Reports!,* 164–165.
[27] Eisenhower to Handy, January 28, 1943, *Eisenhower Papers,* 2: 928.
[28] Roosevelt to Churchill, March 7, 1942, *Collected Correspondence,* 1: 390–391.

if a Soviet collapse appeared imminent (*Sledgehammer*); and a full-scale invasion of France projected for 1943 (*Roundup*). Marshall buttressed his case for
a cross-Channel offensive by arguing that the opening of a European front
would relieve German pressure on the Soviet Union. On April 1, Marshall won
presidential approval for this package of cross-Channel options and was dispatched to London with presidential adviser Harry Hopkins to present them
to the British.

It is impossible to gauge Roosevelt's attitude to the proposals carried to
London by Hopkins and Marshall. In a note to Churchill he was enthusiastic enough, explaining that he supported the plan to "draw off pressure on
the Russians" with "heart and mind."[29] But the problems of *Sledgehammer* –
the operation would be largely British in composition, and even its American
advocates indelicately described it as a "sacrifice" – were hard to ignore.
Moreover, there is plentiful circumstantial evidence that although the president
temporarily ceded the field to the proponents of a cross-Channel invasion, his
interest in North Africa – and in *Gymnast* – continued. At a meeting to formal-
ize the plans Hopkins and Marshall would take to London, Secretary of War
Henry Stimson was alarmed to hear Roosevelt voicing continued interest in the
"Middle East and the Mediterranean Basin." If uncurbed, Stimson feared that
the president's unbroken attachment to the "charming" Mediterranean would
lead to the "wildest kind of dispersion debauch."[30]

In this light it is entirely possible that Roosevelt's support for the Army's
cross-Channel plans in the spring of 1942 was not entirely wholehearted, and
that in his "foxy" way, (as Stimson put it), he may have been gambling on a
British rejection of *Sledgehammer* opening the way for a revival of *Gymnast*.[31]
For their part, the British, relieved that the Americans were not proposing to
dump "Germany first" for the Pacific, expressed initial enthusiasm for the
plans presented by Marshall and Hopkins, but then quickly got to work to
undermine them. British planners concentrated their fire on the "sacrificial"
Sledgehammer. As British criticisms mounted, it became clear to Stimson and
the Joint Chiefs that Roosevelt was preparing to "jump the traces," abandoning the cross-Channel attack in favor of a renewed commitment to *Gymnast*.[32]
He would get the opportunity to do precisely this when the second wartime
summit conference convened in Washington in late June.

In the months between the apparent demise of *Gymnast* in March and its
revival in June, two important developments took place that supported the
case for action in French North Africa. The first involved the initial deployment of American combat units to the wartime Mediterranean, and the second,

[29] Roosevelt to Churchill, Apr. 3, 1942, *Collected Correspondence*, 1: 441.
[30] Henry L. Stimson, *On Active Service in Peace and War* (New York: Harper & Bros.,
     1948), 416.
[31] Ibid., 419.
[32] Ibid.

broader in scope, involved the production of actionable intelligence by Robert Murphy's network in the Maghreb.

In early 1942, the danger of Axis air attacks overwhelming the British island-base of Malta prompted Churchill to request U.S. help in ferrying Spitfire fighter aircraft to the beleaguered garrison.[33] In response, Roosevelt authorized the aircraft carrier *Wasp* to sail into the Mediterranean laden with British aircraft. Before *Wasp* could be dispatched, however, Roosevelt had to squash opposition from Chief of Naval Operations Admiral Ernest King, who complained that London was deliberately understating its own resources in order to secure a U.S. military commitment to the Mediterranean.[34] King's fears of entrapment may have been justified, but *Wasp*'s mission went ahead and forty-eight Spitfires were delivered to Malta on April 20. Most of these reinforcements were soon destroyed on the ground by German attacks, forcing Churchill to request a repeat performance.[35] Responding to Churchill's warning that Malta was being "pounded to bits," Roosevelt quickly authorized *Wasp* to undertake another mission, and the U.S. carrier delivered a further forty-seven aircraft.[36]

Wasp's two sorties had great symbolic significance, indicating – precisely as King feared – America's growing involvement in the Mediterranean. They also underscored the fact that this involvement came in response to British weakness and evidenced the rising military capability of the United States.[37] Given the discussions on Allied strategy underway as *Wasp* sailed, it seems entirely plausible that in authorizing the missions over King's objections, Roosevelt was seeking precisely the opening into the Mediterranean, and hence toward *Gymnast*, that the Joint Chiefs feared. Perhaps alluding to this, Roosevelt's handwritten addition to the telegram to Churchill approving *Wasp*'s second mission observed enigmatically, "time is definitely running in our favor just now."[38]

The president's continued adherence to *Gymnast* throughout the contentious debates in mid-1942 was increasingly succored by the product of the U.S. intelligence network operating in North Africa under Roosevelt's personal oversight. The significance of this covert operation to the resolution of the strategic discussions taking place in Washington and London has been largely overlooked, but without it there would have been no Allied invasion of North Africa. The framework for America's burgeoning covert activity in the Maghreb

[33] See Simon Ball, *Bitter Sea: The Brutal World War II Fight for the Mediterranean* (New York: Harper, 2009), 134–135; Richard Woodman, *The Malta Convoys, 1940–1943* (London: John Murray, 2000), 320.

[34] See Kimball, editorial comment in Warren F. Kimball, *Churchill and Roosevelt: The Complete Correspondence* (Princeton, NJ: Princeton University Press, 1984), 1: 440.

[35] Churchill, *History of the Second World War*, 4: 269.

[36] Churchill to Roosevelt, April 24, 1942, *Correspondence*, 1: 467–468.

[37] See Ball, *Bitter Sea*, 134.

[38] Roosevelt to Churchill, April 24, 1942, *Correspondence*, 1: 470.

was furnished by the Murphy-Weygand trade accord, which reassured French officials in North Africa that they remained central to U.S. plans and gave the vice-consuls diplomatic cover for their clandestine activities. As ever, the accord followed a tortuous course. Quietly resumed in December 1941, shipments were cut again cut in February when officials corroborated British accusations that French officers were supplying Rommel with U.S. food and fuel. When challenged, Vichy reined in their officers, and the State Department announced on April 7 the resumption of economic aid.

True to form, this revival of the trade accord was short-lived. On April 18, Marshal Pétain sidelined Admiral Darlan and handed control of the government back to Pierre Laval. For many U.S. opinion-makers, this concentration of power in the hands of the most openly pro-Nazi wing of the Vichy regime demanded demonstrative action. The *Washington Post* urged recognition of the "De Gaullists" as the "true government of the true France" while the *New York Times* asserted bluntly "Laval is Hitler."[39] Under pressure, Washington finally recalled Ambassador Leahy and suspended the trade accord, but it did not sever diplomatic relations with Vichy. Leahy himself argued strongly for the maintenance of ties in order to facilitate the clandestine effort underway in North Africa.

Opposition to reviving the accord centered on the Board of Economic Warfare (BEW), where policy makers argued that it was better that food did not reach North Africa because undernourished Arabs would blame Vichy for their plight and would welcome U.S. troops as liberators.[40] Leahy, now Roosevelt's personal Chief of Staff and his liaison with the Joint Chiefs, complained that the New Dealers leading the BEW seemed incapable of seeing that U.S. policy in North Africa hinged on cultivating relations with French colonial officials. Finally abandoning attempts at persuasion, he issued a direct order to resume the accord, bluntly informing the BEW that "the President says 'do it!'" On June 11, the State Department quietly resumed shipments to North Africa.[41] Amid reports of Soviet Commissar for Foreign Affairs Vyacheslav Molotov's visit to the United States and news of the victory at Midway, the decision to resume sending aid to North Africa received little attention.

As the debate over Allied strategy continued in Washington, Robert Murphy and his corps of diplomats-cum-spies were still working to secure from French officials a viable "invitation" for American forces to enter North Africa. After Weygand's ouster, Murphy had abandoned the project of working with the aged general in favor of an expanded campaign to cultivate other "well

---

[39] Editorial, *New York Times* April 15, 1942; Editorial, *Washington Post*, April 15, 1942.
[40] See James J. Dougherty, *The Politics of Wartime Aid: American Economic Assistance to France and French Northwest Africa, 1940–1946* (Westport, CT: Greenwood Press, 1978), 45.
[41] William D. Leahy, *I Was There: The Personal Story of the Chief of Staff to Presidents Roosevelt and Truman Based on His Notes and Diaries Made at the Time* (New York: McGraw Hill, 1950), 113.

disposed" French officials.[42] The trade accord, continuing on its rocky road
and revived by presidential fiat, provided the diplomatic framework and cover
for this effort, but the activity of U.S. agents centered increasingly on burnish-
ing the credentials of conspiratorial groups of colonial administrators, military
officers, and business people in the hope that some constellation of these forces
would be able to issue a credible invitation.

In December 1941, Murphy's network was reinforced by the assignment
of former Marine Colonel William Eddy as naval attaché in Tangier. Eddy's
real assignment, received directly from the Coordinator of Information (and
soon to be Office of Strategic Services head) Colonel William Donovan, was
to support Murphy's work by coordinating covert operations throughout
the Maghreb.[43] His importance can be judged by the fact that when he faced
a court martial in 1943 for a lapse of security in letters to his family, Eddy
avoided prosecution on the technical grounds that he was not in the Army
chain of command and therefore not subject to the Articles of War, and on the
actual grounds that his "services" had been secured by "informal arrangement"
between "the Commander-in Chief and Col. Donovan."[44] A decorated veteran
and the Arabic-speaking former head of English at the American University
in Cairo, Eddy plunged eagerly into a *Casablanca*-esque world of espionage, double-cross, and sexual intrigue framed by the fantasies of American
Orientalism.[45] Tangier, Eddy reported, was a "whirlpool" full of "escapees
[from] income taxes and the hangman" and a hive of intrigue where Allied and
Axis agents "mingled freely" at social functions.[46] They also tried to kill each
other; British agents uncovered two plots to bomb Eddy's car.[47] Reflecting on
this unrestrained derring-do, vice-consul Kenneth Pendar recalled that in the
heady atmosphere of the Maghreb "normally sensible" Americans started acting "like Arabs."[48]

Even if they acted like "Arabs," U.S. agents directed their attention firmly
toward Frenchmen. Robert Murphy, reflecting Roosevelt's assurances to Vichy,
emphasized that relations between French rulers and their Arab subjects
were "purely an affair between them," and not a matter of concern to the

[42] Murphy to Hull, November 25, *FRUS 1941*, 2: 479–480; for the best account of U.S. preparations for *Torch*, see Arthur Layton Funk, *The Politics of Torch: The Allied Landings and the
Algiers Putsch 1942* (Lawrence: University Press of Kansas: 1974).
[43] William Eddy, "Spies and Lies in Tangier," unpublished monograph, Eddy Papers, Tangier folder,
Seely Mudd Library, Princeton.
[44] Memo from Judge Advocate Adam Richardson, AFHQ, March 17, 1943, RG 331, Reel 70
(Specialized), NARA.
[45] See Brian T. Edwards, *Morocco Bound: Disorienting America's Maghreb, from Casablanca to
the Marrakech Express* (Durham, NC: Duke University Press, 2005).
[46] Eddy, "Spies and Lies."
[47] British Consul, Tangier, to Childs, April 14, 1942, RG 84, Morocco, Box 4, NARA.
[48] Kenneth Pendar, *Adventures in Diplomacy: Our French Dilemma* (New York: Da Capo Press,
(1945) 1976), 17.

Americans.[49] American agents were warned against "preach[ing] democracy or independence," and Murphy cautioned that any "monkey business" among the Arabs would "enrage" America's French "colleagues" and set back efforts to secure an invitation.[50] Despite these strictures, many vice-consuls found it hard not to sympathize with the Arabs and pursued unofficial political contacts with them. In May 1942, Kenneth Pendar was called to order for his "ill-advised activities among the Moors" by chargé J. Rives Childs, who pointed out that the French were "understandably sensitive" to any hint of U.S. support for Moroccan independence.[51] Pendar's "impropriety," Childs complained, made him a "menace to our work."

Liberal-minded agents were also appalled by the rightist politics of many colonial officials and French settlers or *colons,* some of whom boasted of their ties to the fascistic Cagoulard conspiracy. Even worse, they noted that Murphy seemed to feel at home among them.[52] But Murphy's approach yielded results. Roosevelt confidant Undersecretary of State Sumner Welles was soon receiving glowing reports on his contact with the "able, fearless, young, and experienced" Colonel Jean Van Hecke, allegedly the leader of 26,000 "disciplined, trained, and hardened" young men in the *Chantiers de la Jeunesse Français.* Lest Welles balk at the prospect of collaborating with the Pétainist youth movement, Murphy assured him that it was simply the French equivalent of the New Deal's Civilian Conservation Corps (CCC).[53] Murphy's report built on the work of consul Felix Cole in Algiers, who had noticed the tough "physical and mental conditioning" of the *Chantiers de la Jeunesse* the previous year and had asked the CCC to send information on its activities to Van Hecke.[54] A bemused CCC official duly responded by forwarding material on the organization to North Africa.

Murphy's interest settled on the "Group of Five," a clique of right-wingers that claimed to have extensive contacts within the Vichy administration, the military, and the *colon* community.[55] Led by wealthy businessman and former Cagoule backer Jacques Lemaigre-Dubreuil, the Five saw a coup in North Africa as the first step to the establishment of an independent conservative regime in France that would be led by General Henri Giraud.[56] Captured by the Germans in May 1940, Giraud escaped in April 1942 and returned to France to seek the

---

[49] Robert Murphy, *Diplomat among Warriors* (Garden City, NY: Doubleday & Co, 1964), 92.
[50] Pendar, *Adventures in Diplomacy*, 21; Murphy, *Diplomat among Warriors*, 92.
[51] Childs to Russell, June 16, 1942, RG 84, Morocco, Box 4, NARA.
[52] See Harris R. Smith, *OSS: The Secret History of America's First Central Intelligence Agency* (Berkley: University of California Press, 1972); Hal Vaughan, *FDR's 12 Apostles: The Spies Who Paved the Way for the Invasion of North Africa* (Guilford, CT: The Lyons Press, 2006), 110–111.
[53] Murphy to Welles, March 14, 1942, Welles papers, Box 162, FDRL.
[54] Cole to State, September 26, 1941, RG 59, 851R, 20/13, NARA.
[55] See Vaughan, *12 Apostles*, 111.
[56] See Funk, *Politics of Torch*, 21.

protection of Marshal Pétain, an old friend. Unlike Pétain, however, Giraud was not reconciled to collaboration with the Germans and nor, by virtue of his imprisonment, was he implicated in the French surrender. He quickly became involved in anti-German plots, and after meeting with Lemaigre-Dubreuil in June he agreed to shift the focus of his activity to North Africa and to serve as leader of the Group of Five's planned uprising. Lemaigre-Dubreuil assured him that Washington would provide the necessary funding.

The initial link between Washington and Giraud was made by Robert Solberg, an OSS agent working out of the Lisbon embassy. In early June 1942, acting with Murphy's encouragement but without the approval of OSS chief William Donovan, Solberg met with the Group of Five in Morocco. As he reported to Preston Goodfellow, head of OSS Special Operations, "with a bit of luck and daring" he had opened communication with Giraud, the last "white hope" and a man "capable of getting France into the war again" by inviting an American occupation of North Africa.[57] Solberg and Lemaigre-Dubreuil negotiated an agreement committing Washington to the provision of Lend-Lease to a North African regime headed by Giraud.[58] Solberg left for Washington on June 19 but, having acted without Donovan's approval, his success with Lemaigre-Dubreuil simply resulted in his expulsion from the OSS.[59] Donovan's pique ensured that this initial agreement with Lemaigre-Dubreuil was filed away undiscussed. However, the link between the Five and Giraud uncovered by Solberg was real enough, and the general's name gave the conspiracy a new aura of seriousness.

As these discussions were proceeding, Robert Murphy concluded that the preconditions for an invasion of North Africa were coming into place. His vice-consuls had gathered voluminous intelligence on the disposition of French troops and on beach conditions at possible landing sites. He was connected to what he believed to be an extensive and well-organized conspiratorial network. And now he seemed to have found a link to a charismatic figurehead. None of this was a moment too soon. In May, the Joint Chiefs of Staff, embroiled in its own campaign against *Gymnast*, had refused to authorize arms shipments to the North African plotters, and the failure to deliver American weapons had produced a temporary cooling in relations with the Five. But with Giraud in place, Murphy was confident that he could win the case and Eddy was dispatched to Washington to demonstrate the viability of the North African operation.

On June 11, William Eddy presented an optimistic assessment of the situation in North Africa to the Intelligence Division of the Army General Staff,

[57] Solberg to Goodfellow, June 10, 1942, Box 2, Robert Solberg correspondence 1941–1951, Preston Goodfellow Papers, Hoover Institution Archives.
[58] Funk, *Politics of Torch*, 55. The promise of Lend-Lease support resurfaced at the time of *Torch*; see Murphy to Giraud, November 2, 1942, *FRUS 1942*, 2: 413–415.
[59] Funk, *Politics of Torch*, 57.

suggesting that 35,000 Frenchmen were prepared for "offensive action" in Algeria with 5,000 more readied for sabotage efforts in Morocco.[60] Noting that the covert operation in North Africa was a "purely American" affair and that they had studiously "avoided all contact with the Moors," Eddy stressed the popularity of the United States among the French population, some "75 or 80 per cent" of whom were "hoping for an Allied victory." With the "remarkably efficient" French underground poised to seize Oran and other key ports, Eddy assured Army leaders that American landings would face only "token resistance." "We don't need to be timid about North Africa," he concluded.[61]

The timing of Eddy's report demonstrates that at the precise moment the debate over Allied strategy was moving to a conclusion, senior policy makers had access to intelligence that seemed to offer convincing proof of the viability of a U.S. invasion of North Africa. Eddy's report was everything Roosevelt might have hoped for when he set the North African operation in motion: French North Africa was on the verge of revolt, it had found a capable leader in the incorrigible Giraud, and it was ready to welcome U.S. troops ashore. In this light, the decision to resume the trade accord, taken on the day Eddy presented his report, amounted to a declaration of confidence in the Five's plan to "invite" a U.S. occupation. Murphy certainly saw it as such, hailing the decision as a "splendid step" that would speed military action in North Africa.[62]

The fact that the reports from Murphy and Eddy turned out to be based on gross exaggerations, if not outright falsehoods, has led some historians to conclude that "false optimism" and "amateur" diplomacy produced inaccurate intelligence, and that the decision to invade North Africa was therefore made on false pretenses.[63] There are different potential culprits – some see intelligence reports colored by Donovan's desire to justify the OSS's existence, whereas others blames Murphy's right-wing bias – but the conclusion is the same: faulty intelligence produced a flawed invasion. These assessments miss the point. Perhaps today, when the role of "sexed up" intelligence estimates in preparing the war in Iraq in 2003 is widely recognized, it is easier to see that *useable* and *actionable*, rather than *accurate*, intelligence was in fact the desired product of Murphy's network. Not all the intelligence from North Africa was fabricated or exaggerated, and the reports on beach conditions and French troop deployments were highly accurate. But these were the outer wrappings for political judgments driven by wish-fulfillment, and the wishes originated in Washington, not Africa. Measured by its delivery of the product that Roosevelt wanted, the covert operation in the Maghreb was a resounding success.

---

[60] Eddy, June 11, 1942, transcript of oral report to Army G-2, Box 3, North Africa, Preston Goodfellow Papers.

[61] Ibid.

[62] Murphy to Atherton, July 6, 1942, *FRUS 1942*, 2: 333.

[63] David A. Walker, "OSS and Operation Torch," *Journal of Contemporary History* 22, no. 4 (1987), 676; Leon Borden Blair, "Amateurs in Diplomacy: The American Vice-Consuls in North Africa 1941–1943," *Historian* 35, no. 4 (1973).

These intelligence estimates informed the discussion at the Second Washington Conference when it convened at the end of June. The conference met in the midst of important strategic developments. In the Pacific, U.S. fliers had won a decisive victory at Midway, but in Russia German forces were preparing a new summer offensive toward Stalingrad and the oilfields of the Caucasus and, as the *Wehrmacht* assembled its armored spearheads, Allied leaders again feared for the survival of their Soviet ally. Meanwhile, in North Africa the military balance had again swung sharply against Britain, with Axis forces under Rommel opening a new attack that by early June had Imperial forces streaming back toward Egypt in disarray, leaving an isolated and under-strength garrison behind them in Tobruk.

These developments shaped Anglo-American strategic deliberations. The victory at Midway reinforced U.S. naval opinion that resources should be concentrated in the Pacific in a "Japan first" strategy, but the looming crisis in Russia exercised powerful countervailing pressure. In May, Soviet Commissar for Foreign Affairs Vyacheslav Molotov had visited Washington, painting a grim picture of the threats facing Russia and arguing forcefully for an Allied offensive to relieve the pressure on the Eastern Front. President Roosevelt concurred, committing the United States to opening a "second front" against Germany before the end of the year.[64]

The president's promise of a second front reinforced the "Germany first" approach, but the details remained vague amounting, as the *New York Times* noted, to a "cryptic" pledge simply to tackle the "urgent tasks of creating a second front in Europe in 1942."[65] Probing this question, influential *New York Times* columnist Anne O'Hare McCormick argued that British operations in the Mediterranean *already* constituted a "second front," and even if the fighting there was not as "definite and spectacular" as that in Russia, it was no "sideshow." She backed her assessment by pointing to the bombing of the Ploesti oilfield in Romania recently conducted by bombers based in Egypt in the first U.S. combat operation in the eastern Mediterranean.[66]

McCormick also broached the issue of the postwar order in the region, pointing out that the fall of France had damaged "old Europe" and its imperial system "beyond repair." The question of which power might fill the resulting vacuum in the Mediterranean went unanswered, but the implications for the expansion of American influence were not hard to discern. Anne O'Hare McCormick's writings on questions of American grand strategy are particularly significant given her unparalleled access to Roosevelt, with reporter and president meeting for several extended White House sessions during the war.

---

[64] Robert E. Sherwood, *Roosevelt and Hopkins, an Intimate History* (New York: Harper & Bros., 1948), 563; Roosevelt to Arnold, Hopkins, King, Knox, Marshall and Stimson, memo, May 6, 1942, quoted in Stoler, *Allies and Adversaries*, 78.

[65] Editorial, *New York Times*, June 12, 1942.

[66] McCormick, "Abroad," *New York Times*, June 12 and 17, 1942.

Although McCormick's broad experience and insightful intellect would have made these genuinely two-way discussions, it is reasonable to assume that her columns provided a forum for the unattributed exposition of the president's strategic thinking. More importantly, her standing – in 1936 she became the first woman on the *New York Times* editorial board – made her writings an important component of the foreign policy discourse that both shaped and justified American policy.[67]

Administration thinking on the location of a second front remained shrouded in ambiguity. Addressing a Madison Square Garden rally in support of the Soviet Union on June 22, unofficial national security adviser Harry Hopkins assured the audience that not only was a second front imminent, but that it soon would be followed by "third and fourth" fronts designed to "pen the German Army [in a] ring of our offensive steel."[68] Hopkins did not discuss the location of these fronts, but his comments were closer to Churchill's notion of "closing the ring" by a series of peripheral campaigns than they were to the Army's concentrated cross-Channel attack. Similar ambiguity is evident in Roosevelt's thinking. Discussing Molotov's visit with Churchill, the president argued that the crisis in Russia demanded that *Bolero*, the build-up of U.S. forces in Britain, "proceed to definite action" in 1942, a statement that has been taken as an indication of his support for a cross-Channel assault.[69] But Roosevelt was careful to specify an acceleration of *Bolero*, rather than of *Roundup*, the cross-Channel invasion itself. Exactly where the "definite action" should take place was again left open. It is plausible that Roosevelt focused on the *urgency* of action because he understood that it would push the *location* in a direction that Marshall and the Joint Chiefs would otherwise find unacceptable. If there had to be a "second front" in 1942, and if the British opposed an immediate cross-Channel assault, then *Gymnast* and an invasion of North Africa would necessarily return to center stage.

As it turned out, *Gymnast* returned in the context of a new crisis in the Western Desert that broke during the Second Washington Conference. When the conference assembled on June 19, a very different crisis had seemed to be in the offing. Meeting in Washington while their political masters were at Roosevelt's Hyde Park estate, Allied military leaders formed a common front against any revival of *Gymnast*. What they were *for* remained vague, but the Combined Chiefs were clear on what they were *against*, concluding emphatically

---

[67] Remarkably, Anne O'Hare McCormick lacks a scholarly biography. On McCormick's influence, see Yvonne L. Hunter, "Cold Columns: Anne O'Hare McCormick and the Origins of the Cold War in the *New York Times*, (1920–1954)," MA Thesis, Nipissing University, 2009, especially 11–21; see also Betty Houchin Winfield, *FDR and the News Media* (Urbana: University of Illinois Press, 1990), 63, 67.

[68] *New York Times*, June 23, 1942.

[69] Roosevelt to Churchill, May 31, 1942, *Correspondence*, 1: 503; see, for example, Stoler, *Allies and Adversaries*, 78.

that *Gymnast* "should not be undertaken in the existing situation."[70] They had different reasons for opposing *Gymnast*, with the British focused on the crisis in Egypt and the Americans looking to plow ahead with a cross-Channel assault. But their opposition was unanimous, and it included a discrete jab at the prospect of securing an "invitation" from the French to land in North Africa. Noting that *Gymnast* rested on "the existence of certain psychological conditions" in North Africa, the Combined Chiefs implicitly dismissed Eddy's glowing report by asserting that it was "impossible to predict" how French forces might react to an invasion.[71] With Chief of the Imperial General Staff Alan Brooke expressing his pleasure at achieving "complete unanimity of opinion between the U.S. and British staffs," the Combined Chiefs ratified these conclusions on June 20.[72]

While the military leaders sweated it out in Washington, Roosevelt and Churchill were meeting in the relaxed setting of Hyde Park. Their discussions were conducted without formal record, but it seems likely that their meeting was designed to solidify their common preference for *Gymnast* before embarking on a showdown with the Combined Chiefs. This is certainly what Allied military leaders feared, with Brooke sure that Roosevelt and Churchill were "brewing up" trouble at Hyde Park and that North Africa would "loom large" in their plans.[73] Undoubtedly, what was shaping up was a full-scale collision between Allied military and political leaders over the question of *Gymnast*. This complex inter-Allied and military-political crisis was only averted when an entirely unexpected event, the fall of Tobruk to Axis forces, broke into the conference, redirecting its proceedings and reshaping the course of the war.

News of the fall of Tobruk and the surrender of 28,000 Imperial soldiers arrived in Washington as the conference was getting down to business on June 21. It was a shocking blow, with Rommel's troops battering down the defenses in just three days and opening the road to Egypt and the oilfields of the Middle East.[74] The blow fell particularly heavily on Churchill, whose observation that "defeat is one thing, disgrace is another," reflected a nagging fear that the British Army was simply not up to the demands of modern war.[75] The U.S. response to this moment of British crisis became a mythic symbol of wartime amity, largely through Churchill's own retelling.[76] Within minutes of hearing

---

[70] Record of informal meeting of British and American military leaders, June 19, 1942, *FRUS 1941–1943*, Washington and Casablanca: 428.

[71] Ibid., 427.

[72] Meeting of Combined Chiefs of Staff, June 20, 1942, *FRUS 1941–1943*, Washington and Casablanca: 429.

[73] Brooke diary entry, June 20, 1942, Alex Danchev and Daniel Todman, eds., *Field Marshal Lord Alanbrooke, War Diaries, 1939–1945* (London: Phoenix Press, 2002), 267–268.

[74] On the fall of Tobruk, see Andrew Buchanan, "A Friend Indeed? From Tobruk to El Alamein: The American Contribution to Victory in the Desert," *Diplomacy and Statecraft* 15, no. 2 (2004).

[75] Churchill, *Second World War*, 4: 343–344.

[76] See David Reynolds, *In Command of History: Churchill Fighting and Writing the Second World War* (New York: Basic Books, 2005), 285–286, 302–303.

the news, Roosevelt and Marshall offered to rush aircraft to Egypt, followed by hundreds of Sherman tanks and self-propelled guns. "A friend in need," Churchill moralized, "is a friend indeed"[77]

Given the context of the Second Washington Conference, there was a great deal more going on here than Churchill's account suggests. With Berlin readying its offensive into the Caucasus and popular opposition to British imperial rule in Egypt rising, the danger of German forces breaking into the Middle East seemed all too real, generating broad agreement that Egypt had to be secured. The surrender of Tobruk presented U.S. military leaders with the challenge of defending Egypt without sending a large American army to the region. Before the news of Tobruk broke, Marshall had proposed to dispatch a single division to Egypt, but the British, wary of any U.S. presence in the region, declined the offer. Marshall's new proposal to supply generous quantities of U.S. equipment – the Sherman tank was qualitatively superior to British vehicles – offered an elegant solution, allowing the Americans to help secure Egypt without having to abandon the cross-Channel invasion.

Roosevelt approached the problem from a rather different standpoint. He had arrived back in Washington from Hyde Park ready to do battle for *Gymnast*, and the fall of Tobruk now offered a golden opportunity to take a decisive step toward U.S. engagement in the Mediterranean *without* a bruising fight with his military leaders. Typically, the president bid high, throwing out ideas for an entire U.S. army to "cover the whole front between Alexandria and Tehran," or, as Stimson noted gloomily, for the deployment of a "big force" to Egypt.[78] Falling short of these fanciful projections, the final agreement to supply tanks, guns, and airpower would, as Roosevelt no doubt hoped, be entirely adequate to defend Egypt *and* to turn U.S. strategy decisively toward the Mediterranean.

The immediate crisis in Egypt dominated the Second Washington Conference, and participants agreed simply to "explore" *Gymnast* "carefully and conscientiously," a formula that reflected the Joint Chiefs' continued opposition to an open-ended commitment to the region.[79] The conference, nevertheless, facilitated a decisive shift in U.S. strategy toward North Africa and the Mediterranean. Like Germany, the United States was drawn into the Mediterranean by the crisis of a weaker ally. Unlike Germany, however, the United States had a great deal to gain from its presence there.[80] Moreover, as Anne O'Hare McCormick noted in relation to the U.S. bombing attack on Ploesti, the modest initial involvement of U.S. forces in the Mediterranean "front" carried a weight far beyond

[77] Churchill, *Second World War*, 4: 343–344.
[78] Roosevelt-Churchill meeting, June 22, 1942, *FRUS 1941–1943*, Washington and Casablanca: 436, 438.
[79] Draft press release on Washington conference, June 25, 1942, Map Room, Naval Aide's File, FDRL.
[80] See Douglas Porch, *The Path to Victory: The Mediterranean Theater in World War II* (New York: Farrar, Straus and Giroux, 2004), 280–281.

their limited numbers.[81] After Tobruk, that weight imposed itself irrevocably on America's strategic choices. The question was no longer if, but where, when, and for how long the U.S. military would be in the Mediterranean.

If the Second Washington Conference marked the critical turning point, the road to the final decision for *Gymnast* was still a rocky one, passing through what historian Mark Stoler has described as the "worst civil-military ... clashes of the war" and offering further illustration of Roosevelt's persistent commitment to an invasion of North Africa.[82] No doubt seeing the likely consequences of reinforcing the British in Egypt, George Marshall quickly set out to limit the damage to his cherished plans for a cross-Channel invasion, complaining that although *Gymnast* had been "studied and re-studied," it remained a "poor substitute" for a cross-Channel attack.[83] Even worse, he concluded, the diversion of U.S. resources to North Africa might "emasculate" plans for an invasion of France.

Marshall's protest went unheeded. With British opposition to a cross-Channel venture in 1942 stiffening –Churchill informed Roosevelt on July 8 that no "responsible" British leader could support *Sledgehammer*, the sacrificial attack on the Cherbourg peninsula – Marshall changed tack.[84] Forming a common front with Admiral King, he sent a memorandum to the president on July 10 arguing that if "whole-hearted" British support for *Sledgehammer* was not forthcoming, the United States should "turn to the Pacific and strike decisively at Japan."[85] On Marshall's part, this was undoubtedly a bluff, designed to steer the president away from *Gymnast* and to pressure London into backing *Sledgehammer*. Irrespective of Marshall's intentions, however, the memorandum co-authored with King represented an open challenge to the entire "Germany first" framework of Allied strategy, and it forced the president to show his own hand more openly.

Replying to Marshall and King, Roosevelt expressed support for a cross-Channel attack in 1943 but stressed that the United States could not "wait" to "strike at Germany."[86] He argued that although the Americans were "doing well" in the Pacific, their allies were "losing" in Africa and in Russia, and demanded urgent offensive action against Germany. That meant either "going into Africa through the Red Sea" or launching a U.S.-led invasion of North Africa at the invitation of French leaders there. The president's own preference was for the latter and, although conceding that *Gymnast* would not win the war, he argued that it would "hurt Germany, save the Middle East, and make Italy vulnerable to our air forces."

[81] McCormick, "Abroad," *New York Times*, June 17, 1942.
[82] Stoler, *Allies and Adversaries*, 83.
[83] Marshall to Roosevelt, memorandum, June 23, 1942, Map Room, Box 165, FDRL.
[84] Churchill to Roosevelt, July 8, 1942, *Correspondence*, 1: 520.
[85] Marshall and King memorandum, July 10, 1942, Map Room, Box 165, FDRL.
[86] Roosevelt to Marshall and King, July 11, 1942, Map Room, Box 165, FDRL.

On July 16 – less than a week after their "Pacific first" proposal – Roosevelt dispatched Marshall and King to London with orders to agree on a "definitive plan" of action with the British, concluding "it is of the highest importance that U.S. ground troops be brought into action against the enemy in 1942."[87] Roosevelt added Harry Hopkins to the delegation to give him a trusted back channel of communication to his own military chiefs and to the British. The U.S. delegation was ordered to probe the prospects for *Sledgehammer*, although Roosevelt must have known that, in the face of London's intransigent opposition, this would be a *pro forma* exercise. Assuming a failure to agree on *Sledgehammer*, the delegates carried a list of alternative proposals that included an invasion of North Africa. Roosevelt's instructions thus led unerringly, if circuitously, toward *Gymnast*. The delegation was given one week to conclude its work, and Roosevelt took the unusual step of issuing his instructions in the form of a direct order signed as the commander-in-chief.

Roosevelt's determination to move on *Gymnast* may have been reinforced by a survey of public opinion in French North Africa that reached his desk as he was drafting his instructions to Marshall and King. Conducted by U.S. agents working under Princeton professor Hadley Cantril, the survey had been commissioned by the president himself and organized through the Psychological Warfare Branch of Military Intelligence using the latest "scientific" polling techniques. Despite the narrowness of the sample – agents conducted only 142 "usable" interviews – Cantril concluded that 90 percent of Frenchmen in North Africa favored an Allied victory and 80 percent believed that the United States had no "imperialistic interests" in the region.[88] More than 70 percent would welcome an Allied landing – particularly if it was led by Americans and excluded de Gaulle – and those who resisted would do so "half-heartedly." However dubious its methodology, Cantril's survey added grist to the presidential mill at the precise moment the great debate was being pushed to a conclusion.

Squeezed between British opposition to *Sledgehammer* and Roosevelt's insistence on action in 1942, the discussions in London unfolded along predictable lines. It was with more than a touch of irony that the president noted that early deadlock over *Sledgehammer* had not "wholly taken me by surprise."[89] He reiterated that if there could be no rapid cross-Channel effort then "some other offensive" must "be worked out." In the circumstances, that could only mean some variant of *Gymnast* and Marshall and King, trapped between the British and their president, were finally forced to concede. Fearing that an agreement without a clear timetable would leave room for backsliding by his fellow Americans, Hopkins urged Roosevelt to set a definite date for the

[87] Roosevelt, written instructions to Marshall and King, July 16, 1942, PSF, Marshall, FDRL.
[88] Hadley Cantril, "Evaluating the Probable Reactions to the Landing in North Africa in 1942: A Case Study," *The Public Opinion Quarterly* 29, no. 3 (1965), 406.
[89] Roosevelt to Hopkins, July 23, 1942, PSF, Hopkins, FDRL.

invasion, and the president proposed that it be launched before October 30.[90] On July 25, *Gymnast* was finally adopted and rechristened with the more morally resonant codename *Torch*. The resolution of this long and bitter dispute is often pictured as a triumph for the principle of civilian control of the military; it was also a triumph of politically inspired grand strategy over narrow military nostrums.[91]

---

[90] Roosevelt to Hopkins, July 24, 1942, PSF, Hopkins, FDRL.
[91] See Stoler, *Allies and Adversaries*, 90.

3

Keeping Spain Out of the War

Washington's Appeasement of Franco

As Washington's plans for an invasion of French North Africa took shape, the question of how Spain might respond to such a move began to impose itself on U.S. policymakers and military planners. Although Spain had been devastated by its recently concluded civil war, General Francisco Franco's undisguised pro-Axis sympathies – reflected in Madrid's status as a "nonbelligerent" rather than a neutral power – offered an ever-present threat to Allied operations in the Mediterranean and North Africa. If Spanish troops, perhaps supported by a German expeditionary force, seized Gibraltar, Axis forces could close the Western gateway to the Mediterranean to Allied shipping. Such a move would have disastrous consequences for British forces operating in the Mediterranean and, if made once a U.S.-led invasion of North Africa was underway, it might also lead to the isolation and destruction of U.S. forces there.

When discussion of a U.S.-led invasion of French North Africa began in earnest following the *Arcadia* conference, the threat of Spanish intervention furnished U.S. military leaders, already deeply skeptical of any involvement in the Mediterranean, with a powerful argument against the undertaking. For President Roosevelt and other supporters of *Gymnast*, the fashioning of a policy capable of deterring Spanish entry into the war quickly assumed a special importance. Washington's diplomatic effort to keep Spain out of the European war had begun with its recognition of the Franco government in 1939, but it assumed greater urgency as French North Africa acquired new strategic importance following the fall of France. From the summer of 1940, Washington's Spanish policy was effectively intertwined with its orientation toward Vichy.

Sections of Chapters 3 and 11 are based on my article "Washington's Silent Ally in World War II? United States Policy towards Spain, 1939–1945," *Journal of Transatlantic Studies* 7, no. 2 (2009), and appear here with kind permission of the editor.

The fact that both of these interlinked policies involved the maintenance of close ties with fascist-minded authoritarian regimes led opponents to decry them as unacceptable manifestations of appeasement: no other aspect of Washington's wartime foreign policy aroused as much domestic controversy. Opposition was accentuated by the fact that the administration's wartime policy built on its neutral stance during the Spanish Civil War, a policy that many liberals viewed as being at least partially responsible for Franco's victory.[1] The continuing popularity of the Spanish Republican cause among American liberals ensured that there was a permanent groundswell of opposition to any rapprochement with Madrid. Fueled by a constant drumbeat of criticism in the *Nation* and the *New Republic,* the campaign against the "appeasement" of Franco was strongly reflected in mainstream liberalism, and was espoused by senior policymakers including Vice President Henry Wallace, Treasury Secretary Henry Morgenthau Jr., and Interior Secretary Harold Ickes. These political fault lines, running right to the heart of the administration, overlapped those generated by the policy toward Vichy. The fact that the twin appeasements of Pétain and Franco were pressed forward in the face of such unrelenting opposition underscores the degree to which both formed part of a broader strategic orientation driven forward by the president himself.

When the Spanish Civil War broke out in 1936, the U.S. government expressed sympathy for the democratically elected Republican government. But President Roosevelt and Secretary of State Cordell Hull were also troubled by the potentially revolutionary dynamic of the struggle unfolding in Spain, and in particular by Madrid's policy of arming of "irresponsible members of left-wing political organizations."[2] In the early years of the war, a victory for Franco's Nationalists, if unpalatable from the viewpoint of democratic principles, seemed much less dangerous than a socialist revolution, and the administration's policy of neutrality was crafted to justify blocking the dispatch of war materiél to the Republican government. The United States did not formally sign the arms embargo initiated by London and Paris in July 1936, but it endorsed it in practice. When a U.S. company challenged this "moral" blockade by shipping airplane engines to the Republic, Roosevelt denounced its actions as "unpatriotic" and urged congress to give the embargo the force of law.[3] Congress obliged, passing the Arms Embargo Act in January 1937. The refusal to sell arms to the Republic ensured that it was denied critical supplies

---

[1] On American policy in the Spanish Civil War, see Douglas Little, *Malevolent Neutrality; The United States, Great Britain, and the Origins of the Spanish Civil War* (Ithaca, NY: Cornell University Press, 1985); Dante A. Puzzo, *Spain and the Great Powers, 1936–1941* (New York: Columbia University Press, 1962); Dominic Tierney, *FDR and the Spanish Civil War: Neutrality and Commitment in the Struggle that Divided America* (Durham, NC: Duke University Press, 2007).

[2] Cordell Hull, *The Memoirs of Cordell Hull* (New York: Macmillan, 1948), 1: 60.

[3] *New York Times,* December 30, 1936.

of modern equipment at a time when Germany and Italy were backing the Nationalists with weapons and troops.[4]

As it became clear that German and Italian intervention would facilitate a Nationalist victory, Roosevelt became increasingly worried that Franco's triumph might embolden Berlin and Rome and upset the entire European balance of power. This concern led to a belated willingness to support the Republic, and Roosevelt himself initiated a quixotic and unsuccessful effort to circumvent the arms embargo and ship warplanes to Spain.[5] Reversing his earlier position, Roosevelt informed the cabinet in January 1939 that the arms embargo should have applied only to U.S. ships, leaving the Republican government free to buy arms if it shipped them in Spanish vessels.[6] Roosevelt now argued that U.S. companies should have supplied the Republic with defensive weapons, noting that by blocking such shipments Washington had "indirectly helped the [Franco] revolution."[7] Ironically, this candid admission now legitimized trade with the newly recognized government of General Franco, which would be allowed to trade with the United States on condition that it shipped goods across the Atlantic in Spanish ships.

Whatever Roosevelt's feelings about the outcome of the Civil War, Washington's approach to Madrid in 1939 and early 1940 was governed by an attempt to use diplomatic and commercial inducements to defuse the slide toward a general war in Europe. Efforts to keep Italy out of the war by offering Rome preferential trade deals and recognition of its conquests in Ethiopia came to nothing when Mussolini invaded France in June 1940. It then became imperative to dissuade Spain from following suit. In following this course, Washington marched in step with British policy. London's relations with Spain were governed by the need to safeguard British investments in the Iberian Peninsula, to protect critical supplies of Spanish iron ore and, above all, to keep Madrid out of the war. If Spain joined the Axis, or even simply allowed German troops to cross its territory, then Gibraltar would become untenable. Without Gibraltar, British influence in the Mediterranean would be undermined, the shortest route to India severed, and the entire structure of imperial rule imperiled. Faced with this dire prospect, London utilized its economic influence in Spain to appease Madrid by offering commercial and financial incentives as a reward for neutrality. In September 1939, the two countries signed a trade agreement allowing Spanish ships to pass through the British naval blockade, and supplementary terms agreed in March 1940 adjusted Spanish debts to Britain and extended a £2 million loan for economic reconstruction. As France collapsed, London reinforced this effort by appointing Sir Samuel Hoare, former foreign secretary and

---

[4] See Puzzo, *Spain and the Great Powers*, especially chapter VIII.
[5] See Tierney, *FDR and the Spanish Civil War*, chapter 7.
[6] Harold Ickes, *The Secret Diary of Harold Ickes* (New York: Simon and Schuster, 1954), 569.
[7] Roosevelt press conference, Jonathan Daniels (intro.), *The Complete Press Conferences of Franklin D. Roosevelt* (New York: Da Capo Press, 1972), 15: 459–460.

a leading proponent of "non-intervention" during the Civil War, as its ambassador to Madrid. Hoare understood his task in grand imperial terms, noting that if Gibraltar fell the "maintenance of the British Empire" would be rendered "impossible."[8]

Washington's mounting effort to support Britain led it to step up its own appeasement of Madrid. In May 1939, Under Secretary of State Sumner Welles met with Señor Don Juan Francisco de Cardenas, Madrid's new ambassador to Washington. It was a cordial affair, reflecting a mutual interest in the rapid reestablishment of "friendly and advantageous" diplomatic and economic relations.[9] Welles agreed to support Cardenas's request for a two-year Import-Export Bank credit to fund the purchase of 300,000 bales of American cotton, cautioning only that the full normalization of commercial relations would be dependent on Madrid respecting U.S. investments in Spain. In particular, Welles demanded that Madrid end its harassment of International Telephone and Telegraph (IT&T), the major American company operating in Spain and the former owner of the national telephone network. The Franco government had recently nationalized IT&T's Spanish subsidiary, citing allegations that the company's American managers had favored the Republic to justify the takeover and the expulsion from Spain of company officials.

Over the next several months the gradual resolution of these intertwined issues laid the basis for closer Spanish-American commercial relations. Neither went smoothly. While Welles and the State Department backed the cotton loan, citing Cardenas's assurances that it would reinforce "moderate" elements in Madrid, opposition from Treasury Secretary Henry Morgenthau and Interior Secretary Harold Ickes almost derailed the deal. Roosevelt's personal intervention finally broke the deadlock, and the first cotton left New Orleans for Spain in August 1939.[10] Meanwhile, Madrid moved slowly to resolve the IT&T dispute, with Foreign Secretary Juan Beigbeder and other "moderates" battling the openly pro-Axis Falange led by Interior Minister Serrano Suñer. In August 1939, Franco responded to Washington's approval of the cotton contract by allowing IT&T officials back into Spain to contest the expropriation of the company. Typically, Franco mediated between antagonistic factions within the ruling bloc, resolving conflicting pressures by leaning politically toward the Axis while simultaneously drawing economic sustenance from Britain and the United States.

With the outbreak of the European war in September 1939, the Spanish government proclaimed its "strict neutrality," exchanging diplomatic notes with Washington in which both countries pledged to work to limit the scope of the conflict. Behind the diplomatic flimflam – Cordell Hull embraced Franco's

---

[8] Sir Samuel Hoare, *Complacent Dictator* (New York: Alfred A. Knopf, 1947), 9.
[9] Welles memorandum, May 29, 1939, Welles Papers, Box 166, Folder 3, Europe Files 1933–1943, FDRL.
[10] Welles memorandum, June 28 and July 28, 1939, Welles Papers, Box 166, Folder 3, Europe Files 1933–1943, FDRL.

"moving appeal" on behalf of the world's "humbler classes" – the exchange signaled that despite Madrid's sympathy for the Axis and Washington's support for Britain, both governments would continue to foster their developing bilateral relations.[11] Pushing ahead along these lines, Cardenas proposed that Spain purchase a further 200,000 tons of American wheat, and Sumner Welles agreed to help secure the necessary financing.[12] As a neutral power itself, the United States did not attempt to regulate "private" trade with Spain, and Spanish access to American oil, by far the most important commodity it imported, was limited only by its ability to pay. Under the terms of its own trade agreement with Madrid, London granted the "navicerts" or commercial passports necessary for Spanish oil tankers to pass through the British blockade.

Despite the importance of this Anglo-American trade, in the summer of 1940 Madrid came close to casting off the mask of neutrality and joining the war. Franco proclaimed his support for the Axis loudly and frequently, and – with German victories mounting – Spain agreed to resupply German U-boats in its ports and to open its airfields to the *Luftwaffe*. German military intelligence agents operated freely in Spain, and the German embassy exercised considerable influence over the Spanish press, reinforcing its overwhelmingly pro-Axis basis.[13] When Italy joined the war in July, Madrid abandoned neutrality for "nonbelligerence," a vague status implying active promotion of the Axis cause short of actual war. With Falangist demonstrators attacking the British embassy to demand the return of Gibraltar to Spain, the change in status was widely interpreted as a step toward war. On June 14, Spanish troops occupied the North African city of Tangier with a view to strengthening Madrid's hand in the redistribution of colonial property that would surely follow an Axis victory. With this single bold stroke, Franco overthrew the international protectorate of Tangier established by Britain, France, Italy, and Spain in 1928. Under different circumstances, Franco's action would have caused a major international incident; in the tumultuous summer of 1940 it was barely noticed.[14]

When German troops reached the Pyrenees in June 1940, the stage seemed set for Spain to enter the war. The new British ambassador Samuel Hoare was greeted by rowdy pro-Axis demonstrations, and London advised him to keep an aircraft on hand for a rapid departure if German troops moved into Spain. American ambassador Alexander Weddell, a career diplomat and Virginia gentleman, drew similarly pessimistic conclusions, arguing that the Falangists would now be in a position to "overbear" traditional "conservatives" within

[11] Hull press statement, *Department of State Bulletin*, September 9, 1939.

[12] Welles memo, November 29, 1939, Welles Papers, Box 166, Folder 3, Europe Files 1933–1943, FDRL.

[13] See Christian Leitz, *Sympathy for the Devil: Neutral Europe and Nazi Germany in World War II* (New York: NYU Press, 2001).

[14] See C. G. Fenwick, "The International Status of Tangier," *The American Journal of International Law* 23, no. 1 (1929).

the ruling bloc.[15] His fears were well founded. On June 19, Franco acted on his conviction that a German victory was imminent and proposed to Hitler that Spain enter the war.[16] The German leader demurred on the grounds that the war was already won, and that last-minute Spanish involvement would only complicate postwar relations with Vichy France and Italy, particularly in relation to North Africa, where all three countries had significant territorial claims. It was a decision Hitler would soon come to regret.

When British resistance continued into the fall, Berlin's interest in Spanish belligerency revived. Within the German high command, navy chief Admiral Erich Raeder argued that the destruction of British power in the Mediterranean would help to prepare a final assault on the United Kingdom. With the defeat of the *Luftwaffe* in the Battle of Britain ruling out a cross-Channel assault, Raeder's views won a hearing. The capture of Gibraltar offered particularly favorable opportunities for the rapid dislocation of British power, and Operation *Felix*, an audacious dash across Spain by two army corps to capture the British outpost, was planned for January 1941.[17] The only problem was that the operation required Spanish support, and the factors impelling Berlin toward *Felix* now militated against winning Madrid's approval. Ready to join when victory seemed at hand, the threat of a protracted war now gave Franco good reason to remain nonbelligerent.

In October 1940, Franco and Hitler held a summit meeting at Hendaye in German-occupied France at which the Spanish leader deflected German demands for action by arguing that the economic devastation of the Civil War precluded participation in another extended conflict. After three years of civil war, industrial production stood at barely 70 percent of its 1935 level, and the disruption of agriculture had made Spain dependent on imported food.[18] It was a hard case to answer, and in early December Hitler reluctantly agreed to suspended preparations for *Felix*. With hindsight, it is clear that, by the end of 1940, there was no serious possibility of Spain joining the Axis war effort. But this conclusion was by no means obvious to contemporary observers, with reports of U-boats resupplying in Spanish ports and a constant drumbeat of pro-Axis propaganda in the Spanish press combining to create the impression that Spain might join the war at any time. Madrid was keen to maintain this impression, because Spain's ability to extract the maximum benefit from its pro-Axis nonbelligerency rested on using the threat of military intervention to prod the Allies into providing substantial economic assistance.

Madrid's lurch toward war in the summer of 1940 seemed to challenge Washington's hopes of sustaining Spanish neutrality. Probing the meaning of

---

[15] Weddell to Hull, June 17, 1940, *FRUS 1940*, 2: 798–799.

[16] Leitz, *Sympathy for the Devil*, 122.

[17] See Charles B. Burdick, *Germany's Military Strategy and Spain in World War II* (Syracuse: Syracuse University Press, 1968).

[18] Leitz, *Sympathy for the Devil*, 118.

Spain's new nonbelligerent status, Ambassador Weddell noted that his instructions explicitly tied U.S. trade to Spanish neutrality.[19] Did Spain's new status require new instructions, he asked? In reply, Cordell Hull ordered Weddell to follow his existing instructions and to continue pressing for a comprehensive bilateral trade agreement.[20] At the same time, however, Washington stiffened its negotiating position by restricting the supply of oil, declaring that it was too dangerous for American-registered tankers to carry oil to Spain and requesting that American oil companies keep sales within "customary limits."[21] The resulting constriction of oil shipments quickly yielded results, with Madrid settling the long-running dispute with IT&T in mid-August. Reporting the settlement, Weddell proposed to reward Madrid by resuming unlimited oil shipments, and the State Department concurred.[22] In addition to achieving their immediate goals, these exchanges demonstrated to U.S. policymakers Spain's acute sensitivity to the use of oil as a diplomatic weapon.

With the issue of the telephone company resolved, Weddell argued for an all-round expansion of trade with Spain. Painting a graphic picture of the economic crisis, he proposed extending a further $100 million loan for the purchase of American wheat, gasoline, and cotton. Weddell warned that without this aid Spain could slide into economic chaos, spurring "internal uprisings" that might threaten the government. Franco, the ambassador implied, should be rewarded *both* for keeping out of the war *and* for serving as a bulwark against popular insurrection.[23] In voicing these concerns, Weddell reflected Franco's fear that, despite victory in the Civil War and the terror unleashed against Republicans, the new regime remained unstable. As Ambassador Cardenas explained to Sumner Welles, any direct German intervention in Spain would "unquestionably" produce widespread "revolutionary outbreaks" as Republicans seized the opportunity to reopen the Civil War.[24] Revealing the fear of social revolution that was never far below the surface of U.S. policy, the president and the State Department embraced Weddell's conclusions, and negotiations with Madrid proceeded rapidly. Talks centered on securing a large U.S. loan and on the possibility, floated by Roosevelt himself, of utilizing the Red Cross as a conduit for substantial donations of American foodstuffs.

President Roosevelt intervened personally to remove diplomatic obstacles between the two governments, authorizing Weddell to "modify" a State Department demand that Madrid publicly reaffirm its neutrality by seeking

---

[19] Weddell to Hull, June 13, 1940, *FRUS 1940*, 2: 797.
[20] See Hull to Weddell, June 13 and June 19, 1940, *FRUS 1940*, 2: 798, 800.
[21] See Herbert Feis, *The Spanish Story: Franco and the Nations at War* (New York: W. W. Norton, 1948), 45.
[22] Weddell to Hull, August 19, 1940, and Hull to Weddell, August 30, 1940, *FRUS 1940*, 2: 896–897.
[23] Weddell to Hull, September 7, 1940, *FRUS 1940*, 2: 807.
[24] Welles memo, April 16, 1940, Welles Papers, Box 166, Folder 3, Europe Files 1933–1943, FDRL.

instead only "specific and formal" assurances given in private.[25] With Roosevelt's explicit support – given, not coincidentally, as he was pushing hard for a trade agreement with French North Africa – American trade with Spain looked set for rapid expansion. But the political climate in the United States was quite different from what it had been a year earlier, and whereas the 1939 cotton loan had passed almost unnoticed, meriting just the briefest of references in the *New York Times*, the new commercial negotiations provoked a storm of criticism.[26] These difficulties were compounded by the November presidential elections and by Roosevelt's cautious campaign to prepare American public opinion for war by presenting the world crisis as an irreconcilable struggle between democracy and totalitarianism. It was, to say the least, difficult to square the image of the United States as the "arsenal of democracy" with the stepping up of trade with the pro-Axis dictatorship in Madrid. Roosevelt was no stranger to sublimating contradictions between public policy statements and well-veiled actions, and he may have thought that he could avoid a damaging public fight over trade with Spain. If so, he misjudged the dynamics of a political situation largely of his own making.

Administration liberals – now increasingly refashioned as warhawks – led the charge, with Interior Secretary Harold Ickes scorning the State Department's "appeasement bent" and denouncing the naïve notion that "Spain can be kept from adhering to Hitler if only we send some money in to feed the Spaniards."[27] Ickes urged Treasury Secretary Morgenthau to block the Spanish loan, sending him a letter from radical journalist Jay Allen denouncing the deal as "grotesque and criminal" appeasement.[28] When widely read muckraking journalist Drew Pearson called Morgenthau to announce that he planned to "pan hell" out of the State Department, the treasury secretary agreed that the idea that U.S. trade could keep Spain out of the war was "hog-wash."[29] A flurry of articles denounced the proposed loan, with the *Nation* describing it as a "criminal betrayal" of democracy and asking if Roosevelt had forgotten his own election-time "repudiation" of appeasement.[30] Pearson delivered his promised "panning," noting that Franco had been required to give only private assurances of neutrality rather than a public pledge to "stay out of the war."[31] This hit a sensitive nerve, and Hull called a special press conference to repudiate Pearson's "wholly inaccurate" claims, stating implausibly that he had not even heard of the proposed Spanish loan until questioned about it by a journalist.[32]

[25] Welles to Weddell, November 20, 1940, *FRUS 1940*, 2: 838.
[26] See *New York Times*, August 18, 1939; *New York Times*, September 28, 1939.
[27] Ickes, diary entry, November 23, 1940, Ickes, *Secret Diary*, 373.
[28] Allen to Ickes, October 21, 1940, Morgenthau Diary, 324, 204–208, FDRL.
[29] Pearson to Morgenthau, transcript of phone call, October 23, 1940, Morgenthau Diary 324, 209–210.
[30] Editorial, *The Nation*, October 26 and November 23, 1940.
[31] Pearson, "The Washington Merry-Go-Round," December 13, 1940.
[32] *Department of State Bulletin*, December 21, 1940.

This storm of opposition to the "appeasement" of Franco, breaking just as Roosevelt was stepping up his effort to win public support for U.S. participation in the war, effectively derailed the loan. Modest food relief efforts organized through the Red Cross continued, but the administration felt compelled to bring policy into line with rhetoric, temporarily dropping the pursuit of closer economic ties with Madrid. Washington was keen to stress a globalist vision, typified by Roosevelt's articulation of the struggle for the "Four Freedoms" in his January 1941 State of the Union Address, over the expediencies of appeasement; with this in mind Hull instructed Weddell to throw the weight of his embassy into the "struggle against totalitarian world aggression."[33] The quarrel that resulted from Weddell's attempt to explain his new mission to Foreign Minister Serrano Suñer nearly ruptured diplomatic relations between the two countries and led to the ambassador being frozen out of contact with senior members of the Spanish government for the next six months. Within weeks, the State Department recognized the problem it had created by responding so demonstratively to domestic political pressure and reversed course, authorizing Weddell to restart talks aimed at "broadening and liberalizing" trade.[34] But the damage had been done, and Madrid, where Falangists officials had taken advantage of the opportunity to strengthen their hand against traditionalist conservatives, rebuffed Washington's overtures.

The position of the Falange was further strengthened by German invasion of the Soviet Union in June 1941. The dramatic initial success of Operation *Barbarossa* reinforced Franco's faith in an Axis victory, and in a fiery address to the National Council of the Falange on July 17 he presented the war as a global struggle against communism, expressed contempt for the "plutocratic democracies," and predicted a rapid German victory.[35] For good measure, he also accused Washington of blocking wheat shipments that Spain had already paid for. Madrid quickly sanctioned the establishment of an ostensibly unofficial and all-volunteer force to fight alongside the Germans in Russia, and soldiers of the *División Azul* (Blue Division) began arriving on the Eastern Front in August 1941. More than 20,000 Spanish soldiers served in Russia, making a significant contribution to the fighting around Leningrad.[36] The thin cover offered by the unit's unofficial status allowed Madrid to claim that its operations did not violate its nonbelligerent status. It also allowed Moscow to overlook the potential *casus belli*: a Russian declaration of war against Spain, tempting though it may have been for ideological reasons, would have embarrassed the Allies and wrecked their efforts to appease Madrid. In passing up the opportunity to broaden the war and sharpen its ideological

---

[33] Hull to Weddell, April 19, 1941, *FRUS 1941*, 2: 888.
[34] Hull to Weddell, April 30, 1941, *FRUS 1941*, 2: 893.
[35] Weddell to Hull, July 18, 1941, *FRUS 1941*, 2: 908–909.
[36] See Gerald R. Kleinfeld and Lewis A. Tambs, *Hitler's Spanish Legion: The Blue Division in Russia* (Carbondale: University of Southern Illinois Press, 1979).

character, Moscow thus gave Anglo-American diplomacy vital backhanded endorsement.[37]

Even as it backed away from approving a new loan to Spain, Washington continued to allow unimpeded private trade on condition that U.S. goods were purchased on the open market and shipped in Spanish vessels. In the summer of 1941, however, the administration responded to Madrid's enthusiastic support for the German invasion of Russia by tightening controls over private trade and again limiting shipments of gasoline. Demonstrating that it could utilize trade to punish as well as to reward, Washington enacted measures that were piecemeal but effective. In June, Sumner Welles announced that Spain would be allowed no further imports of tin plate until it showed "greater friendliness," adding that oil shipments would be restricted to the "usual pre-war quantities."[38] Welles ensured that these moves were widely publicized, encouraging articles in the *New York Times* and elsewhere in an effort to counter liberal arguments likening Washington's Spanish policy, as radical journalist I. F. Stone put it, to a matador fighting a bull with a "basket of flowers and a curtsey."[39]

These new measures soon curtailed oil imports and restricted supplies of other critical commodities. Ambassador Weddell warned that a tough line might push Madrid into the arms of the Axis, but Franco, who recognized that Germany could not meet Spain's economic needs, had no interest in severing ties to the United States. In September 1941, Cardenas persuaded Franco to resume discussions with Weddell on a trade agreement, and in late October Madrid received its reward when Roosevelt personally approved a State Department proposal to resume oil shipments to Spain. In exchange for selling oil, the United States would import cork, zinc, and olive oil, goods that, as Sumner Welles explained, "we wish to keep out of German hands."[40] Building on these initial steps, a comprehensive trade agreement was slowly hammered out over the next several months. Washington agreed to supply enough oil to meet Spain's domestic requirements and, in a move that paralleled the deployment of Murphy's vice-consuls in North Africa, established a network of agents in Spain tasked with ensuring that oil was not reexported to Germany. Other American products would be made available as the domestic supply situation permitted and on condition that they were not sold to the Germans.[41] Madrid initially balked at accepting the petroleum agents, but by January 1942 increasing economic difficulties forced its acquiescence. In response, Washington quickly cleared two tankers to load gas for Spain.

[37] See Dennis Smyth, "Franco and the Allies in the Second World War" in Sebastian Balfour and Paul Preston (eds.) *Spain and the Great Powers in the Twentieth Century* (London: Routledge, 1999), 199.
[38] Welles to Atherton, June 23, 1941, Welles Papers, Box 166, Folder 04, Spain, 1941–1942, FDRL.
[39] Stone, "Midsummer Flashes," *The Nation*, August 16, 1941.
[40] Welles to Roosevelt, October 31, 1941, PSF, Box 9, State Department 1941–1942, FDRL.
[41] Hull to Weddell, January 8, 1942, *FRUS 1942*, 2: 248.

Trade negotiations were now concluded in the new conditions created by America's formal entry into the war. While Cordell Hull continued to express reservations about trade with Spain, Roosevelt pressed for the rapid development of commercial relations and worked closely with Sumner Welles to finalize the terms of the agreement. When Welles complained that "subordinate officials" – presumably at Morgenthau's Treasury Department – were intent on blocking "any program which involves the shipment of commodities from the United States to Spain," the president responded by initiating a thorough reorganization of the bodies responsible for economic contact with Spain.⁴² To streamline relations and to minimize the disruptive potential of those liberals who opposed the continuing "appeasement" of Franco, an interdepartmental Iberian Peninsula Operating Committee (IPOC) involving the State Department, the Bureau of Economic Warfare, and the United States Commercial Corporation, was set up under economic advisor Herbert Feis in late March 1942.⁴³

Roosevelt's interest in developing commercial relations with Spain was directly tied to his rapidly forming interest in a U.S. invasion of North Africa. In this he was backed by Churchill, who noted that in the context of "some other ideas we have discussed" it was necessary to "give a few rationed carrots to the Dons to help stave off trouble at Gibraltar."⁴⁴ As the trade agreement was being finalized in March 1942, Roosevelt asked Weddell for an appreciation of the probable Spanish response to a U.S. landing in North Africa.⁴⁵ Although the ambassador ventured nothing beyond the platitudinous observation that Berlin would let out a "howl of moral indignation," Roosevelt's asking of the question shows the degree to which *Gymnast* – and Spain's possible reaction to it – was dominating his thinking. It is particularly significant that Roosevelt's request was made at a time when the Combined Chiefs of Staff had sidelined plans for an invasion of North Africa on the basis of U.S. Army fears of a Spanish intervention cutting off Allied troops within the Mediterranean. Earlier Allied military plans in relation to Spain, prepared by London and endorsed by Washington, had centered on punitive operations against the Azores, the Canaries, and the Cape Verde islands to be undertaken in response to an attack on Gibraltar.⁴⁶ Now, with offensive operations dominating Allied strategic thinking, the issue of neutralizing a hostile Spanish response to U.S.-led landings in North Africa assumed critical importance. In early 1942, Roosevelt sought to use of diplomatic and economic levers to shape Spain's response to

---

⁴² Welles to Roosevelt, March 21, 1942, *FRUS 1942*, 2: 284.

⁴³ See Feis, *Spanish Story*, chapter XXV.

⁴⁴ Churchill to Roosevelt, January 5, 1942, Warren F. Kimball (ed.), *Churchill and Roosevelt: The Complete Correspondence* (London: Collins, 1984), 1: 313.

⁴⁵ Weddell to Roosevelt, March 24, 1942, PSF Box 50, Spain, FDRL.

⁴⁶ Memorandum, "British Plans in the Event of a German Invasion of Spain and Attack on Gibraltar," PSF Box 5, Folder Spain; Smyth "Franco and the Allies," 193–196, 203.

an invasion and to help resolve the long-running debate over strategy with his own military leaders.

The possibility of an Axis attack on Gibraltar during Allied landings in North Africa continued to weigh heavily on Allied leaders even after the decision to proceed with *Torch* had been taken. British Ambassador Samuel Hoare warned that Allied landings in French Morocco would block Madrid's hopes of colonial expansion and push Franco into supporting a German attack on Gibraltar, and Captain Harry Butcher, a senior aide to newly-appointed *Torch* commander General Eisenhower, noted bluntly that the "prospects of the North African invasion depend on continued Spanish neutrality."[47] Summoned to London for a planning conference, the Governor of Gibraltar General Noel Mason-MacFarlane reinforced these concerns by describing the vulnerability of the hundreds of aircraft and millions of gallons of fuel packed into the tiny peninsula. A heavy artillery bombardment, he noted, would cause the "whole damn Rock" to burn.[48] U.S. planners sought to mitigate the danger of Spanish intervention by insisting on a landing outside of the Mediterranean on the Atlantic coast of French Morocco, and by limiting the eastward reach of the landings in Algeria. Plans were also drawn up to invade Tangier and Spanish Morocco if Madrid moved against *Torch*.[49]

As his questioning of Alexander Weddell indicates, President Roosevelt was well aware of these issues – both as actual military dangers and, perhaps more importantly, as potential arguments against *Gymnast* – from early in the planning process. Characteristically, he proposed to utilize trade as the leading edge of a renewed effort to appease Madrid and ensure Spanish neutrality. In April 1942, Roosevelt appointed a new ambassador to Spain to spearhead this campaign, typically entrusting this critical mission not to a career diplomat, but to a man whose standing and experience equipped him for the specific task. Roosevelt's pick for this key post was Columbia history professor Carlton Hayes, and at a White House briefing prior to his departure for Madrid the president made it clear that Hayes would also be functioning as his personal representative. Roosevelt also emphasized that Hayes's appointment was directly connected to plans for an Allied landing in "North Africa close to Spain," and he underscored the necessity of going to "unusual lengths" to prevent Spain taking action against it.[50]

[47] Butcher, diary entry, August 15, 1942; Harry C. Butcher, *My Three Years with Eisenhower: The Personal Diary of Captain Harry C. Butcher, USNR, Naval Aide to General Eisenhower, 1942 to 1945* (New York: Simon and Schuster, 1946), 58.
[48] Diary entry, August 24, 1942; ibid., 71.
[49] CCS 103/13, October 27, 1942, Records of JCS, Operational Plans, Microfilm Reel VI, 0305, 0310.
[50] Carlton Hayes, *Wartime Mission to Spain, 1942–1945* (New York: Macmillan, 1945), 11; see also Charles R. Halstead, "Historians in Politics: Carlton J. H. Hayes as American Ambassador to Spain, 1942–45," *Journal of Contemporary History* 10, no. 3 (1975).

Carlton Hayes was the ideal candidate for the job. Although critical of the openly fascistic Falange, he had backed the Nationalists during the Civil War and was a fervent supporter of the Catholic Church in Spain. In 1936, Hayes coauthored a widely circulated open letter championing Franco's battle against the "anti-religious" Republicans and their attempt to "corrupt" Spain's "national soul."[51] As with his half-joking proposal that Robert Murphy attend mass with Weygand, Roosevelt hoped that Hayes's Catholicism, together with his well-documented support for the Nationalist cause during the Civil War, would allow him to forge a close personal relationship with Franco.[52] Roosevelt gave Hayes broad latitude in the execution of this commission, including the authority to offer Franco the "most sweeping commitments" that the United States would not interfere in the internal affairs of Spain and its overseas territories.[53] Hayes would be ably assisted by Willard Beaulac, a career diplomat newly appointed as consul general in Madrid and a man whose sympathy for the Spanish regime exceeded even his own.[54]

Arriving in Spain in May 1942, Hayes reported to Roosevelt that he found the Madrid government to be quite different from those in Berlin and Rome and that, in contrast to Hitler and Mussolini, Franco was a "taciturn and untheatrical" man who bucked the dictatorial "norm."[55] Not surprisingly, he also found the Spanish dictator to be a "bigger and more able" man than he had expected. Acting on the proven fact of the Spanish government's susceptibility to economic pressure, Hayes set out to build on the existing lines of American economic policy. Addressing the Barcelona Chamber of Commerce in July, the new ambassador sketched out the alluring possibility that "normal commercial relations" might be developed despite wartime restrictions.[56] Unlike his predecessor, who could never be sure that his trade talks would not be spiked by policy shifts in Washington, Hayes moved confident in the knowledge that he enjoyed full presidential backing. In August, concerned that U.S. officials were still delaying oil shipments, Hayes appealed directly to Roosevelt and, despite Herbert Feis's objections, bureaucratic obstacles to Spanish tanker sailings were quickly removed.[57]

Carlton Hayes's position in Madrid improved further in September 1942 when Franco appointed Count Francisco Jordana as Foreign Minister in place

[51] Hayes et al., "Reply of 175 Catholic Clergy and Laymen," *New York Times*, October 14, 1936.

[52] Welles to Hayes, October 11, 1942, *FRUS 1942*, 3: 299.

[53] Hayes, *Wartime Mission to Spain*, 11.

[54] See Willard Beaulac, *Franco: Silent Ally in World War II* (Carbondale and Edwardsville: Southern Illinois University Press, 1986), 52, 58–59.

[55] Hayes to Roosevelt, June 30 and September 3 1942, Box 3, Hayes Papers, Columbia University Library.

[56] Hayes, hand written note of speech Barcelona Chamber of Commerce, July 30, 1942, Box 1A, Hayes Papers.

[57] Feis, *Spanish Story*, 178–179.

of the Falangist Ramón Serrano Suñer. Serrano Suñer's dismissal reflected a broader shift in Spanish policy – known as the *chaqueteo* – as confidence in an Axis victory waned and was replaced by a new willingness to seek rapprochement with the Allies. Hayes was pleased to note the disappearance of Falangist trappings from the foreign ministry, and he quickly formed a positive appreciation of the conservative Jordana. After Myron Taylor (Roosevelt's personal representative to the Vatican) met with Jordana during a stopover in Madrid, he and Hayes agreed that the new minister was committed to "real," and perhaps even "benevolent," neutrality.[58] The numerous letters penned by Hayes to Catholic dignitaries in the United States in an effort to secure employment for Jordana's son attest both to the warmth of their personal relationship and to the ambassador's eagerness to cultivate their friendship. It was all exactly as Roosevelt had proposed.[59]

By October, having secured assurance from Washington that initial plans for an invasion of the Canary Islands had been dropped from Operation *Torch*, Hayes was able to offer Franco a firm guarantee that no Spanish territory would be occupied during the Allied invasion. Assessing the general's response, Hayes concluded that Madrid would not try to impede Allied operations in North Africa.[60] His confidence was well founded. Despite the misgivings of U.S. commanders, Madrid made no moves to oppose the *Torch* landings on November 8 1942, and when Hayes visited Jordana in the middle of the night to announce the landings and to present a message from Roosevelt promising to respect Spanish neutrality, the flustered foreign minister simply expressed his "intense relief" that no Spanish territory was involved. The following morning, Franco confirmed Jordana's reaction, applauding Allies' strategic acumen and thanking the president for his message.[61] With the *Torch* landings successfully completed, the first and most critical part of Hayes's mission in Spain was accomplished.[62]

[58] Hayes to Taylor, November 13, 1942, Hayes Papers, Box 5.
[59] Hayes to Ford, Houget, Paulding, Ready, Rockefeller, Rogers, and Van Renssalaer Wyatt, October 9, 1943, Hayes Papers, Box 5.
[60] Hayes to Hull, October 7, 1942, in Halstead, "Historians in Politics," 390.
[61] Hayes, *Wartime Mission*, 89–92.
[62] Ibid., 95

4

Torch, Darlan, and the French Maghreb

With the decision to invade North Africa finally made, President Roosevelt urged haste, insisting that because *Torch* was now the "principal objective," it should be launched at the "earliest possible date."[1] But substantial disagreements remained. U.S. military planners, still seeking to limit their involvement in the Mediterranean, proposed landing as far to the west as possible. This approach, however, ensured that even if U.S. troops were welcomed ashore by French forces loyal to General Giraud, they could only actually fight Germans after conducting a long and difficult overland march eastward into Tunisia. British leaders, on the other hand, advocated landing much further into the Mediterranean. They had clearer and more urgent goals. The Eighth Army had blunted the Axis advance on Egypt at the First Battle of El Alamein in July 1942, and was preparing a counteroffensive; with an Allied landing in eastern Algeria and Tunisia, Rommel's army could now be trapped in a giant vise.

The argument flared when the Combined Chiefs met in late August. British Admiral Andrew Cunningham argued that the rapid capture of Tunis would help relieve the hard-pressed Russians, facilitate a "satisfactory outcome of the battle for Egypt," and establish a "point of departure [for an] entry into Europe."[2] George Marshall countered by insisting that *Torch* would *not* help the Russians – that was the job of the cross-Channel assault. The invasion of North Africa, he insisted, had much more limited goals, and would simply "relieve" convoy routes to the Middle East while denying Germany access to naval bases in French West Africa. Wary of being drawn into an open-ended commitment to the Mediterranean, American planners favored the westerly landings suited to these more limited objectives, citing dangerously long lines of supply, shipping shortages, and the continuing threat of a German move

---

[1] Leahy to JCS, report on July 30, White House conference, August 1, 1942, Box 325, RG 218, NARA.
[2] CCS #38, August 28, 1942, Box 169, RG 218, NARA.

into Spain. Pointing to the risks faced by shipping passing through the Straits of Gibraltar, Marshall observed bitterly that the British had "strongly emphasized" the dangers of aerial attack when discussing *Sledgehammer*, but seemed blithely indifferent to them when *Torch* faced "similar hazards."[3] The shocking truth was that, barely ten weeks before troops were slated to begin landing, the Allies did not even have agreement on what the invasion was designed to accomplish. It was not an auspicious start.

Having endured a protracted crisis in relations with his senior military officers during the push to secure approval for *Gymnast*, Roosevelt may have felt that he could not challenge the Joint Chiefs' refusal to countenance landings in eastern Algeria and Tunisia. There was a limit to the degree to which he could be seen to side with the British, particularly in matters bearing directly on operational judgment, and having won on the decisive question of an invasion of North Africa, siding with the Joint Chiefs over the location of the landings would now help to reknit collaborative relations. In any case, Roosevelt may have thought that time and the unfolding logic of events would inevitably draw Washington deeper into the Mediterranean. So he focused his attention not on the location of the landings but on their composition, insisting that initial operations be conducted "exclusively" by U.S. troops on the grounds that Anglophobic French officers might take a British presence as an excuse to launch "full resistance."[4]

A heated discussion over the operational details of the campaign ensued, generating a flurry of plans and memorandums derided by Eisenhower as a "transatlantic essay competition."[5] London finally agreed that American troops should lead the invasion and that Washington should take "sole responsibility" for political relations with the French authorities. In return, American planners agreed to add a landing in Algiers, moving *Torch's* center of gravity a little further into the Mediterranean.[6] By carefully picking his battles with both the British and with his military leaders, Roosevelt had succeeded in securing a campaign that extended well beyond the geographical and temporal limits favored by the Joint Chiefs *and* one that would be led by a U.S. supreme commander, spearheaded by U.S. troops, and conducted under U.S. political leadership.[7]

---

[3] Ibid.

[4] Roosevelt to Churchill, August 30, 1942, Warren F. Kimball, *Churchill and Roosevelt: The Complete Correspondence* (Princeton, NJ: Princeton University Press, 1984), 1: 583.

[5] Harry C. Butcher, *My Three Years with Eisenhower: The Personal Diary of Captain Harry C. Butcher, USNR, Naval Aide to General Eisenhower, 1942 to 1945* (New York: Simon and Schuster, 1946), 83.

[6] Roosevelt to Churchill, September 2 and 5, 1942, *Correspondence*, 1: 589, 592.

[7] For a rather different analysis, suggesting that Roosevelt "bargained away" an assault on Tunisia for the "dubious advantage" of taking overall political responsibility for the campaign, see Arthur Layton Funk, *The Politics of Torch: The Allied Landings and the Algiers Putsch 1942* (Lawrence: University Press of Kansas, 1974).

If the operational planning for *Torch* was rushed and divisive, U.S. preparations for the political side of the campaign seemed to be built on somewhat
firmer foundations. Because the operation was premised on the notion that U.S.
troops would enter North Africa at the invitation of French officials, planners
assumed that there would be no break in the continuity of French rule and
therefore no need to establish an Allied military government. Once ashore, it
was anticipated that U.S. forces would work with French authorities without
disturbing the existing governmental structures of colonial rule. This approach
conformed to Washington's assurances to Vichy that it would defend the "integ-
rity of France and of the French empire," and it was popularized in a statement
explaining the invasion prepared for distribution to the population of North
Africa which explained that the "officers and employees of your government ...
will continue their duties as usual."[8] There was, needless to say, no question of
political sovereignty passing into the hands of the Arab and Berber majority.

As preparations for *Torch* advanced, it became apparent that these assumptions masked serious complexities. It was one thing to assert the continuity
French rule, but in whose hands – Pétain's, Giraud's, or de Gaulle's – did the
exercise of that sovereignty lie? By the time Robert Murphy returned to the
United States for a final preinvasion meeting with Roosevelt and Hopkins at
Hyde Park in early September, it had become clear to diplomats that Pétain,
along with several senior officials in North Africa, would oppose any U.S. landing, and that some French military resistance therefore had to be anticipated.[9]
Any significant opposition to the landings by Vichy loyalists would effectively
shatter earlier assumptions of uninterrupted French rule, rupturing political
continuity and requiring the bestowal of sovereignty on some new authority.
In the discussion at Hyde Park, Roosevelt reiterated his opposition to helping
"anyone" who sought to "impose a government on the French people," a statement that Murphy understood as reaffirming Washington's refusal to recognize
de Gaulle's Free French as an alternative bearer of French legitimacy.[10] To minimize the danger of de Gaulle grabbing governmental power in North Africa,
the Free French were to be excluded from preinvasion planning, a move that
would be justified on security grounds.[11]

At their Hyde Park meeting, Roosevelt instructed Murphy to "restrict [his]
dealings to French officials on the local level" and to avoid bestowing official

[8] Hull to Roosevelt, memorandum, "U.S. Position with Respect to French Territory," January 7,
1944," *FRUS 1944*, 3: 770–771; Proclamation in French and Arabic issued as a leaflet to population of French North Africa, Box 325, RG 218, NARA.
[9] Interestingly, the presidential log records Roosevelt's stay at Hyde Park from September 3 to
September 9, 1942, but does not include any mention of Murphy's visit. Murphy writes that he
arrived "quietly and unescorted" on September 4. The discrepancy underscores the delicacy of
the discussion between Murphy and Roosevelt. See "FDR Day by Day," FDRL.
[10] Robert Murphy, *Diplomat among Warriors* (Garden City, NY: Doubleday & Co, 1964),
101–102.
[11] Ibid., 102.

recognition on any higher political authority until the French population could express an opinion through the ballot box.[12] In reality, however, this was simply democratic-sounding window-dressing: having recognized that there would be no seamless continuity of Vichy rule, and deeply antipathetic to de Gaulle's project of restoring French power, American forces would inevitably find themselves choosing, and then upholding, a new regime capable of exercising "French" sovereignty. In doing so, Washington blatantly decoupled its actual practice from the norms of international politics and sovereignty that were supposed to govern it, claiming for itself the right to select which Frenchmen were suitable to rule in an area that it regarded as French territory, even if the majority of the local population did not.[13] This approach was codified in General Order #5, issued by the new Allied Forces Headquarters (AFHQ) in early October, establishing that Allied forces would "retain" the "existing form of government" in French North Africa, but reserving the right to "supplant" local officials judged unsympathetic to the "war aims of the United States."[14]

Acting both as Roosevelt's personal representative and as the head of AFHQ's new Civil Affairs Section, Robert Murphy would enjoy considerable latitude in the implementation of General Order #5. He would need it. As the power to "supplant" recalcitrant officials implied, AFHQ would have the critical task of determining what constituted a legitimate and sovereign French government. To most military officers, these political problems were an unwelcome diversion from the business of fighting the war. Briefing Eisenhower in London, Murphy observed him listening in horror to the "bewildering complexities" of French politics.[15] Eisenhower, his aide Captain Butcher recalled, felt that he was sailing into a "dangerous political sea" where military skill would be of little help in "charting a safe course."[16] Secure in London, Eisenhower could push these complexities to one side for the time being; back in Algiers, Murphy enjoyed no such luxury.

In October, Murphy resumed negotiations with the Group of Five and with General Charles Mast, Giraud's personal representative in Algiers. At the same time, Admiral Darlan sent an emissary to Algiers to negotiate with the Americans. After being removed from power in Vichy in April 1942, Darlan had become convinced that a U.S. invasion of North Africa was imminent and, ever a flexible opportunist, he was keen to explore the possibility of collaborating with Washington. Murphy realized that an agreement with Darlan, undoubtedly an authoritative figure in the eyes of French officers in North Africa, would carry much greater weight than an agreement with Giraud and

---

[12] Ibid.

[13] See Stephen D. Krasner, *Sovereignty: Organized Hypocrisy* (Princeton, NJ: Princeton University Press, 1999), 185.

[14] AFHQ General Order #5, October 12, 1942, Box 325, RG 218, NARA.

[15] Murphy, *Diplomat among Warriors*, 104.

[16] Butcher, *My Three Years*, 84.

the Five. However, in the absence of instructions from Washington and faced with the Five's hostility to any deal with the "double-faced" Darlan, Murphy did not pursue talks with the admiral.[17] Nevertheless, Darlan's approach alerted Murphy to the fact that he might yet become a willing collaborator, and neither AFHQ nor Washington expressed any principled objection to doing business with him. Their decision to stick with Giraud rested on the fact that the conservative and well-connected conspirators seemed a safer bet than the notoriously mercurial admiral.

Having rebuffed Darlan, Murphy struggled to consolidate relations with the Giraud conspiracy. Time was running short. On October 21, and with the invasion force already at sea, Eisenhower's deputy General Mark Clark landed in Algeria for a meeting with General Mast.[18] For all its daring-do – which the publicity-hungry Clark eagerly exploited – the meeting was a comedy of errors, with Mast arguing that Giraud was the indispensable key to North Africa, and the Americans intimating that they were willing to give him command of the entire operation. This was skating on thin ice. Not surprisingly, U.S. leaders had no intention of actually relinquishing command to a virtually unknown Frenchman. American double-speak was exposed after Giraud had been extracted from France and brought to Allied headquarters in Gibraltar. With U.S. troops poised to begin landing, Eisenhower found himself locked in a bizarre "4-hour struggle" with Giraud, who insisted "either I'm Allied C-in-C or I won't play!"[19]

With these critical politico-military questions still unresolved, Allied troops began landing on North African beaches on November 8, 1942. One U.S. task force under General George Patton landed on the Atlantic coast of Morocco, while a second aimed for the Algerian port of Oran. Farther east, a combined Anglo-American force struck at Algiers. On shore, Murphy's operatives carried out numerous "subversive tasks" in support of the inbound forces.[20] Although their actions successfully supported the invasion force, the critical political side of their work proved markedly less successful. With the exception of Algiers, where resistance fighters – ironically, a majority of them Gaullists – secured a number of key facilities, French forces conspicuously failed to welcome the Allied landings. Despite long months of effort to secure an "invitation," Allied troops faced serious French resistance, especially in Morocco. Allied forces suffered nearly 500 casualties as they fought to secure their beachheads.[21]

Back in Gibraltar, Eisenhower continued his tortured negotiations with Giraud, whose compromise proposal to allow the Americans to retain control

---

[17] See Funk, *Politics of Torch*, 133.
[18] See Mark W. Clark, *Calculated Risk* (New York: Harper and Brothers, 1950), chapter 5.
[19] Eisenhower to Marshall, November 7, 1942, Alfred D. Chandler (ed.) *The Papers of Dwight David Eisenhower: The War Years* (Baltimore: Johns Hopkins University Press, 1970), 2: 668.
[20] Instructions to OSS Representatives in North Africa, Entry 97, Box 9, RG 226, NARA.
[21] For an account of U.S. military operations in North Africa, see Rick Atkinson, *An Army at Dawn: The War in North Africa, 1942–1943* (New York: Henry Holt, 2002).

of "base and administrative arrangements" while he took care of combat operations graphically demonstrated the gulf between the two sides.[22] As Giraud negotiated for command, the planned guerrilla operations organized by his supporters in North Africa were proving entirely ineffective. The forces that the Five claimed to have assembled, including the much-vaunted *Chantiers de la Jeunesse Français*, refused to act without direct orders from Vichy, and these, of course, were not forthcoming. Throughout North Africa a majority of French troops remained loyal to Vichy and, although many preferred to await developments before committing themselves to action, those under governor-general Auguste Noguès in Morocco fought tenaciously. With French resistance threatening to unravel the premise that the Allies had been "invited" into North Africa, *Torch* faced disaster. As it became clear that Giraud lacked the political authority to enforce a ceasefire, Murphy and Clark began a desperate search for a French leader capable of stopping the fighting.

In a remarkable coincidence – and one that has fueled numerous conspiracy theories – Admiral Darlan had arrived in Algiers to visit his sick son just two days before the invasion. U.S. leaders now opened talks with him. Over several days of intrigue and negotiation, Darlan drove a hard bargain, finally agreeing on November 13 to end the fighting in exchange for being recognized as High Commissioner for North and West Africa. Darlan bolstered his authority by claiming that his negotiations with the Americans had been conducted with Pétain's approval. In fact, Vichy denounced the deal, but – with the exception of those in Tunisia – most French troops in North Africa accepted Darlan's leadership.

With the deal done, Eisenhower flew into Algiers to add his seal of approval, announcing Darlan's appointment as head of what he termed the "French North African state."[23] Political power across the Maghreb stayed in the hands of former Vichyites, with Noguès remaining Governor General in Morocco and General Alphonse Juin head of the army. A demoralized Giraud was given nominal control of French forces in the region, but Darlan quickly dismissed many of his key supporters, imprisoning some as traitors. Eisenhower justified the deal to the Combined Chiefs on the grounds that a "strong French government" under Darlan was the only alternative to military rule – a step that would incur "tremendous" costs and require 60,000 U.S. troops just to "hold the tribes quiet."[24] He warned that if Washington repudiated the deal it would end any "hope of getting to Tunisia quickly."[25] Although Eisenhower defended the deal with Darlan on the grounds of military necessity, nothing that he or his subordinates did violated the political framework of *Torch* established by Washington. Political decisions in occupied North Africa were always going

[22] Eisenhower to Marshall, November 8, 1942, *Eisenhower Papers*, 2: 670–671.
[23] Eisenhower, quoted in Atkinson, *Army at Dawn*, 158.
[24] Eisenhower to CCS, November 14, 1942, *Eisenhower Papers*, 2: 708.
[25] Ibid., 709.`

to be made on pragmatic rather than ideological grounds – and in any case it would have been difficult to explain how the *Cagoulard* Lemaigre-Dubreuil was more "progressive" than Darlan.

If U.S. military and political leaders were indifferent to the character of the new regime in North Africa – provided that it maintained the continuity of French rule, avoided the necessity of a military government, and kept de Gaulle out – the deal that placed a senior Vichyite at the head of the first territory occupied by U.S. troops provoked a storm of domestic controversy.[26] Initial press reaction to *Torch* had been positive, with *New Republic* announcing joyously "We Begin!" and Anne O'Hare McCormick concluding that the landings had dispelled the torpor of "phony war" and swung public opinion behind the idea of "focus[ing] on Hitler as the principle enemy."[27] The *New York Times* announced that the "turning point of the war has at last been reached" and urged a rapid drive to Tunisia, where victory would give the Allies control of the Mediterranean, the "great waterway which is the historic entrance to Europe."[28] The "Darlan Deal" soured this adulatory outpouring, with many commentators asking how it was possible that the first blow struck in a war against fascism had produced a government headed by the fascist-minded Darlan.[29] Once Roosevelt endorsed the deal – like Eisenhower, he justified it as a "temporary expedient" to "save American and British lives" – mainstream opinion-makers rallied, with influential columnist Walter Lippmann dropping earlier criticisms and welcoming it as "unplanned but wisely improvised."[30] The *New York Times* also highlighted the agreement's "temporary" character, and the Communist Party-influenced *PM* urged its readers not to get too "finicky" about the politics of fellow "United Nations."[31] Government officials used censorship to reinforce their position, blocking the release of newsreel footage of Darlan in relaxed conversation with Eisenhower, Clark, and Murphy.[32]

The administration stifled criticism from liberals within its own ranks by evasion and buck-passing. When Henry Morgenthau questioned Under Secretary of War Robert Patterson about the origin of the deal, Patterson blamed Robert Murphy and the State Department, claiming – not implausibly – "the route was from Murphy to Welles to the White House."[33] Faced with this evidence of

---

[26] Roosevelt to Churchill, November 11, 1942, *Correspondence*, 1: 669.
[27] *New Republic*, November 16, 1942; McCormick, "Abroad," *New York Times*, November 18, 1942.
[28] Editorial, *New York Times*, November 19, 1942.
[29] See Steven Casey, *Cautious Crusade: Franklin D. Roosevelt, American Public Opinion, and the War against Nazi Germany* (Oxford: Oxford University Press, 2001), chapter 4.
[30] Roosevelt, Press conference #861, November 17, 1942, Jonathan Daniels (intro.), *The Complete Press Conferences of Franklin D. Roosevelt* (New York: DaCapo Press, 1972), 20: 244–245; Lippmann, *Washington Post*, November 19, 1942.
[31] Editorials, *New York Times*, November 17 and 18, 1942; Editorial, *PM*, December 3 1942.
[32] Casey, *Cautious Crusade*, 114.
[33] Morgenthau-Patterson telephone conversation, transcript, Morgenthau diary, November 16, 1942, FDRL.

White House complicity, Sumner Welles explained that the deal was a "military question" decided by "military commanders" acting out of "military necessity," and that president was "not aware of the details until they had been arrived at."[34] Patterson, Welles concluded, "doesn't know what he's talking about." The spinning of this Washington merry-go-round left Morgenthau and other liberals confused and temporarily mollified, but the deal nevertheless posed a significant challenge to the entire ideological framework of the war effort. Broadcasting from London, CBS journalist Edward R. Murrow argued that it would encourage "Quislings" everywhere to "rally to our side," thereby undermining the fundamental "principles for which this war is being fought."[35] By permitting the continuation of undemocratic governments, Murrow concluded prophetically, deals of this kind might determine the postwar "political complexion of much of the world;" in Italy, for example, Washington might simply "turn over" power to the House of Savoy.

The suggestion that the war might resolve itself into a series of sordid compromises with right-wing politicians was hard to square with the Atlantic Charter and the "Four Freedoms," and it seemed to many that democratic idealism had collapsed before "temporary expediency," exposing the hard-edged pragmatism at the heart of American policy. While Roosevelt defended the deal on the grounds of military necessity, many officials and opinion-formers fretted that its long-term consequences for the domestic perception of American war aims, and therefore for popular support for the war effort, might be incalculable. Nor was this simply a domestic question. As publisher Henry Luce had argued in his influential "American Century" editorial in *Life* nearly two years previously, it was the *combination* of economic strength, military might, and politico-moral sanctity that rendered the United States uniquely capable of articulating the "war aims of this war" and of championing a new world order with itself at the center.[36] Luce's *Time* now complained that the invasion of North Africa might "set the tone for others to come," asking pointedly "was not freedom to come in the wake of Americans?"[37]

Just as public criticism of the North African deal seemed to be subsiding, it was reignited by Darlan's appointment, with Allied approval, of former Vichy interior minister Marcel Peyrouton to the governor generalship of Algeria.[38] By the time Peyrouton arrived in Algiers, Darlan himself was dead, gunned down by a young anti-Vichy resistance fighter on Christmas Eve 1942. But Peyrouton's appointment, and the roundup of Gaullists and leftists on suspicion

---

[34] Morgenthau-Welles telephone conversation, transcript, Morgenthau diary, November 16, 1942, FDRL.
[35] Edward R. Murrow, November 15, 1942 CBS broadcast from London, transcript, Morgenthau diary, November 16, 1942, FDRL.
[36] Luce, "The American Century," *Life*, February 7, 1941.
[37] Editorial, *Time*, November 20, 1942.
[38] See Casey, *Cautious Crusade*, 116 ff.

of involvement in Darlan's assassination, made it clear that former Vichyites were consolidating their grip on North Africa. Peyrouton's appointment could hardly be justified by military necessity and, far from being a "temporary expedient," the regime was clearly becoming permanent. In this context, the public response to the Peyrouton affair was both sharper and broader than that to the Darlan deal. The *Nation* led the charge, describing Peyrouton as a "model ... Vichy collaborationist" and the author of "savage repression" in France.[39] Mainstream liberals joined the chorus, with the *Washington Post* denouncing Peyrouton's appointment as the "last straw."[40] Exempting Eisenhower from blame – his "hands [were] full with military problems" – the *Post* demanded Robert Murphy's dismissal. Within the administration, Office of War Information head Elmer Davis urged Peyrouton's removal, complaining that his appointment was "extremely difficult to explain to the American people."[41]

Mounting criticism of American policy convinced Roosevelt of the need to affirm that the Allies were fighting for the complete overthrow of the Axis, and not simply for a series of deals with malleable local rightists. In January 1943 he used the final press conference of the Casablanca Conference to announce that the Allies' sought the "unconditional surrender" of their enemies.[42] On his return to the United States, Roosevelt emphasized the point by asserting that Washington would not leave "Quislings or Lavals" in power "anywhere on this earth."[43] These declarations helped to reinforce the image of the war as moral crusade, but Washington still had to deal with the reality of the regime it had established in North Africa. Here, the assassination of Darlan was, as the *Nation* pointed out, a "free gift to the United States," offering a "second chance" to establish a government in French North Africa that could be presented as conforming to its stated democratic war aims.[44] Whether or not the gift was actually "free" remains unclear. Darlan's assassin was railroaded to execution, but his claim to have acted alone appears unconvincing, and evidence points to his involvement in a plot involving some combination of OSS, British Special Operations Executive (SOE) and Gaullist, agents.[45] Whatever the authorship of the assassination, Washington seized its chance to prettify the French colonial regime in North Africa by appointing the reliably anti-collaborationist Henri Giraud as high commissioner.

---

[39] Editorial, *The Nation*, January 23, 1943.
[40] Editorial, *Washington Post*, January 15, 1943.
[41] Quoted in Casey, *Cautious Crusade*, 118.
[42] See Casey, *Cautious Crusade*, 118–120.
[43] Roosevelt, press conference, January 24, 1943, *Complete Press Conferences of Franklin D. Roosevelt*, 12: 78.
[44] Editorial, *The Nation*, January 2, 1943.
[45] See Robin W. Winks, *Cloak & Gown: Scholars in the Secret War, 1939–1961* (New Haven: Yale University Press, 1987), 183–184; see David Reynolds, *In Command of History: Churchill Fighting and Writing the Second World War* (New York: Basic Books, 2005), 328–330.

The effort to smarten up to make the administration of French North Africa took place in the context of an unexpectedly difficult military campaign. Ironically, the Joint Chiefs' insistence on landing in the western Maghreb now militated against realizing their cherished hopes of ending America's Mediterranean sojourn quickly. Allied forces faced a long haul into Tunisia, and as they marched east the Vichy authorities in Tunis were busy facilitating the rapid buildup of Axis forces in North Africa. In late November, Berlin established the Fifth Panzer Army in Tunisia and its veteran troops, reinforced by the remnants of Rommel's German-Italian Panzer Army, waged a vigorous defensive campaign that kept the Allies out of Tunis until May 1943. More than 275,000 Axis soldiers surrendered when "Tunisgrad" finally fell, but the scale of the Allied victory was qualified by the fact that the Axis campaign succeeded in keeping the Mediterranean closed to Allied shipping for several more months and in buying time to strengthen the defenses in southern Europe.[46] Moreover, the protracted struggle in Tunisia ensured that the cross-Channel assault would be postponed until 1944, opening the door to the continuing commitment of large-scale Allied resources to the Mediterranean.

During the North African campaign, the U.S. army went through a rapid process of testing and battle hardening. The *New York Times*'s triumphant proclamation "Victorious Americans in Tunisia Now Veterans" turned out, in the light of experience in Sicily and Italy, to have been somewhat premature, but it was undoubtedly true that U.S. troops emerged from the campaign with a much firmer grasp on the realities of modern mechanized warfare.[47] The campaign also allowed U.S. commanders to begin to come to grips with a series of practical problems that facilitated future operations in Italy and the invasion of France; without this unforgiving process of learning through action in the Mediterranean, U.S. forces would have stood little chance of carrying out a successful cross-Channel assault. From a narrowly military viewpoint, this alone justified Roosevelt's insistence on *Gymnast* over the objections of George Marshall and the Joint Chiefs.

In the context of extended military operations in the Maghreb, the vexed question of the character of French colonial rule there exposed underlying tensions between London and Washington. London approved the appointment of Henri Giraud as Darlan's successor, but Churchill also pressed for de Gaulle to be included in the reformed political set-up in Algiers, urging Roosevelt "to bring them all together [in a] solid and united ... French nucleus."[48] Given Giraud's lackluster performance in Algiers, Churchill no doubt anticipated that de Gaulle would soon control such a "nucleus." Roosevelt's inclination went in exactly the opposite direction. As Eisenhower's aide Harry Butcher noted,

---

[46] See Atkinson, *Army at Dawn*, 539–540.
[47] *New York Times*, May 9, 1943.
[48] Churchill to Roosevelt, December 27, 1942, *Correspondence*, 2: 90.

the "President doesn't want the French to create a single ... central government before the French people can elect one."[49] The emphasis was very much on the first clause, and Roosevelt's opposition to a unified regime rested less on notions of popular sovereignty – Darlan, after all, had enjoyed no such legitimacy – and more on antipathy to de Gaulle and to the strong and independent French state that he personified. De Gaulle himself clearly grasped the thrust of U.S. policy, noting that Roosevelt sought an "American peace" in which the United States would be both "savior" and "arbiter" of a weak and American-dominated France.[50]

London initially supported the "Darlan Deal" out of military necessity, agreeing not to "hamper" Eisenhower's effort to "stamp out" Axis forces in Tunisia by criticizing his political arrangements. Public criticism of the U.S.-sponsored deal, however, soon created new opportunities for Churchill to advance de Gaulle's cause.[51] Buoyed by public hostility to Darlan, the old imperial warhorse struck a positively liberal note, warning Roosevelt that a "permanent arrangement" with former Vichyites would "not be understood by the great mass of ordinary people whose simple loyalties are our strength."[52] In Whitehall, the Darlan deal was widely seen as the inevitable outcome of U.S. leadership and the unhappy product of Roosevelt's hostility to de Gaulle, Murphy's pro-Vichy sympathies, and Eisenhower's political naïveté.[53] British leaders felt that this outcome was at least partly a result of their being underrepresented at AFHQ, a weakness that was itself a reflection of their agreement to allow the United States to take the lead in North Africa. In the new political situation after the landings, it was time to redress the balance, and when Washington announced Robert Murphy's promotion to minister in December 1942, Churchill seized the opportunity to send senior Conservative politician and Colonial Office official Harold Macmillan out to Algiers to "work with him."[54]

Roosevelt readily agreed that Macmillan should have "precisely the same status" as the new American minister, but insisted that he, too, should be attached to Eisenhower's staff.[55] This proposal triggered a protracted exchange over Macmillan's title, whose Monty Pythonesque tone – Churchill proposed styling him "His Majesties (sic) Government's Political Representative at General Eisenhower's Headquarters" – masked the critical question of whether Macmillan would function as London's agent in the field or as an advisor to

[49] Butcher, *My Three Years*, 233.
[50] Charles de Gaulle, *The War Memoirs of Charles de Gaulle: Unity, 1942–1944*, trans. Richard Howard, (New York: Simon and Schuster, 1959), especially 88–89.
[51] Churchill to Ismay, on November 21, 1942, PREM 3/442/10.
[52] Churchill to Roosevelt, November 17, 1942, *Correspondence*, 2: 7.
[53] See Matthew Jones, *Britain, the United States, and the Mediterranean War 1942–1944* (New York: St. Martin's Press, 1996), 81–83.
[54] Churchill to Roosevelt, December 11, 1942, *Correspondence*, 2: 71.
[55] Roosevelt to Churchill, December 19, 1942, *Correspondence*, 2: 85.

the theater commander.[56] Roosevelt finally accepted that as "Minister Resident at Allied Headquarters" Macmillan would act London's man at AFHQ, but he also insisted that Eisenhower have "full veto over all civil officials" and the final say in relations with the French.[57] The whole affair, driven by London's attempt to respond to increased American assertiveness, deepened mutual suspicion between the Allies over their respective plans for French North Africa.[58]

Ironically, the assignment of Harold Macmillan to Algiers was welcomed by U.S. liberals as signaling a shift in Allied policy from "Darlanism to republicanism," and as an "omen of better days" to come.[59] Macmillan himself might have concurred: from his arrival in Algiers he recognized the difficulties created by Giraud's "whoring after the false gods of Vichy."[60] As it turned out, his arrival coincided with a significant shift in U.S. policy, with Washington finally grasping that Darlan's assassination allowed for the forging of a new consensus between Giraud and de Gaulle – hopefully under the control of the former – and for and the de-Vichyfication of French rule in North Africa.[61] In Algiers, the increasingly politically-minded Eisenhower concluded that Giraud was the "medium" though which this "desired rapprochement" could be effected, noting that even the arch-conservative Peyrouton now favored an "accord" between de Gaulle and Giraud.[62] Washington's new openness to the inclusion of de Gaulle in the reformed government of French North Africa was grounded on mounting evidence that the Free French enjoyed widespread support in the region, as well as on the dawning realization that the policy of keeping unpopular Vichy officials "in the saddle" meant that the United States was now running a "poor third" behind the British and the Free French in local public opinion.[63]

Anne O'Hare McCormick noted hopefully that by uniting the French factions, the Allies would also strengthen the "Anglo-American unity" that was critical to all "hopes of victory in war and justice and freedom in peace."[64] But even with the encouragement of both London and Washington, the road to rapprochement was not smooth. When Allied leaders met in Casablanca in January 1943, Giraud and de Gaulle were invited to join them: it was time, as Roosevelt put it, for the "banns to be read and the marriage concluded."[65]

[56] Churchill to Roosevelt, December 23, 1942, *Correspondence*, 2: 87.

[57] Roosevelt to Churchill, December 29, 1942, *Correspondence*, 2: 89, 93.

[58] See Jones, *Mediterranean War*, 78.

[59] Editorial, *The Nation*, January 23, 1943.

[60] Macmillan to Churchill, February 12, 1943, Harold Macmillan, *War Diaries: Politics and War in the Mediterranean, January 1943–May 1945* (New York: St. Martin's Press, 1984), 24.

[61] See G. E. Maguire, *Anglo-American Policy towards the Free French* (New York: Palgrave Macmillan, 1995), 72–73.

[62] Eisenhower to Churchill, December 28, 1942, *Eisenhower Papers*, 2: 870; Eisenhower to Hopkins, January 17, 1943, *Eisenhower Papers*, 2: 907.

[63] Boyd to Eddy, January 13, 1943, RG 226, Box 97, NARA.

[64] McCormick, "Abroad," *New York Times*, January 6, 1943.

[65] Report of meeting of Churchill, Roosevelt, Murphy and Macmillan, Macmillan to Eden, January 17, 1942, PREM 3, 442/16

FIGURE 4.1. The "shotgun wedding." With Roosevelt and Churchill looking on, Henri Giraud and Charles de Gaulle shake hands at Casablanca, January 22, 1943. (Courtesy of Franklin D. Roosevelt Library.)

Even so, the "shotgun wedding" almost collapsed when de Gaulle refused to travel to French-ruled territory at the invitation of the British, only embarking when Churchill threatened to withdraw his support for the French National Committee.[66] Long hours of "arduous debate and considerable pressure" were required before the two leaders were finally cajoled into a handshake for the cameras, and their joint declaration was a model of vacuous brevity. Numerous more fulsome draft statements prepared for them by Allied officials were rejected.[67]

Given the frosty character of the shotgun wedding in Casablanca, the actual establishment of a unified French authority in North Africa remained problematic. In Algiers, Free French and Giraudist factions engaged in long and detailed negotiations; and in London, de Gaulle eyed Anglo-American intentions with suspicion. Amid the mutual hostility, French businessman Jean Monnet worked to reconcile the factions. After the fall of France, Monnet worked in Washington for the British Purchasing Commission, developing a reputation as a "single-minded apostle of all-out production" and forging close relations with leading

[66] Ibid.
[67] Macmillan to FO, January 24, 1943, PREM 3, 442/14.

administration figures including Harry Hopkins and Henry Morgenthau.[68] In December 1942, Monnet sent Hopkins an urgent memorandum on the crisis in North Africa, stressing the importance of moving quickly to overcome the "disorder inherent in the present French situation."[69] Mindful of the political damage done by the deal with Darlan, Monnet argued for a liberalization of the Giraud administration based on making a clean breaking from the "notion of the legitimacy of the Vichy regime." Significantly, Monnet emphasized that only the United States had the political authority to resolve the crisis, concluding that direct presidential intervention would be the "cornerstone of the whole edifice."[70]

Faced during the Casablanca Conference with the seemingly intractable realities of French politics, Roosevelt acted on Hopkins' advice and cabled the State Department to propose that Monnet be dispatched to Algiers to help resolve the crisis. Monnet, Roosevelt argued, had "kept his skirts clear of political entanglements" and was well equipped to help civilianize and liberalize the Giraud regime while mediating with de Gaulle.[71] Moreover, it seemed to Roosevelt that in Monnet he had finally found a French leader who understood the emerging power of the United States and sought to situate France in a suitably deferential position to it. Cordell Hull initially rebuffed the president's proposal, fearing that Monnet was too sympathetic to de Gaulle, but Roosevelt insisted. Monnet sailed for Algiers the following month. Under his guidance Giraud began to clean up his administration, issuing "democratic manifestations," repealing Vichy legislation, and purging Vichyite officials.[72]

Monnet soon became convinced that there could be no lasting solution to the political crisis without overcoming the divisions between Giraud and de Gaulle, and his influential voice was added to those urging unity. De Gaulle recognized the favorable situation developing in Algiers and, evading Eisenhower's mendacious instruction that he should not return until the military situation stabilized, arrived in North Africa to "mass ovations" at the end of May.[73] With de Gaulle forcing the pace, pressure for an agreement finally overcame Giraud's resistance, and the *Comité français de la Libération Nationale* (CFLN) was formed on June 3, 1943, with the two generals as co-chairs.[74] Even then, Washington was not entirely reconciled to the augmentation of de Gaulle's power, and stormy divisions within the CFLN over the control of French forces in North Africa prompted Roosevelt to contemplate briefly the establishment

[68] Robert E. Sherwood, *Roosevelt and Hopkins, an Intimate History* (New York: Harper & Bros, 1948), 288.
[69] Monnet to Hopkins, memorandum, December 27, 1942, Box 330, Hopkins papers, FDRL.
[70] Ibid.
[71] Roosevelt to Hull, January 16, 1943, quoted in Sherwood *Roosevelt and Hopkins*, 678.
[72] De Gaulle, *Unity*, 104–104; see Julian G. Hurstfield, *America and the French Nation, 1939–1945* (Chapel Hill: University of North Carolina Press, 1986), 195–197.
[73] Marc Loris, "The Giraud-de Gaulle Dispute," *Fourth International*, July 1943, 200.
[74] See Macmillan, *War Diaries*, 66, 68.

of Allied military rule. In a striking affirmation of Eisenhower's increasingly confident embrace of the political aspect of his role as supreme commander, this suggestion was firmly rebuffed by AFHQ Algiers.[75]

Under Eisenhower's leadership, American and British officers at AFHQ began pushing for their governments to accord diplomatic recognition to the CFLN as the leadership of the resistance to German occupation and therefore as the putative provisional government of France. Macmillan was convinced that this was his idea – the old Balliol man pictured himself as a clever "Greek" manipulating the "big, vulgar and bustling" American "Romans" – but Eisenhower was clearly moving in the same direction, urging Washington to extend "some kind of limited recognition" to the CFLN.[76] Not for the last time, the British would underestimate Eisenhower's political savvy. By early July, even Robert Murphy had come around, joining Eisenhower on Macmillan's list of the "absolutely sound."[77] The challenge was now to "convert" Washington, and here Murphy deployed a new argument, suggesting that by recognizing the CFLN Washington would actually help to moderate de Gaulle's influence by limiting his opportunities for "personal leadership."[78]

Deepening popular support for the CFLN in North Africa reinforced the case for recognition. Observing an Allied military parade in Casablanca in May, U.S. officials noted the participation of 500 organized Gaullists, who sang patriotic songs and booed Vichy officials before parading to the British and U.S. consulates.[79] OSS analysts concluded that although pro-Vichy sentiment remained strong in the navy, elsewhere groups "claiming to be Gaullists" were quickly becoming dominant.[80] In July, Churchill urged Roosevelt to recognize the CFLN, noting that Macmillan, Eisenhower, and Murphy were all in agreement with the proposal.[81] Roosevelt protested the use of the word "recognition," which he feared might be taken as implying approval of the CFLN as the "government of France." He argued instead for more "limited acceptance" subject to "military requirements."[82] Despite its grudging tone, Roosevelt's response reflected an admission of the fact that the CFLN had established itself in deed as the political authority in French North Africa, and that it would have to be dealt with as such.

---

[75] See Stephen E. Ambrose, *The Supreme Commander* (Jackson: University of Mississippi Press, 1970, 1999), 195 ff; on the rejection of Roosevelt's plan for a military government, see Eisenhower to Marshall, July 2, 1943, *Eisenhower Papers*, 2: 1273.

[76] Macmillan, quoted in Jones, *Mediterranean War*, 80.

[77] Macmillan, diary entry July 5, 1943, *War Diaries*, 141.

[78] Ibid; Murphy to Hull, July 17, 1943, *FRUS 1943*, 2: 173.

[79] Joint Intelligence Center report, May 11, 1943, Entry 97, Box 5, RG 226, NARA.

[80] "Political Situation in North Africa," OSS Report, June 2, 1943, Entry 97, Box 5, RG 226, NARA.

[81] Churchill to Roosevelt, July 8, 1943, *Correspondence*, 2: 310–311.

[82] Roosevelt to Churchill, July 22, 1943, *Correspondence*, 2: 339–340.

The Allies finally extended diplomatic recognition to the CFLN at the *Quadrant* conference in Quebec in August 1943 but, while London welcomed the French Committee, Washington simply acknowledged it as the legitimate administration in "those territories that recognize its authority."[83] Because it was clearly impossible to determine whose "authority" the people of metropolitan France might "recognize," Roosevelt hoped that this circumlocution would keep Washington's options regarding the postwar government of France open. Presented with these divergent statements, René Massigli, CFLN Commissioner for Foreign Affairs, wisely declined to parse the differences, viewing them as "living, not legal, documents" describing an evolving relationship.[84]

Allied recognition coincided with the consolidation of de Gaulle's authority within the CFLN. In July, and with Giraud safely in the United States, de Gaulle secured Monnet's backing for a proposal to separate the functions of the co-presidents, assigning Giraud command of the military while de Gaulle assumed overall political control. Despite having begun the liberalization of the French administration in North Africa, the incorrigibly conservative Giraud became increasingly isolated within the CFLN, and matters headed toward a predictable dénouement. [85] In October, after Giraud organized the capture of Corsica by French troops without seeking prior approval from the CFLN, de Gaulle took advantage his rival's indiscipline to establish himself as sole president, thereby resolving the uneasy "dualism" within the committee.[86]

British policy makers viewed the decision to recognize the CFLN as a victory for their policy of rebuilding a strong France, and in Algiers Robert Murphy witnessed a celebratory Anglo-French "victory lunch."[87] American opinion-formers tended to concur, with the *Nation* saluting the "final end of America's Vichy policy" and the *Washington Post* marking the conclusion of the administration's failed attempt to treat France as a "minor or nonexistent power."[88] Many liberals agreed with journalist I. F. Stone's assertion that the "grudging, cold, and ambiguous" recognition the CFLN had been long delayed by a "steady drift to the right" in U.S. foreign policy.[89] Despite appearances, however, Stone was mistaken. Washington's policy was not becoming more right wing: instead, it was simply hewing to the pragmatic lines on which it had always run. What *had* changed in North Africa was that the abrasive reality of war had stripped away some of the carefully crafted ideological packaging within which policy was customarily wrapped, exposing its pragmatic core.

[83] British and American statements in Macmillan, *War Diaries*, 193.

[84] Macmillan, diary entry August 26, 1943, Macmillan, *War Diaries*, 193.

[85] See Julian Jackson, *France: The Dark Years, 1940–1944* (Oxford: Oxford University Press, 2001), 459.

[86] For de Gaulle's account of these events, see *Unity*, 158–164.

[87] Murphy, *Diplomat among Warriors*, 180.

[88] Editorial, *The Nation*, June 12, 1943; editorial, *Washington Post*, June 8, 1943.

[89] Stone, "The President and Sumner Welles," *The Nation*, September 4, 1943.

Despite their belated recognition of the CFLN, American policy makers maintained an abiding hostility toward de Gaulle. Their antipathy was bolstered by the general's surprising emergence as a "figure of the 'Left.'"[90] The Free French, as de Gaulle explained to the *New York Times*, welcomed "every shade" of opinion from "avowed Communists to Catholic priests," and its policies for postwar France included radical-sounding proposals to regulate big business and to promote a "wider distribution of the national wealth."[91] De Gaulle's ability to refashion himself as a populist rested in large part on the support he received from Moscow and from the French Communist Party (PCF). When Germany invaded the Soviet Union in June 1941, the PCF responded by dropping its earlier opposition to de Gaulle, coming out in support of the Free French and utilizing its own undercover organization to launch armed resistance to the German occupation.

Moscow welcomed the Allies' recognition of the CFLN, and it took a bold step further by stating that the committee represented the "state interests of the French republic." This formula, as the *Washington Post* noted, signaled Moscow's recognition of the CFLN as the "repository of French sovereignty" and as an "equal partner" in the war against Germany.[92] Following this line, Communists throughout North Africa rallied to the Free French, dropping opposition to French colonialism in favor of building broad anti-fascist fronts.[93] U.S. officials took note, with OSS reports highlighting communist efforts to build popular support for de Gaulle. The Algerian Communist Party was particularly effective in this capacity given the "prestige" it had acquired by its unbending opposition to Vichy in the face of "ferocious persecution."[94] In Tunisia, Communist spokesmen protested the CFLN's detention of nationalist Destour Party leaders, but they did so on the grounds that while the nationalists were surely "traitors" to the anti-Nazi cause, their persecution divided the Tunisian people at a time when the unity of the "anti-Hitlerian coalition" was paramount.[95]

To British policy makers, evidence of potential Free French radicalism did not seem so troubling: as senior Foreign Office official William Strang put it, where Washington sought an "anti-Communist and pro-American" France, London hoped for a left-wing government in Paris that would work with the Soviet Union to "contain Germany."[96] Despite its continued antipathy to de

[90] Loris, "The Political Misadventures of the French Bourgeoisie," *Fourth International*, March 1943.
[91] *New York Times*, July 20, 1943.
[92] *Washington Post*, August 28, 1943.
[93] See Roger E. Kanet, "The Soviet Union, the French Communist Party, and Africa, 1945–1960" *Survey* 22, (1976), 76.
[94] "The Political Situation in North Africa," OSS Report, July 2, 1943, Entry 97, Box 5, RG 226, NARA.
[95] Cole to State Department, October 14, 1943, 851S.oo/288, RG 59, NARA.
[96] Strang, August 1943, quoted in Jones, *Mediterranean War*, 82.

Gaulle, however, Washington began to use economic power in the form of military aid to gain influence with the CFLN. This policy unfolded at a time when significant sections of the French elite were modifying their own relationship to de Gaulle and turning, as Jean Monnet's own evolution signaled, toward the Free French.[97] At the same time, de Gaulle began a reciprocal, if veiled, reorientation toward the United States. Meeting with de Gaulle in June 1943, Robert Murphy was surprised to hear him explain that the future of France depended largely on United States. It was on American largesse, de Gaulle argued, rather than on relations with Britain, that the aspirations of a "new France" rested.[98] De Gaulle, Murphy concluded, might never become a "close friend," but he surely understood the shifting balance of power within the Alliance and was orienting himself to it.

By early 1943, powerful evidence of that changing balance of power was pouring into North Africa in the form of U.S. economic aid for the civilian population and materiél for the rebuilding of the French military. Free French forces had initially been equipped by London but, as British resources became exhausted, Washington decided in November 1941 to make a prudent side bet on its Vichy policy by extending Lend-Lease to the Free French. Even then, the Americans avoided direct relations with the Gaullists by insisting that they receive their supplies from British allocations. Under the operational control of the Eighth Army, Free French forces had made a significant contribution to the desert war, and the Combined Chiefs agreed that these troops should remain under British "tutelage."[99] American attention concentrated instead on rebuilding the fourteen poorly equipped divisions of Vichy's African Army.[100] Almost universally referred to as "French," these forces were in their great majority composed of North and West African soldiers under French officers.

Before *Torch*, Washington had declined General Mast's request for equipment to rebuild the French forces in North Africa. Shortly after the landings, however, and with French forces fighting alongside their own troops on the road to Tunisia, the Allies agreed to begin rearming the African Army. On November 14, President Roosevelt facilitated this effort by extending Lend-Lease directly to the French authorities in North Africa while continuing to supply the Free French via London. In mid-December, AFHQ Algiers formed the Joint Rearmament Committee (JRC) to oversee the process, and the committee's composition – four Americans, four Frenchmen, and one Briton – made it clear that the rearmament of the African Army would be essentially

[97] See Charles L. Robertson, *When Roosevelt Planned to Govern France* (Amherst, MA: University of Massachusetts Press, 2011), 81.
[98] Murphy, *Diplomat among Warriors*, 182–183; for a discussion on de Gaulle's positive appreciation of the United States, see Jean Lacoutre, *De Gaulle: The Rebel, 1890–1944*, trans. Patrick O'Brian (New York: W.W. Norton, 1993), 336–337.
[99] See Marcel Vigneras, *Rearming the French* (Washington, DC: Center for Military History, United States Army, 1989). On "tutelage," ibid., 10.
[100] Butcher, *My Three Years*, 58.

an American project. This relationship was underscored at the Casablanca Conference, where Roosevelt met privately with Giraud and pledged, in what became known as the Anfa Agreement, to rearm eleven French divisions.

The Anfa Agreement immediately raised British hackles. In Washington, the British Joint Staff Mission (JSM) reported that U.S. military leaders seemed "embarrassed" by Roosevelt's unilateral action, but they insisted any promises he had made to Giraud had be kept.[101] Churchill assured his Chiefs of Staff that any "promises" made to Giraud came from Roosevelt alone, but he concluded that there was nothing London could do to block what it saw as an American attempt to solidify Giraud's position.[102] British leaders nevertheless argued that it was "militarily unjustified" to divert scarce resources to the French, and Churchill complained to Roosevelt that supplying French forces who would make "no contribution" to the upcoming invasion of Sicily would needlessly exacerbate the shipping crisis.[103] In a similar vein, Foreign Secretary Anthony Eden warned that the Anfa Agreement would put "strong pressure on our imports programme" by channeling American supplies away from Britain.[104]

The Joint Chiefs answered these criticisms by stressing the "important part" that they envisaged French forces playing both in the Mediterranean and in the "ultimate liberation of continental Europe."[105] The American answer made it clear that they, unlike their British counterparts, would welcome the creation of a large and well-equipped French army that could play a role beyond the confines of North Africa. The unstated assumption, of course, was that Washington's role in creating a modern French army would also strengthen its political influence with French leaders. Confident that it could rearm the French while fulfilling its other supply commitments, Washington began shipping matériel to North Africa without waiting for approval from the Combined Chiefs of Staff.

In April 1943, U.S. convoys delivered sufficient supplies to reequip three infantry divisions and two armored regiments, effectively completing the first phase of the Anfa plan.[106] With the American effort already under way, the Combined Chiefs returned to the issue at the *Trident* conference in May, reaffirming the goal of supplying an eleven-division French Army but agreeing to subordinate this task to meeting British and American equipment requirements. This formula appeared to bow to British concerns but, given America's growing ability to meet *all* pressing supply needs, it actually gave Washington significant freedom of action. As British Air Chief Marshal Portal pointed out

---

[101] JSM to War Office, February 27, 1943, PREM 3/441.
[102] Churchill to Ismay, February 28, 1943, PREM 3/441.
[103] COS to JSM, March 10, 1943, PREM 3/441; draft telegram, Churchill to Roosevelt, March 13 1943, PREM 3/441.
[104] Eden to Churchill, March 26, 1943, PREM 3/441.
[105] Minutes of JCS, March 20, 1943, quoted in Vigneras, *Rearming the French*, 55.
[106] Vigneras, *Rearming the French*, 47–48.

gloomily, the "entire project" was "in the hands of the Americans." [107] U.S. control of the equipping and training French forces in North Africa was further underscored on August 7, when the Joint Rearmament Committee was placed directly in the American chain of command.

American confidence rested on the rapidly expanding productive capacity of the U.S. economy and on the competence and drive of American engineers. Arriving in Algiers only days before U.S. supply ships began unloading, Colonel Ernest Suttles and a detachment of forty military engineers set to work, quickly constructing five auto assembly plants with the help of the *Chantiers de Jeunesse*. Soon, one truck was rolling off the new General Motors assembly line every three minutes, and the Jeep plant was building 200 vehicles a day. On May 5, 1943 these auto assembly operations, together with a supply base at Casablanca, were formally handed over to the French authorities. [108] A few days later French troops, wearing U.S. uniforms, manning U.S. guns, and riding in U.S.-manufactured (and French assembled) trucks, joined victory parades in Tunis, Algiers, and Casablanca. By the end of July, AFHQ concluded that the rearmament of the African Army had reached the point at which a French expeditionary force commanded by General Alphonse Juin could be attached to the U.S. Fifth Army for the forthcoming invasion of Italy.

Roosevelt's initial proposal to begin rearming French forces in North Africa may have been driven in part by the hope that the demonstrative supply of U.S. equipment might reinforce Giraud's political standing. Nevertheless, U.S. arms and equipment continued to flow into North Africa even as it became apparent that de Gaulle was mounting a serious challenge to Giraud's leadership. Even the consoling thought that Giraud might maintain military leadership of French forces proved short-lived, and by the time French troops landed in Italy as part of the U.S. Fifth Army, de Gaulle was consolidating his control over the CFLN. Again, a pragmatic effort to strengthen a suitable patron-client relationship with the French leadership in North Africa took precedence over Washington's attitude toward particular French leaders. Moreover, and as the Joint Chiefs' comments about the use of French troops in the "ultimate liberation of continental Europe" indicate, U.S. leaders were already thinking ahead to the role these forces could play in the invasion of France and in post-occupation arrangements there.

At the time that U.S. planners began discussing rebuilding the French army, they were in the process of abandoning their own earlier plans to field an American army of more than 200 divisions in favor of building a 90-division force. In January 1943, the War Department circulated initial plans for a 100-division army, and – in this context – the near-simultaneous decision to equip eleven French divisions reflected a growing realization that Washington could leverage its enormous productive capacity to secure military victory over

---

[107] Ibid., 57.
[108] See Vigneras, *Rearming the French*, 67–69.

the Axis powers *without* having to mobilize a gigantic American army.[109] The "gamble" inherent in reducing the projected size of America's armed forces would thus be offset by arming those of other countries instead. By the same token, London's antipathy to the U.S.-sponsored rebuilding of the French army reflected a dawning recognition that U.S. economic preponderance would have profound political and strategic consequences in hitherto unanticipated areas. Despite Britain's early sponsorship of de Gaulle, the scale of U.S. military munificence would inevitably shift lines of political influence away from London and toward Washington; as Jean Monnet had explained to Harry Hopkins, only the Americans were capable of restoring French power.

Through this effort, Washington was able to forge a favorable relationship with the sections of the French elite as it regrouped around de Gaulle and the CFLN. Given the sharp clashes that continued to mark Franco-American relations to the end of the war and beyond, this may seem an exaggerated claim. But, with its path smoothed by the provision of trade and military aid, Washington shifted its relations from Pétain, to Darlan, to Giraud, and finally to de Gaulle without crippling breakdowns and disjunctures. These shifts were aided by the back-stage efforts of Jean Monnet and others, but they were fundamentally grounded on unwavering U.S. backing for the maintenance of French colonial rule in North Africa and on U.S. support for the restoration of an independent France that – it hoped – would be beholden to the United States. The tortured course of Washington's dealings with the Free French – and the "personality" clashes between Roosevelt and de Gaulle that characterized them – must therefore be seen as part of a broader relationship that also included the U.S. effort to rearm the French. The provision of U.S. civil and military supplies thus helped to establish a connection between Washington and the new French regime taking shape in the physical and political space cleared by Allied arms. The result was a reciprocal relationship that, if plagued by personality clashes, nevertheless laid the basis for the postwar reestablishment of French power and for a revived France capable of playing a key role in the new, U.S.-sponsored, world order.

[109] See Matloff, *Strategic Planning*, 368.

5

The Intricacies of Colonial Rule

As American soldiers and policy makers confronted the complex knot of military and political problems facing them in North Africa, they entered what Anne O'Hare McCormick described as a "political labyrinth unknown to the ordinary American."[1] There they would be exposed to the "complexities of French politics" and the "intricacies of colonial rule." "Stirring currents of Arab nationalism," she warned darkly, would further compound their difficulties, and the problems of the peace would prove more difficult than the achievement of military victory. Nevertheless, with her broad grand-strategic vision and her implicit commitment to protracted U.S. engagement, McCormick concluded that the experience gained in North Africa would be invaluable in preparing U.S. forces for the problems they would inevitably encounter "everywhere in Europe" in the transition from war to postwar. Her words were prophetic: in North Africa, U.S. officials would, by providing economic and political support to the French authorities, facilitate the survival of the old economic and political order, while at the same time they would take every opportunity to extend American interests and influence throughout the region.

U.S. military planners had intended to utilize economic aid to build support for the Allied invasion among the French and Arab populations of North Africa but, in the frantic rush to launch the assault, they had made virtually no provision for the actual supply of aid following the landings. In the early days of *Torch* there was little substance to Roosevelt's bold promise that "no one (in North Africa) will go hungry … if it is humanly within our power to make the necessary supplies available."[2] In practice, U.S. military leaders wanted as little to do with civilian affairs as possible, a stance reflected in the Combined

---

[1] McCormick, "Abroad," *New York Times*, January 16, 1943.
[2] *New York Times*, November 14, 1942; see James J. Dougherty, *The Politics of Wartime Aid: American Economic Assistance to France and French Northwest Africa, 1940–1946* (Westport, CT: Greenwood Press, 1978), 68.

Chiefs' injunction to avoid "economic questions" unless they impinged directly on military operations, leaving them instead to the "Civilian Departments of the United States and United Kingdom governments."[3] In an effort to give this vague assertion some specific content, the Joint Chiefs of Staff urged Bureau of Economic Warfare head Milo Perkins to work with the British Ministry of Economic Warfare to organize the supply of food and other civilian necessities to North Africa. This proposal drew a sharp rebuke from President Roosevelt, who insisted that economic issues in North Africa fell into the "larger field of foreign relations," and that they should therefore be handled by the State Department.[4]

Roosevelt's personal intervention began to establish the organizational framework for the large-scale provision of civilian supplies. With the State Department in the lead, other civilian agencies could be brought into action, and Lend-Lease head Edward Stettinius was soon able to report that the "relationship between BEW, State Department, and Lend-Lease ... is rapidly settling down in a satisfactory fashion."[5] The involvement of the Lend-Lease Administration was itself facilitated by a presidential finding that "the defense of any French province, colony, protectorate, mandated area other territory [was] vital to the defense of the United States," allowing Stettinius to "render more effective Lend-Lease aid to the French people" in North Africa.[6] But simply making French North Africa eligible for Lend-Lease aid did not solve the problem; as Stettinius noted, although previous authorizations had enabled the Free French to receive Lend-Lease supplies, it was "conceivable" that de Gaulle's supporters would not be part of the new setup in North Africa.[7] It would be best, Stettinius concluded, to maintain a "fluid and flexible" attitude as to which French authority was responsible for the distribution of supplies, leaving the final determination to Eisenhower and AFHQ Algiers.

As Washington deliberated, the economy of French North Africa, unhinged by the fall of France and now further disrupted by Allied occupation, plunged into crisis. Only days after the invasion, Robert Murphy sounded the alarm with a warning that the "execution of a program of economic supply" had become a matter of "urgent necessity."[8] Cordell Hull responded quickly, informing Murphy that materials previously ordered under the trade accord were being rushed to North Africa, and explaining the State Department's new role in coordinating the relief operation.[9] With the State Department at the helm, the confusion evident in Washington's initial response to the crisis began to give way to order, and on December 19, 1942 the North African Economic Board

[3] CCS to Eisenhower, October 30, 1942, Box 379, RG 218, NARA.
[4] Roosevelt to JCS, November 11, 1942, Box 379, RG 218, NARA.
[5] Stettinius to Hopkins, November 17, 1942, Hopkins papers, Box 330, FDRL.
[6] Roosevelt to Stettinius, November 13, 1942, Box 5210, RG 59, NARA.
[7] Stettinius to Acheson, November 13, 1942, Box 5210, RG 59, NARA.
[8] Murphy to Hull, November 17, 1942, *FRUS 1942*, 2: 443.
[9] Hull to Murphy, November 18, 1942, *FRUS 1942*, 2: 444.

(NAEB) was established to oversee all aspects of Allied economic engagement with French North Africa.

Established by the State Department, but operating in areas under the jurisdiction of AFHQ Algiers, the NAEB was an uneasy civil-military hybrid. Responsible for everything from the distribution of Lend-Lease supplies to the collection of economic intelligence, commodity purchase, and price control, the board operated under the joint chairmanship of Robert Murphy and General Humfrey Gale, the British chief administrative officer at AFHQ.[10] The NAEB was nominally an Anglo-American body but, with the United States supplying the majority its staff and (with the exception of coal) most of the goods it distributed, it quickly became a vehicle for a broad U.S. intervention into the North African economy.[11]

The establishment of the NAEB coincided with Roosevelt's appointment of Robert Murphy as his personal representative in North Africa with ministerial rank. While continuing to function as the chief civil affairs officer at AFHQ, Murphy's new appointment reinforced his direct relationship to the president. In some ways a formality – Murphy had long had Roosevelt's ear – the appointment of a U.S. minister signaled the strengthening of Washington's engagement with economic and political affairs in North Africa. The new ministerial appointment also relieved Eisenhower of much of the day-to-day responsibility for civil affairs, and the supreme commander was predictably "delighted."[12]

The NAEB faced a daunting task. Reports from U.S. field officers criticized the "low priority" accorded to the relief effort and pointed to a distressing tendency for civilian agencies to work at cross purposes, replicating in North Africa what was "so often the case in Washington."[13] With typical British condescension, Macmillan blamed the NAEB's difficulties on the "extraordinarily low standard of efficiency" of its American staff, who he considered capable of nothing more than the production of "perfectly unintelligible" reports.[14] Macmillan's charges notwithstanding, the board faced substantial difficulties in stepping up the flow of economic aid. Military authorities were reluctant to assign scarce shipping space to civilian supplies, and goods arrived as "filler," packed in around ammunition and military equipment. Lend-Lease supplies were also mixed up with the "barter goods" allocated to the army, and the whole picture was complicated by "unreliable manifests" and confused

[10] John Strawson, "Gale, Sir Humfrey Myddleton, 1890–1971," *Oxford Dictionary of National Biography* (Oxford: Oxford University Press, accessed December 20 2012).

[11] See G. E. Maguire, *Anglo-American Policy towards the Free French* (New York: Palgrave Macmillan, 1995), 120.

[12] Eisenhower to Marshall, December 20, 1942, Alfred D. Chandler (ed.), *The Papers of Dwight David Eisenhower: The War Years* (Baltimore: Johns Hopkins University Press, 1970), 2: 854–855.

[13] Patterson to NAEB, n.d. but by context likely January 1943, NAEB, Box 3, RG 169, NARA.

[14] Harold Macmillan, *War Diaries: Politics and War in the Mediterranean, January 1943–May 1945* (New York: St. Martin's Press, 1984), 62.

unloading procedures.[15] Moreover, with no adequate distribution system in place, supplies that made it across the Atlantic often piled up on the docks in North Africa, subject to the depredations of weather and theft.

Gradually, order emerged. By mid-January 1943, Lend-Lease officials were projecting the importation of 30,000 tons of supplies per month, with shipments of tea, sugar, rice, and cotton cloth arriving along with "consumers goods," including stockings, nail polish, and razors.[16] Under the control of American General Arthur Wilson, port operations were streamlined. Arab dockworkers were hired in large numbers, and Wilson outlined his approach to labor relations in a meeting with Lend-Lease officials in Washington at which he explained that the "natives" could be made to work hard when "treated firmly."[17] Wilson argued that Arab workers should not be given food handouts in case they lost the incentive to work and that – following what he called the French example – a "good kick" usually instilled the necessary work discipline. Warming to his theme, Wilson explained that he hoped to return to North Africa with an "improved paddle" for issue to army overseers. Given the ingrained racism of their American bosses, it is hardly surprising that, even as port operations became more efficient, Arab dockworkers took every opportunity to help themselves to American supplies.[18]

As the influx of U.S. goods increased, officials faced the challenge of doling them out to the civilian population, and the NAEB decided to utilize local *groupements* as vehicles for the distribution of supplies. These associations of merchants, industrialists, and government officials had been established in 1938, and they were later incorporated into the corporatist structure of the Vichy state. U.S. officials were under no illusions about their political character, with one diplomat describing them as "real dictatorships" that controlled "speculation, hoarding imports, and over-bidding prices," while excluding "Jews and Gaullists" from the market.[19] Despite recognizing their "fascist leanings" and open discrimination against the Arab majority, NAEB officials considered that the *groupements* offered the only viable channel for the distribution of supplies and they quickly came to see them as "indispensable" to the conduct of Allied relief operations.[20] In July 1943, the newly formed CFLN formally abolished the *groupements* as part of its effort to clean up the most

[15] Hoehler to Stettinius, n.d. (January 1943?), NAEB, Box 3, RG 169, NARA.

[16] "Civilian Supplies Shipped to North Africa," NAEB memorandum, January 19, 1943, 851R24/27, RG 59, NARA.

[17] "The North African Supply Problem," NAEB memorandum, December 5, 1942, 851R.24/21, RG 59, NARA.

[18] See Joseph Bykovsky and Harold Larson, *The Transportation Corps: Operations Overseas* (Washington DC, U.S. Government Printing Office, 1957), 158 and 182, fn. 141.

[19] Brooks to NAEB, January 22, 1943, FEA, Economic Intelligence Files, numbered subject file 37192, RG 169, NARA; on exclusion of "Jews and Gaullists," see NAEB Manual on Distribution of Supplies in Liberated Areas, August 16, 1943, Box 17, RG 169, NARA.

[20] Brooks to NAEB, Feb 19, 1943, FEA, Economic Intelligence Files, file 37193, RG 169, NARA.

egregiously fascistic elements of the Vichy state, but it was, as an NAEB report noted, largely a "de jure" act that left their essential structure and corporatist functioning intact.[21]

Clearly marked U.S. goods distributed through the *groupements* eventually circulated throughout much of French North Africa, enabling an OSS officer returning from an eight-day trek across the Atlas Mountains in March 1943 to report that American-supplied tea, sugar, soap, and cotton cloth, were all in evidence in even the most remote villages.[22] But the limited quantities of U.S. goods made available to Arab merchants ensured that they were quickly subject to price inflation and black market trading. At the start of the U.S. occupation, Robert Murphy and French official André Bataille had agreed that prices should be pegged at preinvasion levels but, as it was administered by the *groupements*, this agreement proved impossible to enforce. U.S. diplomats were soon reporting the uncontrolled sale of American products at spiraling black market prices, a problems vice-consul Gordon Browne in Fez blamed squarely on "graft practiced by the French authorities."[23] Browne concluded that it had become "practically impossible" for "Moslem" traders to remain outside the black market. NAEB economic advisor Henry Villard agreed, noting that for Arab businessmen and consumers alike, participation in the black market had become "regular and necessary".[24]

Faced with intractable economic problems embedded in the structure of French colonial rule, and fearing that overly close association with French authorities might damage U.S. prestige, by the summer of 1943 NAEB officials were trying to extricate themselves from the distribution business entirely. When the Allies recognized the CFLN in August, U.S. officials agreed that it should be responsible for both ordering and distributing civilian goods. Until this time, the Lend-Lease operation in North Africa been anomalous in that U.S. officials had retained control of supplies until they entered the local distribution network, whereas other Lend-Lease recipients took delivery of their allocated supplies in the United States. Ralph Watkins of the NAEB's Import Division now proposed to bring North Africa into line with standard Lend-Lease practice by having the CFLN take ownership of goods "ship-side" in the United States. Watkins noted that this shift would reassure French officials who were becoming "increasingly sensitive" to "American civilian operations," while allowing U.S. officials to withdraw from their futile efforts to control prices.[25] Assistant Secretary of State Adolf Berle concurred with Watkins's proposal, and the French Supply Council was duly established in the United States in November 1943.

[21] Villard to NAEB, September 15, 1943, Box 17, RG 169, NARA.
[22] OSS memo, March 30, 1943, 31428, RG 169, NARA.
[23] Browne to JICA, June 1943, Entry 97 Box 3, RG 226, NARA.
[24] Villard to NAEB, July 15, 1943, NEA, Box 17, RG 169, NARA.
[25] Watkins to Stettinius, August 31, 1943, Box 17, RG 169, NARA.

FIGURE 5.1. American-made cloth supplied by the North Africa Economic Board is sold at a street market in Zeralda, Algeria. Drawing attention to the sign on display in the background, the original OWI caption explained that prices were set by French authorities and that the market was supervised by the local mayor. In fact, most U.S.-supplied goods ended up on the black market. (Courtesy of Franklin D. Roosevelt Library.)

While discussions on the establishment of the French Supply Council were still going on, Robert Murphy concluded negotiations with René Massigli and Jean Monnet on a "Modus Vivendi" designed to regulate trade between the United States and North Africa.[26] Under this agreement, the French authorities pledged to pay for civilian goods shipped to North Africa and to ensure their equitable distribution there. Not surprisingly, actual cash payments were irregular, and the export of goods from North Africa to the United States – "reverse Lend-Lease" – did not come close to closing the deficit. Despite their obvious weaknesses, however, the "Modus Vivendi" and the French Supply Council set the framework of economic relations between the United States and French North Africa for the remainder of the war. In their own terms, and particularly given Washington's lack of preinvasion planning for economic affairs, they registered the success of the United States' economic effort. Widespread starvation

---

[26] See Dougherty, *Politics of Wartime Aid*, especially chapter 6.

was averted and the economic structure of French colonial rule sustained, while throughout the Maghreb the presence of U.S.-made cloth and U.S.-grown foodstuffs, all emblazoned with a bold "U.S.A.," testified to the capacity and reach of the American economy.

America's economic presence in North Africa advanced simultaneously on other fronts as the massive logistical operation necessary to support the Allied armies in the region exerted its influence. In Morocco alone, U.S. forces built more than thirty military facilities and airfields, including sprawling logistical bases and assembly plants at Port Lyautey and Casablanca. American engineers organized the work, but local workers hired by French subcontractors provided much of the labor. The resulting demand for labor – and the relatively high wages – had a significant social impact, encouraging migration from rural areas to the coastal cities, breaking down longstanding divisions between Arab and Berber populations, and promoting the creation of an urban working class.[27] Huge shantytowns, or *bidonvilles*, sprung up around the U.S. bases, with shacks built from the packing cases and skids in which aircraft parts and military vehicles had been shipped from the United States. In addition to providing housing for thousands of Moroccan workers, the *bidonvilles* quickly became centers of black market trading and – in common with townships around the bases of occupying armies everywhere in the world – of prostitution.

Along with their direct social and economic impact, these sprawling bases played a significant ideological role by introducing Americanism to the native population; nothing like it had been seen in North Africa before, and "America" quickly came to symbolize energy and dynamism, and "Made in USA" to signify quality and modernity.[28] In sharp contrast, the United States would also become widely associated with the continuation of French colonial rule. After U.S. combat forces moved out of Morocco and Algeria and on into Tunisia and then Italy, the United States continued to maintain substantial base facilities in the Maghreb. More than 15,000 U.S. soldiers remained in Morocco until the end of the war, and Algeria provided a key assembly point and logistical base for the Franco-American invasion of the French Riviera. By the end of the war, more than 850,000 tons of weapons and equipment had flowed through America's North African bases, much of it unloaded, assembled, and transported by Arab workers. In addition, U.S. engineers and transportation services upgraded the road network across the Maghreb and modernized the railroad system.[29]

Bases in the French North Africa featured in Washington's early planning for the postwar world. Writing from Casablanca in August 1943, diplomat

[27] See Leon Borden Blair, *Western Window in the Arab World* (Austin, TX: University of Texas Press, 1970), 110.

[28] Ibid., 117.

[29] See Bykovsky and Larson, *Transportation Corps*, especially 166, 170–177.

Earle Russell put the point succinctly when he urged Washington to retain control of its military bases in the region in order to "lay the foundations [for] after-war air communications and commercial development."[30] "The time has come," Russell concluded gravely, "to look after our own interests first." Having already recognized the "acquisition and development" of military bases as a "primary war aim," the Joint Chiefs readily agreed to maintain U.S. bases in Morocco.[31] In fact, U.S. forces withdrew from many of their Moroccan bases in the immediate postwar period, maintaining an active presence only at a key naval communications facility at Port Lyautey. But Earle Russell's strategic foresight was underscored in 1950 when Washington, now faced with the strategic challenges of the Cold War, reactivated its wartime facilities in Morocco and established two Strategic Air Command bases, an early-warning radar system, and other support facilities.[32] Negotiations for the new bases were conducted directly with Paris, but in 1956 Washington reconfirmed their status with the newly independent government of Morocco.

The America's multi-faceted military, political, and economic engagement with French North Africa during the war rested on the assumption that French colonial rule would continue for the foreseeable future. This assumption was neither unspoken nor undocumented: when the administration was discussing the future of French Indo-China in 1944, Cordell Hull was able to furnish Roosevelt quickly with a long list of official statements expressing Washington's clear and unambiguous support for the continuation of French rule over the great bulk of its prewar empire.[33] Nor were these views expressed only behind closed doors, with Roosevelt's broadcast to the French population of North Africa at the start of the *Torch* landings offering assurances that once the "menace" of Axis occupation had been dealt with, U.S. forces would "quit your territory at once."[34] At no point was the idea that North Africa might *not* be French territory ever entertained by the administration; nor, in all the liberal outcry against the deal with Darlan, was there any challenge to the legitimacy of French rule in North Africa.

The fact that these official pledges of support for French imperial rule stood in egregious contradiction to the principles of self-determination heralded by the Atlantic Charter was not lost on U.S. policy makers and opinion-formers. The problematic circle was squared by asserting the subject peoples of North Africa were simply not yet "ready" for self-government, and that benevolent colonial rule was necessary to prepare them for independence at

[30] Russell to State, August 9, 1943, JCSET, Reel 2, North Africa, #0377, Records of the Joint Chiefs of Staff, microfilm.
[31] Minutes of Joint Chiefs of Staff, December 2, 1943, JCSET, Reel 2, North Africa, #0387; see also C. T. Sandars, *America's Overseas Garrisons: the Leasehold Empire* (New York: Oxford University Press, 2000), 6.
[32] See William Zartman, "The Moroccan-American Base Negotiations," *Middle East Journal* 18 (1964); see also *Atlantic Monthly*, November 1952.
[33] Hull, memorandum, January 14, 1944, *FRUS 1944*, 3: 769–772.
[34] Roosevelt, "Message to the French People," White House news release, November 7, 1942.

some future time.[35] For U.S. policy makers, self-determination was not so much a principle as a general approach to be applied selectively, conditionally, and according to the needs of the U.S. government. Writing in defense of the arrangement with Darlan, *New York Times* columnist and Roosevelt confidant Arthur Krock developed this point, arguing explicitly that the deal facilitated the continuation of French rule in North Africa at a moment when the Atlantic Charter, "read in the light of its spirit," might have been taken as pointing to majority rule and an end to French colonialism.[36] Anne O'Hare McCormick followed suit, arguing that Arab North Africa was not yet "ready for independence" and that therefore the United States had a responsibility to promote the development of the region under a "system of responsible trusteeship."[37]

In line with this approach, U.S. officials in North Africa tended to express both broad enthusiasm for French rule and profound skepticism at the prospect of Arab self-government. From Tangiers, for example, diplomat J. Rives Childs insisted that the French had done a "great deal to develop the country," imposing order on tribes that had been "at each others throats for countless generations."[38] The Arabs, in contrast, he considered capable only of "crude and premature nationalistic fanaticism." Some officials took this line of argument to its logical conclusion, noting bluntly that the "Four Freedoms didn't apply to North Africa."[39] Such comments were not limited to U.S. field officers: on his return from Casablanca President Roosevelt praised the beneficial workings of French colonialism, telling reporters that the French were "doing well" by building roads, improving agriculture, and "putting in" education.[40] The Moroccans, he concluded, "liked" their French rulers because they "understand them," and they were not seeking "any change" in the existing colonial setup.

In private, Roosevelt was even more dismissive of Arab capacity for self-government; reporting to the cabinet on his trip to North Africa, he simply noted that they "looked dirty."[41] Army officers in North Africa couched similar observations in even sharper terms. General George Patton, who led the landings in Morocco and whose troops remained in the country to deter an attack from Spanish Morocco, used the unwelcome break from active campaigning to speculate that because everything about Arab life demonstrated chronic "inefficiency," they must surely be the victims of "some sort of arrested

[35] See Warren F. Kimball, *The Juggler: Franklin Roosevelt as Wartime Statesman* (Princeton, NJ: Princeton University Press, 1991), especially chapter 7.
[36] Krock, "In the Nation," *New York Times*, December 10, 1942.
[37] McCormick, "Abroad," *New York Times*, April 14, 1943.
[38] Childs to Hull, June 1943, Box 5, RG 84, NARA.
[39] Russell to Childs, October 12, 1943, Box 5, RG 84, NARA.
[40] Press conference, January 24, 1943, Jonathan Daniels (intro.) *The Complete Press Conferences of Franklin D. Roosevelt* (New York: DaCapo Press, 1972), 21: 139.
[41] Morgenthau, diary entry, February 5, 1943, Morgenthau papers, FDRL.

development."[42] Initially impressed by the Arabs' "quiet dignity," Patton soon concluded that it was in fact a manifestation of "pure dumbness." Given these deep-seated notions of Arab incapacity, it is not surprising that U.S. policy makers readily embraced the idea that they alone were capable of determining whether or not the colonized peoples of the Maghreb were capable of self-government. As the State Department's Advisory Committee on Postwar Foreign Policy put it, "entirely aside from the obvious fact that France will release its hold on Morocco only if compelled to do so by force ... the Moroccans are not capable of governing themselves in a peaceful, orderly way."[43]

The perceptions of U.S. officials were inevitably shaped by a broad range of cultural assumptions about the Arab world that might be described as "American orientalism."[44] The Maghreb seemed impossibly distant to most Americans, a strange land inhabited by an even stranger people, and the setting for a racy mélange of sheik and Foreign Legion films.[45] After *Torch*, North Africa tended to be represented to Americans as a timeless, primitive, and unchanging backdrop against which the modern and dynamic business of war was played out. Darryl Zanuck's 1943 documentary *At the Front in North Africa* captured this sense with its vivid and pointed images of U.S. armored vehicles racing past plodding camel caravans. The distance between the United States and the distant other, and the sense of theatricality that it implied, was summarized in Anne O'Hare McCormick's assertion that the Arabs were "mere spectators" in a war played out in front of them. Warner Brothers' classic wartime romance *Casablanca*, its release fortuitously coinciding with the Casablanca Conference, similarly projected the actions of its American, French, and German protagonists onto the exotic *tableau vivant* of its namesake city; in Bogart's next movie *Sahara*, even these one-dimensional Arabs were replaced by a backdrop of uninhabited sand dunes.

U.S. policy toward North Africa was thus made within an ideological framework in which it seemed entirely natural that Washington's military, political, and economic intervention should proceed without reference to the wishes of the great majority of the population. Pervasive notions of the conflict in North Africa as a "war without hate," fought in uninhabited desert space and without impinging on the lives of civilians, speak to the continued power of these perceptions.[46] In this context, it is unsurprising that the major question

---

[42] George Patton, "Notes on the Arab," January 1943, in Martin Blumenson (ed.), *The Patton Papers, 1940–1945* (Boston, MA: Houghton Mifflin, 1974), 146.

[43] "The Rise and Development of Moroccan Nationalism" (1230-CDA-285), memorandum for State Department Advisory Committee on Postwar Foreign Policy, April 2, 1945, prepared for meeting T-571, July 1945, Notter files, microfilm collection accessed at Alexander Library, Rutgers University, New Brunswick, 33.

[44] See Brian T. Edwards, *Morocco Bound: Disorienting America's Maghreb, from Casablanca to the Marrakech Express* (Durham, NC: Duke University Press, 2005).

[45] Ibid., 41.

[46] Published in 1950, "*War without Hate*" was the title of Erwin Rommel's influential memoir of the North African Campaign.

in America's domestic wartime discourse on North Africa was not *whether* French colonial rule should continue, but rather *which* Frenchmen should rule. Here Arthur Krock's case for the Darlan deal assumes its full force. For Krock, as for the administration, it was essential to avoid the break in the continuity of French rule implied by the establishment of an Allied military government, because such a rupture would create a "knotty post-war problem" when it came time to hand power back to a civilian authority.[47] It was better, Krock argued, to treat with the fascist-minded Darlan today than to risk majority rule tomorrow.

Ironically, even as Washington underscored its support for French rule, many of France's Arab and Berber subjects saw U.S. intervention in the Maghreb as giving them the go-ahead to press for some degree of independence. Untainted by previous colonial involvement in the region and wrapped in the Atlantic Charter's widely-publicized support for self-determination, U.S. forces were seen as a harbinger of sweeping political change and as agents of decolonization. American officials throughout the Maghreb reported on the enthusiastic reception accorded to U.S. forces, with vice-consul Gordon Browne in Fez noting that all of "Moslem society" was impressed by the display of U.S. military power and was "united in praise of America."[48] Others noted that the clearly marked U.S. relief supplies reinforced a positive appreciation of American power. Moreover, although Arab hopes that the United States would back self-determination turned out to be wishful thinking, they were fueled by impressions that U.S. policy makers – including Roosevelt himself – deliberately helped to foster. In fact, even as their actions reinforced French colonialism, U.S. officials actively promoted the idea that Washington stood for a greater measure of Arab self-government.

On January 22, 1943, President Roosevelt took advantage of a brief lull in the proceedings of the Casablanca Conference to host a dinner for Sultan Mohammed V of Morocco. With Winston Churchill listening sullenly – his temper doubtless worsened by an American decision to eschew alcohol in deference to the Sultan's "Moslem code of behavior" – Roosevelt engaged the Moroccan leader in animated conversation.[49] There is no official record of their discussion, but the accounts of other diners suggest that the president expressed support for Morocco's "aspirations for independence," suggesting that U.S. oil companies might help develop the Moroccan economy "on a fee or percentage basis."[50] "Sire," the Sultan's son recalled Roosevelt saying, "I can assure you that ten years from now your country will be independent."[51] Presidential advisor Harry Hopkins was a good deal more circumspect when

[47] Krock, "In the Nation," *New York Times*, December 10, 1942.
[48] Browne to JICA, June 1943, Entry 97, Box 4, RG 226, NARA.
[49] Robert Murphy, *Diplomat among Warriors* (Garden City, NY: Doubleday & Co, 1964), 173.
[50] Ibid.; Elliot Roosevelt, *As He Saw It* (New York: Duell, Sloan and Pearce, 1946), 112.
[51] Crown Prince Moulay Hassan, quoted in Edwards, *Morocco Bound*, 26.

FIGURE 5.2. Dinner in Casablanca, January 22, 1943; (left to right) seated: Sultan Mohammed V, Roosevelt, Churchill; standing: General George Patton, Robert Murphy, Harry Hopkins, the Crown Prince, General Auguste Noguès, French Resident-General of Morocco, Grand Vizier El Mokhri, the Chief of Protocol, Elliott Roosevelt, Captain John McCrea. (Courtesy of Franklin D. Roosevelt Library.)

he met Grand Vizier El Mokhri the following day, carefully balancing a vague assertion that "many peoples" would soon get their "rightful share of the good things of the world" with a warning that the United States saw "no reason to change the present government of Morocco."[52] The contradiction between these statements encapsulates Washington's dual policy toward Arab North Africa: beyond nebulous intimations of support for self-determination and independence, the Moroccans were given nothing more than promises of economic cooperation within the framework of continued French rule.

However ambiguous the promises offered by Roosevelt and Hopkins, many in the Moroccan elite took their words as proof, as vice-consul Kenneth Pendar recalled, of "our sincerity in the Atlantic Charter" and as evidence of U.S. support for Moroccan independence.[53] Washington, they hoped, would now treat Morocco as a "sovereign state," support its economic development with generous financial, industrial, and educational aid, and help prepare it for full independence.[54] It would all mean, as Elliott Roosevelt recounted the Sultan exclaiming, a "new future for my country!"[55] These expressions of hope in the

[52] General Wilbur, memorandum of Hopkins-El Mokhri conversation, January 23, 1943, *FRUS*, Washington and Casablanca, 703.

[53] Kenneth Pendar, *Adventures in Diplomacy: Our French Dilemma*, 1945 (Reprint, New York: Da Capo Press, 1976), 145.

[54] Ibid.

[55] Roosevelt, *As He Saw It*, 112.

anticolonial intentions of the United States were registered in the summer of 1943 by the formation of the Roosevelt Club. Initiated by Abdelatif Sbihi, editor of the leading Moroccan daily *La Voix Nationale*, the club's membership included a broad section of the Moroccan elite, from businessmen to members of the royal family.[56] The Roosevelt Club aimed to promote social contacts between the Moroccan elite and high-ranking U.S. officers, further Arab understanding of American political and economic methods, and foster support for Moroccan independence.

Robert Murphy noted the new mood among the Moroccan elite, reporting on their "growing hope that the United States may intervene on their behalf to relieve them from the French Protectorate."[57] Many hoped that even if they did not get immediate independence, Morocco might be placed under international trusteeship overseen by the United States.[58] Dismayed at the lack of progress in this direction, however, many Moroccans soon concluded that there was no substance to Washington's verbal support for self-government, and founded the nationalist Istiqlal (Independence) Party to press for independence. In early January 1944, a copy of the party's founding Memorial, signed by fifty-eight political figures, religious leaders, and educators, was presented to U.S. officials to be forwarded to President Roosevelt – indicating, perhaps, that illusions in the president outlasted those in American policy.[59] The Memorial was explicitly based on the Atlantic Charter, and advocated an independent Morocco under the leadership of the Sultan. Predictably, U.S. officials in Rabat were "unanimous in deprecating the movement," and Roosevelt and Cordell Hull argued forcefully that it was "inadvisable" for there to be any challenge to the French authorities in what was still considered a war zone.[60] Allied military forces were readied for action in the event of an "active uprising."[61]

Faced with heightened nationalist agitation in Morocco, French officials quickly resorted to open repression. Their efforts were backed by American diplomats who, after warning Istiqlal leaders that Washington could not "look with favor" on any distraction from an "all-encompassing absorption" in the war effort, turned the nationalists' plans over to the French authorities.[62] Chargé Rive Childs acknowledged the moderation of the Istiqlal program – limited as it was to seeking "greater participation ... in the administration of the Protectorate at the close of the war" – but deplored any "premature"

---

[56] See Blair, *Western Window*, 98–99.
[57] Murphy to Hull, June 26, 1943, *FRUS 1943*, 4: 742.
[58] This sentiment was attributed to the Sultan in "The Rise and Development of Moroccan Nationalism" (1230-CDA-285), memorandum for State Department ACPFP, April 2, 1945, prepared for meeting T-571, July 1945, Notter files, 29.
[59] "Our Policy Towards the Nationalist Movement in Morocco," memorandum OEA-3, Department of State Division of African Affairs, January 22, 1944, Notter files.
[60] Ibid., attachment to OEA-3
[61] Ibid., 2.
[62] Mayer to State Department, January 5, 1944, *FRUS 1944*, 5: 528.

application of the Atlantic Charter to Morocco.[63] Demands for even the most modest of reforms, Childs concluded, were "dangerous" when advanced by people "several generations behind Egyptians in political development." Having secured assurances from the French that they would avoid unduly "harsh measures," U.S. officials looked on with approval as the colonial authorities arrested Istiqlal's leaders and then forcibly suppressed the ensuing street protests.[64] Justifying the repression, the *New York Times* blithely repeated unsubstantiated French assertions that the nationalist protests had been initiated by "Frenchmen in the pay of the enemy" who had been parachuted into Morocco to "stir up rebellion."[65]

Even as they backed the suppression of the independence movement in Morocco, however, officials in Washington recognized that their own actions, from the propagation of the Atlantic Charter to the conduct of certain "consular officers and army officials" in the region, had helped to promote the "widespread opinion that the [nationalist] movement is ... backed by the United States Government."[66] This contradiction, the inevitable product of Washington's dual policy, bore down particularly heavily on those officers whose work brought them into close contact with the harsh realities of colonial rule and whose outlook tended to make them sympathetic to the Arab population. Where career diplomats, schooled in maintaining good relations with French officials and in eschewing any involvement in "native affairs," were generally hostile to Arab nationalism, Murphy's vice-consuls and numerous newly-minted OSS agents in the region, untrained in diplomatic protocol and often liberal in political outlook, often struck their superiors as being dangerously pro-Arab.

The career of vice-consul Gordon Browne offers a useful case in point. Browne was assigned to Colonel Eddy's OSS operation in Tangier along with Carleton Coon, and the two men, who had visited the region as young Harvard archeologists and were fluent in Arabic, quickly developed contacts with tribal leaders in the Riff Mountains.[67] Eddy approved their plans for instigating a Berber uprising in support of *Torch* to be led by a tribal chief codenamed "Tassels" but – and not surprisingly given the assurances that had been given to French officials – the scheme did not find favor with Robert Murphy and his superiors in Washington. The plans for *Torch*, as Assistant Secretary Adolf Berle pointed out, did not include any scheme to "raise the tribes," adding that the OSS should develop "native" contacts only as an insurance against the

---

[63] Childs to Hull, December 28, 1943, *FRUS 1944*, 5: 525; Childs to Hull, January 14, 1944, *FRUS 1944, 5:* 534.

[64] Mayer to State Department, January 5, 1944, *FRUS 1944, 5:* 529.

[65] *New York Times*, February 11, 1944.

[66] "Our Policy Towards the Nationalist Movement in Morocco," attachment to OEA-3, Department of State's Division of African Affairs, January 22, 1944, Notter files, 1.

[67] See Hal Vaughan, *FDR's 12 Apostles: The Spies Who Paved the Way for the Invasion of North Africa* (Guilford, CT: The Lyons Press, 2006), 76–78, 187.

"French turn[ing] against us."[68] Undeterred by official disapproval, Browne continued to help run operations by Spanish Republican and Abraham Lincoln Brigade veterans in Spanish Morocco.[69] Reassigned to Fez, Browne's detailed reports on the participation of corrupt French officials in the burgeoning black market led the U.S. consul in Casablanca to warn that his work had acquired a "definite anti-French and pro-Arab Nationalist slant."[70]

To some degree, these clashes reflected bureaucratic infighting between the State Department and the upstart OSS; as one officer reported from Fez, the lack of coordination between different agencies had allowed U.S. policy to "become ambiguous."[71] This problem was exacerbated – at least from the State Department's point of view – by the fact that OSS agents were supervised by army commanders and not by the diplomatic service. As military operations shifted eastward, however, OSS agents in Morocco found themselves in an exposed position, with a State Department report concluding that many of them had become involved in activities that were "not to the best interests of the United States."[72] The problem, J. Rives Childs concluded, was that their actions were leading to an "appreciable" decline in "American prestige in Morocco."[73] Measured in terms of America's standing in the eyes of French officialdom, these concerns were well founded. OSS agents had established an office in Fez that functioned as an unofficial U.S. consulate, and from which Browne and other OSS agents were encouraging "Moslems" to believe that the United States supported their "nationalist activities."[74]

In Morocco, the State Department gained control of the situation as the drawdown of U.S. military forces allowed them to secure the removal of Gordon Browne and other troublesome OSS agents. In Tunisia, however, U.S. policy makers faced a more difficult challenge. Here, criticism of Washington's support for French rule was voiced not by OSS officers, but by Hooker Doolittle, a longstanding career diplomat. Posted to Tunisia in 1933, Doolittle had developed close relationships with French officials, the ruling Husainid dynasty, and leaders of the Liberal Constitutional (Destour) Party.[75] Before the war, Tunisia had been the scene of the first great upsurge of Arab nationalism in the Maghreb, and in 1942 Muhammad VII al-Munsif (known to the Allies as Moncef Bey) had taken the bold step of appointing a Destour Party ministry without first seeking

---

[68] Berle to Atherton, December 16, 1942, 851R20/48, RG 59, NARA.
[69] See Robin W. Winks, *Cloak and Gown: Scholars in the Secret War, 1939–1961.* 2nd ed. (New Haven, CT: Yale University Press 1987), 186–187.
[70] Russell to Childs, October 13, 1943, Entry 350, Box 5, RG 84, NARA.
[71] Callahan to Russell, August 22, 1943, NND 765005, Box 5, RG84, NARA.
[72] Schwartz, memorandum, "OSS Activities in Morocco," October 19, 1943, Entry 350, Box 5, RG 84, NARA.
[73] Childs to Alling, October 18, 1943, NND 765005, Box 5, RG 84, NARA.
[74] Ibid.
[75] Murray to Berle, memorandum, July 27, 1943, 851S.00/257, RG 59, NARA.

French approval.[76] Forced to leave Tunis during the Axis occupation, Hooker Doolittle was shocked to learn that General Giraud planned to remove Moncef Bey on charges of collaboration with the Germans as soon as Allied troops entered Tunis. Doolittle protested to Robert Murphy, arguing that Moncef Bey was in fact sympathetic to the Allies, and that the French were simply taking advantage of the situation to "get rid of a sovereign with a mind of his own."[77] Not surprisingly, Murphy brushed these concerns aside, assuring Giraud that, as he explained to Roosevelt, "American opinion would support any French action against those who had actively aided the Axis."[78]

Given the go-ahead by Murphy, French officials deposed Moncef Bey on May 14, installing a more pliant cousin in his place. Several thousand Destour Party supporters were also arrested. Appalled, Doolittle appealed to Cordell Hull, protesting the French administration's "disastrous" policy – which he described as a "reign of terror" – and criticizing the Allies for "avert[ing] their gaze."[79] In response, Murphy filed a long rebuttal in which he complained that Doolittle had ignored Washington's "general policy [of] cooperation with the French administration," becoming instead an "active partisan" of the Destour Party and of its efforts to secure "increased Arab autonomy [and] better treatment of the Arab population."[80] To Murphy's disgust, Doolittle also seemed to believe that the Atlantic Charter should "include the Arabs." While acknowledging that the French had been "too aggressive in some instances," Murphy assured Washington that Doolittle was the only person who thought that the arrest of "four to five thousand" Arabs amounted to a "reign of terror."[81] Whereas French "methods [were] more drastic than ours," Murphy concluded, there was "no cause for concern" because those arrested had undoubtedly acted "treacherously" during the occupation.[82] Murphy's argument carried the day in Washington, and when General Mast lodged an "informal protest" against Doolittle, Murphy recommended that he should be reassigned.[83] Eisenhower concurred, suggesting pointedly that Doolittle be replaced by a "well-balanced and intelligent officer," and in August he was recalled to Washington and replaced by the reliable Felix Cole.[84]

Despite Murphy's victory, Doolittle's allegations raised serious concerns in image-conscious Washington, and State Department political relations officer Wallace Murray was assigned to review the case. Murray's report noted that

---

[76] See Charles F. Gallagher, *The United States and North Africa: Morocco, Algeria, and Tunisia* (Cambridge, MA: Harvard University Press, 1963), 86–90.
[77] Doolittle to Murphy, Apr. 17, 1943, 851S.001, RG 59, NARA.
[78] Murphy to Roosevelt, May 14, 1943, 851S.001, RG 59, NARA.
[79] Doolittle to Hull, June 6, 1943, 851S.001, RG 59, NARA.
[80] Murphy to State Department, June 6, 1943, 851S.00/258, RG59, NARA.
[81] Ibid.
[82] Murphy to State Department, June 26, 1943, 851S.00/263, RG 59, NARA.
[83] Murphy to Murray, July 29, 1943, 851S.00/267, RG 59, NARA.
[84] Murphy to Murray, July 30, 1943, 851S.00/268, RG 59, NARA.

the dispute between Murphy and Doolittle touched on fundamental questions of policy, concluding that because the "Arab question is vitally connected with methods of winning the war and with our professed post-war aims," Washington could not entirely "escape responsibility" for French actions.[85] Murray concluded that the current policy of giving uncritical support to the French administration would "not to be good enough in the long run," warning "this question may come home to haunt us."

Responding to Murray's report, Adolf Berle reaffirmed that U.S. forces were in Africa to "restore France and fight a war against the Axis," and not to "revamp the French colonial regime." With these concerns in mind, Berle argued, Murphy was undoubtedly "looking at it from the correct angle."[86] But Berle, like Murray, recognized that Washington faced something of a "dilemma;" because, he argued, Moncef Bey had indeed been "unjustly" punished, and because the "treatment of the Arabs" by the French authorities was "anything but nice," Washington was now in danger of being too-closely associated with an undemocratic and repressive colonial regime. Berle therefore concluded that "some kind of clean-up" of the French colonial administration was called for. But here he pulled his punches, warning "we probably ought not be too expansive about it," and proposing only that the French authorities should be encouraged to establish a commission to discuss administrative reforms.[87]

However modest his proposals for action, Berle's recognition of the need to "clean-up" French rule nevertheless marked a new turn in U.S. policy. Prompted by Doolittle's stinging critique of French policy, this new course rested on the successful completion of military operations in Tunisia and on the development of a unified French leadership capable of revamping the colonial administration. With U.S. forces moving on into Sicily – and encountering complex and controversial political questions as they did so – the question of leaving an apparently liberalized North Africa behind them assumed new importance. As Wallace Murray argued, the outcome of America's intervention in North Africa would shape public perception of "our professed post-war aims" in the next phases of the war. Signaling this change, Acting Secretary of State Stettinius explained to U.S. officials in North Africa that the American public was keenly interested in the application of the "broad principles of ... the Atlantic Charter" to the "native situation," even if that application had to be constrained within the framework of continued French rule.[88] Washington, in other words, had an interest in "cleaning up" the public presentation of French colonialism without challenging its fundamental framework.

The actual liberalization of the colonial regime fell short of even the modest cleanup proposed by Berle. In October 1943, the CFLN formed a "purging

[85] Murray report, July 26, 1943, 851S.00/257, RG59, NARA.
[86] Berle to Murray, July 30, 1943, 851S.00/257, RG59, NARA.
[87] Ibid.
[88] Stettinius to Childs, December 1, 1943, Entry 350, Box 5, RG 84, NARA.

commission" to investigate the actions of Vichyite officials, and this led to the arrest of Marcel Peyrouton and a handful of other leading figures. Despite protests from Roosevelt and Churchill, who felt obligated to the former Vichyites for services rendered to the Allies, neither Washington nor London intervened directly on their behalf, and the trials went ahead. Nevertheless, it soon became clear that the CFLN intended to conduct only the most limited of purges necessary to defuse pressure from its own supporters. Many former Vichy officials, particularly in the lower levels of the colonial administration, would continue in office.[89] Peyrouton himself was eventually acquitted by the High Court in 1948. The liberalization of the colonial administration proceeded even more slowly. Felix Cole, Doolittle's replacement in Tunis, reported on French plans to open low-level administrative positions to "Mohammedans," but added that it was considered unlikely that many would be capable of "patient routine labor" necessary to function as a colonial bureaucrat.[90] Cole also noted that French administrators had warned officials against adopting a "bullying" toward the "natives," but he concluded that these measures were intended primarily to head off mounting Arab resentment.[91]

Discussion on more far-reaching reforms, including questions of citizenship and democratic rights, raised issues that were simply irresolvable within the framework of French colonial rule. In March 1943, General Giraud endorsed Vichy's repeal of the 1872 Cremieux Decree, under which Algerian Jews had been granted French citizenship. He justified this egregious anti-Semitism on the grounds that the Cremieux Decree promoted discord between Jews and Arabs, who were also denied citizenship. In meetings with French leaders at the time of the Casablanca conference, Roosevelt had effectively given the green light to Giraud's move, arguing in discussion with General Auguste Noguès, Resident-General of Morocco, that by "overcrowd[ing] the professions" in North Africa, Jews had themselves encouraged anti-Semitism.[92] The situation in French North Africa thus mirrored the "understandable complaints which the Germans bore towards the Jews in Germany." In any event, Roosevelt quipped cynically, "the Jews" need not worry about being unable to vote since "there weren't going to be any elections" in the first place.[93]

In October 1943, the CFLN finally reinstated the Cremieux Decree as part of its "clean-up" of the colonial administration; while reestablishing the citizenship of 140,000 Algerian Jews, however, it did not consider extending it to the Arab majority.[94] The *New York Times* endorsed the CFLN's action, noting that liberalization could not yet be carried to its "logical conclusion" because if

---

[89] See Maguire, *Anglo-American Policy*, 91.
[90] Cole to State, October 16, 1943, 851S.00/290, RG 59, NARA.
[91] Cole to State, October 19, 1943, 851S.00/291, RG 59, NARA.
[92] Notes on Roosevelt-Noguès meeting, Jan 17, 1943, *FRUS*, Washington and Casablanca, 608.
[93] Ibid.
[94] "Cremieux Decree Restored," *Jewish Telegraphic Agency*, October 22, 1943.

Arabs were given the right to vote they would only produce "confusion" – or, presumably, independence.[95] "Whatever might be said for the theoretical democracy of such a step," the *Times* concluded, "it would scarcely help win the war."

Shifting position in the light of the new reality in North Africa, Washington endorsed the reinstatement of the Cremieux Decree. The administration's refusal to press the French authorities to extend the franchise to the Arab majority demonstrated the strict limits U.S. policy makers placed on their efforts to "clean-up" colonial rule, and officials remained extremely cautious about proposing even the most modest reforms to the existing political set-up. When Robert Sherwood, the head of the Office of War Information's Overseas Branch and a presidential speechwriter, returned from a trip to North Africa in May 1943, he proposed to Roosevelt that the government back the establishment of an American University in Fez. Sherwood argued such a move would help to promote education in the Arab world while creating "strong and enduring pro-American sentiment throughout West and North Africa."[96] Cordell Hull strongly disagreed, citing both the proposal's "doubtful practicability" and the "more cogent" argument that the French would simply not permit "foreign religious or philanthropic activity" in Morocco.[97] Ever sensitive to offending French colonial sensibilities, the proposal was shelved.

U.S. policy makers, as their support for the repression of nationalist movements in Tunisia and Morocco demonstrated, clearly did not intend that the democratic principles for which they claimed to be fighting would apply to the Arab majority in North Africa. In squaring this potentially awkward ideological circle, U.S. officials turned increasingly to the notion that they were not rejecting the independence of the North African colonies for all time, but were simply avoiding the "premature" application of the principle of self-determination.[98] President Roosevelt eagerly embraced this notion. Four months after his recall from Tunis, Hooker Doolittle was summoned to the White House where Roosevelt bombarded him with questions concerning the status of the "Moors" in North Africa and their treatment by the French authorities. Doolittle explained that French colonial officials now felt that they were "under observation by foreign forces," and that this international spotlight had resulted in some "relaxation of the active oppressive measures."[99] Doolittle believed that he had initiated this development by "functioning as a conscience," and that in doing so he had acted in accord with president's own sentiments. Roosevelt concurred, thanking Doolittle for his "good work" and outlining his

[95] James, "U.S. Might Shift Position on the Cremieux Decree," *New York Times*, July 4, 1943, E3.
[96] Sherwood to Roosevelt, May 5, 1943, Official File, 203-E, FDRL.
[97] Hull to Roosevelt, June 10, 1943, Official File, 203-E, FDRL.
[98] See above Childs to Hull, June 1943, Box 5, RG 84, NARA; Childs to Hull, January 14, 1944, *FRUS 1944*, 5: 534.
[99] Doolittle, notes on interview with President Roosevelt, November 9, 1943, 851S.00/257, RG 59, NARA.

own belief, ostensibly derived from his discussion with Sultan Mohammed V, that Morocco could become independent within "thirty or forty years." In the meantime, he concluded, the "Moors" needed to be patient and to "educate their young men to be doctors, engineers, and technicians."[100]

Roosevelt's comments on Arab education seem somewhat ironic in the light of his rejection of the plan for an American University in Fez, and he was careful to differentiate between the French protectorates in Morocco and Tunisia, which might eventually become independent, and Algeria, which was constitutionally part of France. But the extended time frame the president projected offered a way out of the intellectual dilemma facing U.S. policy makers, allowing them to justify supporting French colonial rule under wartime conditions while holding out vague promises of independence at some unspecified point in the future. In this context, Roosevelt's approval for the idea that U.S. officials should "function as a conscience" by prodding colonial administrators to make modest improvements to their treatment of the Arabs, seems to have satisfied Hooker Doolittle. By extension, it salved liberal opinion in general, with even radical mouthpieces such as *PM*, the *Nation*, and the *New Republic* focusing on the liberalization of French colonial rule rather than on decolonization and national self-determination.

The final bloody coda to America's wartime engagement with the Maghreb – and the opening chapter of Algeria's war for independence – was written in the town of Sétif on May 8, 1945. On that day, thousands of Arabs, some of them veterans of campaigns in North Africa, Italy, and France, gathered to celebrate the end of the war in Europe and to demand independence for Algeria.[101] Violent clashes with French authorities and *pieds noir* settlers followed, and by the time the army imposed order, more than 100 colonists and as many as 30,000 Arabs had been killed. Meeting with the U.S. minister to Egypt, Abdul Rahman Azzam Bey, Secretary General of the newly formed League of Arab States, held the United States morally responsible for the massacre. It was, he pointed out, "the military forces of the United States which had saved the North African possessions for the French and had reestablished French domination over them."[102] In response to Azzam Bey's protest, the State Department instructed its ambassador in Paris to tell French Minister of Foreign Affairs Georges Bidault that the massacre was a "source of anxiety" to Washington and to the American people.[103] Azzam Bey, meanwhile, was to be informed

---

[100] Ibid.
[101] See Alistair Horne, *A Savage War of Peace: Algeria 1954–1962* (New York: NYRB, (1977) 2006), especially "Prologue;" see also Martin Thomas, "Colonial Violence and the Distorted Logic of State Retribution: the Sétif Uprising of 1945," *Journal of Military History* 75, no. 1, 2011.
[102] Tuck to State, June 21, 1945, *FRUS 1945*, 8, 30.
[103] Grew to Caffery, July 30, 1945, paraphrased in Byrnes to Tuck, October 25, 1945, *FRUS 1945*, 8, 31.

that despite this modest diplomatic protest, Washington did not "accept responsibility for developments in North Africa."[104]

Easy to deny in diplomatic legalese, America's role in the stabilization of French colonial rule in the Maghreb was clear to many of those swelling the ranks of nationalist movements throughout the region at the end of the war. In their eyes, the United States and its armed forces appeared not as liberators, but as indispensable props of continued colonial rule.[105] In the United States, meanwhile, Arab nationalists would no longer be viewed as adjuncts of the Axis powers, but rather as potential agents of the new existential adversary, the Soviet Union. Leading U.S. opinion-formers like *New York Times* journalist C. L. Sulzberger were soon warning darkly that Communists were "playing a strong part in the not unconnected series of maneuvers for native independence" unfolding in an allegedly coordinated manner across the French Empire.[106] This apparent convergence of Moscow-style Communism and anticolonial nationalism would thus justify Washington's continued support for French colonialism, now set within the overall framework of a U.S.-dominated world-system.

---

[104] Acheson to Tuck, October 5, 1945, *FRUS 1945*, 3, 32.
[105] See Dougherty, *Politics of Wartime Aid*, 133.
[106] Sulzberger, "Indo-China Revolt Fateful To France," *New York Times*, December 25, 1946.

6

Senior Partners?

With fighting still raging in North Africa, Allied leaders assembled in Casablanca in January 1943 for the *Symbol* conference, their third major summit meeting of the war. At Casablanca, Allied leaders made the momentous decision to drive deeper into the Mediterranean, agreeing to build on the anticipated victory in Tunis by launching an invasion of Sicily. This decision shaped the entire course of the war in Europe, ensuring that the cross-Channel invasion would be postponed until 1944 and opening the door to the large-scale commitment of U.S. troops to campaigns in Italy and southern France. President Roosevelt and Prime Minister Churchill concluded the conference by congratulating their military commanders on the adoption of the "most complete strategic plan for a world-wide war that has ever been conceived." They then held a press conference at which Roosevelt proclaimed that it was the Allies' intention to seek the unconditional surrender of the Axis powers.[1] Ironically, this announcement, together with a series of important but essentially subordinate decisions on the launching of the combined bombing offensive against Germany and the stepping of Lend-Lease aid to the Soviet Union, have dominated the historiography of the conference.[2]

By the time the conference convened, the outcome of the fighting in Tunisia was no longer seriously in doubt: the question was what to do next. Preparing their arguments in advance of the conference, the Joint Chiefs of Staff reiterated their insistence on moving quickly to launch a "strategic offensive in

---

[1] Brooke diary entry, January 23, 1943, Alex Danchev and Daniel Todman (eds.). *Field Marshal Lord Alanbrooke, War Diaries, 1939–1945* (London: Phoenix Press, 2002), 367.

[2] On Casablanca, see Alan F. Wilt, "The Significance of the Casablanca Decisions, January 1943," *Journal of Military History* 55, no. 4 (1991); for Casablanca and the development of the Allies' Mediterranean Strategy, see Michael Howard, *The Mediterranean Strategy in the Second World War* (New York: Frederick A. Praeger, 1968), 34–36.

FIGURE 6.1. Plenary session at Casablanca, January 18, 1943. From left, standing: unidentified British officer, Gen. Hastings Ismay, Lord Louis Mountbatten, Gen. John Deane, Field Marshall John Dill, Air Chief Marshal Sir Charles Portal, Harry Hopkins. Seated, Gen. H. H. Arnold, Adm. Ernest King, Prime Minister Winston Churchill, President Franklin D. Roosevelt, General Sir Alan Brooke, Adm. Sir Dudley Pound, Gen. George C. Marshall. (Courtesy of Franklin D. Roosevelt Library.)

the Atlantic-Western European theater directly against Germany."[3] Having cleared North Africa of Axis troops, they proposed to transfer "excess forces" to Britain ready for an invasion of France that summer. In a sop to their Mediterranean-minded allies, U.S. commanders argued that building "large scale air installations" in North Africa would facilitate a bombing campaign aimed at "destroying Italian resources and morale, and eliminating her from the war."[4]

When the conference ended on January 24, this approach had been unambiguously rejected and replaced by a strategic plan of action for 1943 that centered on "offensive action" in the Mediterranean.[5] Short of a rapid and unanticipated German collapse, there would be no cross-Channel invasion that year. The rejection of the Joint Chiefs' proposal for an early cross-Channel invasion has led many to view Casablanca as a triumph for the "better-prepared and coordinated" British over their American allies.[6] The reality was

[3] JCS Memo, December 26, 1942, *FRUS*, Washington and Casablanca, 736.
[4] Ibid., 737.
[5] CCS Memorandum, "The Conduct of the War in 1943," January 19, 1943, *FRUS*, Washington and Casablanca, 774.
[6] Mark Stoler, *Allies and Adversaries: The Joint Chiefs of Staff, the Grand Alliance, and U.S. Strategy in World War II* (Chapel Hill: University of North Carolina Press, 2000), 103–104.

more complex. Although U.S. military commanders clearly failed in their effort to avoid an extended commitment to the Mediterranean, the agreement to invade Sicily conformed not only to British wishes, but also to those of the American president.

The main issue here, as it had been in the argument between Roosevelt and his senior commanders over *Gymnast*, was the clash between a narrowly "military" view of strategy and a broader grand strategic approach. The military-strategic nostrums advanced by U.S. military planners were forcefully articulated by General Albert Wedemeyer, participating in the conference as head of the Strategy and Policy Group of the army's Operations Division. Wedemeyer was a persistent advocate of a cross-Channel assault and an acerbic critic of those, from the British to Roosevelt, who advocated what he viewed as wasteful "peripheral" campaigns. Summing up the conference, Wedemeyer famously opined that "we came, we listened, and we were conquered," blaming the defeat on a well-coordinated assault by "swarms" of British staff officers, and on the baneful influence of civilian "drugstore strategists" and "Jews who ... felt bitter against Germany."[7] Wedemeyer complained that, in contrast to the disunity and bureaucratic infighting characteristic of the upper echelons of U.S. policy making, "generations and generations of experience in committee work" ensured that the civilian and military components of the British delegation worked together seamlessly.[8]

Wedemeyer's appreciation of the efficacy of British staff work may have been accurate – the British arrived at Casablanca complete with a specially equipped headquarters ship – but the unity displayed by Britain's top leaders rested not on well-functioning committee work, but on a profound paucity of choice. Faced with tightening economic and manpower constraints, British planners excluded an early cross-Channel attack, concentrating instead on protecting lines of imperial communication in the Mediterranean and on launching attacks on the outworks of Axis power. The limited strategic choices open to London, themselves the product of the decline in British power rather than of some timeless British "way of war," forced British leaders to hone and focus their arguments. Although forced to promise a limited offensive in Burma to smooth the path to American agreement on an invasion of Sicily, "peripheral" operations in the Mediterranean remained absolutely central to London's strategic vision. In the specific conjuncture of January 1943, tightly focused British arguments, pushed forward by the momentum of the campaign in Tunisia, carried the day over the broad strategic reorientation advocated by U.S. military leaders.

In contrast to the increasingly tightened straits that constrained British choices, U.S. leaders found themselves riding on a growing embarrassment of

[7] Albert C. Wedemeyer, *Wedemeyer Reports!* (New York: Henry Holt, 1958), 192, 174, 180; Roberts, *Masters and Commanders*, 344.
[8] Wedemeyer, *Wedemeyer Reports!*, 192.

riches. With war production moving into high gear, and with the Japanese offensive in the Pacific checked at Midway, the United States enjoyed the range of strategic options available only to a rising global power. U.S. leaders were divided, but their divisions were the product of real strategic choices – including over the fundamental question of whether to pursue the defeat of Germany or Japan first – and not primarily the result of organizational weakness. Over the course of 1943, these divisions would be largely overcome through strengthened political-military integration structured, from the middle of the year onward, around a firm agreement to launch the cross-Channel offensive the following summer. At Casablanca, however, this integration of military and political elements into a unified grand strategic approach lay in the future, and Roosevelt's clear preference for pressing deeper into the Mediterranean could only be secured by forming a *de facto* bloc with the British. Roosevelt was able to adopt a rather more low-key role to this debate than he had done in the fight over *Gymnast* but, as Wedemeyer's disgusted reference to "drugstore strategists" indicates, he was nevertheless instrumental in shaping its outcome.

British leaders quickly and thankfully understood that Roosevelt was exercising his powerful personal influence in favor of extended involvement in the Mediterranean. Reporting to the War Cabinet, Churchill noted that whereas Admiral King continued to insist on prioritizing operations in the Pacific, the president was "strongly in favor of the Mediterranean being given prime place."[9] Chief of the Imperial General Staff Alan Brooke concurred, noting "[the] President expressed views favoring operations in the Mediterranean."[10] Conference records indicate that Roosevelt and Churchill held numerous undocumented meetings over the course of the conference, leading some historians to picture the prime minister doggedly "working on" the president to secure his support for Britain's Mediterranean strategy.[11] Such imaginings miss the point: although the two leaders may indeed have been discussing how to win approval for pressing deeper into the Mediterranean, Roosevelt's own well-known and long standing interest in the region made any back-room Churchillian pressure unnecessary.

As the conference progressed, the Joint Chief's increasingly desultory opposition to extended Mediterranean operations was beaten down, with Roosevelt forcing the pace by urging the rapid preparation of operational plans. In fact, as historian James Lacey has recently argued, George Marshall may have been convinced *before* Casablanca that for manpower and logistical reasons there could be no cross-Channel assault in 1943, making his opposition to Mediterranean

---

[9] Churchill to War Cabinet, January 17, 1943, quoted in Warren F. Kimball, *Churchill and Roosevelt: The Complete Correspondence* (Princeton, NJ: Princeton University Press, 1984), 2: 118.

[10] Brooke, diary entry, January 15, 1943, *War Diaries*, 359.

[11] See Andrew Roberts, *Masters and Commanders: How Four Titans Won the War in the West, 1941–1945* (New York: Harper, 2009), 319.

operations at the conference become largely *pro forma*.[12] Meeting with the Combined Chiefs, Roosevelt proposed organizing several operations to mask the intended attack on Sicily, and suggested giving the whole scheme the code-name *Underbelly* – itself surely a provocative and thinly veiled allusion to Churchill's vision of the Mediterranean as the "soft underbelly" of Europe.[13] Pressing this line in the final conference session, Roosevelt urged the Combined Chiefs to launch the invasion of Sicily, now codenamed *Husky*, at an earlier date than either British or U.S. planners had envisioned. His reasons were entirely political. Noting reports of sagging Italian morale, Roosevelt observed that there might soon be outbreaks of popular "revolt" in Italy that it would be necessary to both exploit and control. It was critical, the president insisted, to keep a "flexible mind" and to seize "every opportunity."[14]

As with his advocacy of *Gymnast*, Roosevelt's outlook was shaped first and foremost by politico-strategic rather than narrowly military concerns. At Casablanca the impending collapse of Italy – and also therefore the rapidly emerging question of what political setup might follow the overthrow of fascism – was clearly on the president's mind. In addition to the Italian question, President Roosevelt was, as we have seen, working to broker the agreement between Giraud and de Gaulle that would lead to the establishment of the CFLN, while negotiating the Anfa Agreement on the rearming French forces in North Africa. Neither of these "opportunities," with all of their far-reaching consequences for the postwar order in Europe, could have been pursued if the United States had withdrawn military from the Mediterranean, effectively consigning the region to British control. This is not to suggest that Roosevelt had a hidden master plan for exploiting the Mediterranean "underbelly" or for structuring the postwar order in the region. He did not. But the evidence suggests that he did see clearly, and with the eye of a master opportunist, how initial military success in North Africa created new military and political opportunities in the Mediterranean, and at Casablanca he kept pushing toward those prospects.

Given the weight of the forces ranged against them, the Joint Chiefs offered only modest resistance to the push for extend Allied operations in the Mediterranean. George Marshall initially countered Alan Brooke's insistence on a drive to knock Italy out of the war by questioning whether Mediterranean operations could ever deliver "advantages commensurate with the risks involved."[15] But Marshall did not advance a fully developed proposal for a cross-Channel assault and, boxed in by Brooke's clear presentation of the

[12] James Lacey, "Towards a Strategy: Creating an American Strategy for Global War, 1940–1943," in Williamson Murray, Richard Hart Sinnreich, and James Lacey (eds), *The Shaping of Grand Strategy: Policy, Diplomacy, and War* (Cambridge: Cambridge University Press, 2011), especially 191.

[13] Conference minutes, January 18, 1943, *FRUS*, Washington and Casablanca, 630.

[14] Conference minutes, January 23, 1943, *FRUS*, Washington and Casablanca, 713–715.

[15] Conference minutes, January 14, 1943, *FRUS*, Washington and Casablanca, 545.

choices – either "close down" the Mediterranean or go deeper into it to take advantage of the "many choices" that were opening up – he began to come round.[16] Two days later, while continuing to picture the Mediterranean as a "suction pump" syphoning resources away from the "main plot," Marshall acknowledged that the projected invasion of Sicily offered "attractive" employment for the "excess troops" that would be available in North Africa after the capture of Tunis.[17] Admiral King, who wanted to avoid the large-scale shift of shipping resources from the Pacific to the European theater that would be demanded by a cross-Channel assault, and General Arnold, always alive to the prospects for expanded strategic bombing from Mediterranean bases, concurred.[18]

The argument that the invasion of Sicily could, as Marshall put it, be "financed" by redeploying forces already in North Africa allowed the Joint Chiefs to agree to *Husky* without having to accept London's rationale for extended "peripheral" operations within the Mediterranean.[19] Moreover, as official Army historian Maurice Matloff points out, the forward "momentum" generated by the campaign in North Africa created its own "telling argument" in favor of a follow-up campaign against Italy.[20] President Roosevelt was not unaware of this powerful military logic, and his insistence on holding the conference in North Africa may have been motivated by a hope that proximity to the fighting would help impose that logic on his military chiefs.[21]

After the conference, General Eisenhower – reappointed as Allied Supreme Commander – tipped his own hat to this accelerating military momentum when he noted that the "'big bosses'" could not have "deviated very far from the general course of action they [actually] adopted" at Casablanca given that the cross-Channel attack "could not possibly be staged before August of 1944" and that "inaction in 1943 could not be tolerated."[22] Accurate as Eisenhower's assessment was, however, the "momentum" and "military logic" arguments for *Husky* should not be allowed to overshadow the politico-strategic logic that continued to shape Roosevelt's views. As historian Richard Leighton pointed out, Roosevelt was happy to "let matters take their course" at Casablanca; but, confident though he was that it would to be difficult for American leaders to avoid the military logic unfolding in North Africa, he was also keenly

---

[16] Ibid., 567.

[17] Conference minutes, January 16, 1943, *FRUS*, Washington and Casablanca, 583.

[18] See Matthew Jones, *Britain, the United States, and the Mediterranean War 1942–1944* (New York: St. Martin's Press, 1996), 42.

[19] Conference minutes, January 16, 1943, *FRUS*, Washington and Casablanca, 582.

[20] Maurice Matloff, "Allied Strategy in Europe, 1939–1945," in Peter Paret (ed). *Makers of Modern Strategy: from Machiavelli to the Nuclear Age* (Princeton, NJ: Princeton University Press, 1986), 688.

[21] See Roosevelt to Churchill, December 2, 1942, *Correspondence*, 2: 55.

[22] Eisenhower to Handy, January 28, 1943, Alfred D. Chandler (ed.), *The Papers of Dwight David Eisenhower: The War Years* (Baltimore: Johns Hopkins University Press, 1970), 2: 927–928.

interested in how that building momentum might advance his own grand-strategic perspective.[23]

As President Roosevelt understood, and as American military leaders feared, the continued operation of the Mediterranean "suction pump" would inevitably involve U.S. forces in a great deal more than simply military operations. During *Torch*, American officers had been frustrated by the political complexities of French North African, with Eisenhower complaining bitterly about the difficulty of dealing with "little, selfish, conceited worms that call themselves men."[24] But at least in North Africa the basic principles were clear. Except for the short period when Roosevelt's own frustrations led him to advocate military rule, Washington always insisted that political power remain in French hands and that Allied forces avoid direct involvement in government. This approach did not resolve the complex question of *which* French hands would hold power, but it did ensure that there would be no Allied military government. And, however troublesome they could be, the French could be counted on to keep the "natives" under control. None of this would apply in Italy.

As U.S. planners turned their attention to *Husky* in the weeks after Casablanca, three political issues came to dominate their concerns. First, in Sicily there would be no appropriately legitimate regime with which the Allies could collaborate: as long as Mussolini remained in power there could be no Italian Darlan or Giraud, and Allied forces would therefore have to establish direct military rule. Second, there was already a stream of disturbing intelligence indicating that the Italian people would demand a voice in the post-Fascist political settlement, and that their desires might not align with those of the Allies. Well organized despite years of Fascist rule, it would be harder to marginalize Italian workers than it had been to sideline the North African "Moors." Third, it quickly became clear that although London had been prepared to acknowledge U.S. leadership in North Africa, it would be less willing to do so in Italy, a country it considered critical to its position in the postwar Mediterranean.

The danger that an anti-Fascist revolt in Italy might spill over into a communist-led revolution loomed large in U.S. thinking, with Myron Taylor, Roosevelt's envoy to the Vatican, endorsing the Papal See's concern that "communism might profit from the discontent of people in moments of difficulty."[25] Taylor responded to Vatican Secretary of State Cardinal Maglioni's fear that "upheavals and revolutions" would break out in Italy following an Allied invasion by assuring him that U.S. forces would act firmly to ensure the "immediate establishment of order."[26] Maglioni's concerns were by no means

---

[23] See Richard M. Leighton, "Overlord Revisited: An Interpretation of American Strategy in the European War, 1942–1944," *The American Historical Review* 68, no. 4 (July 1963), 930.

[24] Eisenhower to Smith, November 9, 1942, *Eisenhower Papers*, 2: 677.

[25] Taylor to Roosevelt, September 1941, Box 10, Myron C. Taylor Papers, FDRL.

[26] Taylor to Roosevelt, September 25, 1942, Box 10, Myron C. Taylor Papers, FDRL.

baseless. In March 1943, more than 100,000 workers in the industrial north of Italy braved Fascist repression to launch a series of strikes demanding wage raises and compensation for damage inflicted by Allied bombing.[27] The strikes quickly took on an openly anti-government character, and OSS reports reaching Washington via Berne indicated that the Communist Party of Italy (PCI) was directing the protests.[28] After years of repression, U.S. agents noted that Italian workers seemed highly receptive to radical ideas.

Against this backdrop, the State Department's Advisory Committee on Postwar Foreign Policy, chaired by Undersecretary of State Sumner Welles, prepared a set of guidelines for the political organization of post-Fascist Italy. Welles had been deeply impressed with Mussolini when he met him during his 1940 peace mission to Europe, describing him to Roosevelt as a "man of genius."[29] Welles's enthusiasm for what was seen as the modernizing, anti-communist dynamism of the Fascist regime was not unusual in the American of the 1930s, with fellow Advisory Committee member Anne O'Hare McCormick commenting favorably on Mussolini's leadership in the pages of the *New York Times*.[30] Given this background, it is not surprising that the Advisory Committee proposed that the United States should oversee the establishment of a new political order in Italy that, although shorn of overt Fascist trappings, would nevertheless retain significant elements of the existing regime.

When the Advisory Committee met to discuss the Italian question on January 2, 1943, participants included top State Department officials Sumner Welles and Adolf Berle, businessman-diplomat Myron Taylor and journalist Anne O'Hare McCormick, all of whom were presidential confidants.[31] The Advisory Committee meeting took place days before U.S. delegates set off for the Casablanca conference and, given that Myron Taylor lunched with Roosevelt at the White House shortly afterward, it is reasonable to conclude that both the president's outlook on Italy, and his continued enthusiasm for extended military operations in the Mediterranean, were at least partly shaped by reports of the committee's deliberations.[32] Roosevelt and Taylor were joined for lunch by Charles Poletti, formerly lieutenant governor – and briefly governor – of New York. Poletti had recently accepted a post as special assistant to Secretary of War Henry Stimson and, as a leading Italian-American, he was widely regarded as an expert on Italian politics.

---

[27] See Norman Kogan, *Italy and the Allies* (Cambridge, MA: Harvard University Press, 1956), 18.
[28] OSS reports April 23, May 15, and n.d. mid-May 1943, Box 72, Map Room Files, FDRL.
[29] Welles to Roosevelt, March 19, 1940, Welles Report, PSF, FDRL.
[30] On American perceptions of Mussolini, see John P. Diggins, *Mussolini and Fascism: The View from America* (Princeton, NJ: Princeton University Press, 1972).
[31] Other participants included State Department officials Ray Atherton and Wallace Murray and Office of War Information leader Archibald MacLeish. See James Edward Miller, *The United States and Italy, 1940–1950* (Chapel Hill: University of North Carolina Press, 1986), 42–45.
[32] Transcript of appointments, January 4, 1943, "FDR Day by Day," FDRL.

In preparation for their January meeting, Advisory Committee members reviewed the work of a number of subcommittees, each of which had spent several months researching various aspects of the "Italian question." After reviewing territorial adjustments to the Austria-Italy border, Welles steered the discussion toward the possibility that Italy might, as was the "hope of this Government ... detach herself from Germany and sue for a separate peace."[33] Welles's remarks opened a wide-ranging discussion in which Myron Taylor and Anne O'Hare McCormick argued forcefully for exerting U.S. influence to secure a post-Fascist regime based on the monarchy. Only the king, Taylor insisted, was capable of providing a solid anchor when "everything else [was in] confusion," and McCormick stressed that the monarchy was necessary to contain a "popular uprising."[34]

Archibald MacLeish, a leading liberal and the head of the War Department's Office of Facts and Figures, raised the only dissenting voice. Developing the liberal critique of the deal with Darlan concluded barely two months earlier, MacLeish argued that any arrangement with the House of Savoy would raise new questions for Americans struggling to understand "what the war is about [and] what our war aims are."[35] Adolf Berle responded by arguing that winning the war would necessarily require political compromises with those who "in fact possess power" and, despite MacLeish's protest against such unvarnished pragmatism, the committee endorsed the proposal that Washington pursue the establishment of an Italian government based on the monarchy. A summary produced after the meeting concluded that a royal government would offer a rallying point for the "upper bourgeoisie," military leaders, and the Catholic Church, thereby regrouping major sections of the ruling class in the aftermath of the anticipated collapse of Mussolini's regime.[36]

The Advisory Committee's proposals make it clear that, although the details of the Darlan deal were shaped by local and contingent events, its general character was hardly aberrant. On the contrary, the salient features of the arrangement with Darlan could, it was hoped, be employed elsewhere. What is striking about the committee's proposals for Italy is not just their promonarchical conservatism, but their explicit assumption that the Italian people would play no active part in shaping the contours of post-Fascist Italy. The United States, committee members of all stripes assumed, would be able simply to impose any solution it chose. While reports from Italy were laced with warnings about a "general revolution," the committee concurred with Welles's judgment that there was no "powerful organized group" capable of challenging a reformed monarchy backed by Allied arms.[37]

---

[33] ACPFP minutes of meeting P39, January 2, 1943, Notter Files.
[34] Ibid.
[35] Ibid.
[36] ACPFP document P170, January 7, 1943, Notter Files.
[37] ACPFP minutes P39, January 2, 1943, Notter Files.

If the Advisory Committee saw no immediate threat of communism, it also saw no need to press for the rapid establishment of democracy in Italy. Arguing that democracy had always "failed to take deep root" in Italy, the committee concluded that Italians lacked the necessary "preparation" to "exercise their prerogatives under a liberal government."[38] This problem was, in Welles's view, compounded by the fact that leading anti-Fascist exiles like Count Carlo Sforza lacked the "ability ... prestige ... and rationality of intelligence" to form a government.[39] These judgments were informed by popular cultural notions that pictured Italians as naïve and child-like, uninterested in politics or war, and easily led by forceful leaders, be they Fascists, Communists – or Americans.[40] At a stroke, U.S. planners transposed to Europe the established trope of "native" unreadiness for independence by which they had circumvented the issue of self-determination in North Africa.

U.S. planners focused particular attention to what they saw as a dangerous interregnum between the opening of the Allied invasion of Sicily and the establishment of a new regime in Rome based on the monarchy and capable of dealing directly with the Allied governments. Here the issues of political legitimacy and continuity that had been deployed to justify Washington's relations with Vichy and with Darlan reemerged in modified form. After the proclamation at Casablanca of "unconditional surrender" as the key Allied war-aim, negotiations with the Mussolini government, or with any direct successor, appeared to be ruled out, and planners assumed that some form of Allied military rule would be necessary to bridge the gap until a suitably legitimate Italian government could be put in place.

The Advisory Committee suggested that during this transitional period it would be permissible to incorporate some of the preexisting structures of the Italian state into the apparatus of military rule. Because it was deemed unlikely that the collapse of the Mussolini dictatorship would result in the entire Fascist state being "swept into the discard," many institutions, including the Catholic Church, sections of the state bureaucracy, and the "agencies of local government," could, the committee argued, be purged of "culpable and intransigent Fascists" and thereby rendered "amenable to a new political orientation."[41] In this analysis, Fascism was conceptualized as the "stucco surface" of government rather than as the "cement" binding it together. The conclusion was clear: strip away the stucco and the building itself could be rehabilitated.

As the State Department's Advisory Committee was discussing plans for post-Fascist Italy, army planners were focused on the problem of establishing

---

[38] ACPFP document P170, January 7, 1943, Notter Files.
[39] ACPFP minutes P39, January 2, 1943, Notter Files.
[40] On American constructions of Italianness, see Andrew Buchanan, "'Good Morning Pupil!' American Representations of Italianness and the Occupation of Italy, 1943–1945," *Journal of Contemporary History* 43, no. 2 (2008).
[41] ACPFP document T195, December 17, 1942, Notter Files.

functioning military government in the immediate aftermath of a successful invasion. In North Africa, it had been possible to sidestep this question by simply recognizing the existing structures of French colonial rule and reinforcing their functioning by providing material aid organized largely through civilian agencies. In Fascist Italy, however, the maintenance of the entire preexisting government would clearly be politically unacceptable. Like their civilian counterparts, however, army planners assumed that they would be able to "integrate the local institutions and psychology of the occupied area" into the apparatus of military governments set up amid "utter chaos."[42] They also recognized that it was likely that the end of combat operations would leave the "American army as the sole agency capable of initiating the reconstruction process," and that it was necessary to prepare in advance for the complex economic and political challenges that U.S. troops might be expected to face.[43] In preparation for these eventualities, as well as for the subsequent occupations of Germany and Japan, Provost Marshal General Allen Gullion was instructed to organize the training of army civil affairs officers. The School of Military Government (SMG), situated on the campus of the University of Virginia in Charlottesville, duly admitted its first class in May 1942.[44]

Students at the SMG studied international law and the history of the Axis powers, but their studies focused on America's own practice of military government. Here, they mined a long string of experiences, stretching from the occupation of northern Mexico and the post–Civil War reconstruction of the South to the interventions and occupations in the Caribbean and the Philippines in the early twentieth century, to furnish guidelines for action. Students also reviewed the lessons of the post–World War I occupation of the Rhineland. To some students, these examples seemed hopelessly anachronistic.[45] But, if they appeared remote from the actuality of the unfolding world war, they were far from irrelevant: with the exception of the 1918–1923 occupation of Germany, they all involved the U.S.-sponsored remaking of societies conquered in war. In particular, the establishment of a protectorate in Cuba, the extended occupation of Haiti, and the conquest and pacification of the Philippines, all modeled paths for the advance of U.S. influence and control without direct territorial annexation. In these cases, military intervention and forms of military government provided a critical bridge between armed conquest on the one hand and the establishment of a "nation-based" or "limited-liability" empire on the other.[46]

---

[42] Prospectus of the School of Military Government, March 1942, in Harry L. Coles and Albert K. Weinberg, *Civil Affairs: Soldiers Become Governors* (Washington DC: Office of the Chief of the Military History Department of the Army, 1964), 145.

[43] Wickersham to Gullion, June 17, 1942, Coles and Weinberg, *Civil Affairs*, 12.

[44] See Coles and Weinberg, *Civil Affairs*, chapter 1.

[45] See Thomas R. Fisher, "Allied Military Government in Italy," *Annals of the American Academy* (January 1950), 116, 121.

[46] See Paul A. Kramer, "Power and Connection: Imperial Histories of the United States in the World," *American Historical Review* 116, No. 5 (December 2011), 1368–1369.

FIGURE 6.2. Army Civil Affairs Officers take notes during a lecture at the School of Military Government, Charlottesville, VA, 1943. (Courtesy of Library of Congress)

These were hardly uncontroversial questions, and from its inception the School of Military Government was a lightning rod for intense discussion, both within the administration and beyond, over the character of the postwar order and the road to its establishment. Many liberals feared that, as one Interior Department official put it, the army was "moving in" on postwar planning, insidiously replacing the goal of establishing a "civilian, democratic, and free" world with one "ruled by the armed forces."[47] In particular, they charged General Gullion with packing the school's student body with "Republicans and anti-New Dealers," men who were not "socially minded" and who would be inclined toward establishing military despotisms.[48]

Conservatives attacked the army's preparations for military government from a different angle, suggesting that military rule would be a stepping-stone toward an unwarranted and open-ended commitment of U.S. forces overseas. Graduates of the School of Military Government, the formerly isolationist *Chicago Tribune* argued, would function as pro-consuls and "American

---

[47] Padover to Ickes, memorandum, January 8, 1943, Coles and Weinberg, *Civil Affairs*, 26.
[48] Gullion to Marshall, November 27, 1942, in ibid., 24.

Gauleiters."[49] These exchanges had a highly intemperate tone, with analogies to Nazi Germany and Stalin's Russia being bandied about and with General Gullion warning that civilian agencies might have to appoint "commissars" to keep field commanders in check.[50] The vigor of the language underscored the broad scope of the discussion on U.S. war aims and on the shape of the postwar world that would unfold as Washington marched toward full-scale military engagement in the Mediterranean.

Military leaders did their best to fend off criticisms from both liberals and conservatives and, after William Bullitt visited Charlottesville on Roosevelt's behalf, they secured presidential backing for the work of the School of Military Government. Roosevelt insisted that governing occupied territories would "in most instances" be a "civilian task," but he acknowledged Secretary of War Stimson's argument that the army, as the agency of conquest, would necessarily take the lead in the establishment of a new American-sponsored order.[51] Moreover, despite the heat generated by the prospect of U.S.-led military governments in Europe, no one in Washington doubted either the right of the United States to impose military rule, or the notion that such regimes would furnish powerful instruments with which to begin the reorganization of the occupied countries along U.S.-approved lines. All the important decisions would be taken by U.S. authorities: as the one major study on military government from the Civil War to the Philippines put it, military regimes end by decision of the occupying power, and at the point at which the occupied country exhibits a "satisfactory condition of affairs looking to civil rule."[52] The trick, as one senior war department planner put it, was to view military government as a vehicle for "Good Samaritan internationalism," not as an expression of "American imperialism."[53]

With the invasion of Sicily looming, the operational principles of Allied military government began to be clarified during the early months of 1943. Army civil affairs officers would be attached to frontline units in Sicily, ready to move quickly to take charge in areas cleared of Axis troops. Basing themselves on the existing structures of local government – after those most "tainted" with fascism had been purged – they would assemble local coalitions drawn from the ranks of the Church, local landowners, and other elite figures.[54] To

---

[49] "U.S. Is Training Men to Govern Occupied Areas: School for Pro-Consuls Follows Nazi Patterns," *Chicago Tribune*, December 31, 1942; "American Gauleiters," *Chicago Tribune*, January 8, 1943.

[50] Gullion to Marshall, November 27, 1942, Coles and Weinberg, *Civil Affairs*, 24.

[51] Roosevelt to Stimson, October 29, 1942, in ibid., 22.

[52] William E. Birkhimer, *Military Government and Martial Law* (Kansas City: Franklin Hudson Publishing Company, 1914), 369.

[53] Hyneman to Thomson, University of Colorado, July 6, 1943, in Coles and Weinberg, *Civil Affairs*, 29. Perhaps unconsciously, Hyneman's language reflected Henry Luce's call for the United States to become the "Good Samaritan of the entire world." Henry Luce, "The American Century" *Life*, February 17 1941, reprinted in *Diplomatic History* 23, no. 2 (1999), 170.

[54] C. R. S. Harris, *Allied Military Administration of Italy, 1943–1945* (London: HMSO, 1957), 3.

maintain order, and to ensure civilian passivity, the *Carabinieri* military police
force would be reconstituted under the leadership of Allied police officers. All
public political activity would be banned, there would be no free press, and
other democratic rights would be severely curtailed. Even with these operational principles established, however, AFHQ Algiers was unable to activate
the Allied Military Government of Occupied Territories (AMGOT) until May
1, 1943. The delay was attributable to deep divisions between the Allies over
the new organization's leadership and command structure.

In February 1943, General Eisenhower reported to George Marshall that
because the invasion of Sicily would be the first Allied assault on Axis territory, it would "inevitably establish precedents [and] set the pattern for later
operations in Europe."[55] The British, with their perceived "vital interests in the
Mediterranean," could be expected to argue that they should therefore have
"primary responsibility" for the post-invasion regime. Eisenhower proposed
to counter this challenge by establishing "joint Anglo-American responsibility" for the invasion itself and for the subsequent "conduct of military government." Offering striking confirmation of his growing political confidence,
Eisenhower explained that he was sure that British officers at AFHQ would
accept his plan for "joint responsibility" because he had already discussed it in
detail with Harold Macmillan, London's resident minister.[56]

Eisenhower's plan for "joint responsibility" found little favor in either
London or Washington. Foreign Office officials pressed the case for British political leadership in Sicily, and when Macmillan warned that such "old empire"
thinking might damage relations with Washington, he received a crushing reply
from Churchill. The prime minister set his face against the whole notion of
joint Anglo-American leadership, and insisted that the resident minister take
a firm stand for his "country's rights and the British Empire."[57] An equal and
opposite reaction took place in Washington. Although Secretary of War Henry
Stimson – no friend of an extended U.S. commitment to the Mediterranean –
was "rather for letting [the British] do it," he noted with alarm that President
Roosevelt was pressing an "aggressively American plan" and wanted U.S. officers to "take the leadership of the whole thing."[58]

Matters came to a head in mid-April. Heartened by reports from Field
Marshal Sir John Dill, head of Britain's Joint Staff Mission in Washington, indicating that George Marshall shared Stimson's view that the "Mediterranean is
a British sphere of strategic responsibility" and that London should therefore
decide "what is to be done in occupied enemy territory," Churchill attempted
to exploit these signs of division within Washington.[59] Cabling Roosevelt,

[55] Eisenhower to Marshall, February 8, 1943, *Eisenhower Papers*, 2: 946–947.
[56] Ibid.
[57] Macmillan and Churchill, quoted in Jones, *Mediterranean War*, 85–86.
[58] Ibid., 87.
[59] Jones, *Mediterranean War*, 88.

Churchill proposed that because a British officer, General Harold Alexander, had been slated to command Allied operations in Sicily, the British should also be the "senior partner" in the military government of "Husky-land."[60] Roosevelt quickly issued a tart rejoinder, insisting that the military government of Sicily should be under "joint allied control" with no "senior partner."[61]

Roosevelt backed his rejection of London's claim to seniority with the argument that because many Italians entertained "friendly feelings" toward the United States – a sentiment reciprocated by the "large number of [American] citizens [of] Italian descent" – the military government should be staffed by a "large proportion of Americans" and given "as much of an American character as is practicable."[62] Churchill beat a hasty retreat, explaining implausibly that he had always envisioned *Husky* as a "joint enterprise" conducted on "terms of perfect equality." Accepting the utility of "American ties with Italy," he conceded that "American preeminence" would be beneficial to the "common cause."[63] Churchill concluded this remarkably abject message with a promise that, as in the invasion of North Africa, he would remain the president's loyal "lieutenant."

This exchange paved the way for the establishment of AMGOT at the beginning of May. The command arrangements continued to evolve, however, and by the time they were finalized less than a month before the landings they had acquired Byzantine complexity. A British officer, Lord Rennell (Francis Rodd, an old college friend of Macmillan's), would lead AMGOT, reporting to General Alexander. Meanwhile, an American, Colonel Julius Holmes, would head the Military Government Section of AFHQ, and serve as Eisenhower's channel to Alexander. Holmes would convey Eisenhower's orders on important political questions, ensuring that the supreme commander retained overall control of the political dimensions of the invasion. This arrangement maintained the principle of joint Allied control, but it also displayed a clear inflection toward U.S. predominance. Roosevelt's refusal to countenance any notion of Britain as "senior partner" signaled how quickly and decisively the balance of power within the Alliance had shifted. At Casablanca, only six months earlier, British leaders had envisioned U.S. forces lending powerful support in what would remain fundamentally a British sphere. Now, as plans for *Husky* were readied, Washington was claiming – at the very least – an equal say in the post-Fascist political set-up in Italy.

On the night of July 9–10, 1943, General Alexander's 15th Army Group, composed of Patton's Seventh Army and Montgomery's Eighth, began landing on the southern coast of Sicily. *Husky* was by far the largest seaborne assault yet

[60] Churchill to Roosevelt, April 13, 1943, *Correspondence*, 2: 188.
[61] Roosevelt to Churchill, April 14, 1943, *Correspondence*, 2: 188–189.
[62] Ibid.
[63] Churchill to Roosevelt, April 15, 1943, *Correspondence*, 2: 190.

attempted, and the landings were supported by ships of the Royal Navy and by Vice Admiral H. Kent Hewitt's Eighth Fleet.[64] Formed in March 1943, this new U.S. fleet was a striking symbol of Washington's increasing commitment to the Mediterranean. Operating from a large new base at Oran, recently equipped with dry docks and extensive repair facilities and manned by 4,000 U.S. stevedores and 3,000 Arab workers, the new command oversaw extensive logistical and training operations in preparation for the landings.[65]

Absorbing the harsh lessons of the *Torch* landings the previous November, Allied forces would for the first time be equipped with large "beaching craft" – including the 1,500-ton LST or Landing Ship Tank – capable of delivering troops and heavy equipment directly onto the landing beaches.[66] Despite some appalling blunders – Allied paratroops suffered heavy casualties from "friendly" anti-aircraft fire – the invading armies quickly established solid bridgeheads. German troops fought tenaciously, but their Italian allies quickly collapsed, and Allied troops completed the conquest of Sicily by August 16. Yet despite its dramatic success, the Sicilian campaign heralded problems to come as the Germans demonstrated their skill in defensive warfare, culminating in the evacuation from Sicily of 40,000 German and 70,000 Italian soldiers together with their tanks and equipment.[67]

As planned, Army civil affairs officers arrived hard on the heels of advancing combat troops to begin setting up the structures of Allied military government. Many Italian municipal officers were retained in their posts irrespective of their Fascist past, giving the new AMGOT-led local governments a strongly reactionary character. In a detailed on-the-spot report on the establishment of military rule, the *New York Times* noted that Allied officers exercised "great degree of leniency towards former fascist officials."[68] Not surprisingly, the new local governments sided with landowners against peasants seeking land reform and with employers against workers pressing for better wages and conditions.[69] In the sulfur-mining district, Allied officials asserted their authority in the face of Communist-led mineworkers who had taken advantage of the breakdown of civil government to establish a workers' council. In the face of such challenges, civil affairs officers reached out to the Catholic Church – and perhaps also to

---

[64] For an excellent overview of U.S. military operations in Sicily and mainland Italy, see Rick Atkinson, *The Day of Battle: The War in Sicily and Italy, 1943–1944* (New York: Henry Holt, 2007).

[65] See Barbara Brooks Tomblin, *With Utmost Spirit: Allied Naval Operations in the Mediterranean, 1942–1945* (Lexington, KY: University of Kentucky Press, 2004), especially 113–116; also Joseph Bykovsky and Harold Larson, *The Transportation Corps: Operations Overseas* (Washington, DC: U.S. Government Printing Office, 1957), 157.

[66] See Samuel Eliot Morison, *The Two-Ocean War: A Short History of the United States in the Second World War* (Boston: Little, Brown and Company, 1963), 248–249.

[67] See Robert M. Citino, *The Wehrmacht Retreats: Fighting a Lost War, 1943* (Lawrence, KS: University of Kansas Press, 2012), 195–197.

[68] Matthews, *New York Times*, August 2, 1943.

[69] See Harris, *Allied Military Administration*, 33.

FIGURE 6.3. Citizens of Marsala, Sicily read the proclamation establishing the Allied Military Government, July 28, 1943. (Courtesy of Franklin D. Roosevelt Library.)

the Mafia – for support. Citing the exigencies of ongoing military operations, AMGOT officials suppressed all local newspapers, prohibited the organization of public meetings, and banned other forms of political expression including protests and demonstrations.

Although they did not pose quite such a direct challenge to America's stated democratic war aims as the deal with Darlan, these developments troubled liberal opinion in the United States. In August, a survey of editorial responses to the establishment of military government revealed only a slight majority – thirty-five out of sixty-two – expressing favorable opinions, with the influential *Chicago Tribune* denouncing the whole operation as an exercise in "Gauleiter government."[70] Despite this harsh initial reception, domestic criticism of AMGOT was moderated by the careful packaging of military rule for domestic consumption and by the rapid subordination of events in Sicily to the big political questions posed by the surrender of Italy. A *New York Times* editorial early in the occupation struggled to put a democratic face on AMGOT, explaining that the military government was "dedicated to the eradication of

[70] "Review of Press Views of AMGOT," report by the War Dept. Civil Affairs Division, August 9, 1943, Hopkins Papers, Box 169, folder Civil Affairs in Sicily and Italy, FDRL.

FIGURE 6.4. British and U.S. officers establish military government in the ruins of the town hall, St. Agata, Sicily, August 13, 1943. Listening to the proclamation are a group of clergymen, local notables, former town officials, and an officer of the *Carabinieri*. (Courtesy of Franklin D. Roosevelt Library.)

those political ideologies and their representatives that we fight against" and arguing that the new administrations would "utilize" only those local officials "not too strongly tainted by the Fascist brush."[71] Later articles developed the theme, explaining that because the AMGOT would "operate" through existing local officials, it would not be seen as an "alien" imposition on the Italian people; "towns and provinces," the *Times* enthused, would "virtually run themselves."[72]

Time journalist John Hersey developed these themes in his Pulitzer Prize-winning novel *Bell for Adano*. Hersey accompanied U.S. troops in Sicily and drew on this experience to write the thinly fictionalized story of an American-led local government. Rushed into print in barely six months, this best-selling novel – and the movie and stage play that followed it – offered an uplifting

[71] Editorial, *New York Times*, July 19, 1945.
[72] Editorial, *New York Times*, July 25, 1945, E5.

account of the work of Italian-American civil affairs officer Major Victor Joppolo and of his "wonderful zeal for spreading democracy."[73] Joppolo was, in truth, more benevolent dictator that democrat, but his humanitarian and deeply paternalistic attitude toward the feckless Italians in his care struck a chord with Americans eager for confirmation of the justice of their cause and the rightness of their government's actions. Whatever doubts about the character of U.S.-sponsored "liberation" had been stirred by the Darlan affair, in Hersey's account American forces seemed to the doing the right thing. Hersey, like the State Department's Advisory Committee on Postwar Foreign Policy and the *New York Times* editorial board, presented Italian Fascism as a "taint" on the body politic, a "stucco" surface that could be removed without making – or allowing others to make – fundamental changes to the underlying social structure.

U.S. policy makers and opinion-formers understood that their approach to questions of military government and post-Fascist political organization in Sicily would have profound implications for the postwar reorganization of Italy, Germany, and Japan. Sicily, as journalist Harold Callender explained in the *New York Times*, offered a "working model" of what was "in store" for all the Axis powers, and he pictured a "beneficent" military regime leading the transition to "enlightened and efficient" civil government.[74] Major Joppolo, as Hersey argued in his foreword to *Bell for Adano*, gave dramatic fictional life to this process. A thoroughly "good man," Joppolo symbolized all that liberal public opinion found positive in America's deepening engagement with Europe and in its broader potential for enlightened international leadership. Rejecting more boorish American characteristics, represented in *Bell for Adano* by the Pattonesque General Marvin, Hersey concluded that America would need many "Joppolos" as its armies and "after-armies" pushed deeper into Europe, overthrowing repressive regimes and establishing a liberal new political order.[75]

Hersey's concern for packaging the experience of military government in Italy for a domestic audience was increasingly reflected in the outlook of officers within the ranks of AMGOT itself. Although the practice of British and U.S. civil affairs officers on the ground in Sicily differed little, higher-ranking U.S. officials soon began to argue that the more egregiously undemocratic aspects of the military government were a product of specifically British policies. In September 1943, senior civil affairs officer Charles Poletti (widely held to be the model for Hersey's Joppolo) sent a sharply worded report to the War Department arguing that because AMGOT head Lord Rennell clearly had no intention of "promoting liberal democratic government" in Sicily, he should be packed off home to go "grouse shooting."[76] In such allusions to the conservative

[73] *New York Times*, February 6, 1944.
[74] *New York Times*, August 1, 1943, E3.
[75] John Hersey, *Bell for Adano*, 1944 (Reprint, New York: Vintage Books, 1988), v–vii.
[76] Poletti, quoted in Jones, *Mediterranean War*, 94.

outlook and aristocratic lifestyle of Lord Rennel and other senior British officers, U.S. officials found a convenient excuse for the undemocratic policies that
were in fact the product of mutual agreement and planning. These differences
over the public presentation of the military government in Sicily, if not over the
actual experience on the ground, soon flowed into more substantial divisions
over the character of the post-Mussolini regime in Italy as a whole.

By early 1942, important sections of the Italian elite, including circles
around King Victor Emmanuel III and senior Fascist officials, had begun to
come to the conclusion that an Allied victory was inevitable and that it was
therefore time to explore the options for getting out of the war with their
own power and privileges intact.[77] Assuming that the British would be more
favorable to a new regime based on the monarchy, initial Italian peace feelers
were directed entirely toward London. British leaders, skeptical of the House
of Savoy's ability to rally opposition to Mussolini, brushed them aside. After
the *Torch* landings in November 1942, opposition to Mussolini within Italian
ruling circles deepened rapidly, and by February 1943 London was convinced
that Pietro Badoglio, former Army Chief of Staff and Viceroy of Ethiopia, was
preparing to oust Mussolini. Despite some promising signs, however, tentative
contacts between the Allies and Badoglio did not bear fruit prior to the invasion of Sicily.

The rapid collapse of Italian forces in Sicily, combined with Allied bombing
raids against industrial cities in northern Italy, produced a new political situation in the summer of 1943. The Italian elite now saw danger looming on
two fronts, combining military defeat at the hands of the Allies with a popular insurrection presaged by the wave of strikes and protests in the north. In
this fluid and rapidly developing situation, Mussolini was increasingly viewed
as a liability, and on July 24 the Fascist Grand Council, dormant since 1939,
removed him from office. The following day the former dictator was impris-
oned by King Victor Emmanuel, who then presided over the formation of a
new government under Marshal Badoglio. Popular anti-Fascist forces played
no part in these events: as historian Elena Agarossi points out, the coup against
Mussolini was carried out by men who had come to the conclusion that it was
necessary to "sacrifice" the leader to "maintain the regime he had created."[78]
The new government quickly disbanded the Fascist Party and abolished some
of the most overtly repressive institutions of the Fascist state. Pledging to continue the war alongside Germany, they simultaneously began secret talks with
the Allies.

Many Allied opinion-formers were deeply skeptical of the new Italian government, viewing it, accurately, as essentially a continuation of the Fascist regime

---

[77] See William S. Linsenmeyer, "Italian Peace Feelers before the Fall of Mussolini," *Journal of
Contemporary History* 16, no. 4 (1981).
[78] Elena Agarossi, *A Nation Collapses: The Italian Surrender of September 1943*, translated
Harvey Fergusson II (Cambridge: Cambridge University Press, 2006), 51.

without Mussolini. The *New York Times* scathingly described it as a "military dictatorship resting ... on the shadowy authority of a puppet king," and welcomed statements by Cordell Hull and Henry Stimson calling for increased military action to force an unconditional surrender.[79] Echoing these sentiments, an Office of War Information broadcast to Italy on July 26 denounced the new government, describing Badoglio as a "high-ranking fascist" and Victor Emmanuel as the "moronic little King."

Top Allied leaders were more sanguine. Roosevelt publicly repudiated the OWI broadcast, while Churchill stated bluntly "we should not be too particular in dealing with any Non Fascist Government, even if it is not the one we should like."[80] The British leader expressed a willingness to negotiate with any Italian regime – suitably shorn of the "head devil" – if it could "deliver the goods" in the form of an armistice. Roosevelt concurred, adding a note disparaging "contentious people" who would "make a row if we seem to recognize" the King or Badoglio.[81] The president may have been trying to leave a little semantic ambiguity in his position, perhaps implying a difference between "seem[ing] to recognize" the new Italian government and *actually* recognizing it. However, while cynically reminding Churchill that they should "say something about self-determination ... at the proper time," Roosevelt was equally ready to recognize the political legitimacy of the new government.[82] Journalist Arthur Krock enthusiastically endorsed the president's approach, using his influential *New York Times* column to argue that the Badoglio government could provide the indispensable "bridge" between Italy's Fascist past and its democratic future.[83]

Commenting on the mounting social and political turmoil in Italy, Churchill hoped that the Badoglio government would be able to "make the Italians do what we need" in the face of "chaos, bolshevization or civil war."[84] Allied leaders certainly had good reason to be concerned about "bolshevization," if not yet civil war. Across Italy, and particularly in the industrial north, the ouster of Mussolini opened new opportunities for mass protests actions, allowing working people to envisage the prospect of imposing radical solutions to the crisis, thereby reshaping the entire course and outcome of the war. Although the Italian people had largely been spectators to the final political convulsions of the Fascist regime, the ouster of Mussolini prompted tens of thousands to take to the streets in spontaneous celebrations that spilled over into protest marches,

---

[79] Editorial, *New York Times*, July 27, 1943; see also Steven Casey, *Cautious Crusade: Franklin D. Roosevelt, American Public Opinion, and the War against Nazi Germany* (Oxford: Oxford University Press, 2001), 124–126.

[80] Churchill to Roosevelt, July 26, 1943, *Correspondence*, 2: 348–349.

[81] Roosevelt to Churchill, July 30, 1943, *Correspondence*, 2: 366.

[82] Ibid.

[83] Krock, "Problems Anterior to Italian Peace," *New York Times*, July 27, 1943.

[84] Churchill to Roosevelt, July 31, 1943, *Correspondence*, 2: 369.

strikes, and factory occupations.[85] As the *New York* Times reported, workers' protests demanded pay raises, a purge of Fascist officials, and "Peace Now," and they built on preparations which, as OSS agents reported, involved enraged peasants "killing fascists" and factory workers forming militias in readiness for "anything."[86] Commentating on these developments, the American socialist newsweekly *The Militant* announced boldly "Italy is in the throes of revolution."[87] To Allied leaders on both sides of the Atlantic, this judgment must have seemed alarmingly accurate.

Faced with this wave of popular protest, the Badoglio government declared martial law and ordered the army to suppress street demonstrations. Over the following days, a series of bloody clashes between soldiers and protesters unfolded across the country, with the severity of the government's actions reflecting its fear that the political situation in the north was rapidly slipping out of control. By early August, government forces were getting the upper hand, but intelligence reports reaching Washington indicated that Badoglio remained "preoccupied" with crushing outbreaks of "public disorder."[88] In early August, British bombing raids on Milan, Genoa, and Turin effectively augmented Badoglio's assault on working-class protesters. Hundreds of residents of working-class districts were killed, while thousands more fled to safety in the country.[89] Cloudless skies made for accurate bombing, and returning aircrews reported starting "concentrated fires" that were still burning several days later.[90] Under the combined weight of government repression and British bombing, the anti-government protests collapsed.

London justified the bombing raids on the grounds that they would "intensify [the] pressure on Badoglio" to sue for peace.[91] Writing from Rome, British Minister to the Vatican Sir D'Arcy Osborne challenged this rationale, pointing out that the Badoglio government was not subject to any "Anglo-Saxon democratic process" by which bombed civilians might make their desire for peace felt.[92] In the United States, exiled Italian academic Gaetano Salvemini went a step further, accusing the British bombers of "mowing down and dispersing the crowds who were crying for peace."[93] Roosevelt did not challenge the British bombing. Clearly opposed to the possibility of a working-class insurrection,

---

[85] See Tom Behan, *The Long Awaited Moment: The Working Class and the Italian Communist Party in Milan, 1943–1948* (New York: Peter Lang, 1997).

[86] *New York Times*, August 1, 1943; OSS reports April 23, May 15, and n.d. mid-May, 1943 Box 72, Map Room Files, FDRL.

[87] Editorial, *The Militant*, August 7, 1943.

[88] Harrison to State Dept., August 2, 1943, *FRUS 1943*, 2: 340.

[89] See Behan, *Long Awaited Moment*, 66.

[90] Air Ministry to Churchill, August 13, 15, 16 1943, PREM 3/14/3.

[91] Portal to Tedder, July 30, 1943, PREM 3/14/3; see also Martin Middlebrook and Chris Everitt, *The Bomber Command War Diaries* (Leicester: Midland Publishing, 1990), 419–422.

[92] Osborne to FO, August 18, 1943, PREM 3/14/3.

[93] Salvemini, "What Next in Italy?," *New Republic*, September 20, 1943, 387–388.

like the British he viewed the Badoglio government as a necessary bulwark against revolution. Unlike Churchill, however, Roosevelt did not fully endorse the new political setup in Italy, and he continued to emphasize the unconditional surrender of Italy while stressing the importance of ensuring the "good treatment of the Italian people."[94] In these differences lay the seeds of a much deeper divide over the character of post-Fascist Italy, and one that would deepen as Allied troops moved from Sicily into the mainland.

The rapid success of operation *Husky,* combined with the new political situation created by the ouster of Mussolini, created a powerful argument for launching a rapid invasion of mainland Italy. Meeting in Washington in May for the *Trident* summit conference, Allied leaders had agreed that a campaign to "eliminate Italy from the war" should follow the successful completion of *Husky,* and final approval for the invasion was given at the *Quadrant* conference in Quebec in mid-August. Despite the powerful military logic set in motion by Allied victories in North Africa and Sicily, however, continued divisions over the preparation of a cross-Channel assault combined with the political uncertainty created by the overthrow of Mussolini to impose a short but highly significant pause in major Allied military operations in the weeks following the completion of the Sicilian campaign.

In contrast to the Allies and the Badoglio government, the Germans acted decisively in the weeks following Mussolini's ouster. Convinced that there was no substance in Badoglio's claim that Italy would fight on, Berlin began to move large number of German combat troops into Italy in early August. By the time Mark Clark's Fifth Army began landing at Salerno on September 9, the four original German divisions in Italy had been reinforced by sixteen more, and Field Marshal Albert Kesselring had established a defensive line south of Rome capable of protecting both the capital and the important complex of airfields at Foggia. In northern Italy, German forces completed the work begun by Badoglio and the British bombers, bloodily suppressing what they described as the "communist revolt" in Turin.[95]

The rapid reinforcement of German forces in Italy convinced the Allies to press ahead with the invasion before Kesselring could establish an impregnable position. The decision to invade necessitated bringing desultory talks with the Badoglio government to a rapid conclusion and securing an armistice capable of neutralizing potentially troublesome Italian forces. Until this point, negotiations with the Badoglio government had been hampered both by differences between the Allies and by Italian evasiveness, born of the hope of finding some room for maneuver between Berlin, London, and Washington. Divisions between London and Washington touched on their emerging differences over the character of post-Fascist Italy, with the British insisting on a comprehensive civil-military surrender – dubbed the "long terms" – while the

[94] Roosevelt to Churchill, July 25, 1943, *Correspondence,* 2: 347.
[95] See Agarossi, *A Nation Collapses,* 105.

Americans favored a shorter, purely military text – the "short terms" – that would postpone the resolution of broader political questions to a later date. London's "long terms" had a markedly punitive thrust whereas, as Roosevelt had insisted, the U.S. approach allowed greater scope for "good treatment of the Italian populace." Washington also favored giving greater leeway to Allied leaders in the theater, imparting a degree of flexibility excluded by London's approach.

London finally secured U.S. approval of the "long terms" at the *Quadrant* conference in late August. It was a hollow victory. By the end of August, Allied leaders in the Mediterranean – British and American alike – were convinced that the rapid buildup of German forces in Italy made it imperative to secure an armistice *before* attempting a landing, and that – in this time-dependent context – the "long terms" were an impediment to securing Italian cooperation. Writing from AFHQ Algiers, Harold Macmillan urged the British cabinet to agree that an initial armistice could be concluded solely on the basis of the "short terms." To his relief, London concurred, authorizing the use of the "shorter document" if "military exigencies absolutely required it."[96] The Italian government finally signed the "short terms" on September 3, the same day that the British-led Eighth Army began landing in Calabria.

From the beginning, negotiations between the Allies and the Italians had not gone smoothly, with Badoglio insisting that any armistice be kept secret, ostensibly to give the new government time to prepare a defense of Rome. In fact, beyond a wild scheme to fly U.S. paratroops directly into Rome (Operation *Giant 2),* Badoglio had no serious plan to defend the capital. Instead, members of the new Italian government spent their time organizing their own flight and, when it became clear that there would be no U.S. airborne landing, trying to wriggle out of the armistice altogether. Finally, and with Allied forces already en route to the landing beaches at Salerno, Eisenhower forced the issue by publicly announcing the armistice on September 8. The following day, with the Fifth Army coming ashore, Badoglio fled Rome for the Adriatic port of Brindisi. Secure in the southern resort, Badoglio called for a popular uprising against the German invasion – having, as one OSS officer observed bitterly, spent the previous forty-five days suppressing a similar rising.[97] In the event, poorly led Italian army units and enthusiastic but untrained partisans could offer only token resistance to German troops moving into Rome.

At London's insistence, the Italian government was finally forced to sign the "long terms" on September 29, but both Washington and the Anglo-American leadership in the Mediterranean remained convinced that the imposition of additional terms was unnecessary. However, London had kept Moscow abreast of developments, and on September 25 Washington received a strongly worded letter from Foreign Minister Molotov insisting that the "long terms"

[96] Macmillan, *War Diaries,* 197.
[97] Peter Tompkins, *Italy Betrayed* (New York: Simon and Schuster, 1966), 190.

be implemented. Moscow's first diplomatic intervention into wartime politics in Italy set an important precedent, effectively aligning the Russian government with the most punitive measures and the ones that would have the most detrimental consequences on the conditions facing working people. It is hard not to see Stalin's deep aversion to popular radicalism behind this diplomatic stance. Faced with pressure from both major allies, Washington relented, instructing Eisenhower to secure Italian agreement to the more punitive terms, the text of which would remain secret for the rest of the war lest they harm Allied standing in Italy. Nevertheless, Eisenhower continued to regard the "long terms" as superfluous and, with Macmillan's approval, he sought to soften their impact by referring to them as "additional conditions" rather than "terms of surrender" and by deleting any mention of "unconditional surrender." Roosevelt endorsed these modifications, effectively forcing Churchill to do likewise.[98]

The crisis surrounding the negotiation of the Italian armistice saw the emergence of new forces and alignments that would have long-term repercussions for Allied policy in Italy. First, AFHQ Algiers continued to develop as a semi-independent center in the complex nexus of Allied policy-making, often advocating policies that corresponded to Washington's approach rather than London's. Second, Moscow began to make its voice heard in the formation of Mediterranean policy. While the issue of how much say the Russians would have was yet to be resolved, both Western allies were favorable to some degree of Soviet involvement, not least because it held the promise of a reciprocal relationship in areas that might end the war under Russian occupation. Initially, Moscow sided with Britain on the question of the "long terms," but over time the Russians, too, would come to align themselves broadly with Washington and against London. Third, events on the ground in Sicily and in mainland Italy began to turn Washington away from the initial conservatism of its plans for post-Fascist Italy and toward a more liberal-democratic solution.

---

[98] Roosevelt to Churchill, October 1, 1943, *Correspondence*, 2: 483–484.

7

An "Investment for the Future"

When the U.S.-led Fifth Army came ashore in mainland Italy at Salerno on September 9, 1943, Allied planners anticipated that the landing would be the prelude to a rapid advance on Rome. With the capital in their hands, the Allies hoped to be able to install a new government structured, as the State Department's Advisory Committee on Postwar Foreign Policy had proposed, around the monarchy, the church, and the "upper bourgeoisie."[1] As it turned out, there would be no such rapid progress on either the military or the political front. Fierce counterattacks by the German Tenth Army nearly crushed the beachhead at Salerno, convincing Hitler to approve General Albert Kesselring's plan to confront the Allied invasion south of Rome. Allied troops entered Naples on October 1, but as they pressed slowly north they ran into a series of powerful defensive positions anchored on the Monte Cassino massif. The German "Winter Line" halted the Allied advance and stymied hopes for the rapid capture of Rome. In turn, military deadlock compounded the Allies' political difficulties.

Despite the worsening military situation, the eviction of German troops from Sicily and the far south of Italy and the establishment of the Badoglio government in Brindisi did present the Allies with some limited opportunities for beginning the reorganization of Italian politics. Eisenhower laid out the key political choices facing the Allies in a memorandum to the War Department, arguing that they could either "sweep ... aside" the Badoglio government and establish military rule throughout occupied Italy, or else recognize the Italian regime as a "co-belligerent," place it under Allied political supervision, and collaborate with it under the terms of the armistice.[2] Eisenhower strongly favored the latter policy and, by the time he discussed it with Washington, he had

[1] ACPFP document T195, December 17, 1942, Notter Files.
[2] Eisenhower to War Dept., September 18, 1943, *FRUS 1943*, 2: 367–370.

already began to implement it on the ground by sending a military mission to Brindisi under British General Noel Mason-MacFarlane on September 13.

The notion of "co-belligerency" accorded the Badoglio government a unique status, with the Allies stopping short of accepting it as an ally while recognizing it as a partner in the struggle against Germany. Churchill endorsed the idea, arguing that it would "build up the authority of the King and the Brindisi Administration" and allow Italy to begin to "work her passage" toward becoming a full ally.[3] Italy was formally recognized as a co-belligerent following Badoglio's declaration of war on Germany on October 13. Given the effective dissolution of the Italian army, the immediate military consequences of co-belligerency were negligible, but recognition of the legitimacy of the Brindisi government set the overall political framework for the Allied occupation. Co-belligerency allowed the completion of an Italian version of the Darlan deal, in which the Allies turned nominal political authority over to a viable Italian collaborator.

Developing this policy, Eisenhower decided that while Allied forces would establish "direct" military rule in areas adjacent to the front lines, the Apulian provinces around Brindisi would be governed, subject to "indirect" Allied supervision, by the Badoglio government itself. As Allied forces advanced, direct military rule could be wound up in what were now secure areas behind the front lines, and the additional territory turned over to the government of the "King's Italy." By this means, the entire country would gradually come under the control of the Italian government, which would itself continue to function under "indirect" Allied supervision.

This setup was codified on November 10, 1943 with the establishment of the Allied Control Commission (ACC) under the direction of General Mason-MacFarlane. Operating under the authority of General Eisenhower and AFHQ, the ACC was responsible both for direct military rule in frontline areas and for overseeing the work of the Italian governmental at national, regional and local levels. Given its extensive brief, the ACC quickly developed a substantial bureaucracy that reached into all aspects of Italian civil society, dealing with everything from emergency relief and food distribution to press censorship, labor policy and "defascistization." The Control Commission's staff of more than 1,500 officers, organized into twenty-six sub-commissions and supported by a large secretariat, was installed in the sprawling Bourbon palace at Caserta, outside Naples. Under the direction of this central bureaucracy, teams of army civil affairs officers armed with veto powers worked directly with Italian officials and administrators.[4]

---

[3] Churchill to Roosevelt, September 21, 1943, Warren F. Kimball (ed.), *Churchill and Roosevelt: The Complete Correspondence*, (London: Collins, 1984), 2: 458.

[4] C. R. S. Harris, *Allied Military Administration of Italy, 1943–1945* (London: HMSO, 1957), 110.

In contrast to the state of affairs in North Africa, where the Darlan and his successors presided over a relatively stable domestic situation, powerful popular protests flared across southern Italy in the wake of the Allied landings. On September 9, armed rebellion erupted in Naples and, having weathered a brutal German counter-offensive, the insurgents rose again as Allied troops advanced on the city. OSS agents estimated that there were more than 2,000 fighters under arms and organized in "a revolutionary front."[5] After four days of heavy fighting – the *Quattro giornate di Napoli* – German troops began to withdraw from Naples, and on October 1 Allied troops entered a city already liberated by its own citizens. The "auto-liberation" of Naples, and the political ferment that accompanied it, signaled the rebirth of public political activity in Italy. In the midst of the rising, six parties – Communists, Socialists, Christian Democrats, Labor Democrats, Liberals, and the Party of Action – formed the Committee of National Liberation (CLN) under the leadership of liberal philosopher Bernedetto Croce. Croce had initially placed his hopes in a reformed monarchy, but he now concluded that there could be no genuinely popular democratic government as long as Victor Emmanuel remained on the throne.[6] The "Six" advocated various plans for the removal of the king – ranging from instituting a regency for his son or grandson to an immediate referendum on the future of the monarchy – but all agreed that Victor Emmanuel had to go.

Historians have tended to emphasize the "filth," suffering, and "dejection" that greeted Allied troops entering Naples.[7] However, although there was certainly hardship aplenty, Allied leaders at AFHQ Algiers quickly recognized that insurrectionary outbursts such as that in Naples signaled that, through mass political action and the reemergence of party politics, the Italian people would inevitably impose themselves on the exercise of political power in Italy. In particular, Allied officials saw that a government based only on those sections of the Italian elite represented by the King and Badoglio and constituting what was in effect a police regime backed by Allied guns and devoid of popular legitimacy, would be incapable of commanding the broad political support necessary to buffer further insurrectionary outbursts. Within weeks of the Allied landings, the Advisory Committee's calm assurances that the Italian people would have little say in the post-Fascist order were found wanting.

In Washington, the most astute U.S. leaders had begun expressing "grave misgivings" about a policy that hinged on backing the king and Badoglio shortly after the landings.[8] "It is easy to recognize these people," Harry Hopkins warned prophetically, "but awfully hard to throw them overboard later." Eisenhower was also aware of the problem, arguing in his memorandum

---

[5] Peter Tompkins, *Italy Betrayed* (New York: Simon and Schuster, 1966), 259.
[6] Ibid., 255.
[7] See William I. Hitchcock, *The Bitter Road To Freedom: A New History of the Liberation of Europe* (New York: Free Press, 2008), 233.
[8] Hopkins to Roosevelt, September 22, 1943, Box 160, Italy folder, Hopkins Papers, FDRL.

advocating recognition and co-belligerency that although the Badoglio government had an "unchallenged claim to legality," it would be necessary to strengthen its "national character" by securing an "infusion of representatives of political parties" and by urging the king to abdicate in favor of his son or grandson.[9] Acting along these line, AFHQ instructed Mason-MacFarlane to press Badoglio to build a "broad based anti-Fascist coalition" capable of leading the Italian people as a whole.[10]

While hardly endorsing popular radicalism – Acting Secretary of State Edward Stettinius expressed concern lest the CLN try to fill the "void" created by the collapse of Fascism by forming revolutionary local governments – Washington accepted Eisenhower's case for reforming the Badoglio government.[11] In doing so, the administration veered sharply away from its original monarchy-centric plans, recognizing instead that it had to secure the formation of a government capable of channeling pent-up popular anger into safe constitutional channels. President Roosevelt endorsed this change of course in early November, urging Eisenhower to pursue a "democratic government [in Italy] whether the House of Savoy remains as a figurehead or not."[12] Secretary of State Cordell Hull added his support, noting that he was no longer "at all sympathetic" to keeping Victor Emmanuel on the throne.[13]

As Washington shifted its policy in response to the unfolding situation in Italy, it placed a new emphasis on working with liberal exiles living in the United States, former foreign minister Count Carlo Sforza foremost among them. Arriving in the United States following the fall of France, Sforza joined leftist exiles Gaetano Salvemini and Max Ascoli in the Mazzini Society, a broad anti-Fascist coalition.[14] State Department officials saw the importance of cultivating Sforza and other influential anti-Fascists, and accorded the Mazzini Society what its left-wing critics disparagingly dubbed "semi-official status."[15] The administration also expressed interest in Sforza's plans for an Italian government-in-exile, cosponsoring an international conference of Italian anti-Fascists in Montevideo, Uruguay in 1942. Sumner Welles championed Sforza's case, describing him to Roosevelt as an "outstanding anti-Fascist leader" and endorsing his scheme for a 200,000-strong "Italian Legion" recruited from political exiles and prisoners of war.[16] But Sforza proved to be a demanding

[9] Eisenhower to War Dept., September 18, 1943, *FRUS 1943*, 2: 367–370.
[10] AFHQ to Mason-MacFarlane, September 24, 1943, in Harry L. Coles and Albert K. Weinberg, *Civil Affairs: Soldiers Become Governors* (Washington, DC: Office of the Chief of the Military History Department of the Army, 1964), 428.
[11] Stettinius to Murphy, October 27, 1943, *FRUS 1943*, 2: 414.
[12] Roosevelt to Eisenhower, November 9, 1943, Map Room, Box 34, FDRL.
[13] See Cordell Hull, *The Memoirs of Cordell Hull* (New York: Macmillan, 1948), 2: 1550.
[14] See James Edward Miller, *The United States and Italy, 1940–1950* (Chapel Hill: University of North Carolina Press, 1986), especially chapter 1.
[15] *Fourth International*, June 1943, 175.
[16] Welles to Roosevelt, February 24, 1942, Welles papers, Box 151, FDRL.

protégée, requesting substantial Lend-Lease supplies for his putative "legion," and quickly convincing Welles that he had another egotistical leader like de Gaulle on his hands.[17]

As Italy's war effort faltered during 1942, and with patriotic pressures mounting in the United States after Pearl Harbor, many leading Italian-Americans – or *prominenti* – who had previously backed Mussolini declared their conversion to the anti-Fascist cause. Washington encouraged this development, offering backstage support for an effort by the International Ladies Garment Workers Union to replace the existing social democratic leadership of the Mazzini Society with a coalition of businessmen and labor officials. With their extensive political contacts in Italy and their deep-seated anti-communism, the *prominenti* reinforced the most conservative aspects of Washington's Italian policy, and their rise coincided with the development of the promonarchical course advocated by the Advisory Committee. These developments eclipsed Sforza, with Welles reporting to the Advisory Committee in January 1943 that while he admired the count's "inclinations and beliefs," he would never make a "real leader."[18]

Less than a year later, however, as the realities of Italian politics impelled Washington to think about liberalizing the Badoglio government and removing the King, Sforza suddenly found himself back in favor. At the State Department's urging, Sforza called publicly for broadening the Badoglio government, arguing in the pages of the *New York Times* that "work, peace, and freedom," together with a liberalization of Italian politics, were necessary to head off a communist take-over in Italy.[19] Addressing the Italian-American Labor Council, Assistant Secretary of State Adolf Berle struck a similar note, praising the "common and kindly folk of the streets" who had risen against Mussolini and quoting Sforza on the necessity of making a "common front against Nazi tyranny."[20] Clearly, Sforza's advocacy of a liberalized Italian government joining the Allies in the war against Germany now conformed closely to Washington's own needs.

Washington's new interest effort in liberalizing – or "broadening" – the Badoglio government had the additional advantage of helping to assuage domestic criticism of the administration's Italian policy. In the period after the ouster of Mussolini and the establishment of the Badoglio government, liberal organs like the *Nation*, the *New Republic*, and *PM* had tended – not inaccurately – to view U.S. policy in Italy as an extension of "Darlanism" in North Africa. *New Republic* suggested that Washington had no Italian policy that it "dared announce publicly," resorting instead to "pious platitudes" that covered efforts to "build up the prestige of Badoglio and the King."[21] These criticisms

---

[17] See Christopher O'Sullivan, *Sumner Welles, Postwar Planning, and the Quest for a New World Order, 1937–1943* (New York: Columbia University Press, 2007).

[18] ACPFP, minutes of meeting P39, January 2, 1943, Notter Files, microfiche.

[19] *New York Times*, October 23, 1943, 4.

[20] *Department of State Bulletin*, October 16, 1943, 256–257.

[21] Editorial, *New Republic*, October 4, 1943, 439–440.

reflected a broader unease within the American elite. In early 1943, former Republican presidential candidate Wendell Willkie published *One World*, in which he accused Washington of pursuing "old power politics," acting out of "expediency and apparent practicalities," and losing sight of "what the war is about."[22] *Time* underscored the point, noting sarcastically that the United States was all too "prepared to traffic [with the] miserable little Italian King [and his] reactionary henchman Badoglio."[23] What would follow, the magazine asked: deals with Goering after a putsch against Hitler? As I. F. Stone explained plaintively in *The Nation*, "the Europe that AMGOT would restore is not a Europe in which the Four Freedoms could be achieved."[24]

President Roosevelt had initially dismissed critics of Washington's policy toward Badoglio and Victor Immanuel as "contentious people" whose views could be safely ignored. Now, the new effort to broaden the Italian government gave the administration an opportunity to harness domestic liberalism in support of its Italian policy.[25] The *Washington Post*, for example, welcomed Sforza's call for national unity against the Germans on the grounds that it ended all "doubts about the wisdom of collaborating with Badoglio," thereby justifying Italian Darlanism by giving it an acceptably liberal face.[26] Likewise, the *New York Times* saw in Sforza a leader who "promised well for a future democratic regime in a liberated Italy" and who could dissipate rising tides of "political sectarianism."[27] The *Times*'s real concern, of course, was not with divisive sects or political factionalism, but with the threatening tides of popular insurrection.

Washington's pragmatic adjustment to the realities of Italian politics soon brought it into conflict with London. Although both Washington and Anglo-American leaders at AFHQ saw the necessity of heading off popular protest by establishing a broad coalition government, London persisted in regarding the Italian people as "apathetic" bystanders to the great events unfolding around them.[28] The liberal opposition, Churchill concluded, were nothing more than a gang of ineffectual "professors."[29] Despite claims to favor the establishment of the "broadest based Anti Fascist coalition government possible," Churchill's intransigent defense of the king and his outright hostility to Sforza argued otherwise.[30] In fact, as Washington began to push for a liberalization of Italian politics, London's support for the king and Badoglio hardened; by the spring

[22] Quoted in Steven Casey, *Cautious Crusade; Franklin D. Roosevelt, American Public Opinion, and the War against Nazi Germany* (Oxford: Oxford University Press, 2001), 124.

[23] Ibid., 125.

[24] Stone, *The Nation*, August 7, 1943.

[25] Roosevelt to Churchill, July 30, 1943, *Correspondence*, 2: 366.

[26] *Washington Post*, October 15, 1943.

[27] Editorial, *New York Times*, October 10, 1943, E10.

[28] British Embassy to State, aide-Mémoir, November 23, 1943, *FRUS 1943*, 2: 395

[29] Churchill to Roosevelt, September 21, 1943, *Correspondence*, 2: 458.

[30] Ibid., 458.

of 1944 Churchill was describing Sforza as a "vain and ambitious old man" and Croce as a "dwarf professor," neither of whom should be allowed any role in government.[31]

In the face of British opposition, Washington's campaign to liberalize the Italian government would be a long and difficult one, passing through numerous crises before its eventual triumph in June 1944. Because each discrete crisis ended with the king on the throne and Badoglio entrenched in office, they can be read as a series of victories for British conservatism.[32] Such a conclusion would be mistaken: although the king and Badoglio remained in power, their position, and that of their British backers, was being gradually but irrevocably eroded. U.S. policy makers were characteristically flexible and pragmatic, but they did not, as historian David Ellwood has suggested, "undervalue the significance and weight of the Italian problem even as they were pouring large armies into the country."[33] On the contrary, once Washington had concluded that a liberalization of the regime was necessary, it pushed toward it with dogged tenacity.

In early October, Washington brushed aside British objections and facilitated the return of Count Sforza to Italy, where he would operate as a *de facto* agent of American policy. With American backing, Sforza advocated linking the abdication of Victor Emmanuel in favor of his grandson to the entry of the "Six" anti-Fascist parties into the Badoglio government.[34] The plan foundered on the king's refusal to abdicate; as Robert Murphy pointed out bitterly, Victor Emmanuel had become "*the* obstacle to the formation of a broad-based government."[35] If the king had been acting alone, however, Washington would have had no difficulty in forcing his abdication, but royal intransigence was underwritten by the British. In response to the first U.S. effort to force his abdication, Churchill argued strongly against "breaking up the present King/ Badoglio show," and in favor of postponing any major changes to the Italian political set-up until Rome was in Allied hands.[36] Faced with London's resistance, Washington backed down. In November, Badoglio formed a new government, but its new members were former civil servants recruited into a "cabinet of experts," not representatives of the "Six."

In the early fall of 1943, Allied leaders still assumed that Rome would soon be in their hands, but the military situation soon turned against them. Of the two Allied armies in Italy, the U.S.-led Fifth was exhausted after its struggle in the Salerno beachhead, and the British-led Eighth, despite receiving Polish and French reinforcements, had lost much of its drive after years of hard fighting

[31] Churchill to Noel Charles, April 20, 1944, PREM 3/241/2.
[32] See Paul Ginsborg, *A History of Contemporary Italy* (New York: Palgrave, 2003), 10; David W. Ellwood, *Italy 1943–1945*, (New York: Holmes & Meier, 1985), 47.
[33] Ellwood, *Italy*, 47.
[34] See Robert Murphy, *Diplomat among Warriors* (Garden City, NY: Doubleday, 1964) 200–201.
[35] Murphy to Hull, November 2, 1943, *FRUS 1943*, 2: 417.
[36] Churchill to Roosevelt, November 6, 1943, *Correspondence*, 2: 587.

in North Africa.[37] The Germans, meanwhile, reaped the benefit of Hitler's decision to make a stand south of Rome as they settled in to the strongly forti-
fied Gustav Line – part of the Winter Line complex – in the hill country of
the Rapido and Garigliano valleys. After forcing a crossing of the Volturno in
October and pressing slowly northward, the Allied offensive stalled out in front
of the Gustav Line. Allied troops would be there for the next six months.

Faced with this stalemate, the Allies proposed an ambitious amphibious
operation to outflank the German positions by landing behind the Gustav Line
at Anzio and opening the road to Rome. Churchill, who understood that with
the cross-Channel invasion now scheduled for May 1944 protracted deadlock
in Italy would put paid to his hopes for extended operations in the Eastern
Mediterranean, was an early and enthusiastic proponent of the Anzio operation. But the Anglo-American force that landed on January 22, 1944 was too
weak and too poorly led to unlock the strategic impasse. Instead of a rapid
breakout toward Rome, U.S. General John Lucas's Sixth Corps was forced to
wage a desperate battle simply to hold on to its beachhead, followed by further deadlock and immobility. Churchill was bitterly disappointed, complaining that while the Allies had hoped to "land a wildcat," they had managed only
to "strand a vast whale."[38] Evoking imagery of World War I as a metaphor for
hopeless stalemate, senior British diplomat Sir Alexander Cadogan observed
that the war in Italy now resembled "a Passchendaele."[39]

Irrespective of the deadlock at the front, Italian politics continued to evolve.
On January 1, 1944, the Combined Chiefs of Staff, acting on an American
recommendation that was a response both to popular protests in Italy and to
vocal criticism at home, rescinded the ban on public political activity in Italy.
Henceforth, Italians would be allowed to "participate in such political activities as do not lead to rioting and disorder."[40] Acting with U.S. encouragement,
the Committee of National Liberation in Naples overcame British opposition
to organize an anti-Fascist congress in Bari at the end of January. Derided
by London as the so-called Committee of Liberation, the congress rejected
a radical proposal that it immediately assume governmental powers, but it
unanimously demanded the abdication of the king and the formation of a government based on the six parties of the Naples CLN.[41] An executive Junta of
the "Six" was elected to pursue these goals.

The Bari Congress had a profound effect on many of the civil affairs officers, both American and British, assigned by the Allied Control Commission to

---

[37] See Carlo D'Este, *Fatal Decision: Anzio and the Battle for Rome* (New York: Harper Collins, 1986), 42.
[38] Brooke diary, February 29, 1944, Alex Danchev and Daniel Todman, eds., *Field Marshal Lord Alanbrooke, War Diaries, 1939–1945* (London: Phoenix Press, 2002), 527.
[39] Cadogan diary, March 25, 1944, David Dilks (ed.), *The Diaries of Sir Alexander Cadogan, 1938–1945* (New York: G. P. Putnam's Sons, 1972), 613.
[40] CCS to AFHQ, January 1, 1944, R363, FO 371/43836, National Archives (NA).
[41] Foreign Office to Churchill, January 24, 1944, PREM 3/240/5.

work with Italian officials. Although London remained implacably hostile to any liberalization of Italian politics, many British officers on the ground were caught up in the surge of popular enthusiasm for radical change. Psychological warfare officer I. G. Greenfield, dispatched to oversee the running an Italian radio station in Bari, caught the mood of the congress. Observing "liberation filled us with hope," Greenfield reported that his Italian coworkers believed that the defeat of Fascism "meant the beginning of a new and better world in which democratic values would reign triumphant."[42] Hauled before Control Commission head General Mason-Macfarlane for participating in the Bari Congress in violation of a military directive prohibiting attendance, Greenfield found himself the subject of only the mildest of rebukes, followed an assurance from the British general that "he would have done the same thing." Mason-Macfarlane, Greenfield concluded, was a remarkably "liberal-minded man."[43]

In January, the Bari Congress, combined with early optimism that the Anzio landings would unlock the military deadlock, convinced Washington to resume its push for political reform. Cordell Hull duly instructed American officials at AFHQ that it was now "imperative [that the] reconstruction of the Italian government on a broad political basis should be undertaken without further delay."[44] But British opposition and the souring of the Anzio operation again forced Washington to back down, with Roosevelt halting the liberalization effort on February 12, pending an improvement in the military situation.

The Fifth Army's assault on German positions at Monte Cassino in late February stimulated fresh hopes for a breakthrough, triggering a new U.S. reform effort. This time, senior British figures in the Mediterranean, including General Sir Henry Wilson, newly appointed to succeed Eisenhower as supreme commander, joined their U.S. counterparts in advocating liberalization. Mason-Macfarlane, the "liberal-minded" head of the Allied Control Commission, warned the Combined Chiefs that unless representatives of the Junta were incorporated into the government, the possibility of a "moderate solution" would slip away and Communist-led partisans would began taking matters into their own hands.[45] Wilson endorsed this argument, concluding that the Allies either had to back the Junta and move against the king, or else prepare to repress the popular opposition by force. The decision, he emphasized, could not be held hostage to "progress [in] the battle for Rome."[46] Not surprisingly, Churchill reacted vigorously to these proposals, informing the House of Commons that the Junta lacked either "elective" or "constitutional" authority," and emphasizing that there could be no new government in Italy

[42] Major I. G. Greenfield, "Memoirs of an Anglo-Italian," Greenfield papers, Imperial War Museum (IWM).
[43] Ibid.
[44] Hull to Reinhardt, January 25, 1944, *FRUS 1944*, 3: 1007.
[45] AFHQ to CCS, February 19, 1944, Map Room, Box 30, FDRL.
[46] Wilson to CCS, February 19, 1944, Map Room, Box 34, FDRL.

until Rome was captured.[47] His messages to Wilson were even more pointed, and Harold Macmillan had to take the "poor general" aside to explain "all the trouble he had got himself into with the P.M."[48] In the face of British opposition the reform effort stalled again. This time, however, several senior British officers in the Mediterranean had shown themselves to be openly sympathetic to the U.S. approach. It was striking evidence of the shifting balance in the relationship between London and Washington.

Again, the British seemed to have emerged triumphant, but again the ground was slipping away beneath them and their cherished "King/Badoglio show." In late February, the king finally agreed in principle to abdicate once Rome was in Allied hands, at which point the "Crown Prince would proceed to form a new government on a broad base."[49] More importantly, Italian working people responded to London's continued opposition to political reform by again seizing the initiative. Deftly exploiting divisions among the Allies, the Socialist, Communist, and Action parties in Naples called a ten-minute strike on Saturday, March 4 to protest Churchill's House of Commons speech attacking the Junta. The proposed strike was a somewhat tepid affair – workers were instructed to "work 15 minutes overtime in lunch hour to compensate" – but AFHQ nevertheless banned it on the grounds that it was "inimical to the war effort."[50] The three parties agreed to cancel the strike, instead calling a mass rally in downtown Naples to launch a petition campaign demanding the king's abdication and admission of the "Six" to the government. For the Control Commission, Mason-MacFarlane argued that it was "essential" that Italians be allowed a "lawful and orderly" means of protest, while Macmillan noted with characteristic cynicism "a few public meetings are a source of innocent pleasure to a people deprived of these amusements for twenty years."[51]

As this political crisis was unfolding in Naples, popular resistance was gathering momentum in German-occupied northern Italy as thousands of workers struck for higher wages, increased rations, and an end to forced labor in Germany. Led by the Italian Communist Party (PCI), these strikes demonstrated the confidence and organizational ability of its cadres in the factories. After years of enforced isolation from the collaborationist "popular front" policies emanating from Moscow in the 1930s, many PCI members believed that the strikes would lead to a generalized insurrection against the German occupation and Italian capitalism.[52]

[47] Churchill speech to House of Commons, February 22, 1944, Winston S. Churchill, *The Second World War*, in 6 vols. (Boston: Houghton Mifflin, 1948–1954), 5: 498–499.
[48] Macmillan, diary entry March 9, 1944, Harold Macmillan, *War Diaries: Politics and War in the Mediterranean, January 1943–May 1945* (New York: St. Martin's Press, 1984), 382.
[49] Wilson to CCS, February 29, 1944, Map Room, Box 34, FDRL.
[50] Wilson to CCS, February 29, 1944, Map Room, Box 34, FDRL.
[51] Wilson to CCS, March 5, 1944, Map Room, Box 34, FDRL; Macmillan to Churchill, March 21 1944, PREM 3/243/8.
[52] See Tom Behan, *The Long Awaited Moment: The Working Class and the Italian Communist Party in Milan, 1943–1948* (New York: Peter Lang, 1997).

Renewed industrial militancy among urban workers overlapped with the growth of armed resistance in many parts of the north. Organized by local Committees of National Liberation under the overall leadership of the Milan-based National Committee for the Liberation of Upper Italy (CLNAI), some 20,000–30,000 partisans were under arms by the spring of 1944.[53] Where partisans confronted forces of the Italian Social Republic, the puppet government established by Berlin after German paratroops rescued Mussolini from captivity in September 1943, the fighting took on the character of a brutal civil war. The power of the struggle unfolding in the north and its potential anticapitalist dynamic was apparent to the Allies; while cheering the "reckless courage" of the Italian workers, the *New York Times* warned darkly that the "Europe that will rise when Germany is defeated may have ideas for the future that will not always fit into the plans of the Great Powers."[54]

The rising militancy displayed by workers in northern Italy in the spring of 1944 – the *New York Times* estimated that at least 3 million people took part in strike actions – underscored for Washington the urgency of establishing a popular government that could buffer and defuse the rising tide of social protest.[55] The alternative, as Roosevelt saw all too clearly, was that Allied forces would end up using "force against the anti-Fascist leaders and groups," with unpredictable consequences for both Italian and domestic politics.[56] With strikes raging in Italy in early March, the president reopened discussion on the thorny question of reforming the Italian government, arguing that the political crisis was outrunning the prospects for a military solution, and that "major political decisions" would therefore have to be taken *before* the capture of Rome.[57] Tellingly – and, to Churchill's discomfort, accurately – Roosevelt pointed out that "both British and American" officials at AFHQ now favored giving "immediate support to the program of the six opposition parties."

At this critical juncture, Washington's reform project received unexpected and decisive assistance from Moscow. On March 8, 1944, the Soviet Union unilaterally and without prior discussion with the Allies established limited diplomatic relations with the Italian government. At the same time, and in a closely related move, Stalin sent veteran Italian Communist leader Palmiro Togliatti home from exile in Moscow with instructions to lead the PCI into the Badoglio government.[58] Moscow's actions stemmed from a desire to gain some political leverage in response to Allied efforts to deny it any real say in Italian affairs: as Stalin explained, the Soviet Union did not intend to settle for the role

---

[53] See Ginsborg, *Contemporary Italy*, 17.
[54] Editorial, *New York Times*, March 9, 1944, 16.
[55] Ibid.
[56] Roosevelt to Churchill, March 9, 1944, *Correspondence*, 3: 29.
[57] Roosevelt to Churchill, March 13, 1944, *Correspondence*, 3: 41.
[58] See Silvio Pons, "Stalin, Togliatti, and the Origins of the Cold War in Europe," *Journal of Cold War Studies* 3, no. 2 (2001).

of a being a "third, passive observer."[59] As Washington's anger at this surprise diplomatic maneuver subsided, however, it became clear that Moscow's move could help break the logjam in Italian politics and open the road to a solution of the governmental crisis. At the end of March, General Wilson reported that Communist members of the Junta had "completely changed their attitude," abandoning efforts to organize a petition demanding the abdication of the King in favor of advocating that the opposition parties join a "strong government" led by Badoglio.[60]

The Soviet Union's intervention into the Italian political crisis occurred within the framework of the evolving triangular relationship between London, Moscow, and Washington. At Washington's initiative, the Allies had since the summer of 1943 sought to involve the Russian government in Italian affairs by making it privy to discussions on the armistice. The obvious payoff, as Ambassador John Winant pointed out from London, was that "we will want to influence the terms of capitulation and occupation" once Russian armies entered Eastern Europe.[61] The Russian leadership approved the terms of the armistice with Italy in August 1943, "empower[ing]" Eisenhower to sign on its behalf and establishing the political basis for the tripartite supervision of Italian affairs.[62] This relationship was codified at the meeting of Allied foreign ministers in Moscow in October 1943, where it was decided to set up an Advisory Council – initially termed the "Military-Political Commission" – for Italy.

The Advisory Council, composed of representatives of the British, U.S., and Russian governments and of the French Committee for National Liberation, was set up to offer nonbinding political advice to the Allied Control Commission. Despite this genuflection in the direction of tripartite decision making, neither London nor Washington intended to grant Moscow a decisive voice in Italian affairs, and they made it clear that the supreme commander, acting through the Control Commission, would have the final say in all disputed questions. Moscow's participation in the Advisory Council, one Foreign Office official smirked, would burden it with a "share of the responsibility" for Allied policy in Italy, while allowing it no real say in determining that policy.[63]

While chaffing at these restrictions, Moscow recognized that they were simply part of the price of establishing a relationship with the Allies that would ultimately permit the division of Europe into clearly defined spheres of

[59] Lydia V. Pozdeeva, "The Soviet Union: Territorial Diplomacy," in David Reynolds, Warren F. Kimball, and A.O. Chubarian, *Allies at War: The Soviet, British, and American Experience, 1939–1945* (New York: St. Martin's Press, 1994), 366–367.

[60] Wilson to CCS, March 25 1944, Coles and Weinberg, *Civil Affairs*, 448.

[61] Winant to Hull, July 26, 1943, *FRUS 1943*, 2: 335.

[62] Hull to FDR, August 29, 1943, *FRUS 1943*, 2: 357.

[63] Foreign Office to Macmillan, January 22, 1944, R1167, FO 371/43836, NA; see also Geoffrey Roberts, *Stalin's Wars: From World War to Cold War, 1939–1953* (New Haven, CT: Yale University Press, 2006), 175.

influence. In this sense, the establishment of the Advisory Council for Italy built on the tripartite recognition of the CFLN in August and on Russian approval for the Italian armistice in September, and it helped pave to way to the Tehran Conference in November.[64] Moreover, the exclusion of Russia from actual decision making was at least partially offset by an outward show of cooperation that projected a powerful public image of amity and unity.

Such tripartite collaboration as was possible under the agreement proceeded rapidly. In early 1943, Moscow had dispatched senior diplomat Alexander Bogomolov to Algiers to represent Russian interests to the French CFLN, and when the Advisory Council was set up he was assigned to represent Russia on it. Robert Murphy quickly formed a positive appreciation of "Bogo," while Averell Harriman concluded after meeting him in Algiers that the Russians had finally "made up their minds to play ball."[65] In November 1943, Moscow further strengthened its representation at AFHQ by assigning Senior Vice Commissar for Foreign Affairs Andrei Vyshinsky to the Advisory Council. At Roosevelt's request, Murphy developed a close relationship with Vyshinsky and, although initially alarmed by his "ice-cold" reputation, he soon warmed to the former lead prosecutor of the Moscow show trials.[66]

The congenial relations established between U.S. and Soviet diplomats in Algiers reflected in microcosm the emerging global framework that was registered at the Tehran conference in November 1943. In many ways, Tehran (discussed in more detail in chapter 8) was a watershed moment in the evolving balance of forces within the Grand Alliance, marking the relative decline of the Anglo-American relationship and the rise of the Washington–Moscow axis.[67] With an eye to the postwar division of Europe, and having concluded that Italy would lie in the American sphere, Moscow was prepared to help Washington secure a stable and pro-capitalist Italy. Stalin's policy here, as elsewhere in Western Europe, was directed not toward establishing communist regimes, but rather at securing a divided and docile continent partitioned between the new global superpowers. The Russian government was therefore prepared to help establish a government in Italy capable of absorbing the revolutionary pressures that, as Moscow and Washington both saw, were building rapidly.[68] This was not a new position; during the mass demonstrations following the ouster of Mussolini, Moscow-inspired leaders of the PCI had explained "it is stupid and incorrect to identify this movement ... as a Communist movement ... it is

[64] See Pozdeeva, "The Soviet Union," 366–367.
[65] Murphy, *Diplomat among Warriors*, 207; Harriman to Eisenhower, November 11, 1943, Harriman Papers, Box 170, Library of Congress.
[66] Murphy, *Diplomat among Warriors*, 210–211.
[67] See Mark Stoler, *Allies and Adversaries: The Joint Chiefs of Staff, the Grand Alliance, and U.S. Strategy in World War II* (Chapel Hill: University of North Carolina Press, 2000), 165; Mary E. Glantz, *FDR and the Soviet Union; The President's Battles over Foreign Policy* (Lawrence, KS: University of Kansas Press, 2005), 155–158.
[68] See Pons, "Stalin, Togliatti, and the Origins of the Cold War in Europe," 5.

FIGURE 7.1. The "Grand Alliance" in North Africa: Mr. Teherniaguire, First Secretary of the Russian Embassy in Algiers, addresses a gathering celebrating the opening of the Stalingrad-Leningrad exhibition in Oran, Algeria, in this undated 1943 photograph. The ceremony was attended by senior Allied officers, including General Pence of the Mediterranean Base Section, and by representatives of the French Committee for National Liberation. (Courtesy of Franklin D. Roosevelt Library.)

a national movement [and] if anyone believes that the Communists are fighting for a socialist revolution then he should be locked in a cage."[69]

In reward for its cooperation in Italy, the Allies agreed at Teheran that Moscow should receive some of the spoils of victory in the form of a portion of the Italian navy. With typical acidity, Chief of the Imperial General Staff Alan Brooke observed that the deal, struck "during moments of special friendship fomented by wine," offered the British "nothing but disadvantages."[70] The vague agreement at Teheran gave Roosevelt an opportunity to demonstrate publicly his good will toward Moscow by announcing at a March 3, 1944 press conference that the Russians would get a full third of the Italian navy. To some observers, the president's comments seemed to have been made

---

[69] PCI statement quoted in *The Daily Worker*, August 7, 1943.
[70] Brooke, diary entry, January 11, 1944, *War Diaries*, 28.

"without forethought, and perhaps even inadvertently."[71] The British, who had not been consulted before Roosevelt made the announcement, were inclined to agree, not least because they were under the misapprehension the question had already been settled.[72]

When British and American leaders had discussed the matter after Teheran, it had become apparent that simply giving Italian ships to the Russians was unworkable both on operational grounds – the ships were "quite unsuited for Northern waters" – and because it seemed likely to provoke a mutiny by Italian sailors. Churchill therefore proposed to substitute Allied warships for Italian, and it was agreed to hand over to the Russians the "crewless" old battleship *Royal Sovereign*, eight destroyers, and four submarines, together with the U.S. cruiser *Milwaukee* and four merchant ships.[73] The warships were old – the destroyers were former American vessels sent to Britain in 1940 – but Churchill assured Roosevelt that they could still "steam and fight."[74] Stalin remained dubious of ships' "fighting qualities," but accepted the switch after an extended diplomatic exchange.[75] In haste to conclude the deal, London and Washington issued operational orders for the ships to sail in early February.[76]

Roosevelt's March 3 announcement of a plan to send one third of the Italian fleet to Russia therefore reopened a settled question – so settled, in fact, that the *Milwaukee* was already at sea en route to the Soviet Union. Churchill was incredulous when he received word of the presidential statement, dashing off a telegram to Roosevelt demanding, "can this be true?" and adding – in a paragraph deleted before dispatch – that "if so … it is a complete departure from all our arrangements and agreements."[77] Under this barrage, Roosevelt beat a retreat, agreeing that no Italian ships would be sent to Russia "at present" and endorsing Churchill's parliamentary statement reaffirming the substitution of British and American vessels for Italian.[78] But the question of *why* Roosevelt raised this issue at a public press conference remains unanswered. To Churchill, he implied that he had been flustered by "insistent questioning."[79] This seems implausible. Roosevelt was familiar with the detailed discussion on the disposition of the Italian fleet and he was skilled at handling the press. It seems more likely that his announcement was a piece of political theater designed to show Moscow that Washington wanted to meet Soviet demands in full but that London was blocking its generous impulse.

---

[71] Crider, "Stalin Seeks a Third," *New York Times*, March 4, 1944, 1.
[72] Halifax to Churchill, March 4, 1944, PREM 3/240/5.
[73] Churchill to Eden, January 10, 1944, PREM 3/240/5.
[74] Churchill to Roosevelt, February 3, 1944, *Correspondence*, 2: 699.
[75] Stalin to Churchill and Roosevelt, January 29, 1944, Map Room files, Box 35, FDRL.
[76] Leahy (for Roosevelt) to King, February 10 1944, Map Room Files, Box 35, FDRL; Admiralty to Flag Officer in Command, Tyne, February 7 1944, PREM 3/ 240/ 5.
[77] Churchill to Roosevelt, March 3, 1944, *Correspondence*, 3: 15.
[78] Roosevelt to Churchill, March 7, 1944, *Correspondence*, 3: 27–28.
[79] Roosevelt to Churchill, March 3, 1944, *Correspondence*, 3: 14–15.

This interpretation conforms to Roosevelt's desire to strengthen the Washington–Moscow axis following Tehran, and reflects Washington's interest in utilizing its developing relationship with Russia to strengthen its hand in Italy. Commenting on this question in late March, Harold Macmillan noted that as Russian influence in Italy – both direct and mediated through the PCI – increased, British and U.S. policy was "in danger of drifting apart"; in a caustic comment scrawled on Macmillan's memorandum, Foreign Secretary Anthony Eden observed "it is already far apart."[80]

Within days of the resolution of the imbroglio over the Italian fleet, Moscow recognized the Italian government. Taken by surprise, the Allies protested that Moscow had violated diplomatic protocol by failing to discuss its move in the Advisory Council. In response, the Russians explained that their initiative was designed to help resolve the Italian impasse and that, because the western Allies could not agree on forcing the king's abdication, Moscow would instead facilitate the Junta joining the existing government.[81] Despite its disapproval of Moscow's methods, and setting aside its concern that Russia planned to establish military bases in Italy, Washington quickly grasped that the Russian initiative would help shift the entire framework of Italian politics in its favor. Moreover, while appearing to bolster Badoglio and the king and therefore to register another success for London, Moscow's move actually prepared a solution along the lines advocated by Washington. As Averell Harriman noted, Russia's support for Badoglio "solved our difficulty" in Italy by making possible the outcome "we wanted from the beginning."[82]

Palmiro Togliatti's return to Italy followed hard on the heels of the opening of diplomatic relations between Moscow and Brindisi. Arriving in Naples on March 27, Togliatti sought to carry out Stalin's instructions to "intensify ... the war against the Germans ... by unifying the Italian people" by urging both the PCI and the other members of the Junta to join the Badoglio government.[83] Backed by the authority of the Kremlin, Togliatti drove the new course through the PCI leadership in what became known as the "Salerno switch." The new line, however, was not simply imposed on the PCI from outside; it also undoubtedly appealed to the desire of many party leaders to champion a broad process of national renewal and, after years of Stalinist leadership in the Comintern had overturned the old Leninist orthodoxies, it seemed acceptable to them to replace proletarian internationalism with Italian nationalism.[84] The results of the new course quickly became evident, and U.S. observers noted with satisfaction that Togliatti's "strong line" prevented radical socialists and

[80] Macmillan to Eden, March 21, 1944, R4999, FO 371/43836, NA.
[81] Soviet Embassy to State Department, March 19, 1944, *FRUS 1944*, 3: 1062–1065.
[82] Harriman, press conference, May 4, 1944, Harriman papers, Box 172, LC.
[83] Quoted in Roberts, *Stalin's Wars*, 176.
[84] See Allesandro Brogi, *Confronting America: The Cold War between the United States and Communists in France and Spain* (Chapel Hill: University of North Carolina Press, 2011), chapter 1.

the Party of Action from "dislocating" the government and "upsetting" the war effort; as Robert Murphy observed, for Togliatti "the war always [came] first."[85]

Many rank-and-file PCI members were less impressed with Togliatti's new line. As U.S. diplomats reported, "large masses" of Italians were responding to the social and political crisis by turning "towards communism" and the PCI was growing rapidly, leading many cadres to believe that the socialist revolution was at hand.[86] Presented with Togliatti's new and explicitly anti-revolutionary line, many preferred to think that it was all a crafty double policy aimed at accommodating the Allies and Badoglio in public while secretly preparing an insurrection against them.[87] At the same time, many Communists felt deeply ambivalent toward the United States; encouraged by Moscow to esteem Roosevelt and attracted by American modernity, they nevertheless resented the high-handed and undemocratic actions of their "liberators."[88]

The Socialists and the Party of Action were critical of the concessions to the old elite implied by the Salerno Switch, but the relationship of forces within the Junta soon forced them to follow Togliatti into the Badoglio government. Events now moved rapidly to a denouement. Acting on Roosevelt's instructions, Robert Murphy led Harold Macmillan and General Mason-Macfarlane into an April 10 meeting with Victor Emmanuel at which the king finally gave a definitive promise to abdicate once Rome fell. In an aside that demonstrates the degree to which senior British leaders in the Mediterranean now concurred with Washington's policy, Macmillan told Murphy that he was acting on his own initiative and "without specific instructions" from London.[89] Once the King had announced his impending abdication, Sforza, Togliatti, and other Junta leaders joined Badoglio's cabinet, accepting the "long terms" of the armistice sight unseen. When a "beaming" Badoglio told Murphy that the PCI had played a decisive role in bringing about the new "broad-based Liberal government," the U.S. diplomat noted astutely that Togliatti was acting as an "intelligent national patriot" rather than as a Communist.[90] He might have added that Togliatti was also acting in complete conformity with Moscow's plans and priorities.

In the summer of 1944, military developments would finally allow Washington's political plans to be brought to fruition. General Alexander's plan for a summer offensive – codenamed *Diadem* – called for a renewed assault on Monte Cassino with the goal of breaking through the Gustav

---

[85] Reinhardt to Hull, March 29, 1944, *FRUS 1944*, 3; 1082; Murphy, *Diplomat among Warriors*, 215.

[86] Tittman to State, PSF, Italy, Box 41, FDRL.

[87] See Pons, "Stalin, Togliatti, and the Origins of the Cold War in Europe," 10; Behan, *Long Awaited Moment*, 75.

[88] See Brogi, *Confronting America*, 36–40.

[89] Murphy to Hull, April 14, 1944, *FRUS 1944*, 3: 1100.

[90] Murphy to Hull, April 22, 1944, *FRUS 1944*, 3: 1103.

Line, pushing into the Liri Valley, and opening the road to Rome. Once this attack was underway, 6th Corps, now under General Lucien Truscott, would break out of the beachhead at Anzio and drive into the rear of the German Tenth Army, trapping it between the two Allied forces and annihilating it.[91] Alexander's operational orders did not specify which force would take Rome, leaving that question to be answered as the battle unfolded. There was, however, no ambiguity about the basic plan, with 6th Corps being clearly tasked with an offensive on the "general axis Cori-Valmontone" designed to block the "withdrawal of the Tenth Army."[92] Fifth Army commander Mark Clark, keen to secure approval for a U.S. drive on Rome, disagreed with several aspects of Alexander's plan, but he was clearly subordinate to the British officer in the Allied chain of command and was forced to accept his allotted role. There is no doubt that both Clark and Truscott fully understood Alexander's plan of campaign and the part their forces were expected to play in it.[93]

Operation *Diadem* opened on May 11, and one week later Monte Cassino finally fell to the Polish II Corps. Then, with the Moroccan and Algerian *goumiers* of General Juin's French Expeditionary Corps plunging through the mountains to the south, Allied forces finally began to break into the Liri Valley. On May 23, Truscott launched his breakout from Anzio, with U.S. forces driving across the rear of the German Tenth Army as Alexander had planned. Two days later, however, and with Truscott poised to block the German's line of retreat, Clark ordered him to halt his advance into the rear of the Tenth Army and to swing his forces northward into the Alban Hills and on toward Rome. "Dumbfounded," Truscott tried unsuccessfully to find Clark to have him personally verify the new order.[94] Unable to secure Clark's confirmation, he nevertheless began to execute the new order. Overcoming stiff German resistance in the Alban Hills, Truscott's troops – now accompanied by Clark himself – entered Rome on June 4. Partisans blocked German efforts to sabotage roads, bridges, and aqueducts, and Communist and other CLN leaders ensured that as the Germans pulled out, Rome passed quickly and more or less peacefully into U.S. hands.[95] Unlike in Naples, there would be no popular insurrection and no "auto-liberation" before the arrival of U.S. troops.

With Truscott's troops heading for Rome, the German Tenth Army was able to escape the trap that had been set for it. Alexander, who was not informed of

[91] See Field Marshal Earl Alexander of Tunis, *The Alexander Memoirs* (New York: McGraw Hill, 1962), especially 127ff; Shelford Bidwell and Dominick Graham, *Tug of War; The Battle for Italy, 1943–45* (London: Hodder and Stoughton, 1986), especially chapter 15.

[92] Alexander, Operational Order #15, May 15, 1944, Alexander Papers, WO 214/33, NA.

[93] See Mark W. Clark, *Calculated Risk* (New York: Harper & Bros., 1950), especially 342, 351; Lt. General L. K. Truscott, *Command Missions* (New York: E. P. Dutton, 1954), especially 368–369.

[94] Truscott, *Command Missions*, 375.

[95] See Robert Katz, *The Battle for Rome* (New York: Simon & Schuster, 2003), 308–313; Tompkins, *Italy Betrayed*, 308–312.

Clark's drive for Rome until it was too late to stop him, was naturally outraged by his subordinate's actions. Historians have generally echoed his sentiments.[96] It is clear that Clark had long been determined to lead the Allied capture of Rome: as Truscott reports, he considered it the "only important objective."[97] Despite Alexander's assurances that U.S. troops would lead the way into Rome, Clark feared that the British general would push the Eighth Army out ahead at the critical moment. Alexander subsequently concluded that the "lure of Rome" led Clark to violate his direct and unambiguous orders, and many commentators have elaborated this line, stressing Clark's vanity and hunger for publicity. There is no doubt Clark enjoyed being lionized in the American press – he held a public command conference after entering Rome that was effectively a photo opportunity – but it seems unlikely that this alone could justify the risk of defying a direct order issued clearly and unambiguously through the established Allied chain of command.

Mark Clark explained his actions by asserting that the elite Herman Goring Division had blocked Truscott's drive into the rear of the Tenth Army, and that the turn northward toward Rome offered the only opportunity for continuing the advance. Moreover, he argued, the reorientation toward Rome was permissible because the instructions given to him by Alexander's 15th Army Group were in the form of general "suggestions," rather than direct and binding orders.[98] These explanations are highly implausible. In fact, only light elements of the Herman Goring Division were present at the moment when Clark ordered Truscott to change the axis of his attack, and while the division's main force was on the move into the area, it was under heavy air attack and in no position to block Truscott's advance.[99] The planned line of advance into the rear of the Tenth Army, as Truscott himself recalled, lay "wide open" before his advancing troops.[100]

A more plausible explanation for Clark's actions can be pieced together from his own memoirs and from circumstantial evidence. When the initial planning for *Diadem* had begun in mid-April, Clark had been summoned to the United States for discussions on the upcoming offensive.[101] Traveling in great secrecy – even his wife was not informed that he would be in Washington – Clark met with George Marshall and then enjoyed a few days rest at White Sulfur Springs before flying to South Carolina to meet with Roosevelt at presidential confidant

[96] See Carlo D'Este, *Fatal Decision: Anzio and the Battle for Rome* (New York: Harper Collins, 1986), 366; Matthew Jones, *Britain, the United States, and the Mediterranean War 1942–1944* (New York: St. Martin's Press, 1996), 165.

[97] See Alexander, *Memoirs*, 127; Truscott, *Command Missions*, 369; D'Este, *Fatal Decisions*, 388.

[98] Clark, *Calculated Risk*, 357–359.

[99] See F. M. Sallager, *Operation "Strangle": A Case Study of Tactical Air Interdiction* (Santa Monica, CA: RAND Publications, 1972), 72–73.

[100] Truscott, *Command Missions*, 375.

[101] Clark, *Calculated Risk*, 335–337.

Bernard Baruch's country estate.[102] Clark recalled that Roosevelt displayed a "surprising knowledge" of the Italian campaign, offering his own ideas and "plans for reaching Rome."[103] Roosevelt, of course, did not allow written records of such meetings, and the only corroborative account is an off-the-record comment by the president at a May 16 press conference acknowledging that Clark had "come down to see me" and that they had "talked the whole thing over."[104] It is impossible to know exactly what passed between Roosevelt and Clark, but – in the context of the ongoing political crisis in Italy and the forthcoming Allied offensive – it is entirely possible that the president stressed the political importance of having *American* troops capture Rome. It would not have been difficult to get the point across given that Clark's preexisting desire to claim Rome as his prize. What Clark needed was political encouragement to do it, and protection from the resulting fallout.

Following his interview with the president, Clark held a secret briefing for senior politicians, including Vice President Henry Wallace and House Speaker Samuel Rayburn, at which he explained how he planned to take Rome. The events of the subsequent campaign would unfold, he recalled with satisfaction, in "about the way I forecast."[105] This evidence points toward Clark being given strong political encouragement for a direct move on Rome, a course of action to which he was already inclined for reasons of personal prestige. One vital consequence of acting at the president's behest was that Clark could expect some political cover for his insubordination, effectively enabling him to violate direct orders with impunity. Moreover, if Clark had presidential backing then the diplomatic strictures of the Anglo-American alliance would ensure that the real issue at stake – Washington's political interest in securing U.S. control of Rome – could not be addressed without causing a damaging Anglo-American rift. Alexander would be left to fume, and Clark's remarkable *post facto* transformation of specific and detailed orders into general "suggestions" would be allowed to go essentially unchallenged.

The political significance of establishing U.S. control of Rome quickly became apparent. As he had promised to do, Victor Emmanuel abdicated as soon as Rome was in Allied hands. On June 8, four days after the capture of Rome, Crown Prince Umberto, together with Badoglio, his entire cabinet, and Allied Control Commission head General Mason-Macfarlane, flew into the city. Everything was done, Mason-Macfarlane recalled, with the "greatest

---

[102] The date of the meeting is unclear. Roosevelt was at Hobcaw Barony, in Georgetown, SC from April 9 to May 6. Presidential logs do not record Clark's visit. As with Murphy's visit to Hyde Park before *Torch*, some sensitive meetings were simply not recorded. See "FDR Day-By-Day," FDRL.

[103] Clark, *Calculated Risk*, 335–337.

[104] Roosevelt, press conference #950, May 16, 1944, Jonathan Daniels (into.) *The Complete Press Conferences of Franklin D. Roosevelt* (New York: Da Capo, 1972), 23: 174–175.

[105] Clark, *Calculated Risk*, 337.

possible speed" to prevent the leaders of the Roman CLN establishing a "self-appointed" leftist government in Rome.[106] London concurred with Mason-Macfarlane's plan to move the government to Rome on the grounds that it would be beneficial for Badoglio and Prince Umberto to "show themselves" to the people of the capital.[107] But British officials were thin on the ground in Rome. On Mark Clark's orders, no Allied civilians were allowed into the city and Sir Noel Charles, London's representative on the Advisory Council and de facto ambassador to Italy, was left stranded idly in Naples. As a later post-mortem on these events prepared by Churchill's Private Office noted bluntly, "Sir Noel Charles was not in Rome at the time of the crisis because General Mark Clark had refused to allow any civilians to go there."[108] Charles himself explained that he had been unable to get to Rome because of "General Clark's interdiction."[109]

When Badoglio's cabinet met with the leaders of Rome CLN on June 9, Mason-Macfarlane made a few introductory comments urging them all to "sink [their] party disputes" and then withdrew, leaving them, as an exasperated Churchill complained, "to it."[110] In Mason-Macfarlane's absence the meeting took a dramatic turn as the Italians bucked the mechanisms of Allied political control and took matters into their own hands. By the end of the day, CLN leaders from Naples and Rome had pushed Badoglio aside and established a new government under former prime minister and liberal anti-Fascist Ivanoe Bonomi. Out maneuvered, Badoglio refused a cabinet post in the new government and tendered his resignation to Prince Umberto. Meeting with Bonomi the following day, Mason-Macfarlane endorsed the new government, intervening only to block Count Sforza's appointment as foreign secretary and to ensure that the service ministries remained in military hands.

As it became clear that the Italian government had been reconstructed along lines long favored by Washington, London reacted angrily. Stunned by this "very surprising development," Foreign Office Under Secretary Alexander Cadogan argued that Mason-MacFarlane should have "put the brake on hard," delaying any public announcement of the new cabinet until it had been approved in London.[111] Churchill was predictably furious, demanding that the Bonomi government be suspended pending Allied approval, and seeking to enlist Stalin's support for this maneuver. "Since when," he thundered, "have we admitted the right of the Italians to form any government they please?"[112]

---

[106] Noel Mason-Macfarlane, Notes on Chapter XVIII of Badoglio's *Italy in the Second World War*, Mason-Macfarlane papers, Reel 2, IWM.
[107] Foreign Office to Charles, June 1, 1944, R8617, FO371/43793, NA.
[108] Memorandum by Churchill's Private Office, June 14, 1944, PREM 3/241/12.
[109] Charles to Foreign Office, June 10, 1944, R9394, FO371/43793, NA.
[110] Charles to Foreign Office, June 9, 1944, R9121, FO371/43793, NA; Churchill to Mason-Macfarlane, June 11, 1944, PREM 3/ 241/2.
[111] Cadogan minute, June 9, 1944, R9122, FO371/43793, NA.
[112] Churchill to Charles, June 10, 1944, R9289, FO371/43793, NA.

Despite Churchill's bluster, the force of the fait accompli in Rome quickly became apparent, with Macmillan arguing that it was not possible to "put Humpty Dumpy in his place again after our officers MacFarlane and Sir Noel Charles have allowed him to tumble off."[113]

After talking it over with General Wilson, Mason-Macfarlane, and Robert Murphy, Macmillan reaffirmed that there was no way to "undo what has been done."[114] At the Foreign Office, Under Secretary Sir Orme Sargent added a sardonic minute to Macmillan's message, noting that the "Americans have never shared our affection for Badoglio and will not be in the least bit sorry to see him replaced by a pre-Fascist politician like Bonomi."[115] Sargent's assessment was accurate. On June 15, Roosevelt cabled Churchill, shedding crocodile tears over Badoglio's "withdrawal," but arguing that it would be a "grave mistake" to block the installation of the Bonomi cabinet, particularly because it had already accepted the "long terms" terms of surrender favored by the British.[116] Moreover, the president noted, the governmental reorganization in Rome would help "allay criticism at home and abroad of our Italian policy," adding disingenuously that any other course would "be in direct violation of our announced policy" of allowing the Italian people to "choose their own government."

Roosevelt's argument here stood in sharp contrast to his refusal to recognize the legitimacy of de Gaulle and the CFLN without electoral confirmation, but it left London with no choice but to accept what Churchill described as the "untrustworthy band of non-elected political come-backs" then in office in Rome.[117] Churchill vented his spleen on Mason-Macfarlane, pledging to prevent him holding "any post of the slightest military or political responsibility."[118] Noel Charles also came in for savage Churchillian criticism, having shown himself to be a "helpless kind of person" by sitting passively in Naples instead of defying Clark's order and going to Rome.[119] None of this would have happened, Churchill concluded, had Macmillan been in Rome.

Churchill's intemperate outbursts demonstrate that there was no doubt in Whitehall that, either by omission or commission, leading British officials in Italy had allowed the Americans to get the maximum political advantage from their temporary control of Rome. There is a good deal of logic to this argument, as a more substantial British presence in the Rome during this critical period

---

[113] Macmillan to Foreign Office, June 13, R9397, FO371/43793, NA
[114] Macmillan to Foreign Office, June 15, R9424, FO371/43793, NA.
[115] Sargent minute, June 15, 1944, R9424, FO371/43793, NA.
[116] Roosevelt to Churchill, June 15, 1944, *Correspondence*, 3: 188–189.
[117] Churchill to Eden, June 20, 1944, PREM 3/243/12.
[118] Churchill was unable to carry out his threat: recalled to Britain and invalided out of the army, Mason-Macfarlane was elected Labour Party MP for Paddington North in the 1945 general election. See Ewen Butler, *Mason-Mac: The Life of Lieutenant General Sir Noel Mason-Macfarlane* (London: Macmillan, 1972), chapter 17.
[119] Churchill to Eden, June 16 and 20, 1944, PREM 3/243/12.

would undoubtedly have limited both Washington's and the CLN's room for maneuver. It seems unlikely, however, that Washington directly organized the ouster of Badoglio in collaboration with Mason-Macfarlane and other senior British officials. For his part, Mason-Macfarlane insisted that he had been presented with a fait accompli by the Italians, and blamed "cumbrous" communications between Rome and the Allied capitals for allowing the situation to slip out of control.[120] Nevertheless, anyone familiar with Italian politics would have known that the politicians assembled in Rome on June 9, 1944 would produce some spectacular fireworks. By facilitating their meeting, Mason-Macfarlane and the Americans working with him knowingly set in motion the final act of a long-running political drama, even if the precise outcome was unscripted and unknown to them beforehand.

Mason-Macfarlane's claim that speed was necessary to avoid the Roman CLN setting up a radical government of their own in the capital also seems unwarranted. There are no indications that the Roman CLN was planning such a coup. As Mason-Macfarlane was well aware, any move of this kind would have required the support of the Communist Party and that, given Moscow's clearly stated policy, would not have been forthcoming. In contradiction to Mason-Macfarlane's exculpatory assertions, it seems more likely that the haste was necessary to take full advantage of the window of opportunity opened by the U.S. occupation of Rome: after all, General Clark could not keep British civilians out of the capital indefinitely. This was, in essence, Badoglio's own conclusion, expressed in his insistence that events were pushed with "undue haste."[121]

Even if there is no evidence of direct collusion between U.S. officials and Mason-Macfarlane, it is clear that by early 1944 several key British leaders in the Mediterranean were in broad agreement with Washington's approach to Italian politics, and that they were prepared to act on this conviction. The unfolding political crisis had convinced them that it was necessary to make significant concessions to popular militancy to head off more deep-going social conflict. Generals Wilson and Mason-Macfarlane had been advocating a thoroughgoing liberalization of the Italian government since February 1944, and by March Harold Macmillan was privately in agreement.[122] Despite Churchill's lament that things would have turned out differently had Macmillan been in Rome, it is striking that the resident minister made no effort to go to the capital or otherwise involve himself in Italian affairs at this critical juncture. Instead of challenging Clark's ban on travel to Rome and rushing to the city as the crisis unfolded, he busied himself with other matters before intervening after the event to smooth London's acceptance of the Bonomi government.[123] While

[120] Quoted in Butler, *Mason-Mac*, 190–191.
[121] Pietro Badoglio, *Italy in the Second World War* (London: Oxford University Press, 1948), 164–166.
[122] Macmillan, diary entries, March 23 and April 8, 1944, *War Diaries*, 394–396, 412–414.
[123] Macmillan, diary entries June 8–14, 1944, *War Diaries*, 459–465.

Macmillan remained in Churchill's good graces, an "unrepentant" Mason-Macfarlane returned to Britain on medical leave in July 1944. He would, Macmillan noted, undoubtedly have been fired had an old back injury not allowed his removal on medical grounds.[124]

Despite the Churchill's enmity, Mason-Macfarlane had many supporters, several of whom rushed to express their appreciation for his work in Italy. Harold Caccia, British head of the Allied Control Commission's Political Section, pointedly thanked him for his role in establishing a "broadly based Italian government," adding that it was "our monument," even if it was one sadly "[un]appreciated by those at home."[125] Captain Ellery Stone, the American second in command at the ACC, noted gushingly that the Mason-Macfarlane was the "greatest man and leader I have served under."[126] From Washington, Cordell Hull offered his gratitude, wishing the British general a speedy recovery and thanking him for his "outstanding service on behalf of this government;" tellingly, the phrase "as well as the British government" was deleted before the note was sent.[127]

These testimonials to Anglo-American collaboration at AFHQ offer striking confirmation of the degree to which leading British officials in the Mediterranean – the apparently quintessentially "British" theater – were by the summer of 1944 increasingly following a general policy course originating in Washington rather than in London. For all Churchill's bluster and vengeful slaps at Mason-MacFarlane and Noel Charles, Clark's bravura stroke, most likely pre-approved in Washington, allowed a political solution to the Italian crisis that opened the door to ever-greater U.S. involvement in Italy and to a concomitant decline in British influence. On June 5, 1944, Roosevelt broadcast to the American people welcoming the capture of Rome as an "investment for the future" that would enable the "salvage" of the Italian people to begin.[128] He knew full well that American resources and capital flowing into Italy under U.S. leadership and direction would soon redeem that investment.

[124] Macmillan, diary entry, June 16, 1944, *War Diaries*, 467.
[125] Caccia to Mason-Macfarlane, letter, August 20, 1944, Box 23, Mason-Macfarlane papers, IWM.
[126] Stone to Mason-Macfarlane, letter, August 20, 1944, Box 23, Mason-Macfarlane papers, IWM.
[127] Hull to Mason-Macfarlane, August 23, 1944, 740.00119 Italy/8-2344, RG 59, NARA.
[128] Roosevelt, text of "Fireside Chat," June 5, 1944, FDRL.

8

The Tehran Conference and the Anglo-American Struggle over the Invasion of Southern France

Two days after the capture of Rome, Allied troops began the long awaited cross-Channel assault on June 6, 1944. With the landings in Normandy underway, America's military effort in Europe became focused primarily – although by no means exclusively – on northern France and then on Germany. This simple military fact has long underpinned the notion that with the launch of Operation *Overlord*, a relieved United States finally put its diversionary excursion into the Mediterranean cul-de-sac behind it, and set off on the high road to victory long advocated by its military leaders. But if the political and economic dimensions of U.S. grand strategy are considered, this picture changes dramatically with the Mediterranean – and Italy in particular – continuing to remain central to Washington's concerns. From this vantage point, the capture of Rome and landings in Normandy mark a *broadening* of U.S. engagement with Europe on several increasingly interlocked fronts rather than a simple *switch* from one front to the other. Throughout the Mediterranean, this process increasing involved emphasizing the economic and political aspects of grand strategy over the specifically military, consolidating Washington's emerging hegemony and registering its advancing predominance over London.

Many of these elements had begun to come into focus around the time of the first meeting of the "Big Three" in Tehran in November 1943. Crossing the Atlantic in the fast battleship *Iowa* on their way to Tehran, U.S. leaders took advantage of their enforced idleness to hold a series of wide-ranging discussions. Barely ten months earlier at Casablanca, U.S. military leaders had felt themselves outmaneuvered by the highly organized British; this time they would be well-prepared and united. In forging this new unity, the president and his military leaders finally began to resolve their longstanding differences over strategy in the war against Germany.[1]

---

[1] See Mark Stoler, *Allies and Adversaries: The Joint Chiefs of Staff, the Grand Alliance, and U.S. Strategy in World War II* (Chapel Hill: University of North Carolina Press, 2000), 161.

To the relief of the Joint Chiefs, Roosevelt's enthusiasm for extended Mediterranean operations finally seemed to be waning and in their discussions on the *Iowa* American leaders agreed to make the cross-Channel invasion, newly renamed Operation *Overlord*, the "primary U.S.-British ground and air effort against Germany" in the coming year.[2] In Italy, the Joint Chiefs assumed that Rome would soon be in Allied hands, and they proposed that Allied forces should advance north of capital to a line from Pisa to Rimini, halting south of the major industrial centers. Having knocked Italy out of the war and resolved the political crisis through the capture of Rome, the primary military mission of Allied troops there would be to support *Overlord* by tying down German troops and by supplying forces for an invasion of southern France. This new operation would be organized in conjunction with the "bulk of the re-equipped French army."[3]

In turning toward *Overlord*, American leaders were explicitly turning away from major campaigns in the Balkans or eastern Mediterranean. U.S. planners argued that these areas were fundamentally "unsuitable" for large-scale operations aimed at Germany's "European fortress," adding warily that even "limited objective operations" there seemed to demand disproportionately large resources. Allied actions in the Balkans, they concluded, should be strictly limited to efforts to supply Greek and Yugoslav resistance fighters with arms and equipment; to "minor" commando raids; and to bombing strikes on strategically important targets.[4] Roosevelt approved this approach, signing off on the Joint Chiefs' proposals for the Balkans with an emphatic "Amen!"[5]

In typical Rooseveltian manner, this question was perhaps not settled quite as categorically as the Joint Chiefs might have hoped, and during the *Iowa* talks – and even more alarmingly at the Tehran Conference – the president occasionally lurched back toward the Balkans, perhaps motivated by an urge to support Soviet troops then poised to enter Rumania and, in doing so, to limit Russian domination of the region.[6] However, while Roosevelt's residual attraction to Balkan adventures continued to give military leaders some worrying moments, the overall thrust of U.S. policy codified during the *Iowa* talks was clear, and the united front between the president and his military leaders unshakable.

The strategic approach adopted on the *Iowa* was the product of the Joint Chief's vigorous and protracted insistence on the centrality of the cross-Channel assault. Temporarily deferred during *Torch* and at Casablanca, it was forcefully reasserted during the Anglo-American conferences at Washington

---

[2] JCS Operational Proposals, November 18, 1943, *FRUS*, Cairo and Tehran, 211–212.
[3] Ibid.
[4] JCS 558, Strategy in Balkans-Eastern Mediterranean, November 18, 1943, *FRUS*, Cairo and Tehran, 210.
[5] Roosevelt meeting with JCS, minutes, November 15, 1943, *FRUS*, Cairo and Tehran, 195.
[6] See Roosevelt meeting with JCS, minutes, November 19, 1943, *FRUS*, Cairo and Tehran, 259.

(*Trident*) in May 1943, and Quebec (*Quadrant*) in August. These summit meetings approved major Allied actions in the Mediterranean – the invasion of Sicily at the former, and of mainland Italy at the latter – but they had also placed these operations firmly within the framework of a commitment to launching the cross-Channel invasion of northern France in the summer of 1944. As they approached the conference at Tehran and the preconference meeting with the British in Cairo (*Sextant*), U.S. policy makers were determined to draw a firm line against any major new operations in the Mediterranean, making an exception only for the projected Franco-American invasion of southern France. As they anticipated, securing this strategic approach would involve another fight with the British; but this time, and in sharp contrast to Casablanca, it would be the Americans who would be aided by divisions among their ally.

In the months before Tehran, significant disagreements opened up among top British leaders. After the surrender of Italy, London ordered General Henry Wilson's Middle East Command to occupy the Italian-held Dodecanese islands in the Aegean. After some initial successes, however, German troops evicted them from Kos in October 1943 and secured the key island of Rhodes.[7] Churchill demanded that AFHQ Algiers reinforce British operations in the Dodecanese, but Eisenhower refused to divert resources from Italy. Churchill's insistence on sending more troops to the eastern Mediterranean also ran into opposition from the British Chiefs of Staff. Echoing Eisenhower, Alan Brooke noted bluntly that "commitments in Italy" precluded "serious operations in the Aegean," and he lamented the time wasted arguing with Churchill over his "Rhodes madness."[8] Brooke concluded that Churchill's "frenzy of excitement" demonstrated that he was becoming "less and less well balanced," a shocking judgment that surely reflected the prime minister's profound frustration with Britain's declining strength and influence.[9]

Two major factors underlay this changing reality, and together they shaped the Tehran conference. First, 1943 saw America's wartime production move into top gear. Now, as the increasingly over-stretched British economy faltered, America's growing material preponderance substantially reinforced its voice in Allied decision making. Second, the months between Casablanca and Tehran saw the Red Army's successful counterattack at Stalingrad, its destruction of the offensive power of the *Wehrmacht* at Kursk, and its subsequent advance to the Dneiper, and with these decisive victories the strategic initiative on the Russian front passed firmly and permanently into Soviet hands. By the time the "Big Three" met at Tehran, the question was no longer whether Germany would be defeated, but when and precisely how the victory would be

---

[7] See Matthew Jones, *Britain, the United States, and the Mediterranean War 1942–1944* (New York: St. Martin's Press, 1996), 100.

[8] Brooke, diary entry, October 6 and 7, 1943, Alex Danchev and Daniel Todman, eds., *Field Marshal Lord Alanbrooke, War Diaries, 1939–1945* (London: Phoenix Press, 2002), 458.

[9] Ibid., 459.

accomplished. Moreover, as the end of the war began to come into sight, the question of "concert[ing] plans for the destruction of the German forces" was increasingly overshadowed by discussion on the contours of power in postwar Europe, and on Roosevelt's vision of a new world order guaranteed by the "four policemen."[10]

As the discussion at Tehran unfolded, it quickly became apparent that propaganda images of the three leaders in smiling amity concealed an emerging bipolarity in which Churchill found himself increasingly marginalized by Roosevelt and Stalin. As the conference opened, Foreign Office official Alexander Cadogan was aghast to hear Averell Harriman "lecturing" Anthony Eden on the conduct of international conferences; "I've forgotten a great deal more about that than he ever knew," he sniffed.[11] By the end of the conference, however, even Cadogan was forced to recognize that the Americans now held the whip hand, confiding to his diary that Churchill now pictured himself as a "poor little English donkey" squeezed between the "great Russian bear" and the "great American buffalo."[12] Unfortunately for London, Churchill's belief that only the donkey "knew the right way home" carried less and less weight. Stalin rejected Churchill's proposals for operations in the Balkans and the eastern Mediterranean – now packaged as a way to ease neutral Turkey into the war – and instead threw his weight behind U.S. plans for a cross-Channel invasion, backed by supporting operations in Italy and southern France.[13] This convergence meant that the Tehran conference was characterized by what Mark Stoler has described as an "extraordinary confluence of Soviet-American strategic interests."[14] Not surprisingly, the British took a more jaundiced view, with Cadogan observing bitterly "the President promised everything that Stalin wants in the way of an attack in the West."[15]

Soviet-American agreement on military strategy at Tehran rested on an emerging political understanding, in which Washington accepted that the Russians would be the predominant power in postwar Eastern Europe, and Moscow recognized that the United States would be hegemonic in the west. This willingness to think in terms of dividing Europe into spheres of influence stemmed in turn from a mutual recognition of the fact that, as Stalin explained to Yugoslav Partisan leader Milovan Djilas, "whoever occupies a territory also imposes on it his own social system."[16] Stalin's blunt statement reflected the simple reality

[10] *New York Times*, December 7, 1943; see also Warren F. Kimball, *The Juggler: Franklin Roosevelt as Wartime Statesman* (Princeton, NJ: Princeton University Press, 1991, especially chapter V.

[11] Cadogan, diary entry, November 27, 1943, David Dilks (ed.), *The Diaries of Sir Alexander Cadogan, 1938–1945* (New York: G.P. Putnam's Sons, 1972), 579.

[12] Ibid., 582.

[13] Winston S. Churchill, *The Second World War*, in 6 vols., (Boston: Houghton Mifflin, 1948–1954), 5: 355.

[14] Stoler, *Allies and Adversaries*, 167.

[15] Cadogan, diary entry, November 29, 1943, *War Diaries*, 580.

[16] Milovan Djilas, *Conversations With Stalin* (New York: Harcourt, Brace & World, 1962), 90.

that areas occupied by the Red Army at the end of the war would come under Russian political control, furnishing Moscow with a defensive glacis while being gradually assimilated into its centrally planned economic system. The reverse, of course, would also hold true. Countries under U.S.-led occupations would emerge from the war oriented politically toward the West and increasingly integrated into an American-dominated capitalist world economy. The genesis of this division, giving Stalin a free hand in Eastern Europe in exchange for Allied predominance in Western Europe and the Mediterranean, can be found in the Anglo-Soviet treaty of May 1942.[17] By the time of Tehran, however, it was the Americans, not the British, who were making the running on the Allied side.

President Roosevelt's approach to the Russians at Tehran – encapsulated in his notion that Stalin was "get-at-able" – rested on his acceptance of this putative division of Europe into spheres of influence.[18] Roosevelt expressed some concern over the domestic political consequences of agreeing to Russian domination of Poland and the Baltic States, but assured Stalin that most Americans would be satisfied with some modest demonstrations of local support for Soviet rule. Talking to vice president Henry Wallace after the conference Roosevelt went further, "defend[ing] Stalin's attitude to Estonia, Latvia, and Lithuania" and Russian policy toward Finland and Poland.[19] This did not sit well with Secretary of State Cordell Hull, the self-appointed guardian of Wilsonian idealism. While Hull did his best to block the codification of the spheres of influence outlined at Tehran, however, his views commanded little support within the administration. His standing on this issue can be gauged by his exclusion from the U.S. delegation to the Tehran and by the fact that Roosevelt prepared for the conference by holding a series of discussions with de facto national security advisor Harry Hopkins – a supporter of Moscow's "legitimate aspirations" in Eastern Europe – rather than by consulting the briefing books provided by the State Department.[20]

If Hull's Wilsonian idealism was out of fashion within the administration, it nevertheless conformed more closely to the liberal-democratic war aims articulated in the Atlantic Charter than did Roosevelt's pragmatic recognition of the emerging power of the Soviet Union. As such, it remained an important component of the domestic discourse on foreign policy, where liberal opposition to spheres of influence – held to typify old-style great power politics – converged

[17] See Albert Resis, "Spheres of Influence in Soviet Wartime Diplomacy," *The Journal of Modern History* 53, no. 2 (1981), 431–436.

[18] See Lloyd Gardner, *Spheres of Influence: the Great Powers and the Partition of Europe, from Munich to Yalta* (Chicago: Ivan R. Dee, 1993), 176.

[19] Wallace, quoted in John Morton Blum (ed), *The Prince of Vision: The Diary of Henry A. Wallace, 1942–1946* (Boston: Houghton Mifflin, 1973), 283–284.

[20] Robert E. Sherwood, *Roosevelt and Hopkins, an Intimate History* (New York: Harper & Bros., 1948), 641–643; Keith Eubank, *Summit at Tehran* (New York: William Morrow & Co., 1985), 238–239.

with conservative opposition to making apparent concessions to Moscow. Faced with the prospect of substantial domestic opposition to the potential postwar consequences of the relationship with Moscow registered at Tehran, Roosevelt declined to mount a public defense of the proposed division of Europe, despite Stalin's advice that he undertake substantial "propaganda work" on the issue.[21] As a result, domestic discussion on the shape of the postwar world remained wrapped, as Herbert Feis noted, in "vaguely formulated possibilities."[22] Where Roosevelt recognized the inescapable reality of the situation on the ground and was ready to make pragmatic adjustments to the actuality of Soviet power, many Americans continued to display, as Alexander Cadogan noted with the condescension of a diplomat schooled in great power politics, "an astonishing phobia about spheres of influence."[23]

A significant difference between the potential political leverage exercised by the western Allies on the one hand, and by their partner in the east on the other, also bore down on the process of dividing Europe. Simply put, where the Allies lacked any vehicle for direct political intervention within the Soviet Union and Eastern Europe, Moscow could stimulate the activity of hundreds of thousands of Communist Party members and supporters throughout Western Europe. Soviet diplomatic initiatives could thus be backed – and Allied plans disrupted – by popular mobilizations within the west. This potential, not surprisingly, reinforced Washington's long standing concern that wartime dislocation might open the road to social revolution, a fear exacerbated by the rapid radicalization of Italian politics in the fall of 1943. It also underscored the importance of striking a deal with Moscow on the shape of postwar Europe.

From this point of view, Washington's willingness to accept a division of postwar Europe that left the east under Russian domination was reinforced by the hope that Moscow would use its political influence in Italy and elsewhere to contain and tamp down working class radicalism. Roosevelt's belief that Stalin was "get-at-able" thus reflected an understanding that, as Herbert Feis put it, the Russian leader was "working for Russia rather than for the cause of international communism."[24] Stalin himself was at pains to make precisely this point, publically signaling his opposition to any extension of socialist revolution by dissolving the Communist International in May 1943 and by instructing national Communist Parties to become "radical patriots."[25]

---

[21] Eubank, *Summit at Tehran*, 484.

[22] Herbert Feis, *Churchill, Roosevelt, Stalin: The War They Waged and the Peace They Sought* (Princeton: Princeton University Press, 1967), 271.

[23] Eubank, *Summit at Tehran*, 484; Cadogan quoted in Gardner, *Spheres of Influence*, 188.

[24] Feis, *Churchill, Roosevelt, Stalin*, 275.

[25] See Geoffrey Roberts, *Stalin's Wars: From World War to Cold War, 1939–1953* (New Haven, CT: Yale University Press, 2006), 168–174; Lydia V. Pozdeeva, "The Soviet Union: Territorial Diplomacy," in David Reynolds, Warren F. Kimball, and A.O. Chubarian, *Allies At War: The Soviet, British, and American Experience, 1939–1945* (New York: St. Martin's Press, 1994), 365.

This overt abandonment of socialist revolution codified the inward-looking and nationalist character of the Stalinist regime that had been evident – despite occasional ultra-leftist binges – since its consolidation in the late 1920s. Moscow would continue to use national Communist Parties under its influence as instruments for the application of political pressure in Western Europe but, in the framework of the grand accommodation that emerged in Tehran, this influence would be used to ensure that popular hostility toward discredited social and political systems did not give rise to revolutionary upsurges. Once the framework had been established at Tehran, the details would be quickly fleshed out, with Palmiro Togliatti's return to Italy in the spring of 1944 paving the way for the entry of the PCI into the Badoglio government, the liberalization of Italian politics, and the muffling of popular revolutionary sentiment. Nor would Moscow's restraining hand be exercised simply to finesse a division of Europe with the Americans. As historian Geoffrey Roberts notes, Stalin viewed "Bolshevik revolution" in Europe as a threat to his own power as well as to that of his Allies.[26]

The *New York Times* greeted Tehran as the "Victory Conference," and columnist Walter Lippmann was struck by a new tone of confidence that was quite different from the old "nervous anxiety."[27] This new mood, Lippman concluded, was the product of America's "ample and ever-growing resources" and of the string of "victories that turned the tide of war at Stalingrad, El Alamein, Tunisia, and Sicily." Several opinion-makers drew attention to the lack of detail in the descriptions of the postwar arrangements in Europe sketched out at Tehran, but only formerly isolationist papers like the *Chicago Tribune* sounded a seriously discordant note by warning of the advance of "Red" power. This generally positive portrayal of the Tehran conference did not fare well in the early Cold War, when many commentators claimed to see a reprise of prewar appeasement in the emerging Washington-Moscow axis. In this Cold War iteration, a naïve – or worse – president sacrificed Eastern Europe to cozy up to Stalin. In particular, commentators like Hanson Baldwin and Chester Wilmot argued that the military strategy adopted at Tehran scuppered Churchill's prescient plan for a bold advance from Italy, through the Ljubljana Gap in Yugoslavia, and on to confront the Red Army on the Danube.[28]

The reality was more complex. As Michael Howard argues, the fact that the "glittering vistas" opened by the ouster of Mussolini had already begun to dissipate as the advance on Rome bogged down should not obscure the fact that by the time of the Tehran Conference the Allies had actually achieved all of their agreed aims in the Mediterranean.[29] Allied convoys could pass freely from

---

[26] Ibid., 222.

[27] Editorial, *New York Times*, December 7, 1943; Lippman, "Today and Tomorrow," *Washington Post*, December 7, 1943.

[28] See Hanson W. Baldwin, *Great Mistakes of the War* (New York: Harper, 1950); Chester Wilmot, *The Struggle for Europe* (New York: Harper, 1952).

[29] Michael Howard, *The Mediterranean Strategy in the Second World War* (New York: Frederick A. Praeger, 1968), 48, 49.

Gibraltar to Suez, saving scarce shipping resources as vessels previously forced to detour around Africa once again utilized the Suez Canal.[30] Much of the southern and eastern littoral of the Mediterranean was under Allied control, and the Italian and Balkan peninsulas were active battlefields. Allied bombers, based in North Africa and later on the airfields around Foggia, were attacking targets in southern Germany and Central Europe. Nearly fifty German divisions were tied down in Italy and the Balkans. Above all – and exactly as outlined in ABC-1 back in 1941 – the Allies had accomplished the "early elimination" of Italy.[31]

Although Rome remained in German hands, these were substantial achievements, and they were duly noted by the ever-perceptive Anne O'Hare McCormick. Highlighting the "decisive importance" of Allied victories in the Mediterranean, McCormick concluded, in an implicit swipe at the Joint Chiefs' enthusiasm for a cross-Channel assault, that it was now as "clear as light [that] no full-scale [cross-Channel] expedition" could have been launched from Britain until the "Mediterranean was safe."[32] McCormick also celebrated the role of the Mediterranean campaigns in "welding together … the British and American fronts."

In terms of the development of a strong, unified, and well-organized military command structure, McCormick's comments were undoubtedly accurate, but the unity at AFHQ concealed new lines of cleavage and contest that were emerging between the Allies. America's expanded presence in the Mediterranean involved a complex of military, political, and economic elements that necessarily began to pose a long-term challenge to the reestablishment of British hegemony in the region. From this point of view, while Tehran marked the fulfillment of the Allies' initial goals in the Mediterranean, it also signaled the deepening *divergence* between the *different* Mediterranean strategies advocated by London and Washington. The United States had not exhausted its interest in the region, as the simplistic *Overlord*-versus-Mediterranean interpretation would have it, but rather had begun to refocus it: what was rejected at Tehran was not the notion of Mediterranean operations per se, but London's proposals for extended operations in Italy, the Balkans, and the Eastern Mediterranean.

While rejecting Britain's Mediterranean plans and finally forcing London to – as Admiral Leahy put it – "fall into line" with *Overlord*, the plan of action for the war against Germany adopted at Tehran still included a substantial Mediterranean component.[33] Urged on by Stalin, initial U.S. ideas for an invasion of southern France developed into Operation *Anvil*, a Franco-American

---

[30] Simon Ball, *Bitter Sea: The Brutal World War II Fight for the Mediterranean* (New York: Harper, 2009), 216.

[31] *ABC-1*, Ross, *War Plans*, 70.

[32] McCormick, "Abroad," *New York Times*, December 29, 1943, 16. There is no evidence that McCormick's comments here directly reflected Roosevelt's thinking – their most recent meeting was two months earlier, on October 21, 1943 – but it is nevertheless likely that her assessment that the Mediterranean strategy had been vindicated would have been endorsed by the president. FDR day-by-day, FDRL.

[33] Admiral William D. Leahy, *I Was There*, (New York: McGraw Hill, 1950), 209.

landing on the Riviera to be followed by a bold advance up the Rhône Valley. Tasked with supporting the cross-Channel assault by opening the ports of Marseilles and Toulon to Allied shipping and by providing the "anvil" against which German forces in northern France might be smashed, *Anvil* also had an explicitly politico-military function. With the exception of General Leclerc's 2nd Free French Armored Division, which would land alongside the Americans in Normandy, the great majority of the French Army, much of it recruited in North and West Africa and reequipped by the United States, would enter France from the Mediterranean.

In addition to its immediate military functions, *Anvil* would therefore also open the door to the reestablishment of the armed power of the French ruling class on its native soil: American leaders recognized that the creation of a well defended government and state would be critical to the establishment of a solidly based post-occupation political setup in France. In particular, the reintroduction of substantial French forces would facilitate the disarming of partisan fighters in the burgeoning ranks of the French Resistance, thereby neutralizing potential rival centers of political power. Moreover, this last critical piece of the war in the Mediterranean would take place under U.S., not British, oversight.

The issue of the reintroduction of French forces to France was central to U.S. thinking about the invasion of southern France from the beginning of the planning process. During the *Iowa* discussions, Admiral Leahy, since his days as ambassador to Vichy a consistent opponent of U.S. collaboration with de Gaulle, expressed concern that in organizing *Anvil* the Americans would simply give the French leader a "lever with which to enhance his own position" and the firepower with which to "take charge of the government of France by force."[34] Roosevelt countered Leahy's comments by observing that while London hoped to rebuild France as a "first class power," the fact was that the French could not actually hope to achieve great power status again for "at least" another quarter century. The president's remarks underscored the idea that a relatively weak France oriented toward Washington was much preferable to a strong one allied with London, and they suggested that this goal might eventually be accomplished by backing the formation of a de Gaulle government beholden to the U.S. and dependent on it for military equipment and supplies. In subsequent discussions, and after Roosevelt had reassured the Joint Chiefs that the United States would not become directly involved in "reconstituting France," Leahy conceded that "if we want to let de Gaulle have France, then all well and good."[35]

At Tehran and at the follow-up Anglo-American meeting in Cairo, the British expressed half-hearted approval for the proposed landings in southern France, agreeing to them being spearheaded by U.S. troops withdrawn from Italy. However, as it became clear over the following months that the allocation

---

[34] JCS minutes, November 15, 1943, *FRUS*, Cairo and Tehran, 194.
[35] JCS minutes, November 19, 1943, *FRUS*, Cairo and Tehran, 254–255.

of troops for *Anvil* would weaken the campaign in Italy and effectively scupper any hope of major operations in the Balkans, London's lukewarm approval curdled into bitter opposition. The ironic result of the Tehran conference was thus that the British, the long-time advocates of Mediterranean strategy, ended up waging a protracted struggle *against* the last major Mediterranean operation of the war, while the Americans, often portrayed as opponents of all things Mediterranean, championed it. In this sense, Tehran did not curtail Allied efforts in the Mediterranean so much as it refocused and redirected them, with the resulting campaign in southern France signifying the triumph of Washington's Mediterranean strategy and the wreck of London's.

In the early months of 1944, *Anvil* became one element of in complex series of Anglo-American strategic deliberations, the unlikely currency of which was the tank landing ship, or LST. Developed after the *Torch* landings, and capable of disgorging tanks and heavy equipment directly onto a beach, LSTs soon became indispensable to large-scale amphibious operations. More than 1,000 LSTs were built during the war, most of them in the United States, but there were never enough to support *all* desired operations; consequently, their availability became a decisive element of operational planning, determining how many landings could be conducted and how large the forces involved could be. The relative shortage of LSTs thus acted as a form of strategic rationing, forcing policy makers and planners to make hard choices between competing operational plans. Moreover, given that most LSTs were produced in the United States and were crewed by Americans, control over the allocation of this scarce resource tended to reinforce Washington's voice in strategic policy making.

The shortage of LSTs was not simply the result of objective limitations on their manufacture – unlike larger warships, they were quick to build – but rather it was the product of American decisions on production priorities. Churchill raised this question in early 1944 in a letter to George Marshall in which he expressed his "deep concern" at the "strong disinclination of the American Government to ... keep the manufacture of LSTs at its full height."[36] Churchill implied that the "absurd" shortage" of LSTs was allowing Washington to use its economic preponderance to resolve strategic questions. The "shortage" of LSTs helped create a bewildering merry-go-round of logistical and strategic difficulties whose solution always seemed to favor the Americans.

At the *Sextant* conference in Cairo prior to Tehran, Roosevelt promised Chinese leader Chiang Kai-shek an amphibious assault in the Bay of Bengal – operation *Buccaneer* – in support of a planned Chinese offensive into northern Burma. Then at Tehran, the "shortage" of landing craft created by assigning LSTs to *Buccaneer* was used to justify U.S. arguments against Churchill's plans for amphibious operations in the Aegean and Adriatic. Finally, at the Cairo meeting held after Tehran, the demand for landing craft created by the

[36] Churchill to Marshall, April 16, 1944, Churchill, *Second World War*, 5: 514.

decision to proceed with both *Overlord* and *Anvil* forced the cancellation of *Buccaneer*. Lord Louis Mountbatten, the Allied commander in Southeast Asia, was now told to "do his best" with his existing forces, while the Chinese were left to fume at the deprioritization of the war in Burma.[37] For London, the new arrangement was sweetened by the fact that the LSTs released for *Anvil* by the cancellation of *Buccaneer* could be utilized in the interim to help unlock the stalemate in Italy by facilitating the landing at Anzio.

When U.S. planners first began to discuss an invasion of the South of France in the summer of 1943, they looked on it primarily as a means by which Allied successes in Italy might be used to reinforce the upcoming cross-Channel offensive. The first invasion plans, produced by the Joint War Plans and the Joint Strategic Survey (JSSC) committees of the Joint Chiefs of Staff, envisaged land-based operations launched from northern Italy, with the JSSC version suggesting that the southern campaign might actually eclipse the Normandy landings. Both plans emphasized that operations in southern France would feature the French forces rearmed by Washington. Not surprisingly, the Joint Chiefs' rejected the JSSC's challenge to the fundamental structure of *Overlord*, but they approved the general idea of a subordinate operation in the South of France designed to support the cross-Channel attack by pinning down German forces and opening southern ports to Allied shipping. The British approved this outline at the *Quadrant* conference in Quebec in August 1943, despite concerns that it might divert resources from the Italian campaign. It was agreed that the preconditions for *Anvil* would include the surrender of Italy, the elimination of all Axis forces south of Rome, and the successful occupation of Corsica and Sardinia.

As planners worked on the details of *Overlord* in the weeks following *Quadrant*, it became apparent that, in the light of U.S. commitments in the Pacific, the shortage of LSTs would preclude conducting simultaneous large-scale landings in both northern and southern France. Moreover, by the fall of 1943 optimistic projections of a rapid Allied advance on Rome had collapsed in the face of vigorous German resistance. As the prospects of achieving the necessary preconditions for *Anvil* in time to launch it in conjunction with *Overlord* receded, Eisenhower approved a new plan for *Anvil* that simply called for a one-division "threat" designed to pin down German forces in the Riviera. While Roosevelt and the Joint Chiefs of Staff continued to view an invasion of the south as critical to the speedy return of French troops to France, operational planners had already downsized it to a demonstration; by the time Allied leaders met in Cairo prior to Tehran, *Anvil* was not even on the agenda.[38]

Anvil's prospects were revived at Tehran by Stalin's enthusiastic support for simultaneous attacks in northern and southern France. The Russian leader's

---

[37] CCS minutes, December 4, 1943, *FRUS*, Cairo and Tehran, 676.
[38] Jeffrey C. Clark and Robert Ross Smith, *Riviera to the Rhine: The European Theater of Operations* (Washington, DC: Center for Military History, U.S. Army, 1993), 11.

desire for an effective "second front" was undoubtedly matched by his interest in keeping Allied troops occupied in the western Mediterranean and hence
out of the Balkans. Whatever his motives, Stalin's intervention ensured that
Anvil was incorporated into the strategic plan adopted at Tehran, duly taking its place alongside *Overlord* as one of the two "supreme operations" projected for 1944.[39] In his last major act as Supreme Allied Commander in the
Mediterranean, Eisenhower oversaw the production of a new plan for a three-
division assault in southern France that was approved by the Joint Chiefs on
December 23, 1943.[40]

Despite its revival at Tehran, *Anvil*'s hold on life remained tenuous. In January
1944, Allied planners in the combined cross-Channel planning staff (COSSAC)
in London argued that the projected margin of success for *Overlord* was so
slender that the Normandy landings had to be strengthened at the expense
of those in the south, again reducing *Anvil* to a "threat."[41] With his own eyes
increasingly fixed on the projected landings in Normandy, Eisenhower concurred. COSSAC's draft plan, submitted to the Combined Chiefs on January
23, noted that *Anvil* might make an "important contribution" to *Overlord* but
concluded that the need for a five-division assault in Normandy meant that
the southern attack could only be "maintained as a threat until enemy weakness justifies its active employment."[42] On February 7, with the difficulties of
the Anzio landings placing their own heavy demands on shipping resources,
Eisenhower noted in his diary "it looks like *Anvil* is doomed."[43]

Eisenhower's pessimism over the prospects for *Anvil* did not sit well in
Washington, where George Marshall was becoming increasingly concerned
that the supreme commander was bending to British hostility to the invasion
of southern France. In early February, Marshall cautioned Eisenhower not
to allow the "localitis" produced by working in London to "warp" his judgment.[44] Eisenhower's defensive response to Marshall's suggestion that he might
be "surrender[ing]" his convictions in the "interests of local harmony" had
the tone of a man caught in the act.[45] Marshall's intervention thus kept *Anvil*
alive, and over the following weeks Eisenhower's planners juggled with the
deployment of LSTs to maintain a two-division assault in southern France. At
the end of February, Eisenhower approved a new plan in which *Anvil* would
be launched after *Overlord*, instead of simultaneously with it, and on this basis
he persuaded the British to delay final judgment on the operation for a further
month. Eisenhower's resolve in this critical period was stiffened by a cable

---

[39] CCS #423/2, December 5, 1943, *FRUS 1943*, Cairo and Tehran, 796.
[40] JCS #639, December 23, 1943, Box 50, RG 218, NARA.
[41] COSSAC memo, January 8, 1944, Box 50, RG 218, NARA.
[42] Eisenhower to CCS, January 23, 1944, Alfred D. Chandler (ed.), *The Papers of Dwight David Eisenhower: The War Years* (Baltimore: Johns Hopkins University Press, 1970), 3: 1675.
[43] Eisenhower, diary entry, February 7, 1944, *Eisenhower Papers*, 3: 1712.
[44] Marshall to Eisenhower, February 7, 1944, *Eisenhower Papers*, 3: 1708.
[45] Eisenhower to Marshall, February 9, 1944, *Eisenhower Papers*, 3: 1715.

sent by the Joint Chiefs at Roosevelt's behest, arguing darkly that since *Anvil* had been adopted in consultation with the Russians, it could not be cancelled "without taking up the matter with that third power."[46]

Roosevelt's personal intervention into the increasingly acrimonious inter-Allied argument over *Anvil* demonstrates once again his willingness to uphold the Mediterranean dimension of U.S. strategy. In contrast to the line-up in previous rounds, however, this time the president was arrayed alongside the Joint Chiefs and in opposition to Churchill and to Eisenhower's "localitis." Despite Washington's unwavering support for *Anvil*, however, the combined effects of a shipping shortage exacerbated by the loss of five LSTs, the continued failure to capture Rome, and the necessity of reinforcing the planned beachhead in Normandy, all continued to limit Eisenhower's room for maneuver. On March 20, he reported to Marshall "*Anvil* as we originally visualized it is no longer a possibility."[47]

Eisenhower then presented this conclusion – accompanied by a rider that the "abandonment" of *Anvil* would not "lessen [the] intention of operating offensively in the Mediterranean" – to the British Chiefs of Staff.[48] Not surprisingly, British leaders embraced Eisenhower's report, eagerly informing General John Dill, head of the British Joint Staff Mission in Washington, that *Anvil* had finally been "cancelled."[49] Again the Joint Chiefs fought back, arguing that *Anvil* should be postponed rather than cancelled and stressing the importance of the operation to the Russians and the French.[50] The Joint Chief's also decided to make an additional twenty-six LSTs, previously allocated to the Pacific, available for use in the Mediterranean. This unprecedented transfer of U.S. resources from the Pacific to the Mediterranean underscored the importance Washington attached to *Anvil*, and it forced London to recognize this "earnest and sacrificial" proposal by agreeing to postpone *Anvil* rather than cancel it.[51]

This new compromise still failed to resolve the debate over *Anvil*, as British leaders seized on the assignment of additional LSTs to the Mediterranean to argue that the invasion of southern France was only one of several strategic options that would open up after the capture of Rome.[52] Privately, they complained that the Americans were using their "extra resources" to impose their own "Mediterranean strategy" by implying that the additional LSTs would "not be forthcoming" unless London agreed to Washington's plans.[53] The accusation that the Americans were using their material resources to impose their

---

[46] JCS to Eisenhower, February 21, 1944, *Eisenhower Papers*, 3: 1743–1744.
[47] Eisenhower to Marshall, March 20, 1944, *Eisenhower Papers*, 3: 1775.
[48] Eisenhower to Marshall, March 21, 1944, *Eisenhower Papers*, 3: 1777.
[49] COS to JSM, March 22, 1944, PREM 3/ 271/4.
[50] JSM to COS, March 24, 1944, PREM 3/ 271/4.
[51] Eisenhower to Marshall, March 27 1944, *Eisenhower Papers*, 3: 1793.
[52] COS to JSM, March 28, 1944, PREM 3/271/4.
[53] COS to JSM, March 31, 1944, PREM 3/271/4.

preferred strategy on the British – and in the Mediterranean of all places! – vividly illustrates the growing tensions within the alliance. In Washington, General Dill, ever sensitive to American opinion, was acutely aware of the problem British leaders were making for themselves. U.S. leaders, Dill warned his superiors in London, had offered to allot additional shipping to the Mediterranean in a spirit of "broadminded generosity," and they were "shocked and pained" at "how little we appreciated their magnanimity and how gaily we proposed to accept their legacy while disregarding the terms of their will."[54]

In early April, Churchill entered the fray, writing to George Marshall detailing his opposition to *Anvil* on the grounds that it was not "practicable" to mount an advance up the Rhône in time to "influence our main operations" in northern France.[55] Instead, the prime minister argued that the breakout from the Anzio bridgehead should be timed to "accord harmoniously" with the landings in Normandy, so that "all available forces" would "be in heavy action on both fronts simultaneously." More importantly, Churchill insisted that the main thrust of Allied operations after the capture of Rome should be "a vigorous pursuit" of the retreating Germans, backed by another Anzio-like "amphibious cats-claw" in northern Italy.

As Churchill saw it at this time, the choice facing the Allies lay between a concentrated offensive in Italy or diversion into southern France. In later iterations, his opposition to *Anvil* became associated with the idea of a strategic thrust from Italy, through the Ljubljana Gap in Yugoslavia, and on to confront the Red Army before Vienna.[56] But this was not how the debate was framed at the time, and in this sense the Ljubljana Gap plan came to offer a convenient post facto rationalization for what was in fact a much more straightforward clash of strategic priorities. Moreover, it seems entirely plausible that the great heat generated by the debate over *Anvil* was a product not of the depth of the strategic division itself, but of the fact that it represented Washington's insistence on making Allied strategy in the Mediterranean its own.

Unable to resolve their differences, Allied planners conducted a further acrimonious exchange as they struggled to produce an agreed directive to guide supreme commander General Wilson's planning for operations in the Mediterranean theater. Finally, and as it became obvious that Rome would not be captured in the near future, Eisenhower met with Churchill and the British Chiefs to hammer out a temporary agreement that was then incorporated into a new set of instructions to Wilson issued on April 19. The supreme commander in the Mediterranean was now directed to launch an early and all-out offensive on Rome; to develop an effective "threat" to pin German forces in the south of France; and to make the "best possible use" of the available shipping either

---

[54] Dill to COS, April 1, 1944, PREM 3/271/4.
[55] Churchill to Marshall, April 12, 1944, PREM 3/271/4.
[56] For a critique of Churchill's Ljubljana Gap scheme, see Howard, *Mediterranean Strategy*, 66–67.

by developing operations in Italy or by a landing in the Riviera.[57] These were very open-ended instructions, and they served primarily to postpone a final resolution of the debate over *Anvil* until after the initial battles in Normandy had secured the beachhead there.

In the weeks following the D-Day landings, the debate over the invasion of southern France resumed. U.S. leaders, who had never agreed to the cancellation of *Anvil*, now deployed powerful new arguments in its favor. First, Allied armies in Normandy faced an increasingly precarious logistical crisis: the struggle in the *bocage* country around the beachheads had given the Germans time to destroy the ports of Cherbourg and Le Havre; the temporary "Mulberry" harbors had been badly battered by storms; and the capture of the more northerly Channel ports was clearly going to be delayed. With the tenuous logistical lifeline across the Normandy beaches working at full capacity, Eisenhower and Marshall recognized that additional dock facilities were urgently needed to meet the needs of the invading armies. Such facilities could only be provided by capturing the ports of Marseilles and Toulon. Second, the capture of Rome by U.S. forces on June 4 and the subsequent installation of the Bonomi government meant that Washington's immediate military and political objectives in Italy had been accomplished, freeing U.S. units to be redeployed for *Anvil*. The Americans now had a decisive operational justification for an invasion of southern France and they had the forces necessary to carry it out.

On June 24, the Joint Chiefs proposed that the post-Rome advances underway in Italy should be halted short of the German Gothic Line defenses in northern Tuscany. Relieved of the task of attacking this new defensive line, Mark Clark's Fifth Army would detach a substantial force for the invasion of southern France. By posing the issue in terms of a direct and explicit choice between Italy and the South of France, the Joint Chiefs provoked a new round of acrimonious debate that could only be resolved at the highest level. Writing to Roosevelt on June 28, Churchill accepted the necessity of taking "speedy and effective" measures to "help General Eisenhower," but he rejected any suggestion that this required the "complete ruin of all our great affairs in the Mediterranean" that would result from the redeployment of Allied troops in Italy.[58]

Churchill's note crossed with one from the president expressing his support for the Joint Chiefs' proposal, registering his opposition to "moving into northern Italy and from there to the northeast," and urging the "consolidation" of Allied operations instead of greater dispersal.[59] With the alternative courses clearly laid out, Churchill penned an extensive exegesis of his views, developing his opposition to the "bleak and sterile … Toulon-Marseilles operation"

[57] JSM to COS, April 19, 1944, PREM 3/271/4.
[58] Churchill to Roosevelt, June 28, 1944, Warren F. Kimball (ed.), *Churchill and Roosevelt: The Complete Correspondence* (London: Collins, 1984), 3: 212.
[59] Roosevelt to Churchill, June 28, 1944, *Correspondence*, 3: 213.

in increasingly hyperbolic language and over several closely argued pages.[60] "Confronted with superior forces at every step we advance up the Rhone valley," Churchill argued, *Anvil* would fail to succor *Overlord* while "wreck[ing] one great campaign for the sake of another."

Washington replied with a detailed statement drafted by the Joint Chiefs and closely edited by the president himself. While Roosevelt's messages, like Churchill's, strove to maintain a degree of cordiality – "My dear friend, I beg you, let us go ahead with our plan" – the overall tone of the exchange revealed the deep divergence at its heart.[61] Roosevelt underscored his support for *Anvil*, and he again broadened the argument by pointing to commitments made to the Russians and the French. The Russians, Roosevelt argued, had approved *Anvil* at Tehran, and any fundamental change of plan would therefore have to be approved by Stalin. For their part, the French were unlikely to agree to the use of their troops in Italy or in the Balkans if *Anvil* were cancelled. Roosevelt's belief that Moscow would oppose major Allied operations in the Balkans, and his insistence on submitting any changes in the basic strategic plan adopted at Tehran for Russian approval, demonstrate his understanding of the practical utility of the spheres of influence that had begun to be hammered out in Tehran. No doubt with this agreement in mind, Roosevelt brusquely rejected any notion of an advance on the Ljubljana Gap, suggesting that while Allied commander in Italy General Alexander was looking in this direction for "natural and very human reasons," his ideas were at variance with both agreed-upon strategy and with practical reality.[62]

The following day, Churchill drafted a reply that revealed the central issues at stake with great clarity. After making a bathetic offer to resign "if my departure from the scene would ease matters," Churchill laid out his understanding of the basic Anglo-American division of responsibility, claiming "you would have the command in *Overlord* [and] we have to have command in the Mediterranean."[63] This division, with its insistence on British primacy in the Mediterranean, was fundamental not only to British strategic thinking, but also to its standing as an *equal* partner with the Americans. Churchill had already become concerned that the Americans were trying to subvert this division by winning General Wilson, like Mason-MacFarlane before him, to their side, and he had blasted the supreme commander for "contradicting my arguments and undermining my influence with the President."[64] Not content with bending Wilson to their will, the Americans now seemed intent on overturning British leadership in the Mediterranean by taking direct control of what would clearly be the last major strategic operation in the theater.

[60] Churchill to Roosevelt, June 28, 1944, *Correspondence*, 3: 217–218.
[61] Roosevelt to Churchill, June 29, 1944, *Correspondence*, 3: 223.
[62] Ibid.
[63] Churchill to Roosevelt, June 30, 1944, *Correspondence*, 3: 225–226.
[64] Churchill to Wilson, March 7, 1944, PREM 3/272/11.

Even as Churchill was penning this note, the British Chiefs of Staff concluded that they had no choice but to accede to U.S. demands. "Further discussion," they told Churchill in a successful effort to block the dispatch of his note to Roosevelt, "is useless."[65] The Chiefs of Staff attributed U.S. intransigence to domestic political pressure in the United States, noting Roosevelt's own observation that "I would never survive even a slight setback in *Overlord* if it were known that fairly large forces had been diverted to the Balkans."[66] But in his diary, Alan Brooke probed the bigger underlying issue, noting that:

> The situation is full of difficulties. The Americans now begin to own the major strength on land, in the air, and on the sea. They therefore consider that they are entitled to decide how their forces are to be employed.[67]

Sir Alexander Cadogan, typically precise in his appreciation of power, noted simply that "P.M. has had to give way to Americans, and we shall have to skin poor Alex [General Alexander] for *Anvil*," adding that Churchill "really had no alternative but to submit" in the face of Roosevelt's "imperious" demands.[68]

On July 1, Churchill finally relented. In another long note to Roosevelt, he reprised his objections to *Anvil*, mimicking (perhaps unconsciously) earlier U.S. criticisms of London's Mediterranean strategy by describing the Rhône Valley as a "cul-de-sac" and by observing that the movement of the rearmed French Armée B into France would allow de Gaulle to get his "talons pretty deeply dug into France."[69] Bewailing the "first major strategic and political error for which we two have been responsible," Churchill concluded weakly "we shall do our best to make a success of anything that is undertaken." The following day the Combined Chiefs issued operational orders to General Wilson to launch a three-division invasion of southern France by August 15. Churchill launched a final, incoherent attack on *Anvil* in early August when he tried to persuade Eisenhower to switch the assault from the Riviera to Bordeaux. He finally conceded defeat on August 11, just in time to arrive off the coast of the Riviera in a Royal Navy destroyer as American landing craft headed for the shore to begin the invasion, now renamed Operation *Dragoon*.

[65] COS to Churchill, June 30, 1944, PREM 3/271/8.
[66] Roosevelt to Churchill, June 29, 1944, *Correspondence*, 3: 223.
[67] Brooke, diary entry, June 30, 1944, *War Dairies*, 564.
[68] Cadogan diary entries, June 30 and July 6, 1944, *War Diaries*, 644–645.
[69] Churchill to Roosevelt, July 1, 1944, *Correspondence*, 3: 227–229.

9

Invasion, Insurrection, and Political Settlement in France

The question of the participation of French troops in the freeing of their country from German occupation posed Allied policy makers with something of a dilemma. Since the *Trident* conference in May 1943, they had recognized that it was "politically ... of great importance" to have French troops "represented" in the forthcoming invasion.[1] At the same time, however, planners were distinctly unenthusiastic about having substantial forces under Gaullist command too close to the main center of action in Normandy, fearing that their presence would limit the Allies' political room for maneuver. Only one French division was included in the order of battle for *Overlord* and, although popular support, de Gaulle's persistence, and the importance of mastering Paris, would finally force the Allies to make concessions to the Free French in the north, the great bulk of the French army entered the country via the *Dragoon* landings in the south. The opening of what Eisenhower described as a southern "gateway ... into France" through which the French troops rearmed by the United States in North Africa might pass was therefore seen as central aspect of *Anvil/Dragoon* from early in the planning process.[2] Without this gateway, Eisenhower concluded, "all of our French investment [would] have been wasted".

The French troops based in Algiers and slated to take part in *Dragoon* were organized into *Armée B*, under the command of Marshal Jean de Lattre de Tassigny, in December 1943. De Lattre summed up the political importance of his assignment by noting that his army was a "living representation of the whole empire" charged with "bringing freedom to the homeland and restoring

---

[1] Conference minutes, May 24, 1943, *FRUS*, Washington and Quebec, 191; see also G. E. Maguire, *Anglo-American Policy towards the Free French* (New York: Palgrave Macmillan, 1995).
[2] Eisenhower to Marshall, January 17, 1944, Alfred D. Chandler (ed.), *The Papers of Dwight David Eisenhower: The War Years* (Baltimore: Johns Hopkins University Press, 1970), 3: 1662.

FIGURE 9.1. French paratroops with U.S.-supplied uniforms and equipment on parade in Rabat, Morocco, September 14, 1943. (Courtesy of Franklin D. Roosevelt Library.)

it to its place in the world."[3] *Armée B* would also be responsible for assimilating members of the Resistance – the *Maquis* – into the armed forces of the reconstituted French state, a task critical to establishing the stability and popular legitimacy of the new government.[4] In early 1943, resistance leader Jean Moulin had succeeded in forming the *Conseil National de la Resistance* (CNR), bringing the five disparate resistance organizations operating in France under the overall direction of the CFLN. Political tensions nevertheless continued to plague relations between the combatants in France and the leadership in Algiers, and to disrupt the work of the Council itself.

Based on the port city of Marseilles, the southern Resistance had a markedly left-wing slant, with the Communist Party's guerilla fighters, the *Francs-Tireur*

[3] Jean de Lattre de Tassigny, *History of the French First Army* (London: George Allen and Unwin, 1952), 30–31.
[4] See Arthur Layton Funk, *Hidden Ally: The French Resistance, Special Operations, and the Landings in Southern France, 1944* (Westport, CT: Greenwood Press, 1992), especially Part One.

et Partisans, being particularly active.[5] As S. Pinkney Tuck, the newly appointed American consul in Marseilles reported in 1942, the Communist-led resistance was the "best organized outfit in France."[6] The development of Resistance activity in southern France overlapped with a revival of popular political protest. In July 1943, 50,000 people took to the streets of Marseilles to protest the German occupation, and in early 1944 underground Socialist and Communist cadres helped organize a series of strikes protesting food shortages. As in Italy, Allied planners were inclined to see such actions as harbingers of dangerous political instability and, in addition to helping to expel the Germans from southern France, they tasked *Armée B* with establishing political order in this volatile region. In particular, they hoped to head off the prospect of local Resistance forces seizing the insurrectionary moment to establish rival centers of political power.

General Eisenhower, now with experience of the complexities of North Africa and Italy under his belt, was well aware of the political side of his responsibilities as supreme commander, and before leaving the Mediterranean to assume command of the preparations for *Overlord* he worked to establish a working relationship with de Gaulle. In late December, U.S. ambassador to the CFLN Edwin Wilson and British resident minister Harold Macmillan visited de Gaulle to discuss the outline plan for Operation *Anvil*. This meeting produced an initial agreement on the involvement of French troops in *Anvil*, organized under the overall authority of the Combined Chiefs of Staff and the operational direction of the Allied Supreme Commander in Europe. With this agreement in place, Eisenhower and de Gaulle exchanged cordial Christmas greetings, with the former observing hopefully that the "misunderstandings" that had long disrupted collaboration between AFHQ and the CFLN had now been "largely eliminated."[7]

Before Eisenhower left the Mediterranean for SHAEF, he and de Gaulle followed their exchange of seasonal niceties with a face-to-face meeting on December 30. Described by Harry Butcher as a "love fest," the meeting built on initial discussions with Wilson and Macmillan by establishing – at least according to de Gaulle's recollection of events – that in the "political sphere" the supreme commander would recognize no French force other than the CFLN.[8]

---

[5] See Hilary Footitt, *War and Liberation in France: Living with the Liberators* (New York: Palgrave Macmillan, 2006), 99–104.

[6] Tuck to Matthews, August 20, 1942, in David Mayers, *FDR's Ambassadors and the Diplomacy of Crisis: From the Rise of Hitler to the End of World War II* (Cambridge: Cambridge University Press, 2013), 154.

[7] Eisenhower to de Gaulle, December 29, 1943, *Eisenhower Papers*, 3: 1637.

[8] Butcher, diary entry, January 20, 1944, Harry C. Butcher, *My Three Years with Eisenhower: The Personal Diary of Captain Harry C. Butcher, USNR, Naval Aide to General Eisenhower, 1942 to 1945* (New York: Simon and Schuster, 1946), 473; Charles de Gaulle, *The War Memoirs of Charles de Gaulle: Unity, 1942–1944*, trans. Richard Howard (New York: Simon and Schuster, 1959), 240–241.

If de Gaulle's version is accurate, and Eisenhower's subsequent actions suggest that it is, the supreme commander was effectively pledging to recognize the CFLN as the provisional government of France. Butcher also noted that de Gaulle's desire for closer military collaboration with the Allies stemmed in part from his fear of the "radical and Communist elements" that had gathered in his "coterie of supporters" in Algiers and in the Resistance movement in France.[9] On this question, Allied leaders and de Gaulle were in full agreement.

Shortly after arriving in London to take command of SHAEF, and buoyed by his cordial new relationship with de Gaulle, Eisenhower pushed for an "immediate crystallization of plans relating to civil affairs in Metropolitan France."[10] Sketching an approach to civil affairs modeled on that pursued in Italy, Eisenhower suggested that while "military control" should be maintained in combat zones, areas "not essential for military operations" should be "turn[ed] over to French control at the earliest possible date." This approach, of course, assumed the presence of "properly accredited French authorities" ready to take political control, and here Eisenhower "assume[d]" that "such authorities will be representatives of the Committee of National Liberation."[11] Building on the collaboration with de Gaulle begun in Algiers, Eisenhower proposed that the French leader be asked to assign a delegation of CFLN leaders to work out the details of this arrangement directly with SHAEF in London. Eisenhower's chief of staff Bedell Smith underscored the point in a note to Civil Affairs Division head General John Hilldring explaining that, while he was not particularly "pro-de Gaulle," some French "vehicle" would be required to handle civil affairs after the invasion, and he "didn't see a better one" than the CFLN.[12]

Eisenhower's and Smith's arguments for structuring post-invasion French politics in collaboration with de Gaulle and the CFLN reflected their own increasing confidence in handling political affairs. But, if their approach seemed commonsensical at SHAEF, its implied recognition of the CFLN as the provisional government of France did not find approval in Washington.[13] Writing to Eisenhower at the end of January, Assistant Secretary of War John McCloy explained that Roosevelt supported taking "whatever steps you feel desirable to make this resistance as helpful to you as possible," but warned that no decisions had yet been taken on "matters of civil administration."[14]

---

[9] Ibid.

[10] Eisenhower to Combined Chiefs of Staff and Combined Civil Affairs Committee, January 19, 1944, *Eisenhower Papers*, 3: 1667.

[11] Ibid.

[12] Smith to Hilldring, January 7, 1944, Harry L. Coles and Albert K. Weinberg, *Civil Affairs: Soldiers Become Governors* (Washington, DC: Office of the Chief of the Military History Department of the Army, 1964), 665.

[13] For a new and clear-sighted discussion of Franco-American relations in this critical period, see Charles L. Robertson, *When Roosevelt Planned to Govern France*, (Amherst: University of Massachusetts Press, 2011), especially chapters 4, 5, and 6.

[14] McCloy to Eisenhower, January 25, 1944, Coles and Weinberg, *Civil Affairs*, 666.

McCloy's note conveyed an uneasy dualism in Washington's policy, approving close military cooperation with the CFLN and the Resistance, while avoiding recognizing the committee as the provisional government of France. This approach was codified in a March 15 presidential memorandum authorizing Eisenhower to determine "where, when, and how the Civil Administration in France shall be exercised by French citizens," and to work with the CFLN on the selection and installation of local civilian administrations.[15] At the same time, however, Eisenhower was instructed not to "deal exclusively with said Committee," and to ensure that his actions did not imply any recognition of the CFLN as "the government of France, even on a provisional basis."

Eisenhower, who believed that *Overlord* "very badly" needed the support of the CFLN-led Resistance, lamented that the presidential directive threw the question of political power "back in my lap" while prohibiting the one act – the recognition of the CFLN as a provisional government – that would make genuine collaboration possible.[16] Leading administration figures including Cordell Hull, who gave a speech on April 9 explaining that he was now "disposed" to see de Gaulle "exercise leadership," tried unsuccessfully to persuade Roosevelt to recognize the CFLN as a government-in-exile.[17] His continued refusal to do so meant that the Allied invasion of France would be conducted in something of a political vacuum. Roosevelt again cited allegedly immutable principles of sovereignty and legitimacy to justify his view that the CFLN could not be recognized as a provisional government, explaining that "no existing group outside of France" could be given "domination over the French people" lest it prejudice the "free expression of a choice" in a postwar election.[18] Roosevelt does not seem to have felt it necessary to square this decision with his own recognition of the legitimacy of regimes headed by Franco, Pétain, Darlan, and Badoglio, all of which governed – and were recognized by the United States – without recourse to elections.

The dual track character of U.S. policy created particular problems for the operational control of French forces. At their meeting with Wilson and Macmillan in December, CFLN leaders had welcomed the inclusion of substantial French forces in Allied plans for *Anvil*, and had agreed to place them under Eisenhower's operational control and under the overall command of the Combined Chiefs of Staff. But problems arose when it came to detailing the terms of this agreement. On March 11, Allied military leaders instructed General Henry Wilson, now supreme commander in the Mediterranean, to explain to the French that their forces would be placed under the control of

[15] Roosevelt to Eisenhower, March 15, 1944, Coles and Weinberg, *Civil Affairs*, 667–668.
[16] Eisenhower, diary entry, March 22, 1944, *Eisenhower Papers*, 3: 1784.
[17] Cordell Hull, *The Memoirs of Cordell Hull* (New York: Macmillan, 1948), 2: 1429; see also Julian G. Hurstfield,. *America and the French Nation, 1939–1945* (Chapel Hill: University of North Carolina Press, 1986), 212.
[18] Roosevelt to Eisenhower, May 13, 1944, Coles and Weinberg, *Civil Affairs*, 670.

the Combined Chiefs of Staff as the result of an agreement between two *committees*, the CCS itself and the CFLN. This was unacceptable to the French, who pointed out that the Combined Chiefs had been established by agreement between the British and U.S. *governments*, and that the placing of French troops at its disposal must similarly – and logically – involve a government-level political agreement between the CFLN and the Allies.[19]

Not surprisingly, this French counter-proposal was unacceptable in Washington, where it was viewed as a backdoor maneuver to establish the CFLN as the provisional government of France. Writing to George Marshall, Roosevelt argued that command arrangements had to be made solely on the basis of agreement between the Supreme Commander and the CFLN, and not between "one sovereign government in full possession of its sovereignty and another government that has no *de facto* sovereignty."[20] It is striking that Roosevelt used the word "government" in the singular; British members of the Combined Chiefs were, like the Foreign Office, inclined toward recognizing the governmental authority of the CFLN. With the Combined Chiefs divided, the issue remained unresolved, and the invasions of France in June and August 1944 took place without any formal agreement on the operational control of French troops.[21] This fudge was, perhaps, Roosevelt's preferred solution: when the Joint Chiefs discussed the matter again in September, the president simply noted "I think this can be further delayed," arguing that it was still "premature" to resolve the question at the "political level."[22]

Much had been made of Roosevelt's antipathy toward de Gaulle, and there is no reason to doubt the depth of his personal animosity. Roosevelt's correspondence is studded with acerbic comments about the French leader, of which his sarcastic expectation that de Gaulle would "perform … in accordance with his previous record of lack of cooperation in our effort to liberate France" during his July 1944 visit to Washington is typical.[23] But great affairs of state are rarely determined by personal animosities, and Washington's policy toward France was not driven by Roosevelt's dislike of de Gaulle. De Gaulle symbolized the restoration of a strong and independent France, a goal that was antithetical to Washington's pursuit of a relatively weak nation oriented toward the United States. It was this substantive policy question that drove the personal animosity, not vice versa . For his part, de Gaulle recognized that Roosevelt sought an "American peace" in which the United States would be the "savior and arbiter" of France and that France's revival as a "sovereign and independent nation … in the heat of battle" would necessarily "thwart [these]

[19] See Marcel Vigneras, *Rearming the French* (Washington, DC: Center for Military History, United States Army, 1989), 149–151.
[20] Roosevelt to Marshall, March 28, 1944, quoted in Vigneras, *Rearming the French*, 150.
[21] See Vigneras, *Rearming the French*, 151.
[22] Roosevelt to Leahy, September 22, 1944, Box 50, RG 218, NARA.
[23] Roosevelt to Churchill, June 9, 1944, *Correspondence*, 3: 173.

intentions."[24] Roosevelt's refusal to recognize a CFLN provisional government left open the possibility that political forces capable of blunting the perceived dangers Gaullism might yet emerge, possibly led by former president Albert Lebrun or even, as Leahy suggested, by Pétain himself.[25] "Premature" recognition of a CFLN provisional government would foreclose on this possibility, locking Washington into de facto support for Gaullist revanchism.

The fact that events did not work out quite as Roosevelt had hoped – there was simply no credible force in French politics able and willing to challenge de Gaulle – does not mean that his policy, judged by its own lights, was erroneous. Washington's refusal to recognize the CFLN, first as a government-in-exile and then as a provisional government, kept Washington's options open for as long as possible, and at no great cost. While de Gaulle chafed against the fact that Washington's combination of political nonrecognition and military collaboration effectively codified France's dependent status, he was realist enough to recognize that without American assistance his stirring image of France reborn in the flames of battle had little substance. Without substantial U.S. aid, he lacked the material resources to realize his vision, particularly in the face of a potential challenge from the left. De Gaulle could not walk away from the Americans, however vexations their treatment of him might be; without American support offered on American terms, de Lattre's army would have been left sitting in North Africa, unarmed, ill-trained, and without the means to return to metropolitan France. As it was, these issues would now be resolved in the context of the unfolding Allied invasion of France.

In early August 1944, the resolution of the final great Anglo-American battle over Mediterranean strategy allowed the Franco-American invasion of the South of France to move forward. On August 1 – barely two weeks before the landing – AFHQ Caserta established the 6th Army Group, composed of the American Seventh Army and de Lattre's *Armée B*, under the command of American General Jacob Devers.[26] Enjoying overwhelming air superiority, American bombers of the 15th Air Force had already begun disrupting road and rail communications throughout southern France. On the ground, the *Force Françaises de l'Interior* (FFI) – composed of the Communist-led *Francs-tireurs et Partisans* (FTP) and the Gaullist AS (*Armée Scrète*) – intensified its attacks on German outposts. In May, AFHQ had established the Special Project Operations Center (SPOC) at Algiers, tasked with expanding Allied assistance to the Resistance.[27] SPOC's activities ranged from the dispatch of

[24] De Gaulle, *Unity*, 88–89; for an extended discussion on this question, see Jean Lacoutre, *De Gaulle: The Rebel, 1890–1944*, trans. Patrick O'Brian (New York: W. W. Norton, 1993), chapter 27.

[25] On Allied approaches to Lebrun in the summer of 1943, see de Gaulle, *Unity*, 182–183; on schemes involving Petain, see Robertson, *When Roosevelt Planned to Govern France*, especially 181.

[26] AFHQ moved from Algiers to the Bourbon palace at Caserta, near Naples, in July 1944.

[27] See Funk, *Hidden Ally*, 32–35.

three-man "Jedburgh" teams assigned to collaborate with the Resistance on specific projects, to the deployment of platoon-sized OSS Operational Groups. Provided with weapons by Allied airdrops and by disarming German soldiers, and backed by SPOC teams, FFI fighters provided invaluable assistance to the invading armies throughout Operation *Dragoon*. They would also play a crucial role in shaping post-occupation politics.

On August 15, the three experienced divisions of Lucian Truscott's VI Corps began landing on the Riviera, backed by *Armée B*'s three divisions and an armada of nearly 1,000 ships.[28] U.S. and French troops beat off a weak German counterattack and, in contrast to the desperate beachhead battles at Salerno, Anzio, and in Normandy, began moving quickly inland. As *Dragoon* got underway, the long-awaited break out from Normandy was gathering momentum, creating a dangerous situation for German troops throughout southern France. On August 18, Hitler ordered German forces to abandon the Riviera and to begin a general withdrawal up the Rhône Valley, leaving behind only the garrisons of Marseilles and Toulon to delay the Allied advance and to wreck the port facilities. Allied troops pressed rapidly up the Rhône Valley; far from becoming a "cul-de-sac" as Churchill had warned, the valley offered 6th Army Group a broad avenue of advance into central France. On September 10, having fought their way through several rearguard actions and captured more than 100,000 German soldiers, advance elements of the Seventh Army linked up with patrols from General Patton's Third Army near Dijon.

Under the pressure of events, several of the most vexatious issues in Allied-French relations had begun to be resolved during the six-week interval between D-Day and *Dragoon*.[29] A week after the Normandy landings, the Allies finally allowed de Gaulle to visit France, where he made his way to an enthusiastic popular reception Bayeux.[30] Seizing the moment, de Gaulle presented himself to the large crowd as the president of a free France. Then, after appointing a top aide as the new government's commissioner in Normandy, he returned to Britain. Allied officers were blindsided by de Gaulle's audacity, but – faced with undeniable evidence of his popularity and authority – they quickly reconciled themselves to the fait accompli. Although both London and Washington refused to accord the emerging Provisional Government formal diplomatic recognition, increasing collaboration between Allied officers and officials of the new regime, first at local and then at regional and national levels, quickly

---

[28] See Jacob L. Devers, "Operation Dragoon: The Invasion of Southern France," *Military Affairs* 10, no. 2 (Summer 1946), especially 11; for an overall account of the *Dragoon* landings and subsequent operations, see Rick Atkinson, *The Guns at Last Light: The War in Western Europe, 1944–1945* (New York: Henry Holt, 2013), 189–219.

[29] See Maguire, *Anglo-American Policy*, 132.

[30] See Hilary Footitt and John Simmonds, *France 1943–1945* (New York: Holmes & Meier, 1988), 71–73.

established the overall political framework within which the next stages of the invasion of France would unfold.[31]

These developments in Normandy simplified the political dimensions of *Dragoon*. As U.S. and French troops pushed inland after the initial landings in the Riviera, they encountered FFI fighters and local CFLN leaders who had stepped up to fill the political vacuum created by the rapid collapse of the German occupation. The chief civil affairs officer of the American 36th Division reported enthusiastically that the invading army was "moving so fast we cannot set up [i.e. establish military governments] all towns falling into our hands," adding that the FFI was "doing a wonderful job of German collaborator and political cleanup."[32] The political situation, he concluded, "looks to be alright." Similar assessments multiplied in the following days, with Seventh Army reporting to AFHQ Caserta "in each town the FFI was completely organized and prepared to take over the government, install a Marie, and care for civilian needs."[33] Throughout the region, many such transitions took place as local political power passed seamlessly into the hands of the CFLN. By mid-September, Seventh Army civil affairs officers were sufficiently confident of the political situation to give up any attempt to establish Allied military governments even in frontline areas, replacing them with small groups of liaison officers assigned to work with the new French authorities.[34]

As American troops swung northward up the Rhône, much of de Lattre's *Armée B* turned west toward Toulon and Marseilles. These cities, with their port facilities and their large, well-organized, and militant working classes, were critical to the overall strategic, military, and political goals of the entire campaign.[35] Their importance was further underscored by events further north. On August 18, with *Dragoon* underway and as Allied troops fought to close the last escape routes available to German forces in Normandy, a general strike broke out in Paris. The following day, FFI fighters in the capital launched an armed revolt against the German occupation forces. Although largely unplanned, the power of the uprising, and the prominence of Communist activists within it, alarmed both Allied leaders and CFLN officials. Abandoning earlier plans to bypass Paris, Eisenhower ordered General Philippe Leclerc's 2nd Free French Armored Division to advance directly into the city. There was a special urgency to Leclerc's mission, as a temporary ceasefire agreed between FFI fighters and German General Dietrich von Cholitz was set to expire in two days, and a resumption of fighting in the capital could have unpredictable

---

[31] See Julian Jackson, *France: The Dark Years, 1940–1944* (Oxford: Oxford University Press, 2001), 551–553.

[32] CAO, 36th Div., n.d., Coles and Weinberg, *Civil Affairs,* 757.

[33] Seventh Army to AFHQ, August 18, 1944, Coles and Weinberg, *Civil Affairs,* 757.

[34] Official History of CA Operations in Southern France, quoted in Coles and Weinberg, *Civil Affairs,* 754.

[35] See Footitt, *War and Liberation,* 102.

FIGURE 9.2. French Resistance fighters on parade in Toulon, summer 1944. (Courtesy of Franklin D. Roosevelt Library.)

military and political consequences. As the 2nd Armored Division advanced, Leclerc met with de Gaulle at Rambuillet. Both French leaders clearly understood the stakes: urging haste, de Gaulle insisted bluntly "we can not have another Commune".[36]

On August 24, Leclerc's French troops swept into Paris, overcoming rapidly weakening German resistance and encountering a tumultuous popular reception as they advanced toward the city center. The following day, Leclerc accepted von Cholitz's capitulation in the name of the Provisional Government, grudgingly allowing Parisian FFI leaders to add their signatures to the articles of surrender. De Gaulle arrived in Paris later the same day, and he marched in triumph down the Champs-Elysées to a mass in Notre Dame on August 26. Defying orders from his U.S. superiors to move out of Paris in pursuit of the Germans, Leclerc deployed his troops along the line of the parade. With his political standing reinforced by control of the capital, de Gaulle quickly reestablished Paris as the seat of new Provisional Government of the French Republic. At the same time, he distanced himself from local Resistance forces by arguing that his authority

---

[36] De Gaulle, quoted in John Keegan, *Six Armies in Normandy: From D-day to the Liberation of Paris, June 6–August 25 1944* (New York: Viking Press, 1982), 306.

and legitimacy derived from decisions of the CFLN in Algiers and not from the domestic insurrection. Visiting Paris, Eisenhower readily agreed that the 2nd Armored Division should remain temporarily in the city to help secure the new government against any potential domestic challenge.

On the same day that workers began to move into action in Paris, Resistance leaders in Marseilles initiated a general strike. FFI fighters, many wearing the armband of the Communist-led FTP, were soon operating openly in the city. On August 21, the Vichyite regional prefect was arrested, and a new Departmental Liberation Committee proclaimed the end of the collaborationist regime and the triumph of the "general insurrectional strike."[37] Two days later, regular French forces, spearheaded by the *gourmiers* of the 7th *Régiment Tirailleurs Algeriens*, were in de Lattre's words "literally … drawn in" to the city by huge crowds.[38] It took several more days of heavy fighting before the army and the FFI finally overcame the last German units ensconced in strong waterfront bunkers, but by August 27 – and more than a month ahead of schedule – Marseilles was in French hands. As historian Hilary Footitt explains, in Marseilles as in Paris the French people "reconquer[ed] their urban space" by tearing down symbols of the occupation and establishing new organs of government.[39] Even before the fighting was over, local newspapers began to appear, marking the reemergence of public political discourse and giving it a strongly radical bent.

As they prepared for the forthcoming occupation of Marseilles, U.S. civil affairs officers had been wary of the potential challenges posed by a city whose population, according to the official army history, was composed of the "dregs of six continents" and the "flotsam of many races."[40] In the event, the auto-liberation of Marseilles reduced U.S. civil affairs officers to virtual bystanders, reporting on events but exercising little control over them. Entering Marseilles under small arms fire with a detachment of the 2678th Civil Affairs Regiment on August 25, Colonel Henry Parkman reported that "Resistance elements seem to be in control of the departmental and municipal governments and appear to be working well."[41] As urban life returned to "normalcy," with side-walk debris cleared and stores reopened, U.S. officials noted that law and order was in the hands of the FFI, with "truck loads [of] Vichyites [being] carried away to 'imprisonment.'"[42]

The overwhelming predominance of political forces associated with the CFLN meant that the big questions of civil government in the south were quickly settled, leaving U.S. officers to concentrate on arranging supplies of food and medicine, and on working to reopen port facilities to Allied shipping. As soon

[37] Footitt, *War and Liberation*, 99.
[38] De Lattre, *French First Army*, 101.
[39] Footitt, *War and Liberation*, 99.
[40] Official History of CA Affairs, Coles and Weinberg, *Civil Affairs*, 762.
[41] Parkman to Seventh Army, August 25, 1944, Coles and Weinberg, *Civil Affairs*, 761.
[42] 2678th CA Regt. to AFHQ, August 27, 1944, Coles and Weinberg, *Civil Affairs*, 763.

as German resistance in the Marseilles was overcome, U.S. military engineers of the Continental Base Section began work on the docks. Army civil affairs officers hired more than 12,000 French civilian workers to help with the work of clearing the extensive damage caused by battle and by German sabotage. These efforts ran into numerous difficulties. U.S. officials complained bitterly about the "notorious laziness" of the Marseilles workers who, echoing similar complaints against Arab workers in North Africa, they claimed demanded two-hour lunch breaks and refused to work in the rain.[43] For their part, French workers, who had seen wage levels driven relentlessly down under the Vichy regime, took the opportunity to join the Communist-led *Confédération Général du Travail* and to press for better wages and conditions, resulting in considerable "worker unrest" numerous "spontaneous stoppages."[44]

In early October, U.S. officials finally sidestepped these problems by turning responsibility for the hiring and payment of dockyard workers over to the French authorities.[45] They also sought to counter labor militancy by setting 14,000 Italian prisoners of war to work in the Marseilles docks, a policy approved by French officials with the proviso that none of the existing workforce would be discharged.[46] Despite these difficulties, the rehabilitation of the port moved quickly, and Allied ships began unloading on September 15, 1944. By the end of the month, eighteen berths were operational and military supplies were pouring in. Between September and November 1944, the ports of Marseilles and Toulon handled some 40 percent of the total tonnage of military equipment discharged in France, and although this percentage declined after the opening of Antwerp in December, the southern ports continued to make a major contribution to Allied logistical operations.

By October 1944, the popular enthusiasm that had greeted U.S. troops in southern France was, as the official history delicately put it, "starting to wane."[47] Strained labor relations between U.S. officers and French workers; delays in meeting civilian food needs; a burgeoning black market often connected to members of the military; resentment of the purchasing power of Allied soldiers; and endemic complaints about dangerous American driving in French towns and on French country roads, all generated first tension and then outright hostility. With U.S. officers often regarding FFI fighters as little better than armed hoodlums, clashes between American soldiers and members of the Resistance inevitably developed, sometimes with lethal consequences.[48] Despite these difficulties, however, U.S. officers were generally satisfied with the progress of civil

[43] "History of CA Operations," quoted Coles and Weinberg, *Civil Affairs*, 779.

[44] Ibid.

[45] See Provisional Directive for Civilian Labor, October 3, 1944, 7th Army CAHQ, Coles and Weinberg, *Civil Affairs*, 781.

[46] Regional Relief Officer, Marseilles, to AFHQ, September 26, 1944, Coles and Weinberg, *Civil Affairs*, 779.

[47] History of CA Operations, Coles and Weinberg, *Civil Affairs*, 796.

[48] See Footitt, *War and Liberation*, 111–121.

affairs and with the development of French civilian government. Few had any desire to plunge into French politics, and throughout the Riviera the successful establishment of CFLN-led local governments allowed them to avoid having to do so. Reflecting increasing political stability, U.S. officers reported in early October that summary executions of former Vichy officials had ceased and that the number of collaborators arrested was "not excessive."[49]

The rapid establishment of stable civilian government in the South of France in the weeks following *Dragoon* owed a great deal to the actions of the French Communist Party and its armed wing, the FTP. At every step, Communist leaders worked closely with other political groupings in the CFLN and with the Americans, enabling Seventh Army's Civil Affairs Department to report happily that "local Communist leaders have continued their policy of working with other political groups in the city and with the departmental and regional officials ... officers of the *Sécurité Militarire* declare that the Communists are creating no problems."[50] Clearly – and not surprisingly, given the respective spheres of influence established between the Allies and the Soviet Union – Communist Party leaders showed no interest in harnessing the power of popular uprisings in Paris and Marseilles to bid for power at a regional or national level.

Where Communist leaders took positions in the emerging structures of local and regional government, they did so as loyal members of the CFLN. This approach was reflected at a national level in November 1944, when PCF leader Maurice Thorez returned to Paris from exile in Moscow with orders from Stalin to back de Gaulle and to work for the rehabilitation of the French economy.[51] As with Togliatti's return to Italy, Thorez's class-collaborationist policy underscored Moscow's commitment to the stability and security of capitalism in Western Europe. As in Italy, Stalin's policy also conformed to the patriotism – sometimes referred to as "National-Thorezism" – of many party leaders. In fact, since 1943, French Communists had been arguing enthusiastically for the restoration of France's "power, grandeur, and universal mission."[52]

As *Armée B* consolidated its control of southern France, de Lattre moved to curb the independent power of the Resistance, disarming some fighters and assimilating others directly into French army. The Communist Party, as Seventh Army headquarters reported in early September, participated fully in the process of "regularizing" the FFI, insisting that its own FTP guerilla fighters – who U.S. officials considered the "shock troops" of the Resistance – hand

---

[49] Quoted in Footitt, *War and Liberation*, 108.
[50] Seventh Army to SHAEF, September 3, 1944, Coles and Weinberg, *Civil Affairs*, 772.
[51] Geoffrey Roberts, *Stalin's Wars: From World War to Cold War, 1939–1953* (New Haven, CT: Yale University Press, 2006), 176.
[52] Quoted in Allesandro Brogi, *Confronting America: The Cold War Between the United States and Communists in France and Spain* (Chapel Hill: University of North Carolina Press, 2011), 16.

over their weapons to the new authorities.[53] U.S. officers continued to fear the disruptive potential of the FFI, its ranks swollen by enthusiastic young people who had joined the uprisings in Marseilles and elsewhere and who did not necessarily come under the strict party discipline of the PCF. These concerns abated, however, as de Lattre pushed ahead with "amalgamation," often bringing entire FFI units directly into *Armée B*'s ranks. In addition to helping to tame the Resistance, this policy had the added benefit for the new government of allowing the Arab and African soldiers who had borne the brunt of the fighting thus far to be replaced by native-born Frenchmen. This "whitening" of the army – the term was used unblushingly – enabled de Gaulle to present the final struggle to drive German forces out of the country as an all-French affair, thus beginning the long marginalization of the contribution of the colonial troops. By the time *Armée B* – now redesignated the French First Army – reached the German border it was possible, as de Lattre cynically joked, to "search in vain for a black soldier" in regiments that still bore the title "Senegalese."[54]

For these critical political reasons, as well for as the more obvious military and logistical factors, *Dragoon* was an unqualified Franco-American success. German troops were driven from southern France well ahead of even the most optimistic U.S. projections; the ports of Marseilles and Toulon were soon funneling indispensable supplies to the advancing Allied armies; and the political authority of the new French government was established without major conflict or confrontation. The danger of post-occupation chaos or even civil war that had so concerned U.S. policy makers had been avoided, although the price, as Admiral Leahy had warned, was that de Gaulle strengthened his grip on the country.

The relationship between Washington and Charles de Gaulle's "dictatorship by consent" in Paris was, predictably enough, a rocky one.[55] True to his goal of reestablishing France as a great power, de Gaulle sought to shape an independent foreign policy, concluding a general treaty of friendship with Moscow in late 1944. Paris did not share London's willingness to embrace American free trade principles, and the nationalization of key economic sectors, together with the foundation of an extensive welfare state, prompted U.S. fears of expanded state control and a socialized economy. As tension between the United States and the Soviet Union deepened, however, Paris came around. By early 1946, de Gaulle was out of office, and in April 1947, the Communist Party was expelled from the government. With its path eased by U.S. concessions to French oil interests, and encouraged by access to Marshall Plan funds, the French government tacked back toward Washington, joining the newly formed NATO alliance in 1950. While never a docile junior partner, Paris arrayed itself firmly

[53] Seventh Army to SHAEF, September 3, 1944, Coles and Weinberg, *Civil Affairs*, 772.
[54] de Lattre, *French First Army*, 176–177.
[55] Footitt and Simmonds, *France*, 245.

in the emerging consortium of the capitalist west under the overall leadership of the United States.[56]

Despite its not inconsiderable role in the establishment of a stable, capitalist, and – in general – pro-American France, *Dragoon* remains little known and largely unsung. This eclipse was largely the product of Churchill's unrelenting hostility to *Anvil/Dragoon*, a stance he continued in his own influential history of the war. While grudgingly admitting that operations in the South of France "eventually" assisted Eisenhower's advance, Churchill nevertheless insisted that the removal of Allied troops from Italy for *Dragoon* prevented the Allied armies there from "reach[ing] Vienna before the Russians."[57]

In private, and particularly in correspondence with close friend and collaborator South African General Jan Smuts, Churchill was more blunt. In July 1944, he complained to Smuts that the "major hopes in Italy" had been "ruined by the American insistence on concentrating on a minor project," adding in August, even as Franco-American forces were exploiting the German collapse in the Riviera, that the campaign was an "abortion" premised on "breaking [the] full career" of the Allied armies in Italy.[58] Whether or not Allied armies in Italy were ever in "full career," Churchill's purpose was to elaborate the notion that *Dragoon* had destroyed the prospect of confronting the Russians in Central Europe. Smuts concurred, warning in late August 1944 that Russian influence in the Balkans could only be countered by rushing Allied troops to the region.[59]

To many newly minted cold warriors in the immediate postwar period, Churchill's apparent insistence on facing down the Russians in Austria, instead of charging off into the Rhône "cul de sac," seemed to have been remarkably prescient. Churchill's scheme for a move through the Ljubljana Gap to Vienna benefited greatly from never having to stand the harsh test of implementation. More importantly, it also acted as a cover for the real issues at stake. These had been outlined by Churchill in an unsent telegram to Harry Hopkins drafted after finally acceding to U.S. demands for *Dragoon* back in July. Here, in his anger and frustration, Churchill got to the crux of the matter, complaining that "Marshall, King, and Arnold [now] run one part of the war through Eisenhower and run the Mediterranean part themselves without the slightest regard for the opinion of the British Commander there, or of the Chiefs of Staff, or of His Majesty's Government."[60] For the prime minister, the real issue was not an imaginary march on Vienna – a fantasy that appalled the British

[56] See Anand Toprani, "The French Connection: A New Perspective on the End of the Red Line Agreement, 1945–1948," *Diplomatic History* 36, no. 2, (April 2012).

[57] Winston S. Churchill, *The Second World War*, 6 vols. (Boston: Houghton Mifflin, 1948–1954), 6: 90–91.

[58] Churchill to Smuts, July 5, 1944, PREM 3/271/5; Churchill to Smuts, August 25, 1944, PREM 3/271/6.

[59] Smuts to Churchill, August 30, 1944, PREM 3/271/6.

[60] Churchill to Hopkins, unsent draft, July 7, 1944, PREM 3/271/9.

Chiefs of Staff – but the question of whether London or Washington controlled the course of Mediterranean strategy. With *Dragoon*, the Americans had unambiguously asserted their predominance.

Churchill chewed this question over with his chief military adviser General Hastings Ismay as he prepared his blistering note to Harry Hopkins at the conclusion of the argument over *Anvil/Dragoon*. "I think that [Hopkins] ought to know that we consider they have done us a great wrong," the prime minister complained, "and that we will not tolerate their mastery of the Mediterranean."[61] The problem was that London was no longer in any position to challenge U.S. "mastery" in the Mediterranean or anywhere else. Unable to counter growing U.S. predominance, Churchill vented his spleen on the French, predicting that the landing craft "stolen" for the "tomfoolery" of *Dragoon* would wash up "sprawling in the suburbs of Marseilles."[62] Protesting the American withdrawal of seven divisions from Italy for use in *Dragoon* – the force actually comprised "3 American and 4 Frog blackamoors" – he implicitly recognized the significance of the Franco-American axis. After everything that London had done for de Gaulle – often in the face of U.S. opposition – it now seemed that, courtesy of the "abortion" on the Riviera, the United States had positioned itself to exert a powerful influence in postwar France.

General Brooke and other senior British leaders feared that this powerful mélange of bitterness, foiled ambition, exhaustion, and strategic fantasy, might unhinge Churchill entirely. In his discussions with Ismay in early July, Churchill threatened to "break the Allied Command in the Mediterranean [into] an American sphere playing the fool at *Anvil* [and a] British sphere doing the best it can towards Trieste."[63] Such a move would have had enormous and unpredictable consequences for the entire Allied command structure as it approached some of the most complex military and political challenges of the war. In the end, calmer voices prevailed, blistering telegrams were left unsent, and Churchill's public effort to vindicate his strategic approach was postponed to the battle of memoirs in the early Cold War. But his dogged opposition to *Anvil/Dragoon*, and his desperate grasping for alternatives in the Balkans, reflected a new reality: what the fight over *Anvil* demonstrated with absolute clarity was that, even in the Mediterranean, Washington was now the senior partner.

---

[61] Churchill to Ismay, July 6, 1944, PREM 3/271/9.
[62] Ibid.
[63] Churchill to Ismay, July 6, 1944, PREM 3/271/9.

10

Italy Enters the Postwar Period

The U.S. capture of Rome in June 1944 marked a critical turning point in the war in the Mediterranean. The long-awaited victory finally enabled Washington to prevail over London in the debate over Allied strategy in the Mediterranean, securing the shift of Allied forces out of Italy and into the invasion of southern France. Churchill's fear that *Dragoon* would hobble Allied operations in Italy proved accurate. Deprived of three U.S. and four French divisions, the Allied advance ground to a halt in August. In the fall, Allied forces launched a series of attacks on the German Gothic Line in the Apennine Mountains, but they no longer had the strength to achieve a decisive breakthrough. Contrary to much historical writing, however, the stymied military campaign did not turn Italy into a backwater.[1] The installation of the Bonomi government in Rome opened wide the road to the advance of American political and economic influence and, even as the main locus of the fighting moved into France, many of the key contours of postwar Western Europe continued to take shape in Italy. Moreover, if Italy was one of the key sites for the consolidation of America's postwar hegemony, it was also a place where the eclipse of British power became starkly evident.

In July 1944, James Dunn, director of the State Department's Office of European Affairs, outlined this fundamental shift in discussion with General John Hilldring, head of the army's Civil Affairs Division. Dunn argued that with an "anti-Fascist, pro-United Nations and democratic" government in place in Rome, Italy could begin to "enter … the post-war period."[2] With northern Italy

[1] For a new iteration of the reduction of the campaign in Italy to the status of a "dismal backwater," see Rick Atkinson, *The Guns at Last Light: The War in Western Europe, 1944–1945* (New York: Henry Holt, 2013), 189–190.
[2] Dunn to Hilldring, July 6, 1944, Harry L. Coles and Albert K. Weinberg, *Civil Affairs: Soldiers Become Governors* (Washington, DC: Office of the Chief of the Military History Department of the Army, 1964), 497.

still in German hands and harsh fighting awaiting Allied troops on the Gothic Line, this was a bold observation, but it reflected Washington's confidence that measures to rebuild Italy – and to secure U.S. influence within it – could now be put into place at an accelerated pace. In August, State Department planners discussed plans for "converting" Italy into a "stable, peaceful, and constructive element among the nations of Europe" by integrating its economy into "multilateral and non-discriminatory foreign trade" and by encouraging the "direct participation of American industries in Italian enterprises."[3] This approach emphasized the reconstruction and "rehabilitation" of Italian society over the wartime battle for survival in the face of hunger and disease, and it privileged the integration of the country into the emerging U.S.-led international order over London's strident demands for its continued punishment.

Not surprisingly, British policy makers disagreed, and their reaction to the advance of U.S. influence at the expense of their own illuminates critical aspects of a process that American policy makers were reluctant to discuss – at least in writing – in quite such unvarnished terms. In July 1944, Sir Noel Charles, London's representative on the Advisory Council for Italy, warned Whitehall that U.S. officials were giving the new government in Rome "full license" to take ever-greater control of Italian political and economic affairs, and he urged London not to "slavishly" follow Washington's lead.[4] British officials did not need much prompting. At the Foreign Office, Sir Orme Sargent concurred with Charles's memorandum, noting bluntly that Washington's "attitude" ran contrary to "our long-term interests" and arguing that Britain should play the "predominant" role in Italian affairs.[5] Unfortunately for London, while it was easy enough to revive visions of Britain being the "senior partner" in the Italian affairs, it turned out to be impossibly difficult to summon the material resources necessary to challenge the actual advance of U.S. predominance.

Harold Caccia, British head of the Control Commission's Political Section, offered one solution to this dilemma. Writing in October 1944, Caccia made a great leap of optimism, arguing that with Britain incapable of supplying aid on the same scale as the Americans, it was in London's "interests to see that the U.S.A. provides what we cannot," because by so doing "they will be indirectly serving our interests."[6] Caccia concluded that Britain should "welcome and encourage" large-scale U.S. economic assistance, while at the same time seeking to moderate the influence it might purchase in Rome by ensuring that British "brains" and "organizing ability" were available on "loan" to advise the Italian government.

[3] "The Treatment of Italy," memorandum, State Dept. Interdivisional Country and Area Committee, CAC#248, August 31, 1944, microfilm T1221, NARA.
[4] Charles to Foreign Office, July 22, 1944, R12663/53/22, FO371/43837, NA.
[5] Orme, minute on Charles to Foreign Office, July 22, 1944, R12663/53/22, FO371/43837, NA.
[6] Caccia to Foreign Office, October 26, 1944, R19126/691/22, FO371/43915, NA.

Caccia's comforting fantasy of British brains offsetting American brawn – or even, judo style, of turning it to Britain's advantage – was shared by other British officials, including Harold Macmillan.[7] There could be no doubt, however, about the sheer weight of U.S. economic aid flowing into Italy. Even before Rome was in Allied hands, U.S. aid vastly outweighed that provided by Britain, with the United States supplying more than 414,000 tons of civilian relief supplies between August 1943 and March 1944, whereas Britain provided only 49,000 tons, more than half of it in seed potatoes.[8] Building on this impressive start, in the period between 1943 and 1945 the United States would supply more than four fifths of all civilian relief supplies for Italy.[9]

Buoyed by this economic effort, and with the establishment of the new government in Rome behind them, U.S. policy makers argued for a radical reorientation of Allied policy in Italy. Building on James Dunn's vision of relations with Italy entering the "post-war" period, the State Department began pressing for the "demilitarization" of the Allied Control Commission and for the "infiltration" of American civilian business and technical experts into its organization.[10] U.S. officials in Italy concurred, with Robert Murphy noting in August "there is no doubt that the ACC should be demilitarized."[11] "Demilitarization" had much to commend it to U.S. policy makers, because it would release the army from the business of government while allowing the full capacities of official and unofficial civilian aid agencies to come into play. Moreover, and as British observers realized to their horror, U.S. officials linked demilitarization to a broader move away from a purely palliative relief effort, and toward a "new emphasis on rehabilitation," centered on a U.S.-led effort to rebuild the Italian economy.[12]

British officials resisted Washington's combined drive for demilitarization and rehabilitation, arguing that it was impermissible to rebuild the economy of a former enemy while allied countries were still under German occupation. Their efforts met with some initial success, derailing a July 1944 U.S. proposal to invite the Italian government to the United Nations Monetary and Financial Conference at Bretton Woods.[13] "The British people haven't forgotten," Foreign Secretary Anthony Eden sniffed, "which country was our ally and which our enemy, ... and neither have I."[14] Despite this temporary reverse, the Americans persisted, with the War Department forcing the pace by announcing

[7] See Matthew Jones, *Britain, the United States, and the Mediterranean War 1942–1944* (New York: St. Martin's Press, 1996), 80.

[8] Charles to Foreign Office, April 28, 1944, R7239/53/22, FO 371/43837, NARA.

[9] Gabriel Kolko, *The Politics of War: The World War and United States Foreign Policy* (New York: Pantheon Books, 1990), 60.

[10] OEA Memorandum, July 31, 1944, Coles and Weinberg, *Civil Affairs*, 487.

[11] Murphy to State Department, August 22, 1944, RG 59, 740.00119 Italy/8-2244, NARA.

[12] Campbell to Foreign Office, August 11, 1944, R12488/95/22, FO 371/43863, NA.

[13] "The Italian Situation," State Department briefing paper, n.d., *FRUS, Quebec,* 1944: 209.

[14] Eden memorandum, Charles to Foreign Office, July 10, 1944, R11177/15/22, NA.

that in the fall of 1944 it would stop funding relief efforts outside of those areas under direct military rule. The announcement provoked an unseemly scramble in Washington as various civilian agencies competed to fill the vacuum. As was often the case, interagency rivalry gave U.S. policy making a seemingly chaotic character, with one British observer at a particularly heated bout of bureaucratic infighting involving State Department, Foreign Economic Administration, and Lend-Lease officials, reporting sarcastically "what a party!"[15]

Despite these difficulties – and perhaps, given the eagerness of rival agencies to get involved in the rehabilitation of Italy, because of them – U.S. intervention pressed forward. Moreover, with the growing weight of America's economic might behind it, it began to move with irresistible force. Washington's drive for demilitarization and rehabilitation reached a critical turning point at the *Octagon* summit conference in Quebec in September. By this time, U.S. officials viewed the conjuncture in Italy as one laden with both great danger and great opportunity. The dangers were all too obvious: as Anne O'Hare McCormick reported from Rome, continuing economic dislocation threatened to produce "large-scale rioting and social disintegration" on a scale that could generate "repercussions throughout Europe" and undermine "the political position of the United States in the post-war period."[16] Again, the specter of social revolution was haunting U.S. officials.

In a presidential briefing paper prior to the *Octagon* conference, General O'Dwyer, head of the Control Commission's Economic Section, argued that decisive action was necessary to avert these insurrectionary dangers and to lay the basis for the long-term political and economic stability of Italy.[17] The State Department echoed O'Dwyer's conclusions, concurring with the Army's "wish to be relieved" of the responsibility for civilian aid and producing plans for the "de-militarization" of the ACC and the "rehabilitation" of the Italian economy. [18] These moves, department officials proposed, should be linked to full diplomatic recognition of the Italian government, an expansion of the Italian army, and the inclusion of Italy in international bodies such as the International Labor Office.

State Department officials also noted, with considerable understatement, that many of the "physical problems" in Italy had been "augmented by divergences in British and American views."[19] At the *Octagon* conference, and later during follow-up discussions between Roosevelt and Churchill at Hyde Park in late September, these "divergences" were substantially – if superficially – resolved, with London reluctantly approving Washington's new approach to

---

[15] Marris to Treasury, August 10, 1944, R13019/95/22, FO 371/43863, NA; see also David W. Ellwood, *Italy 1943–1945* (New York: Holmes & Meier, 1985), 129.

[16] McCormick, "New Relief Scheme for Italy is Urged," *New York Times*, September 7, 1944, 7.

[17] O'Dwyer, memorandum, September 8, 1944, *FRUS*, Quebec 1944: 210–211.

[18] "The Italian Situation," State Department briefing paper, September 6, 1944, *FRUS Conference at Quebec, 1944*, 207–210.

[19] Ibid., 207.

the rehabilitation of Italy. On September 26, 1944, Roosevelt and Churchill jointly issued the Hyde Park Declaration, stating that the Italian people had amply "demonstrated their will to be free," thereby proving their fitness to exercise "an increasing measure of control" over their domestic affairs.[20] By the same token, they had earned access to the economic assistance necessary to rebuild an economy devastated by Fascist "misrule" and German occupation. Allied leaders agreed that the new United Nations Relief and Rehabilitation Administration (UNRRA) should be allowed to operate in Italy, and that civilian engineers, technicians, and industrial experts should be dispatched to help the country's economic recovery. To signify this new departure – quickly dubbed the "New Deal" – the word "control" was dropped from the title of the leading Anglo-American supervisory body in Italy, which would now be known simply as the "Allied Commission."

The Hyde Park Declaration marked a turning point both in Allied relations with the Italian government and in relations between London and Washington. The declaration registered the advancing political and diplomatic rehabilitation of the Italian government under Allied tutelage, but it also marked the unambiguous ascendancy of Washington's approach to the key political and economic questions in Italy. Only weeks after asserting its supremacy in strategic decision making in the Mediterranean by forcing approval of *Anvil/Dragoon*, Washington effectively claimed the mantle of "senior partner" in Italy as well. This bitter pill was made somewhat more palatable to London by the appointment of Harold Macmillan, formerly British resident minister at AFHQ, as acting president of the rechristened Allied Commission. It was a hollow victory. In common with his predecessor, Allied Supreme Commander and ACC head Henry Wilson, on most major questions Macmillan would accommodate to U.S interests, effectively putting a British face on an American-inspired project. As soon as he assumed office, Macmillan issued a statement amplifying the Hyde Park Declaration and arguing that the dropping of the word "control" would only have "real meaning" if the Allies stuck to the "path of generosity."[21] In an implicit swipe at his superiors, Macmillan concluded that if the Allies resumed a punitive policy – of the type long advocated by London – then Italy would slide into "despair, anarchy, and revolution."

The reformulated and U.S.-inspired policy toward Italy embodied in the Hyde Park Declaration continued to face considerable economic and political challenges. On the economic front, the Allied and Italian governments confronted the cumulative consequences of the breakdown of the Fascist economy, the German occupation, the destruction wrought by combat and bombing, and presence of enormous Anglo-American armies and their (relatively) well-paid

[20] Roosevelt and Churchill, joint press statement, September 26, 1944, Coles and Weinberg, *Civil Affairs*, 499.
[21] Macmillan, "Allied Policy toward Italy," memorandum, December 1944, Coles and Weinberg, *Civil Affairs*, 509.

soldiery. The result was a deepening spiral of social and economic dislocation, unemployment, inflation, and – particularly in southern Italy – a food crisis verging on outright famine. A survey made by British intelligence officers of letters sent to prisoners of war by their families in Italy offered a graphic picture of civilian life dominated by severe shortages of basic consumer goods and bread riots, and encapsulated – pointing to the combined effects of the black market, prostitution, and the mafia – in the conclusion that "a good many people have given up living honestly."[22] In April 1944, Noel Charles reported that the average calorific intake in Naples had fallen to around 600 per day, in sharp and unfavorable contrast to an average of 1,378 calories per day under German occupation.[23] Rampant inflation added to the economic breakdown, with U.S. officials estimating that the cost of living in Naples had risen from 48 liras per week in July 1943 to more than 360 liras by February 1944.[24] Under these conditions – graphically described by Norman Lewis in his memoir *Naples '44* and by John Horne Burns in his autobiographical novel *The Gallery* – normal civilian life began to disintegrate, with potentially dangerous consequences for the establishment of stable postwar order.

A young American merchant seaman shipping military supplies into Naples captured the popular mood, noting that "disease is widespread," and prostitution the "most flourishing industry," but adding that "the streets of Naples are full of political literature – socialist, Stalinist, Marxist" and that leftist parties are "holding mass meetings."[25] Scrawled slogans hailing President Roosevelt were heavily outnumbered by those proclaiming "Long Live the Red Army!" U.S. officials witnessed the same conditions, with Colonel Charles Poletti, now military governor of Rome, reporting that Italians were "bitterly disappointed" by the Allies' failure to deliver "freedom from want."[26] By November, Alexander Kirk, U.S. representative on the Advisory Council (he would be appointed ambassador to Rome in December), was warning that civilian morale was "spiraling downward," prompting the emergence of revolutionary groups that were "much more extremist" than even the "Russians may desire."[27] These comments reflected the nagging fear that economic and social breakdown might, in a situation where the old political elite was almost entirely discredited, give rise to revolutionary impulses beyond the control of the compliant Italian Communist Party and of its masters in Moscow. In assessing the degree to which these concerns weighed on U.S. officials, it is important to set aside our knowledge that popular social revolution did not break out in Italy:

[22] "Conditions in Italy from Postal Censorship," memorandum, April 3, 1944, R5543/53/22, FO 371/43836, NA.
[23] Charles to Foreign Office, April 28, 1944, R7239/53/22, FO 371/43837, NA.
[24] FEA Intel. Memo #18, September 12, 1944, Entry 179, Box 1, RG 169, NARA.
[25] William Hill, "An Eyewitness Looks At Italy Under the AMG," *The Militant*, June 10, 1944.
[26] Poletti, quoted in FEA Intelligence Memo #16, August 29, 1944, Entry 179, Box 1, RG 169, NARA.
[27] Kirk to State, November 27, 1944, 740.00119/11–2744, RG 59, NARA.

in 1944 such a development seemed entirely possible, not only to U.S. policy makers but also – and more importantly – to many Italians.

This grim economic reality, and the political fears that it generated among U.S. policy makers, cast a long shadow over the cheerful vision of Italy moving smoothly into the "postwar world." But it also reinforced Washington's determination to press ahead with the civilianization of the Allied Commission (AC) and with the demilitarization of relations with the Italian government. In this process, the AC would in effect sustain the Italian state, providing the bureaucratic structure and material resources that permitted its recomposition.[28] On the economic front, it had become apparent to U.S. officials that earlier plans to provide civilian relief at a level designed simply to alleviate "disease and unrest" were woefully inadequate, leading them to advocate increased levels of relief and to argue for the rapid rebuilding of the Italian economy so that it could help meet the desperate shortages of food and consumer goods from its own resources. These conclusions meshed with the liberalization of political relations with Italy and, not coincidentally, with hopes for augmenting of U.S. influence. A great deal of American aid flowing into Italy would be channeled through Rome's Fascist-era *Istituto per la Ricostruzione Industriale,* a corporatist planning and finance agency. Ironically, Italian Communists hoped to transform the *Istituto* into a "central organ for state control of industry."[29] Either way, U.S. policy makers judged that the reestablishment of free-market capitalism would initially have to be nurtured by the centrally planned distribution of American largess.

It was easier to discuss the rehabilitation of the Italian economy than it was to accomplish it. By the end of 1944, acting AC director Harold Macmillan had accepted that levels of civilian relief should be governed by a "liberal" interpretation of the old "disease and unrest" formula, and he had approved the proposal to launch a program of "industrial first-aid."[30] It remained unclear, however, precisely how this would be organized and paid for. Despite Macmillan's earnest hope that "His Majesty's Government will be willing to provide their share of the cost," the parlous state of the British economy meant that little funding would be forthcoming from that source. Foreign Office officials recognized that conditions in rural Italy were "similar to those of the Dark Ages," but they were forced to concede that Britain's "capacity to assist Italy in the restoration of the economy is strictly limited."[31] In contrast, in Washington the newly formed Foreign Economic Administration (FEA) was already busy promoting itself as the lead agency responsible for the provision of "essential civilian items" and

---

[28] See Ellwood, *Italy 1943–1945,* 237.

[29] Dunn to State, May 7, 1947, *FRUS 1947,* 3: 899; also see Allesandro Brogi, *Confronting America: The Cold War Between the United States and Communists in France and Spain* (Chapel Hill: University of North Carolina Press, 2011), 73.

[30] Macmillan, "Allied Policy toward Italy," memorandum, December 1944, Coles and Weinberg, *Civil Affairs,* 509–513.

[31] "Report on Situation in Italy," November 1944, R18758/691/22, FO 371/43915, NA.

for supply of the equipment and machinery necessary to "promote economic rehabilitation."[32]

Initially, the FEA proposed to meet these new responsibilities by extending Lend-Lease to Italy, but the administration decided in the summer of 1944 against such a move. Significantly, opposition came primarily from business interests concerned that the bureaucratic entanglements generated by Lend-Lease operations would militate against the development of private trade.[33] Even as the proposal to extend Lend-Lease was being debated and rejected, policy makers were elaborating a more radical plan that called for compensating Rome in dollars for monies that it had paid out in wages for U.S. servicemen serving in Italy, as agreed under the terms of the armistice. Under this new plan, the Italian government could use these dollar remittances to purchase both food aid and capital goods from the United States. This proposal would simultaneously strengthen the finances of the Italian government and give it, under AC guidance, a greater say in the allocation of its resources. Not coincidentally, it would also strengthen U.S. economic ties to Italy. The problem was that, at a stroke, it unilaterally scrapped the armistice requirement that Italy fund the Allied occupation.

Not surprisingly, Washington's proposal to subsidize the Italian government in this fashion met with strong British opposition, both on grounds of principle – they argued that the defeated enemy *should* meet the costs of the occupation – and on grounds of practicality – London simply could not afford to make equivalent Sterling remittances to cover the pay of British and Commonwealth troops. As Foreign Office officials complained, any such British remittances would lead to Italy accumulating large Sterling holdings, making for an "intolerable conclusion" to the war.[34] Yet again, however, Washington forged ahead undeterred by British opposition. On October 10, President Roosevelt announced the implementation of the scheme to "make available to the Italian government the dollar equivalent of the Italian lire issued up to now and hereafter as pay to United States troops in Italy."[35] The presidential statement made it clear that the Italian government was expected to spend these funds on the purchase of "essential civilian supplies" from the United States. With nonchalant ease, Washington had utilized its economic might to reinforce economic ties with Italy, strengthen its own standing with the Italian government, and *en passant* to give to London another lesson on the shifting balance of power.

As it pushed to demilitarize the relief effort and to strengthen the government's role in economic reconstruction, Washington also worked with nongovernmental agencies to alleviate the social and political consequences of

---

[32] FEA "Economic Program With Reference to Italy," July 25, 1944, Entry 172, Box 2, RG 169, NARA.

[33] See Ellwood, *Italy 1943–1945*, 132–133.

[34] Meeting of Committee on Armistice Terms, July 5, 1944, R10999/95/22, FO 371/43862, NA.

[35] Roosevelt Press Statement, October 10, 1944, *Department of State Bulletin*, October 15, 1944.

economic breakdown. Chief among them was UNRRA, founded by forty-four Allied governments in November 1943 and led by former New York governor Herbert Lehman. Fittingly, given the decisive role played by the United States in the leadership, organization, and financing of UNRRA – more than 73 percent of the agency's funding came from the United States – the inaugural address was given in the White House by President Roosevelt.[36] Roosevelt explained that UNRRA's goals were "to assure a fair distribution of available supplies among all of the liberated peoples [and] to ward off death by starvation or exposure among these peoples."[37] Beyond this immediate humanitarian mission, U.S. policy makers viewed UNRRA as an instrument for securing postwar stability in war-torn Europe and for heading off, as Assistant Secretary of State Dean Acheson put it, the "emergency that will come when the fighting is over."[38] Given Washington's constant association between economic hardship and communist insurrection, there is no doubt about the kind of "emergency" UNRRA was intended to defuse.

As economic and social breakdown deepened in Italy in the summer of 1944, the State Department suggested to British ambassador Lord Halifax that the two governments approach Herbert Lehman to propose that UNRRA begin organizing relief operations in Italy.[39] In line with London's general opposition to expanding relief efforts in Italy – and setting aside the absurdity of making an Anglo-American "approach" to what was in all practical terms an arm of the U.S. government – Halifax was instructed to "stall."[40] UNRRA, the Foreign Office argued, had been set up to help "liberated peoples," and as former enemies the Italians did not qualify.[41] As on the issue of dollar remittances, however, London soon found itself waging a rearguard action in the face of relentless U.S. pressure and, following the *Octagon* conference and the proclamation of the "New Deal," British leaders finally agreed to allow UNRRA relief operations in Italy. Notifying British delegates to the second UNRRA council of the change of policy, the Foreign Office explained that on "political grounds" Churchill now believed that it was "desirable to accord a greater measure of economic assistance to Italy."[42] Churchill's note to the Foreign Office captured the reality of the situation more accurately, arguing simply "the President agrees it should be done."[43]

[36] See William I. Hitchcock, *The Bitter Road To Freedom: A New History of the Liberation of Europe* (New York, Free Press, 2008), 220.

[37] Quoted in George Woodbridge, *UNRRA: The History of the United Nations Relief and Recovery Administration* (New York: Columbia University Press, 1950), 1:3.

[38] Acheson, radio broadcast December 18, 1943, text in *Department of State Bulletin*, December 18, 1943, 421; see also Hitchcock, *The Bitter Road to Freedom*, 218.

[39] Halifax to Foreign Office, June 30, 1944, R10303/95/22, FO 371/43862, NA.

[40] Foreign Office to Halifax, July 6, 1944, R10303/95/22, FO 371/43862, NA.

[41] Ibid.

[42] Foreign Office to British delegation, September 19, 1944, R14371/95/22, FO 371/43864, NA.

[43] Churchill to Foreign Office, September 16, 1944, R14888/95/22, FO 371/43864, NA.

British support for Washington's proposal ensured that the UNRRA's council, meeting in Montreal in September, approved extending operations to Italy. It was not an entirely one-sided discussion, with the Yugoslav delegation expressing its opposition to the proposal on the basis that that because Italy had not been a "victim of the war," measures that would "improve the political status of the Italian government" were inappropriate.[44] In response to this division within the council, and out of sensitivity to continued British unease, Washington scaled back its initial proposal, and the final resolution limited UNRRA's operation in Italy to $50 million worth of aid directed specifically to the care of displaced persons, children, and expectant mothers. An initial UNRRA mission arrived in Italy in November 1944, but protracted negotiations with the Italian government, which insisted that it participate as an equal in this United Nations undertaking, as well as extensive discussions with AFHQ and the Allied Commission, were necessary before aid finally began to flow in February 1945.[45]

As it pressed for UNRRA operations in Italy, Washington also took unilateral action to raise the civilian food ration in areas of the country where supplies were, as Roosevelt euphemistically explained in an October 4 press statement, "below the standard necessary to maintain full health and efficiency."[46] The president followed this announcement with an instruction to the War Department to provide the additional shipping necessary to raise the bread ration in Allied-occupied Italy from 200 to 300 grams per day. The Combined Chiefs of Staff, facing a worldwide shipping shortage, opposed the increase, while AFHQ and the AC, under pressure from the unfolding social crisis in Italy, supported it.

Predictably, London opposed any increase in the bread ration. Churchill pointed out to Roosevelt had he had "jumped a good many fences" in making such a unilateral decision, and he warned against giving "our ex-enemies in Italy more than our allies in Greece and Yugoslavia."[47] Reflecting London's weakness in the face of increasing U.S. unilateralism, one Foreign Office official complained that Roosevelt had simply taken the whole matter "out of our hands."[48] In fact, British opposition – Churchill's "non-concurrence in the proposed directive to the theater" – blocked the implementation of Roosevelt's order until March 1, 1945, by which time increased shipping capacity made further resistance impossible.[49] London still had the ability to delay Washington's

[44] UNRRA Council II, Doc. 246, Lot 52 D 408, Box 1, RG 59, NARA.
[45] See Woodbridge, *UNRRA*, 2: 262–263.
[46] Roosevelt statement, October 4, 1944, Coles and Weinberg, *Civil Affairs*, 500.
[47] Churchill to Roosevelt, November 12, 1944, Warren F. Kimball (ed.), *Churchill and Roosevelt: The Complete Correspondence* (London: Collins, 1984), 3: 387.
[48] Charles to Foreign Office, November 5, 1944, R18289/95/22, FO 371/43866, NA.
[49] Hilldring to Stimson, February 8, 1945, Coles and Weinberg, *Civil Affairs*, 519; FEA Intelligence Bulletin #40, February 13, 1945, Entry 179, Box 1, RG 169, NARA.

plans, but it could neither derail them entirely nor implement an alternative of its own.

British policy makers were also alarmed by the flow of nongovernmental U.S. aid to Italy, particularly that organized by American Relief for Italy Inc. This charitable fund, sponsored by President Roosevelt and led by Ambassador to the Papal See Myron Taylor, circumvented bureaucratic obstacles to the mobilization of civilian resources to disperse more than $37 million in aid. Given UNRRA's Italian relief budget of $50 million, this was hardly an insignificant sum.[50] Reporting on conversations with Myron Taylor, Britain's representative to the Vatican Sir D'Arcy Osborne noted sniffily, if not inaccurately, that Taylor's "charitable instincts" coincided with the pursuit of publicity designed to win Roosevelt Italian-American votes.[51] Taylor's efforts, Osborne added, had secured a Papal contribution of some 5 million lira, and had garnered widespread and favorable publicity in Italy. Osborne told Taylor that there would be no reciprocal British effort, both because "all materials were needed at home" and because public opinion in Britain would "not tolerate contributions to an ex-enemy."[52]

On these various and interlocking fronts, Washington took advantage of the political opportunities opened by the establishment of the Bonomi government in June 1944 to move beyond simply providing aid to stave off "disease and unrest" and to begin exporting plant, equipment, and know-how necessary for economic recovery. Aid, capital inflows, and U.S. political influence advanced together. There were limits to how far this process could go under wartime conditions, and the Italian economy at the end of the war remained deeply scarred by war and by the German and Allied occupations. But despite all the difficulties and delays, U.S. economic engagement advanced significantly in the last months of the war, and in doing so it prepared the ground for American business interests poised to take advantage of the economic opportunities created by the demands of postwar reconstruction once the fighting finally stopped.[53]

These U.S. advances were made in the face of dogged British opposition. From dollar remittances for troop pay, to raising the bread ration, to the operation of UNRRA, London's initial reaction to was to denounce U.S. proposals as "unacceptable" and "intolerable." Political and economic considerations combined to shape this response, with British policy reflecting both a concern that a former enemy was being "rehabilitated" too rapidly, and the realization that Britain simply could not match America's influence-buying largess. British policy makers hoped that their U.S. counterparts would either be too disorganized to press their economic policies effectively, or that they could be made to

---

[50] See James Edward Miller, *The United States and Italy, 1940–1950* (Chapel Hill: University of North Carolina Press, 1986), 105ff.

[51] Osborne to Eden, October 6, 1944, R15955/95/22, FO 371/43865, NA.

[52] Ibid.

[53] See Ellwood, *Italy 1943–1945*, 234–235.

understand that growing American economic influence in Italy would create an "open divergence" between the Allies.[54] In fact, U.S. policy makers understood this very well, but they also knew that the invariably positive Italian response to their proposals for economic reconstruction ensured that it would be the British who would be under pressure to close ranks to avoid a damaging public split. Both on the discrete issues, and on the overarching policy of "rehabilitation," the British were gradually, grudgingly, but inevitably forced to give ground as U.S. influence grew.

British policy makers were also forced to contend with the fact that U.S. economic aid gave Washington considerable political leverage within Italy.[55] As late as the fall of 1944, Noel Charles was still clinging to the belief that the Italian government preferred British "commonsense and political judgment" to American "immaturity in international affairs," but even he was forced to admit that the "enchantment of dollars" was exercising powerful countervailing pressure.[56] Moreover, Charles and other British officials were becoming increasingly out of touch with Italian politics as the United States began reaping the rewards of its economic primacy and of its role – well known to Italian politicians of all stripes – in the ouster of Badoglio and the formation of the Bonomi government. The Italian government's appreciation of this emerging Washington-Rome axis was signaled by Bonomi at the end of September when, during a meeting with Alexander Kirk to discuss the Hyde Park statement, he noted that while Italy had to "work out its own salvation," it would rely on U.S. aid and guidance to do so.[57]

As they consolidated their influence with the Italian government, U.S. policy makers became increasingly hostile to what Ambassador Kirk, referring to renewed British efforts to block Count Sforza's entry into the government, unblushingly described as "sporadic incursions from abroad into the internal politics of Italy."[58] Typically, Washington viewed British intervention as being external and self-interested, while that of the United States was organic and disinterested. In December, new Secretary of State Edward Stettinius publicly rebuked London for meddling in Italian politics, prompting Churchill to complain to Roosevelt about the "acerbity" of his comments.[59] Despite reminding Roosevelt of the support he had given him during the Darlan crisis – a strange analogy for Italy in late 1944 – Churchill elicited only the most modest of presidential apologies, accompanied by a pointed reminder that the prime minister's efforts to block Sforza's appointment to the cabinet had been made with-

---

[54] Foreign Office to Halifax, August 19, 1944, R12994/95/22, FO 371/43863, NA.
[55] See Emily Rosenberg, *Spreading the American Dream: American Economic and Cultural Expansion, 1890–1945* (New York: Hill & Wang, 1982), 222.
[56] Charles to Eden, October 26, 1944, R12126/691/22, FO 371/43915, NA.
[57] Kirk to State Department, September 30, *FRUS 1944*, 3: 1155.
[58] Kirk to State Department, November 28, 1944, *FRUS 1944*, 3: 1158.
[59] Churchill to Roosevelt, December 5, 1944, *Correspondence*, 3: 438.

out U.S. approval.[60] As with the political crises earlier in 1944, this clash also helped to reinforce Washington's standing in Rome at London's expense.

On December 14, 1944, the United States welcomed the establishment of a new government in Rome. Again led by Ivanoe Bonomi, the cabinet was remade after the withdrawal of Socialist and Party of Action leaders in protest at the slow pace at which former Fascists were being purged from the state apparatus, and it now featured increased Communist and the Christian Democratic participation. With Palmiro Togliatti as deputy prime minister, the new cabinet was well placed to conclude negotiations with the largely Communist-led resistance movement in German-occupied northern Italy, and on December 26 the government and the National Committee for the Liberation of Upper Italy (CLNAI) signed the Protocols of Rome. Under this agreement, partisans in the north would receive Allied money and military assistance – but not formal political recognition – in exchange for promising to operate under Allied military command. Critically, all territory liberated from the German occupation was to be turned over to allied military rule as soon as conditions permitted. To help Rome – and the Allies – get a grip on the partisans, a senior Italian army officer was appointed supreme commander of all the resistance forces in the north.

The Protocols of Rome created the political framework that would enable the Allies and the Italian government to absorb and contain the massive popular upsurge that greeted Allied troops as they finally pushed through the Gothic Line and into northern Italy in early 1945. Here, too, Washington's politico-strategic understanding proved superior to London's. If Allied troops had advanced into northern Italy in the summer of 1944 as Churchill had demanded, they would have arrived before relations between the new government in Rome and the resistance forces in the North could be consolidated, an eventuality that might well have resulted in clashes between Allied troops and resistance fighters engaged in "auto-liberation." As it was, the idea that local CLN committees might "set themselves up as an alternative government" during the "vacuum period" between the withdrawal of German forces and the arrival of Allied troops continued to worry Allied planners.[61] The stakes here were very high; as the new American head of Allied Commission Rear Admiral Ellery Stone pointed out, the structures of political power established during this "vacuum" would "affect the political future of Italy for a considerable period."[62] The solution, AFHQ decided, was that army civilian affairs officers would have to "persuade local committees and bands to preserve law and order pending the arrival of Allied forces" and the establishment of local military governments.[63] This approach to heading off the dangerous prospect

[60] Roosevelt to Churchill December 6, 1944, *Correspondence*, 3: 443.
[61] Stone to AFHQ, September 29, 1944, 331.1000/136/286, RG 331, NARA.
[62] Stone to Alexander, September 1, 1944, 331.1000/136/286, RG 331, NARA.
[63] Stone to AFHQ, September 17 and 29, 1944, 331.1000/136/286, RG 331, NARA.

FIGURE 10.1. As Allied troops advanced into northern Italy in the spring of 1945, Italian partisans organized by the CLNAI turned over their arms to the occupation authorities. In Verona on April 25, 1945, American fighter pilot Captain James "Rabbit" Hare watched and photographed one such ceremony. Squads of partisan fighters bearing signs announcing their home towns and villages marched into the Verona Arena and paraded in front of a reviewing stand decked with the U.S., British, Russian, and French flags (above) before throwing their weapons into U.S. trucks (below). (By kind permission of JC and James "Rabbit" Hare.)

of the Italian people taking their future into their own hands was set on solid political foundations by the signing of the Protocols.

The long-anticipated partisan rising – the "wind from the north" – would indeed blow fiercely in the spring of 1945, with resistance fighters, often led by Communist Party activists, establishing their own local governments as German troops abandoned northern Italy. In Genoa, Milan, Turin, and other northern cities, striking workers and partisan fighters fought running battles with Germans forces, culminating in the "auto-liberation" of these industrial centers and in the establishment of CLNAI-led local governments. But in cities, towns and villages across the North, partisan fighters then turned their arms over to arriving Allied troops. The Italian Communists, by remaining in the government even as the Socialist and the Action parties resigned in protest at Bonomi's increasingly moderate, pro-Allied, and pro-capitalist stance, thus ensured that Allied fears of "irresponsible communist activities" erupting during the final struggle against the German occupation would come to naught.[64] Acting within the architecture of global division established between Moscow and Washington at Tehran and consolidated at Yalta in February 1945, the PCI played a decisive role in preserving liberal democracy and capitalist social relations in Italy.

London finally recognized that it had become the junior partner in Italy.[65] Italy was not specifically discussed at the Yalta Conference in February 1945, but U.S. officials complained in private that London continued to obstruct the reconstruction of Italy. In an atmosphere of strained relations – Roosevelt ensured that Anglo-American preconference talks in Malta focused only on narrowly military questions – the president claimed that senior British and U.S. officials had reached agreement on Italy. "It is surely in our joint interest," Roosevelt argued, to provide the "spiritual and material food ... to foster [Italy's] gradual recuperation by developing a return to normal democratic processes."[66] The alternative, he cautioned darkly, was to allow "those who fish in troubled waters" to take advantage of Italy's "semi-servitude." With Roosevelt referring obliquely to the increasingly chilly relations with Moscow at the end of the war in Europe, Churchill was left little room for maneuver. He conceded in late February, announcing in parliament "we look forward to Italy's return under a truly democratic regime to the community of industrious and peace-loving nations."[67] Bold as ever, he also made the startling claim that he had "taken the lead" in promoting Italy's rehabilitation. Despite his bravura performance, Churchill's speech nevertheless marked the public abandonment of London's punitive policy toward Italy. The prime minister's

---

[64] Stettinius to Roosevelt, October 25, 1944, PSF, Vatican, Box 52, FDRL.
[65] See Moshe Gat, *Britain and Italy, 1943–1949: the Decline of British Influence* (Brighton: Sussex Academic Press, 1996), 103–107.
[66] Roosevelt to Churchill, February 11, 1945, *Correspondence*, 3: 533–534.
[67] Churchill speech February 27, 1945, *Parliamentary Debates*, 5th Series, 408, 1286.

sincerity can be gauged by the fact that only two weeks earlier he had rebuffed General Alexander's claim to be fighting to improve the lot of the Italians with an angry assertion that *he* was fighting "to secure the proper respect for the British people."[68] His public words now more accurately reflected the real relationship of forces.

American policy now came fully into its own. Celebrating the capture of Rome in June 1944, Roosevelt had described the long-anticipated event as an "investment for the future" that would permit the "salvage" of the Italian people.[69] His unspoken assumption was that the United States would furnish the means of "salvage," and that the "investment" would pay long-term dividends by advancing U.S. diplomatic, political, and economic influence in Italy. No one in Washington envisioned this influence being structured around a long-term military presence; instead, the success of U.S. arms would open the doors through which, as John Hersey put it so optimistically in the preface to *Bell for Adano*, the United States would get "on its way into Europe, ... full of knowledge and enthusiasm and ready to rebuild a shattered world on new foundations."[70] This would not be a project of military domination – although that would be necessary at the start – but of liberal paternalism, rebuilding with U.S. economic aid and under U.S. tutelage, and integrating the country into a U.S.-dominated world order.

Washington did not advance in a straight line toward these goals. On the contrary, its course unfolded through a series of opportunistic lurches and pragmatic adaptations that were themselves shaped by the contingencies of war, the complexities of relations with Britain and the Soviet Union, and development of Italian politics. In Italy, as in the rest of the Mediterranean, Washington was feeling its way into a politico-military situation of great complexity. It began its Italian campaign with a political approach that, like its initial policies toward Vichy, Madrid, and Algiers, was essentially conservative and promonarchical. But within weeks of the Salerno landings, this approach had to be jettisoned as policy makers, prompted by those closest to the action, responded to the mounting tide of popular rebellion in Italy. Having grasped the urgency of the unfolding crisis, Washington pursued a thoroughgoing liberalization of Italian politics with determination and through a series of interim compromises to the eventual triumph, courtesy of U.S. arms and Russian cooperation, in Rome.

After Rome, the character of U.S. engagement with Italy shifted, with less emphasis placed on the military aspects – the U.S.-led Fifth Army was stripped of seven divisions for the invasion of the French Riviera – and more on the political and economic. The twin banners under which this shift occurred were

---

[68] See Gat, *Britain and Italy*, 104–107; Cadogan, diary entry, February 13, 1945, David Dilks (ed.), *The Diaries of Sir Alexander Cadogan, 1938–1945* (New York: G. P. Putnam's Sons, 1972), 711.

[69] Roosevelt, "Fireside Chat," June 5, 1944, FDRL.

[70] John Hersey, *Bell for Adano*, 1944 (Reprint, New York: Vintage Books, 1988), 2.

"civilianization" and "rehabilitation," with Washington demilitarizing the occupation, putting significant political power back into Italian hands, and beginning the rebuilding of the Italian economy. As with the liberalization of Italian politics, this course was advanced in the teeth of British opposition, developing unevenly, pragmatically, and without any clear overall plan. But advance it did, from the "New Deal," via the reestablishment of Italian government finances by dollar remittances for troop pay, to the development of projects to rebuild Italian industry. It all turned out to be more difficult – and far more costly – than U.S. planners anticipated, but through this process Italy became the first former Axis power to be integrated into the emerging U.S.-led world economy.[71]

None of this would have been possible without the active support of Moscow and the actions of the Italian Communist Party. Togliatti, as Mason-Macfarlane had noted, played an absolutely "indispensable" role in establishing a broadly based government and in buffering the potentially revolutionary crises that accompanied the end of Fascist rule and German occupation.[72] Moscow's diplomatic and political initiatives in Italy developed within the overall architecture of the agreements reached at Tehran and, after some initial hesitation, they were welcomed and encouraged by Washington. Initial suggestions that London would be the beneficiary of Soviet recognition of the Badoglio government proved illusory, and the PCI's entry into Badoglio's cabinet in April 1944 was a critical step on the road to the establishment of the Bonomi government in June. If anything, the importance of collaboration between Washington, Moscow, and Rome increased after the establishment of the new liberal-Communist government. In late 1944, the PCI provided the critical link between Bonomi's cabinet and the CLNAI, facilitating the Protocols of Rome and, more importantly from the viewpoint of Italian capital, the relatively harmless exhaustion of the "wind from the north" the following spring.

After the potentially insurrectionary shocks of the "auto-liberation" had been buffered, however, and in the context of the end of the war in Europe and the rapid emergence of the lines of Cold War polarization, a new political situation opened up in Italy. For Washington, its alliance with Moscow – and hence with the PCI – was now a waning asset, and policy makers turned instead to the centrist and conservative forces around the emerging Christian Democracy Party and the Vatican. This shift had been prepared by alarmist reports on the advance of Russian influence in Italy, signaled in September 1944 by William Bullitt's warning from Rome that "hordes of invaders" from the East were set

---

[71] See Melvyn P. Leffler, *A Preponderance of Power: National Security, the Truman Administration, and the Cold War* (Stanford, CA: Stanford University Press, 1992), 71–73; Kolko, Politics of War, 60.

[72] Mason-Macfarlane, Notes on Chapter XVIII of Badoglio's "Italy in the Second World War," Mason-Macfarlane Papers, Reel 2, 3, IWM.

to prey on the prostrate country.[73] U.S. diplomats echoed these sentiments, with Alexander Kirk, since December 1945 U.S. ambassador to Rome, cautioning that without sustained "material and moral" support from the United States Italy would turn toward the "group of police states extending westwards from Russia."[74] With typical paternalism, journalists and policy makers worried that Italian "racial traits" and their "pacific ... attitude" made them particularly susceptible to political manipulation.[75] In a pointed hint that Italians could flip from one dictator to another, the *Saturday Evening Post* reported slogans proclaiming "Long Live Il Duce" being painted over with "Viva Stalin."[76]

In the immediate postwar period, Italy passed through a series of political crises as first Party of Action leader Ferruccio Parri and then Christian Democrat Alcide De Gasperi struggled to form workable governments.[77] The Allied military occupation ended in December 1945, but U.S. political and economic engagement continued to deepen, with political leaders in both Rome and Washington viewing it as the key to the maintenance of the social and political order. Thus the wartime occupation regime morphed seamlessly into a postwar relationship of U.S. hegemony, with the so-called empire by "invitation" resting firmly on military government and direct intervention into the affairs of another ostensibly sovereign state. Ambassador Kirk recognized this potentially troubling ideological bind but eased it to one side, noting "with full admission of the principle of non-intervention in the internal politics of another country" it was nevertheless necessary to "facilitate" democratic and pro-American government by "some means more efficacious than the statement of generalities and the emission of pious wishes."[78] In the following years, such economic, political, and covert "means" would culminate in Washington's successful effort secure a Christian Democrat victory in the critical 1948 election.

[73] Bullitt, "The World From Rome: The Eternal City Fears a Struggle Between Christianity and Communism," *Life*, September 4, 1944, 96, 104, 106.

[74] Kirk to Grew, July 11, 1945, Records of the Office of Western European Affairs, Box 3, RG 59, NARA.

[75] Bullitt, "The World from Rome"; State Dept. Country and Area Committee, CAC#242, August 31, 1944, microfilm T1221, NARA.

[76] Raymond, "We Run Third in Italy," *Saturday Evening Post*, June 17, 1944.

[77] See Paul Ginsborg, *A History of Contemporary Italy* (New York: Palgrave, 2003), chapter 3; Gat, *Britain and Italy*, 107ff.

[78] Kirk to Byrnes, February 22, 1946, *FRUS 1946*, 5: 881. See also Ellwood, *Italy 1943–1945*, 223.

Spain, Wolfram, and the "Liberal Turn"

In early 1943, the military rationale for the appeasement of Madrid evaporated as the success of *Torch* ruled out the possibility that Franco would risk entering the war on the Axis side. Within its own framework, Washington's policy toward the Franco government in the first two years of the war had been a complete success. Now, with the threat of Spanish belligerency gone, Washington was able gradually to abandon a course that long been the target of strident domestic criticism. For the remainder of the war, the administration adopted a more critical stance toward Franco's Madrid, focused in particular on efforts to block the continued sale of tungsten ore – or wolfram – to Germany. None of this happened quickly, but as Washington became more openly critical of the Franco government, its Spanish policy came into line with the liberal political framework evident in the proclamation of the "New Deal" in Italy. As these policies intertwined in late 1944, the administration's approach to the entire region – with the exception of its continuing support for French rule in North Africa – finally came into conformity with the democratic-sounding war aims enunciated in the Atlantic Charter.

Following the success of the *Torch* landings, Washington's relationship with Madrid came under renewed scrutiny. The deal with Darlan sharpened this process, as Washington's willingness to work with the former Vichy leader suggested to many that the policy of appeasement evident in America's relationship with Franco might now be being projected into other areas under Allied military occupation. Explicitly linking Darlan and Franco, the *Nation* warned of a "Europe studded with Quisling governments" and cautioned that "democratic elements all over the world" were becoming increasingly alarmed by the prospect of "marching ... side by side with their enemies."[1] In this context, press criticism of Washington's Spanish policy, muted prior to *Torch* in deference to

---

[1] Kirchwey, "Darlan and American Liberals," *The Nation*, November 28, 1942.

the military, now resumed with full force. The *Nation*, which together with other liberal mouthpieces had given Ambassador Carlton Hayes the "benefit of some rather grave doubts" prior to the invasion, now pointed in alarm to his pledge to Franco that the Spanish regime would not be jeopardized by an Allied victory.[2] If promises to sustain fascist-type regimes into the postwar period were being given, the editors argued, then the entire war was being fought for "strange and uncertain ends."

While liberal criticism along these lines intensified in early 1943, it took time for Washington to shape a new course. In the immediate aftermath of the landings, policy makers and opinion-formers alike warned against "counting" on Spanish neutrality, and the policy of using economic inducements to secure Spanish neutrality continued.[3] In December 1942, Roosevelt overrode objections from Henry Morgenthau's Treasury Department and approved Ambassador Hayes's proposal to permit currency transfers into previously frozen Spanish bank accounts in the United States.[4] The following month, the Joint Chiefs of Staff approved a State Department plan to push Germany out of the market for Spanish wolfram by using a "preclusive purchasing" campaign to force the price up to new heights.[5] Wolfram was a critical element in the production of armor plate and armor-piercing shells, and the effort to block German acquisition of this precious resource had obvious military significance. The preclusive purchasing campaign rested on the assumption that Spanish demand for U.S. oil would give Washington continued economic leverage, but it also required the maintenance of relatively amicable political relations between the two countries. In the politically charged atmosphere of the war in the Mediterranean, this amity would become increasingly controversial.

Less than a month after the start of the preclusive purchasing campaign, officials at the State Department's inter-departmental Iberian Peninsula Operating Committee (IPOC) noted that U.S. oil exports to Spain were increasing rapidly. Fearing that American-supplied fuel might be reaching Axis forces, IPOC concluded that the tide of accommodation with Madrid was "running too fast."[6] Cordell Hull agreed with IPOC's proposal to cut oil shipments to Spain from 135,000 to 100,000 tons per month, and instructed the embassy in Madrid not to authorize Spanish tanker sailings scheduled for May. When the embassy failed to implement this order, Hull asked the Joint Chiefs if there were any "military considerations" that necessitated the maintenance of such high levels

[2] Editorial, *The Nation*, January 23, 1943.

[3] Editorial, *Christian Science Monitor*, December 10, 1942.

[4] Roosevelt to Morgenthau, December 4, 1942, PSF, Box 50, Folder Spanish Diplomatic Correspondence, FDRL.

[5] Hull to JCS, December 22, 1942; JCS to Hull, January 14 1943, JCS 179, JCS Records, European Theater, Reel VI.

[6] Herbert Feis, *The Spanish Story: Franco and the Nations at War* (New York: W. W. Norton, 1948), 198.

of oil supply.[7] Assured that there were none, Hull repeated his instructions to the embassy in Madrid.[8] Carlton Hayes responded by informing the Secretary of State that he planned to ignore these instructions and authorize further tanker sailings. Efforts to curtail oil shipments, Hayes warned, threatened "our entire policy toward Spain," and he announced that he would appeal the matter directly to Roosevelt.[9]

Buoyed by his apparent success at preventing Spanish interference with *Torch* and by his direct line to the president, Hayes clearly felt empowered to ignore direct orders from Washington. The strength of his position is evidenced by the fact that the State Department overlooked his insubordination and backed down, with Assistant Secretary Dean Acheson notifying the Joint Chiefs that the department considered it inadvisable to recall tankers already at sea under Hayes's authorization lest it provoke "unwelcome political repercussions."[10] Admiral Leahy reiterated the Joint Chief's view that there was no military reason not to cut oil shipments, but added that the whole matter was more "political than military."[11] Hayes's appeal to the president resulted in petroleum attaché Walter Smith being recalled from Madrid for talks at the State Department and the Bureau of Economic Warfare. These resulted – not surprisingly – in an agreement to continue supplying U.S. oil to Spain at the higher levels. Clearly, even if support was building in Washington for a tougher line toward Madrid, the White House was not yet ready to change course.

Hayes's efforts to maximize oil shipments to Spain reflected his conviction that good commercial relations would help secure Franco as a "potential military ally."[12] Addressing a meeting of Spanish businessmen in February 1943, Hayes explained that the United States was willing to support the development of a strong "peace economy" capable of overcoming the "set backs" inflicted by the Civil War.[13] Hayes elaborated this approach in near-identical letters to Myron Taylor and Sumner Welles in which he argued that expanded U.S. trade would reinforce "moderates" within the government, help Madrid weather threats of "radical rioting and violent revolution," and secure Spain as a postwar "ally" (letter to Welles) or "satellite" (letter to Taylor).[14] On these questions, bearing directly on the creation of a stable postwar order with the United States at its head, Hayes's thinking seems to have paralleled that of the president. The problem was that the character of the Franco regime did not allow matters to unfold along quite such straightforward lines.

[7] Hull to JCS, Apr. 24, 1943, JCS 308, Records of JCS, European Theater, Reel VI.
[8] Hull to Hayes, April 27, 1943, *FRUS 1943*, 2: 676.
[9] Hayes to Hull, April 29, 1943, *FRUS 1943*, 2: 678.
[10] Acheson to Leahy, May 12, 1943, Records of JCS, European Theater, Reel VI.
[11] Leahy to Acheson, May 22, 1943, Records of JCS, European Theater, Reel VI.
[12] Hayes to Hull, June 22, 1943, *FRUS 1943*, 2: 697.
[13] Hayes speech, February 23, 1943, Box 1A, Hayes papers, Columbia University.
[14] Hayes to Taylor and Hayes to Welles, April 29, 1943, Box 5, Hayes Papers.

Hayes's ability to use U.S. trade to help forge closer political ties with Madrid rested directly on Roosevelt's willingness to back his ambassador to Spain. In early 1943, Hayes's standing in Washington was reinforced by several diplomatic successes that reflected Franco's growing recognition that Allied victories from North Africa to Stalingrad signaled a decisive shift in the military balance to the detriment of the Axis powers. Typically, Franco kept his options open by concluding a new accord with Berlin in December 1942, but he also responded positively to U.S. overtures on a number of important questions. In February 1943, Madrid permitted the repatriation of Allied airmen who had made their way to Spain after being downed over Europe. Then in May, Franco bucked German pressure and opened the Pyrenean border to thousands of French people, many of them Jews, who were fleeing the German occupation of southern France following *Torch*.[15] Hayes presented these Spanish concessions as very much the product of his own diplomatic virtuosity; even while negotiating with Madrid on the question of refugees, he refused to allow the War Refugee Board to base one of its officers in the embassy, leading WRB head James Mann to speculate on Hayes's own anti-Semitism.[16] Nevertheless, working in conjunction with the Red Cross, and backed by a $100,000 contribution from the president's Emergency Fund, the embassy persuaded Madrid to allow as many as 40,000 refugees to pass through Spain.[17] Of these, some 16,000 Frenchmen headed for North Africa where many joined the Free French forces being reorganized and rearmed there.[18]

Hayes built on these steps, meeting with Franco in July 1943 to secure a pledge that Madrid was willing to "alter" its policy on a number of key questions, including dropping "non-belligerency" in favor neutrality, ending anti-Allied bias in the Spanish media, and withdrawing the Blue Division from Russia.[19] Hayes assured Franco that, while he shared the dictator's "repugnance" for Communism, the U.S. government could not condone Spanish interference in Russia's internal affairs. Madrid announced its neutrality on October 3, 1943, and, while some Spanish soldiers stayed in Russia as volunteers in the German army, the bulk of the Blue Division began pulling out of the front lines and preparing for repatriation the following week.

Despite these successes, however, criticism of Washington's Spanish policy continued to mount. Allegations in *The Nation* that Spain was funneling American oil to Germany were echoed in the mainstream press, and the *New York Times* expressed concern that Hayes was going "a little far out of his

---

[15] See Emmet Kennedy, "Carlton J. H. Hayes's Wartime Diplomacy: Making Spain a Haven from Hitler," *Diplomatic History* 36, no. 2, (April 2012), 252–253.

[16] See David Mayers, *FDR's Ambassadors and the Diplomacy of Crisis: From the Rise of Hitler to the End of World War II* (Cambridge: Cambridge University Press, 2013), 327, fn 13.

[17] See Kennedy, "Carlton J. H. Hayes's Wartime Diplomacy," 244, 253.

[18] Carlton Hayes, *Wartime Mission to Spain, 1942–1945* (New York: Macmillan, 1945), 119.

[19] Hayes to Hull, July 29, 1943, *FRUS 1943*, 2: 612.

way" in praising Franco.[20] These criticisms stung the ambassador, who viewed them as evidence that the U.S. press was under the influence of a secret cabal of Communists and Spanish Republicans that the State Department was either "unable or unwilling" to challenge.[21] But the shrill tone of Hayes's complaints suggests that he was aware that, despite his recent victories and his relationship with the president, the tide was turning against him. He had reason for concern. As they reviewed strategic options in preparation for the *Quadrant* conference at Quebec in August 1943, the Joint Chiefs discussed the possibility of invading Europe via Spain.[22] The scheme was shelved, but the critical new approach to Spain that underpinned it led them to concluded "the time is now ripe [to] adopt a stern and frankly demanding" policy aimed at stopping the export of Spanish wolfram to Germany.[23] Reflecting this new interest in breaking Madrid's ties to Berlin, a British briefing paper highlighted the critical role of tungsten in arms manufacture, concluding that German production of armor-piercing ammunition would grind to a halt within six months if shipments of Spanish wolfram ended.[24]

By the time of the *Quadrant* conference, the preclusive purchasing campaign had pushed prices of Spanish wolfram to such heights that Germany had been virtually driven from the market. Intense competition for this scarce resource increased Spain's income from wolfram sales from £73,000 in 1940 to £15.7 million in 1943, creating a super-heated bubble in an otherwise desolate economy. Madrid was understandably keen to maintain prices at this inflated level, and that meant ensuring continued competition. To this end, and motivated by economic pragmatism as much as by pro-Axis sentiment, Madrid facilitated Berlin's reentry into the market in the fall of 1943 by advancing it a 100 million Reichsmark line of credit.[25] The resumption of German efforts to buy wolfram qualified the success of the preclusive purchasing campaign, leading to demands in the United States for measures to force an end to wolfram exports to the Reich once and for all. In mid-October, the State Department instructed Hayes to offer Madrid U.S. wheat in exchange for the complete cessation of wolfram shipments to Germany. Hayes demurred, arguing for a less confrontational stance and pointing out that the British shared his approach.[26]

Hayes's ability to deflect mounting pressure for a radical shift in U.S. policy was undermined by a particularly maladroit move by the Franco government.

[20] Editorial, *New York Times*, May 13, 1943.
[21] Hayes, *Wartime Mission*, 136.
[22] William D. Leahy, *I Was There: The Personal Story of the Chief of Staff to Presidents Roosevelt and Truman Based on His Notes and Diaries Made at the Time* (New York: McGraw Hill, 1950), 165–166.
[23] CCS 303, August 9, 1943, PREM 3/405/4.
[24] CCS 321, August 20, 1943, PREM 3/405/4.
[25] Christian Leitz, *Sympathy for the Devil: Neutral Europe and Nazi Germany in World War II* (New York: NYU Press, 2001), 130–135.
[26] Hull to Hayes, October 15, 1943; Hayes to Hull, October 21 1943, *FRUS 1943*, 2: 643–645.

On October 18, 1943, the Spanish government sent a telegram to Filipino politician José Laurel congratulating him on his appointment as head of the new Japanese-sponsored government in the Philippines. The telegram, quickly reprinted in the German press, suggested that Madrid's enthusiasm for the Axis cause remained strong. An embarrassed Hayes explained to Roosevelt that although "ill-advised and stupid," the telegram was the work of a single disgruntled Falangist in the Foreign Ministry.[27] That may – or may not – have been so, but the note had gone out over foreign minister Francisco Jordana's signature, thus giving those in the administration who wanted to take a harder line with Spain the *cause célèbre* they needed. And now, as U.S. officials prepared a new campaign of economic pressure to force the complete cessation of wolfram exports to Germany, it appeared that Roosevelt was also ready to adopt a more confrontational stance toward Franco.

In November 1943, the Joint Chiefs of Staff approved the new campaign to constrict oil shipments to Spain in an effort to force Madrid to end wolfram exports to Germany; and in January 1944, the State Department instructed Hayes to notify the Spanish authorities that further tanker loadings had been "suspended."[28] The oil embargo was on. Washington's tough new line received enthusiastic press support, with the *New York Times* hoping that it might lead to the overthrow of Franco's "totalitarian" regime.[29] Longtime opponents of Franco were encouraged by the change in U.S. policy, with Congressman John Coffee of Washington calling for the United States to work for the overthrow of Franco so that Spain could rejoin the "world family of democratic countries."[30]

From Madrid, Carlton Hayes warned darkly that the oil embargo might produce the kind of economic dislocation that could reopen the Civil War and provoke a new Spanish revolution.[31] As oil shortages began to take effect, Hayes tried desperately to craft a compromise solution, presenting Washington's demands to Madrid in the most apologetic manner possible and promising to compensate for the loss of lucrative German wolfram contracts by increased trade with America.[32] There was no compromise to be had and, with Roosevelt swinging firmly onto an anti-Franco tack – the president even complained to Churchill that Hayes seemed overly inclined to "accept some compromise short of a complete embargo" – it was clear that the ambassador no longer enjoyed the support of the White House.[33]

[27] Hayes to Roosevelt, November 15, 1943, Box 3, Hayes Papers.
[28] Leahy to Stettinius, November 14, 1943, JCS 538/1, Records of JCS, European Theater, Reel VI; Hull to Hayes, January 27, 1944, *FRUS 1944*, 4: 304.
[29] Editorial, *New York Times*, January 20, 1944.
[30] Coffee speech, February 24, 1944, *Congressional Record* 90, part 2, 78th Congress, 2nd Session, 2040.
[31] Hayes to Hull, January 28, 1944, *FRUS 1944*, 4: 306.
[32] See Hayes, notes on meeting with Jordana, January 3, 1944, Box 3, Hayes Papers.
[33] Roosevelt to Churchill, February 15, 1944, Warren F. Kimball (ed.), *Churchill and Roosevelt: The Complete Correspondence* (London: Collins, 1984), 2: 728.

The deepening divide between Washington and Hayes was mirrored within the Madrid embassy, where relations between the ambassador and more liberally inclined officers assigned by the Office of Strategic Services and Office of War Information were particularly bad. Hayes suspected the OSS Madrid station of plotting with Spanish Republicans to overthrow Franco, while for its part the intelligence agency felt compelled to run many of its Spanish operations from Lisbon to circumvent the ambassador's policy of identifying U.S. agents to the Spanish authorities.[34] In early 1943, the OSS had survived a formal complaint from Hayes to the Joint Chiefs demanding that Donovan withdraw his agents from Spain. Not surprisingly, relations between the OSS and the ambassador did not improve after that.[35] To compound the increasingly dysfunctional nature of the Madrid embassy, Office of War Information officials assigned to the press office contrived to give official press releases a markedly anti-Franco slant.[36] These problems did not pass without notice; in the summer of 1944, Congressman Emanuel Celler of New York demand Hayes's recall for his continued refusal to aid the work of the War Refugee Board.[37]

As well overcoming the resistance of their own ambassador, U.S. policy makers also had to contend with British efforts to maintain close relations with the Franco government. During 1942, the preparations for *Torch* had ensured that the two allies had pursued similar policies toward Madrid, but after the landings divergent pressures came to bear. At the time of the *Quadrant* conference in August 1943, Foreign Secretary Anthony Eden had expressed general agreement with U.S. efforts to be "firmer with the Spaniards" but noted, by way of a get-out clause, that the question was "how and when?"[38] London remained torn between accepting Washington's new line, and urging caution lest the Spanish respond by cutting trade with Britain and "deny[ing] us our iron ore."[39] Given Britain's own economic difficulties, the latter consideration prevailed. When initial effects of the oil embargo failed to persuade Spain to end sales of wolfram to Germany, London advocated accepting a "slight compromise" to escape the "present deadlock."[40]

London's refusal to force the issue bolstered Spanish resistance, and in April 1944 Roosevelt abandoned the effort to stop all shipments of Spanish wolfram to Germany, accepting instead a compromise that limited the trade but did not stop it entirely.[41] Despite Churchill's offer to ease Washington's "difficulties

---

[34] See Smith, *OSS*; Mark Byrnes, "Unfinished Business: The United States and Franco's Spain, 1944–1947," *Diplomacy and Statecraft*, 11, no. 1(2000), fn28, 158.

[35] See Douglas Waller, *Wild Bill Donovan: The Spymaster Who Created the OSS and Modern American Espionage* (New York: Free Press, 2011), 159–163.

[36] On discord in the Madrid embassy, see memoir by former OWI officer Abel Plenn, *Wind in the Olive Trees* (New York: Bonni and Gaer, 1946).

[37] See Mayers, *FDR's Ambassadors*, 327, fn. 13.

[38] Eden to Churchill, August 22, 1943, PREM 3/405/4.

[39] Churchill to Eden, February 18, 1944, PREM 3/405/7.

[40] Churchill to Roosevelt, March 30, 1944, *Correspondence*, 3: 66–68.

[41] Roosevelt to Churchill, April 25, 1944, *Correspondence*, 3: 114.

about public opinion" by taking responsibility for the compromise, Cordell Hull feared that a resumption of oil shipments to Spain without a clear-cut victory would provoke a "press outburst" in the United States.[42] When he finally acquiesced to Roosevelt's efforts to secure a compromise, the State Department issued a curt statement announcing that the deal to limit Spanish wolfram shipments to Germany had been struck in response to an "urgent request" from London.[43]

It looked as though Carlton Hayes had emerged victorious once again. Some liberal journals certainly took this view and attacked both Hayes and the deal, while mainstream media voices hailed the compromise as a "signal victory" and heaped renewed praise on the ambassador.[44] Over the following months Carlton Hayes registered further diplomatic successes. With the military situation making Madrid more responsive to U.S. approaches, Hayes secured the expulsion of German agents from Tangier and the regularization of commercial airline services to Spain.[45] But, notwithstanding these modest successes, there could be no return to the old policy of appeasement. Despite ending in compromise, the wolfram crisis marked a definitive turn in Washington's Spanish policy and the adoption of a course characterized by increasing public hostility toward the Franco regime: as Leo Crowley, director of the Bureau of Economic Warfare, remarked excitedly, the crisis signaled "a new change of thought over there [at the State Department]."[46]

Senior State Department official Perry George spelled out the consequences of this "new change of thought" to Carlton Hayes during a visit to Madrid at the height of the wolfram crisis.[47] In an extensive memorandum written in preparation for his discussion with Hayes, George situated American relations with Madrid in the context of the rapidly emerging postwar world. Arguing that Spain had placed itself outside of the broad democratic "rehabilitation" of the world that was Washington's main goal, he concluded that Franco's removal was a necessary precondition for Spain's diplomatic reintegration.[48] George also insisted that this was the most sensitive international issue facing the United States, and that the "natural shortness of temper" evident in the domestic discourse on Spain made it imperative to avoid any further taint of appeasement.

[42] Churchill to Roosevelt, April 22, 1944, *Correspondence*, 3: 107–108; Halifax to Foreign Office, April 18 and 27, 1944, PREM 3/505/2.
[43] "Agreement with Spain on Certain Outstanding Issues," *Department of State Bulletin*, May 6, 1944, 412.
[44] Editorial, *New York Times*, May 6, 1944.
[45] See "Agreement Between the United States and Spain Relating to the Operation of International Air Transport Service," *Department of State Bulletin*, December 3, 1944, 674–676.
[46] Transcript of telephone call, Crowley to Morgenthau, April 28, 1944, Morgenthau Diary, 725: 39–41, FDRL.
[47] Hull to Hayes, April 4, 1944, *FRUS 1944*, 4: 377–378.
[48] George to Hayes, April 11, 1944, Box 1, Hayes Papers.

Grasping the direction in which Washington was heading, Hayes attempted to convince Madrid to "reorient ... before it was too late."[49] Speaking as a "friend of Spain" he appealed directly to Franco but, given the turn in U.S. policy, he was unable to offer any new material incentives to promote expanded cooperation with the Allies. Reading the writing on the wall, Hayes resigned his ambassadorship in November 1944, arguing that his "wartime mission" had been successfully completed, and pleading a desire to return to academia. Typically, he spent his final weeks in Spain attempting to block Operation *Safehaven*, a joint Treasury, State Department, and Foreign Economic Administration project to disrupt the dispersal of German assets in neutral countries.[50] After returning to the United States, he was stung by an extensive article in *Harper's Magazine* that was critical of his ambassadorship, and he quickly took sabbatical leave to pen his own exculpatory account of his work in Spain.[51] Unlike the *Harper's* journalists, however, he was not granted access to State Department files.

In the context of Washington's developing plans for the postwar world order, the true significance of the wolfram crisis had little to do with the actual quantities of tungsten ore shipped to Germany. As U.S. leaders well knew, the pending invasion of France would soon make it physically impossible to ship any more Spanish ore to Germany, thereby rendering the whole question moot. Instead, the wolfram issue provided a serviceable focus for a significant redefinition of U.S. policy in relation both to Spain and to the broader postwar order. President Roosevelt took the appointment of Hayes's successor, career diplomat Norman Armour, as an opportunity to develop these themes. In a letter to Armour, later published in the *New York Times* to buttress Washington's anti-Franco credentials, Roosevelt argued that the Franco regime was a product of German and Italian aid and was "patterned" along similarly "totalitarian lines."[52] The forthcoming defeat of Germany, he concluded, must bring with it the "extermination of Nazi and similar ideologies" elsewhere: there was to be no place in the "community of nations" for governments based on "fascist principles." While genuflecting before the principle of noninterference in the internal affairs of other countries, Roosevelt made it clear that Armour's embassy would have an explicitly anti-Franco mission. Hayes wrote to the president to protest the new course, arguing that Franco's "cautious cleverness" had served the Allies well and that it would be a grave mistake to press

---

[49] Hayes, notes of meeting with Jordana, June 30, 1944, Box 3 Hayes Papers.

[50] See Donald P. Steury, "Tracking Nazi Gold: the OSS and Project *Safehaven*, Center for the Study of Intelligence, CIA website, https://www.cia.gov/library/center-for-the-study-of-intelligence/kent-csi/docs/v44i3a04p.html, 3 and fn. 6.

[51] See Ernest K. Lindley and Edward Weintal, "How We Dealt with Spain," *Harper's Magazine*, December 1944.

[52] Roosevelt to Armour, March 10, 1945, PSF, Box 50, FDRL; Reprinted in *New York Times*, September 25, 1945.

for his removal.[53] His plea, so patently at odds with the liberal gloss on U.S. policy at the war's end, was ignored.

Washington's vocal opposition to Franco also became an important element in the deepening political divide between the United States and Britain in the closing stages of the war. The compromise solution to the wolfram crisis allowed Washington to place the blame for the failure to achieve a total embargo squarely on London, reinforcing the image of the British as conservative defenders of the old order, and of the United States as the champion of a democratic new world purged of all taint of fascism and appeasement. These divisions deepened in May 1944 when Churchill addressed "kindly words" to Spain in the House of Commons, recognizing Madrid's "services" to the Allied cause and looking forward to "increasingly good relations" in the future.[54] In an implicit swipe at Washington, Churchill suggested that the war had become less "ideological" as it had progressed.

In a pointed public reply, made on behalf of an administration interested in making the war *more* ideological and less overtly pragmatic, Roosevelt noted that Spanish neutrality had always been "less than satisfactory." "With a bit of a twinkle in her eye," Eleanor Roosevelt joined in, observing "Mr. Churchill has thought the same way for sixty years and doesn't want to change."[55] As was often the case, Anne O'Hare McCormick drew out the big picture, arguing that Churchill's "kindly words about Spain" and his assertion that Madrid would be a "strong influence for the peace of the Mediterranean" indicated that Britain was "looking beyond the war to the strengthening of her ties with Western Europe."[56] It would be "surprising," McCormick assured her readers, "if either the Spain or the Europe emerging from the crucible will be the Europe tentatively sketched by Mr. Churchill."

Despite this intensified public criticism of Franco, U.S. policy makers studiously avoided giving any indication that they favored either a return of the Republic or – even worse – a resumption of the Civil War. On the contrary, as a 1945 State Department Advisory Committee on Postwar Foreign Policy paper put it, they concluded that the United States could not put "much faith" in the establishment of a "successful republic" in Spain because such a government would inevitably have "leftist tendencies."[57] The utility of this approach became clear at the Potsdam conference in July 1945. Here Washington combined verbal hostility toward Franco with actual opposition to any outside intervention in Spanish affairs. This carefully nuanced policy allowed the new Truman administration to steer between British support for the Nationalist

---

[53] Hayes to Roosevelt, February 1945; Roosevelt to Hayes, March 29, 1945, PSF, Box 50, FDRL.
[54] "Text of Churchill's Survey," *New York Times*, May 25, 1944.
[55] "Roosevelt Criticizes Spain, Takes Issue with Churchill," *New York Times*, May 31, 1944.
[56] McCormick, "Abroad," *New York Times*, May 27, 1944.
[57] ACPFP, "Spain: Possible Restoration of the Monarchy under British Auspices," Doc.T-536, January 11, 1945, Notter Files, Microfiche.

regime – suitably prettified by a return of the monarchy – and Russian insistence on international action to remove Franco.[58] The final Potsdam commu-
niqué reflected this uneasy compromise, noting that the Franco dictatorship
had been established with Axis support and opposing Spanish membership of
the United Nations, but stopping short of any proposal for action against the
regime. This balancing act enabled Washington to step forward as the champion of a democratic postwar order without having to take action against
overtly undemocratic regimes in Spain and elsewhere.

The corollary of this policy was that while Washington had maintained discrete relations with former Spanish Republican leaders throughout the war,
U.S. policy makers never gave any serious consideration to working with them
to launch a struggle against the Franco dictatorship. On the contrary, U.S.
officials maintained that any resumption of the Civil War, perhaps triggered by
a German invasion or by economic hardship, would create dangerous instability, military complications for the Allies, and opportunities for Communist
advance. From this point of view, and despite the gyrations in policy toward
the Franco government, Washington always made clear its willingness to underwrite Spanish capitalism; as Carlton Hayes assured the Spanish government,
U.S. aid would help Spain solve the economic problems that might otherwise
"encourage the growth of communism."[59]

On this critical question, Washington enjoyed the implicit support of the
Russian government, reflecting Stalin's view that Spain lay unequivocally within
the U.S. sphere of influence. Moscow's stance was of vital importance in two
instances. First, Moscow effectively turned a blind eye to Madrid's involvement in the dispatch of the Blue Division to the Eastern Front in 1941, thereby
avoiding the prospect of a Russian declaration of war on Spain with all of its
disruptive consequences for Allied diplomacy. Second, as thousands of former
Republican fighters crossed the Pyrenees from France into Spain in late 1944,
Moscow refused to back a renewal of armed action against Franco, acting
through the Spanish Communist Party to tamp down the incipient revolt. With
Moscow again underwriting the stability of a key western country, the United
States stood aside as the Spanish army crushed the guerrillas. Carlton Hayes
reassured Roosevelt that the insurgents, many of whom had fought with the
French resistance, were no better than "cattle rustlers" and "thieves."[60]

Washington's Spanish policy during World War II has been described as a
series of lurches from "war-inspired idealism" to "realism" and back again.[61]
In an effort to avoid a German-dominated Europe, Washington first used
trade-based appeasement to secure the neutrality of the Franco regime. In early

---

[58] See Byrnes, "Unfinished Business," 139–143.
[59] Hayes to Jordana, October 21, 1943, *FRUS 1943*, 2: 623.
[60] See Paul Preston, *Franco: A Biography* (New York: Basic Books, 1994), 518; Hayes to Roosevelt,
    "Memorandum on the Spanish Situation," February 1945, PSF Box 50, FDRL.
[61] See Byrnes, "Unfinished Business," especially 148–149.

1941, this "realist" policy was terminated amidst a flurry of domestic criticism and, in the context of Roosevelt's campaign to paint the world crisis in starkly Manichaean terms, replaced by trade sanctions and vocal anti-Francoism. Another sharp turn unfolded in 1942 as Washington prepared for the invasion of North Africa, with Carlton Hayes, backed by Roosevelt, ably executing a policy of unabashed appeasement. During 1943, the global military situation enabled Washington to begin sketching out a new world order based on liberal democracy and free trade under U.S. hegemony, and this in turn necessitated drawing a clear line against the Franco regime. Given Carlton Hayes's opposition to the new course, this policy transition was a long and difficult one, but it was signaled by efforts to stop the export of wolfram to Germany in early 1944, and was finally cemented by Hayes's resignation and the appointment of Nelson Armour in March 1945.

Both "realism" (appeasement) and "idealism" (anti–Francoism) were thus different phases and successive aspects of a single, fundamentally pragmatic, policy. While liberals in the media and in the administration maintained a constant barrage of opposition to appeasement, their efforts were not responsible for the anti-Franco tacks adopted in early 1941 and again in mid-1943. Instead, the liberal critique served to popularize a course that the administration, for entirely pragmatic reasons, had already fixed upon. When "realism" was in the ascendancy, in 1939–1940 and again during 1942–1943, these domestic critics were effectively marginalized. This zigzag course makes it clear that "idealism" was not in some way the real character of Roosevelt's foreign policy, buried out of necessity for extended periods but reemerging when the administration finally won the "luxury" of "indulging" in it.[62] In fact, "realism" and "idealism" were equally Rooseveltian traits, deployable according to specific circumstances.

In its general outline, the evolution of Washington's Spanish policy parallels broadly similar developments in relation to Italy and France. In Italy, initial State Department projections for a post-Mussolini regime built around the monarchy were quickly discarded as reentry of the Italian people into politics made it clear that a more broadly based and politically liberal solution was necessary to buffer popular radicalism. The opportunity to implement such a course arrived with the capture of Rome in June 1944, an event that in turn opened the door to greater U.S. political and economic involvement in Italy. In France, Washington's policy of appeasing Vichy and then of backing Darlan and Giraud was only gradually replaced by one that recognized the leadership of the CFLN and, even more reluctantly, of Charles de Gaulle. But, if Washington lagged in responding to the new political reality represented by the formation of the CFLN, it displayed no such reticence when it came to rearming and reequipping the substantial French army under de Gaulle's command in North Africa. This dual policy of extending

<hr />

[62] Ibid., 131.

military support to the CFLN while withholding political recognition carried Washington into the invasion of southern France in the summer of 1944 and facilitated, courtesy of the enormous armed might marshaled in the Mediterranean by the United States, the establishment of a post-occupation government in Paris that would be essentially pro-American in character and orientation.

The evolution of U.S. policy in the Mediterranean signaled by these broadly parallel shifts in relations with Italy, France, and Spain during 1944 can be loosely described as a "liberal turn," and as it unfolded it began to impart a progressive ideological coloration to Washington's approach to the entire region. With hindsight, and because the liberal turn brought the political form of Washington's Mediterranean policy into conformity with the ideological war aims presented in the Atlantic Charter and popularized by the "Four Freedoms," this might seem unremarkable. But in contrast to Washington's earlier political relationships in the region, marked by the appeasement of Franco, relations with Vichy and Darlan, and support for Badoglio and Victor Emmanuel, the shift was dramatic and profound.

The "liberal turn" enabled Washington to conclude its wartime engagement with the Mediterranean by putting the compromises with assorted "Quislings," characteristic of the early years of the war, behind it. With this belated seizure of the moral high ground, Washington was able to bury the actual history of its political intervention in the Mediterranean deeply and – at least in terms of popular public perception – permanently. In fact, of course, political action in support of rightist and undemocratic figures had not ended, as the escalating covert intervention in Italian politics and the rehabilitation of Franco in the name of "Western" security would soon reveal, but the place of the Mediterranean in the construction of the "Good War" was secured.

The approval of Moscow, and the active assistance of the Communist parties in France, Italy, and Spain, was critical to the construction of the liberal turn. Once Europe had been divided into spheres of influence, tentatively at Tehran and with more assurance at Yalta, Washington could proceed secure in the knowledge that if the workers' revolts it had feared for so long actually erupted, it would have powerful Russian support in containing or suppressing them. This assurance was particularly important in Italy, where knowledge that the "wind from the North" would be controlled by its own leaders allowed Washington to press ahead with the civilianization of Italian politics and the advance U.S. economic and political interests, while simultaneously releasing the combat units necessary for the invasion of southern France. In France, collaboration with the French Communist Party enabled U.S. and French troops, acting in conjunction with the CFLN, to master the turbulent political situation in Marseilles and throughout southern France and to integrate the fighters of the *Maquis* into the military apparatus of the new regime. In Spain, meanwhile, Spanish Communists ensured that there was no substantial resurgence in Republican activity at the end of the war.

One inevitable consequence confluence of the Soviet-American strategic interests registered at Tehran was the declining influence of the Anglo-American axis.[63] It is not surprising, therefore, that every aspect of the "liberal turn" was carried through in the face of British opposition: In Italy, the British sought to maintain a political setup centered on the King and Badoglio and, when this failed, to block "civilianization" and "rehabilitation"; in Spain, London strove to maintain ties with the Franco regime and to avoid a sharp clash over the export of wolfram; and in France, Churchill conducted a desperate struggle against *Anvil/Dragoon*. On top of their failures to block U.S. policy in these key areas, the British saw their own hopes for the development of the war in the Mediterranean, from plans for extended operations in the Aegean to the fanciful scheme of a drive through the Ljubljana Gap to Vienna, scuppered by Washington with Moscow's approval. Washington's complete and unambiguous victories over its British ally on all these key questions in the summer of 1944 illustrate the degree to which the Americans had now emerged as the driving force in the Mediterranean

---

[63] See Mark Stoler, *Allies and Adversaries: The Joint Chiefs of Staff, the Grand Alliance, and U.S. Strategy in World War II* (Chapel Hill: University of North Carolina Press, 2000), 167.

12

The Culbertson Mission and the Open Door

As U.S. policy makers worked to shape the emerging contours of postwar power in the Mediterranean, they also began to press for a loosening of the bureaucratic controls over economic activity in the region that had been characteristic of the early years of the war. Officials were guided in this effort by a deep-seated belief in the efficacy of free trade and in the consequent necessity of establishing "open door" access to overseas markets.[1] However, while Secretary of State Cordell Hull had long viewed the promotion of free trade as the cornerstone of U.S. foreign policy, the new drive to end wartime regulation did not imply simply pursuing a return to prewar conditions. On the contrary, with the economies of both allies and enemies debilitated by war, with the old structures of imperial control shaken, and with American businessmen eager to explore a broad range of commercial opportunities opened up by U.S. military and diplomatic engagement, the United States was poised to become the predominant economic power in the Western Mediterranean. In this context, the project of establishing a U.S.-dominated regime of "free" trade and open door access to markets throughout the Mediterranean inevitably pointed toward the restructuring of the economy of the entire region under American leadership and for America's benefit.

A key agent in this new campaign was American attorney, diplomat, and expert on international trade William S. Culbertson. Culbertson arrived in Algiers on August 9, 1944 on the first leg of an economic mission sponsored by the State Department and the Foreign Economic Administration, which would take him on a broad sweep through the Mediterranean world from French North Africa and the Middle East to Italy and France.[2] Culbertson's

---

[1] See Lloyd Gardner, *Economic Aspects of New Deal Diplomacy* (Madison: University of Wisconsin Press, 1964), especially chapter 13.

[2] For an overview of the Culbertson Mission, see John A. DeNovo, "The Culbertson Economic Mission and Anglo-American Tensions in the Middle East, 1944–1945," *The Journal of American History* 63, no. 4 (1977); also Gardner, *Economic Aspects*, 220–226.

FIGURES 12.1 AND 12.2. America's deepening economic and cultural involvement in the Mediterranean took many forms. (above) Six Women's Army Corps soldiers enjoy a day on the beach in Algeria, June 26, 1944. Although – presumably – on a private beach, their behavior demonstrates a striking lack of concern for local mores. (below) Sampling the Orient in safety: U.S. airmen admire Arab trinkets on display in the PX store on an unidentified base in Cairo, Egypt. (Courtesy of Franklin D. Roosevelt Library.)

team included leaders of the National Foreign Trade Council, together with businessmen representing leading exporters in the drug, chemical, automotive, and steel industries. His brief was to review current economic conditions in the Mediterranean countries and to outline the steps necessary to "restore" trade to its normal "commercial channels."[3] The barely concealed subtext was that this process would involve the rapid dismantling of the bureaucratically controlled and centrally planned distribution of Lend-Lease and other wartime economic aid, and the reinstitution of the open door and bilateral free trade. As an ardent free trader, Secretary of State Cordell Hull gave enthusiastic support to the Culbertson Mission, underscoring its importance by persuading President Roosevelt to accord its leader ambassadorial status.

The dispatch of the Culbertson Mission signaled a key turning point in the development of Washington's grand strategy in the Mediterranean. In nearly two years of fighting, the "gales of war" had, in Lloyd Gardner's memorable phrase, "blown open the door," clearing the way for the emergence U.S.-dominated systems of bilateral and multilateral trade throughout the region.[4] But during this first and primarily military phase of U.S. engagement, operational and political imperatives had led Washington to participate in the most unfree of regulatory bodies, including the Middle East Supply Center (MESC), the North African Economic Board (NAEB), and the various bilateral agreements governing Lend-Lease. Through these various bodies, and in ways that seemed to many to contradict the basic principles of U.S. capitalism, the state itself had taken a leading role in economic life. The primacy of the state in economic affairs does not mean that Washington's participation in these forms of centrally planned economic activity was inimical to U.S. business interests. It was not; although individual businessmen often railed against the restrictions placed on unfettered free trade, the picture looked rather different from the standpoint of America's overall economic development. In fact, the contacts made and the experience gained by participation in MESC and the NAEB, often in areas where prewar U.S. trade penetration had been weak or nonexistent, were invaluable when it came time to shift back to unrestricted free trade.

By 1943, the Middle East Supply Center had come, as its historian Martin Wilmington put it, to "dominate the entire Middle East economy."[5] Established by London in April 1941 and headquartered in Cairo, MESC was initially set up to ensure that sufficient shipping capacity was set aside from the task of moving soldiers and military supplies to facilitate the provision of essential civilian goods to the countries of the Middle East. London's motivation had nothing to do with philanthropy, stemming instead from a fear that food shortages would reinforce nationalist and anti-British sentiment throughout the

---

[3] *Department of State Bulletin*, July 30, 1944.
[4] Gardner, *Economic Aspects of New Deal Diplomacy*, 220.
[5] Martin W. Wilmington, *The Middle East Supply Center* (Albany: State University of New York Press, 1971), 141.

region. The United States joined MESC in April 1942, dispatching Frederick Winant, former head of the wartime Export Control Office, to Cairo together with three staff members drawn from the Board of Economic Warfare, the Lend-Lease Administration, and the Department of Agriculture. While their numbers were limited – the British had more than 100 officers working at the supply center's headquarters – the fact that the Americans were backed by a war economy then moving into top gear allowed them to have a substantial impact on policy. As well as organizing to fill orders for much-needed civilian goods with American-made products, Winant's team also promoted import substitution efforts that used U.S. machinery and technical know-how to help local businessmen set up manufacturing and assembly plants.

As U.S. participation in MESC expanded, and as American war matériel and Lend-Lease supplies flooded into the region, U.S. diplomats became accustomed to hosting high-level government delegations interested in trade and economic development.[6] The work of a special military-economic mission established in the summer of 1942 under the leadership of Colonel Harold Hoskins, the Beirut-born son of U.S. missionaries, former textile executive, and friend of the president's, was of particular importance.[7] Envisioned as a contribution to the defense of British positions in the Middle East in the face of Rommel's advance on Suez, the Hoskins Mission was based in Cairo and operated throughout the region. Its mission, according to Cordell Hull, was to "capitalize on the existing goodwill towards the United States" to build support for a "United Nations victory" in the Arab world.[8]

Given that the Hoskins Mission would clearly also be developing contacts useful to U.S. business, the War Department cautioned against sending such a mission into a region in which Britain had long been the predominant power. President Roosevelt, however, claimed to see no contradiction between building support for the United Nations and capitalizing on opportunities to strengthen U.S. business. In fact, as Cordell Hull explained, the fact that a long history of American philanthropic and missionary work in the Middle East demonstrated that U.S. efforts were not "tarnished by any material motives or interests" rendered the United States uniquely capable of building support for the Allies in countries under some degree of British control.[9] "No other member of the United Nations," Hull added pointedly, could make a "claim" to enlightened disinterest.

Developing this theme, plans were made for the Hoskins Mission to be accompanied by an Office of War Information campaign designed to boost U.S.

[6] Ibid., 60.
[7] See Phillip J. Baram, *The Department of State in the Middle East 1919–1945* (Philadelphia: University of Pennsylvania Press, 1978), 189; Andrew Buchanan, "A Friend Indeed? From Tobruk to El Alamein: The American Contribution to Victory in the Desert," *Diplomacy and Statecraft*, 15, no. 2 (2004), 295–296.
[8] Hull to Winant, August 27, 1942, *FRUS 1942*, 4: 27.
[9] Ibid.

propaganda activities in the region "enormously and quickly in both volume and effectiveness."[10] U.S. diplomats would place news items and photographs in the Arab press, while distributing pamphlets and – rather mysteriously – "gadgets" outlining U.S. policies. Taking their distance from the policies of British and French colonialism, these propaganda materials would assure the people of the Middle East that a United Nations victory over the Axis powers would advance the cause of national self-determination "in line with American foreign policy and the Atlantic Charter."[11]

Given the anticolonial tone of these proposals, it is hardly surprising that U.S. ambassador to Britain John Winant's initial efforts to secure British approval for the mission proved unsuccessful. Foreign Secretary Anthony Eden feared – not unreasonably – that the proposed mission was simply the leading edge of a broader effort to establish U.S. influence throughout the Middle East, and he argued that London should block its dispatch. Instead, he suggested, Washington should be encouraged to appoint "specialized personnel to work with the appropriate British authorities."[12] Eden particularly objected to Washington's "stress on the promotion of 'liberty' and 'freedom'" in a region where, he claimed, both already existed, "qualified only by the exigencies of the war situation." In a remarkable twist of logic, Eden concluded that U.S. pledges to hasten political liberty and national independence would play into Axis hands by implying that these freedoms did not already exist. In particular, Eden fretted, Jews and Arabs could both "misinterpret" the American statement in ways that "could hardly fail to have dangerous repercussions" in Palestine.[13]

Despite British opposition and War Department doubts, Roosevelt – looking beyond the immediate crisis and toward the promotion of America's long-term interests – insisted, and in late October Sumner Welles bluntly informed the Joint Chiefs "the President feels ... that the British authorities should be told that this government desires the mission to proceed to the Near East."[14] After further discussion extracted a State Department pledge not to conduct the proposed propaganda campaign, the Combined Chiefs of Staff finally approved the mission, and Colonel Hoskins left for Cairo in November 1942. Unable to operate on the same level as London's Minister of State in the Middle East – U.S. involvement in the region had yet to develop to the point at which its political representation could equal that of the British – the Hoskins Mission was nevertheless able to develop contacts with key political and business figures throughout the region.[15] The mission's effectiveness, however, was somewhat

---

[10] Ibid., 27–28.

[11] Ibid., 28

[12] Eden to War Cabinet, memorandum, September 14, 1942, PREM 3/312/1.

[13] Ibid. See also Sir Llewellyn Woodward, *British Foreign Policy in the Second World War* (London: HMSO, 1962) 385.

[14] Memorandum Welles to Leahy, October 20, 1942, *FRUS 1942*, 4: 34.

[15] See Baram, *The Department of State in the Middle East*, 189.

compromised by its leader's unexpected sympathy for European colonialism; as Simon Ball notes, Washington's first "take" on becoming a power in the Levant rested on copying British and French methods.[16]

In September 1943, Washington replaced the Hoskins Mission with the American Economic Mission to the Middle East (AEMME), also based in Cairo. AEMME leader James Landis, former dean of Harvard Law School, also served simultaneously as the chief U.S. representative to the Middle East Supply Center. Signaling Washington's increasing engagement with the region, Landis was given the rank of minister, according him equal diplomatic status with Richard Casey, the British minster resident in Cairo. More than fifty U.S. officials were assigned to work under Landis's direction in Cairo, and many of them also assumed leading positions in the supply center. Even as U.S. participation in MESC expanded, however, Washington was preparing to take American economic policy in the region in a very different direction. Landis announced this impending shift on his arrival in Cairo, explaining "all policies must have long-range objectives [that] go beyond immediate war objectives and into a period of peace."[17]

Landis's statement made it clear that, as the tides of war ebbed away from the Middle East, the time had come to end wartime regulation and begin a return to free trade. In the Middle East, as in Italy, policy makers would view the war and the postwar not as hermetically sealed categories, but as points on a continuum. Working closely with Ambassador Alexander Kirk, Landis personally championed this approach in Egypt, cultivating ties with Egyptian political and business leaders, and aggressively promoting U.S. economic interests. This effort had administration backing at the highest level. Stopping over in Cairo after the Tehran conference, Harry Hopkins met with Kirk to discuss the establishment of a U.S. bank in Egypt. Such a venture, Kirk explained, would "service and promote American business interests in Egypt and the Middle East" while generating considerable profits for its owners.[18]

U.S. interest focused initially on two projects of critical importance to Egyptian economic development: the establishment of a chemical industry tied to the production of fertilizers, and the construction of a massive hydroelectric plant on the Nile.[19] U.S. involvement in these key sectors posed a direct challenge to London's cherished neocolonial project, which rested on parlaying its dominant hand in Egyptian politics into investment opportunities for British business. By early 1944, British and U.S. officials were engaged in

[16] Simon Ball, *Bitter Sea: The Brutal World War II Fight for the Mediterranean* (New York: Harper, 2009), 164.

[17] Landis, quoted in Gardner, *Economic Aspects of New Deal Diplomacy*, 221.

[18] Kirk to Hopkins, January 15, 1944, Box 139, Egypt folder, Hopkins Papers, FDRL.

[19] See Robert Vitalis, "The 'New Deal' in Egypt: The Rise of Anglo-American Commercial Competition in World War II and the Fall of Neocolonialism," *Diplomatic History* 20, no. 2, (1996).

a fierce struggle to secure major contracts for plant and equipment but, with London's political predominance shaken by its armed intervention into Egyptian politics in April 1942, and with British firms unable to compete with their U.S. rivals in terms of price and delivery times, it was a struggle that the old colonial power was bound to lose.[20] As historian Robert Vitalis has shown, the consequent establishment of a series of American-Egyptian joint ventures amounted to a veritable "new deal" for Egypt, laying the groundwork for a massive influx of U.S. investment – Westinghouse, Kodak, Coca-Cola, and Ford were all involved – in the immediate postwar period.[21]

The change of course signaled by Landis's appointment did not imply that that it had been a mistake for the United States to involve itself in the centrally planned economic order of MESC in the first place. On the contrary, U.S. participation proved invaluable, not only in helping to head off economic crises and social dislocation that would have been detrimental to the Allied war effort, but also – and as London had feared – in preparing the next steps in U.S. economic penetration of the region. It was also extremely lucrative: in Egypt alone U.S. trade increased eightfold in this period.[22] As the Axis threat to the Middle East waned, however, private business interests could once again come to the fore, and U.S. businessmen could begin to edge the British out of what were fast becoming critical markets in an increasingly critical region. Moreover, as private businessmen pressed into areas previously outside of the main circuits of U.S. trade, they would, as in Egypt, receive a great deal of support from State Department officials who had acquired their local knowledge and business contacts through their work in MESC and through the far-flung distribution of Lend-Lease supplies.

The first open clash between Washington and London over the operation of MESC came in January 1944, when the Foreign Economic Administration, citing practices that were held to discriminate against U.S. goods, denied the supply center jurisdiction over the export of U.S. textiles to Middle Eastern countries not under direct British control. Writing to James Landis in March, President Roosevelt underscored this approach by explaining, in a striking leap of policy definition, that the United States had a "vital interest" in the Middle East and that the "special privileges" previously enjoyed by the British would have "little place in the type of world for which this war is being fought."[23] Reaffirming Washington's commitment to free trade and its opposition to systems of imperial preference, Roosevelt instructed Landis to oppose any "discrimination" in the "exchange of goods and resources." Despite diplomatic niceties – Landis was instructed to avoid giving the impression that the United States was trying to "steal the economic position away from other nations" – Roosevelt clearly

[20] Ibid., 221, 233.
[21] Ibid., 234.
[22] Gardner, *Economic Aspects of New Deal Diplomacy*, 220.
[23] Roosevelt to Landis, March 6, 1944, *FRUS 1944*, 5: 2–3.

favored the rapid establishment of regimes of free trade in which the United States could expect to enjoy significant competitive advantages.

As Washington began the transition from wartime regulation to postwar free trade in the Eastern Mediterranean and Middle East, U.S. officials were facing a similar set of issues in relation to the operation of the North African Economic Board. Here Washington faced the double challenge of shifting responsibility for the receipt and distribution of Lend-Lease supplies onto the French Committee for National Liberation, while simultaneously preparing for a return to unregulated free trade that would, given the comparative health of the U.S. and French economies, necessarily favor the former. The United States therefore wanted to extricate itself from the business of directly underwriting French colonial administration – particularly, as one U.S. official reported, as the French were becoming "increasingly sensitive to American civilian opera-tions" – while leveraging the experience and contacts gained through the NAEB to strengthen U.S. trade with both North Africa and metropolitan France.[24]

In making this transition, Washington faced the problem that, like all sub-stantial bureaucracies, the Middle East Supply Center and the North African Economic Board had developed self-justifying lives whose momentum mili-tated against making a clean break with wartime regulation. The supply center, for example, had stalwart defenders not only in London, where officials saw it as a bulwark against unrestrained American economic penetration of the Middle East, but also among its own U.S. staff members, many of whom cher-ished liberal notions of ongoing involvement in disinterested regional planning and economic development in the Middle East.[25]

The North African Economic Board had likewise evolved into a highly sophisticated moderator of regional trade, regulating such matters as the export of Italian hops to Tunisia (to brew beer for British soldiers), the import of chemical fertilizers and tartaric acid into Sicily (to promote the "olive oil campaign"), the export of oak bark and salt from Corsica, the provision of fishing nets for Sardinian fishermen, and the supply of drilling equipment for exploratory oil wells in Tripolitania.[26] These issues, discussed and managed in minute detail, offer graphic evidence of the NAEB's bureaucratic momen-tum as it took onto itself the responsibility for organizing economic activity throughout the Western Mediterranean.

If this degree of economic micromanagement – with its implied challenge to Roosevelt's open door vision of the "type of world for which this war is being fought" – was not enough to alarm U.S. advocates of free trade, then evidence of a growing convergence between MESC and the NAEB surely was. In June 1943, a top-level MESC delegation arrived at AFHQ Algiers to begin a series of

[24] Watkins to Stettinius, August 31, 1943, NAEB, Box 17, RG 169, NARA.
[25] See Wilmington, *Middle East Supply Center*, especially chapters 8, 9, and 10.
[26] NAEB Inter-Territorial Sub Committee minutes, April 5, 1944, NAEB, Box 14, RG 169, NARA.

discussions with NAEB officials with a view to integrating the work of the two bodies.[27] The initial meeting consisted largely of an exchange of information on the functioning of the two organizations, but an underlying push toward the integration of their work, and hence toward an ever-greater degree of bureaucratic oversight of trade throughout the Mediterranean and the Middle East, was clearly evident. Moreover, as Allied military advances increasingly limited Axis capacity to interfere with shipping in the Mediterranean, the prospects for tying the entire Mediterranean basin into an integrated economic system would improve dramatically. To American business interests, and to U.S. officials steeped in the principles of free trade, this vision of sprawling networks of centralized economic planning stretching the length of the Mediterranean was not an appealing one.

The dispatch of the Culbertson Mission to the Mediterranean in the summer of 1944 signaled Washington's determination to reject this vision by breaking from the strictures of wartime centralization and pushing, as Culbertson's instructions put it, for the resumption of "bilateral trade through commercial channels."[28] The State Department instructed diplomats throughout the Mediterranean to support Culbertson's efforts to secure an immediate increase in U.S. trade while working on "long-range plans" for closer bilateral commercial relations.[29] After a series of "mutually helpful and cordial" meetings with French officials in the Maghreb, Culbertson and his colleagues moved on to Cairo in mid-September.[30] Reviewing Culbertson's report on French North Africa, U.S. officials in the region quickly embraced his conclusions, with J. Rives Childs writing from Tangier to endorse his plans for the "decentralization" of U.S. trade, the "liquidation" of the North Africa Economic Board, and a rapid but "orderly" return to "private trade."[31]

After completing his work in the Middle East, and after an important visit to Italy discussed later in this chapter, William Culbertson traveled to Paris to present his conclusions on the organization of U.S. trade with France and French North Africa to the French government, newly recognized by Washington. While Culbertson was in the Middle East, U.S. policy makers had concurred with the recommendations of diplomats in the Maghreb, and had endorsed the mission's proposals for North Africa. In December, new Secretary of State Edward Stettinius instructed the embassy in Paris to work with Culbertson to secure French cooperation in the deregulation of trade. U.S. officials in Paris prepared for the traveling ambassador's arrival by urging the French government to "assist in the resumption of private trade [by] promoting direct contact between U.S. and French buyers and suppliers," and by lifting travel restrictions

---

[27] NAEB/MESC joint meeting, minutes, June 27, 1943, NAEB, Box 14, RG 169, NARA.
[28] Draft orders to Culbertson Mission, July 14, 1944, 033.1151R/7–1444 RG 59, NARA.
[29] State Department to Chapin, August 2, 1944, 033.1151R/8–244 RG 59, NARA.
[30] Cole to State, August 30, 1944, 033.1151R/8–3044 RG59, NARA.
[31] Childs to State, October 9, 1944, 033.1151R/10–944 RG 59, NARA.

on U.S. businessmen operating in North Africa.[32] Behind the felicitous language urging a restoration of "normal commercial relationships," Washington made it clear that the supply of civilian goods to North Africa under Lend-Lease would cease as of June 30, 1945, and that the promotion of dollar-earning exports from the French colonies was therefore a matter of some urgency if the flow of consumer goods was to continue into 1946.

When Culbertson met with Herve Alphand of the French Foreign Ministry on December 16, their discussion covered both Franco-American economic relations and the organization of bilateral U.S. trade with French colonial territories. As Washington had anticipated, their proposals for a rapid liberalization of trade with the French colonies and protectorates touched on broader political issues. Alphand, Culbertson reported, displayed an "emotional concern" over the condition of the French economy, noting the devastating impact of war and German occupation and complaining at length about France's disadvantageous economic position vis-à-vis the United States.[33] Culbertson came away from the meeting deeply concerned about the new government's plans for the French economy – he detected a dangerously socialistic impulse in plans for "government trade and government industry" – but heartened by Alphand's assurance that Paris favored an "enlargement of the open-door regime in the colonies." This stance, Culbertson concluded, reflected a "tendency [that] we should do all we can to encourage."[34]

Applying this approach to the Middle East, Culbertson concluded that the Middle East Supply Center had outlived its usefulness and should be disbanded. Having traveled extensively throughout the region, mission members praised MESC's work in organizing the distribution of scarce resources during the crisis years of 1941 and 1942, and welcomed its work in providing technical support for agricultural, industrial, and public health projects. Nevertheless, Culbertson and his colleagues agreed that centralized economic controls were now becoming a brake on U.S. commercial interests – and hence, in their view, on the common good – particularly in the increasingly critical areas of oil and civil aviation. Culbertson also warned that any continuation into the postwar period of the currency and exchange controls managed by MESC could only serve to tie the Middle East into the "Sterling area" and hence into British-dominated trade networks, to the detriment of U.S. business. Addressing this question, the U.S. petroleum attaché in Cairo warned Culbertson that the postwar maintenance of the Sterling area would reinforce British control over the majority of Middle Eastern oil. Reviewing the long-term importance of Persian Gulf oil, he outlined steps to weaken Britain's hold on this increasingly

[32] Stettinius to Embassy Paris, December 1, 1944, 033.1151R/12–144 RG 59, NARA.
[33] Culbertson, memorandum on meeting with Herve Alphand, December 18, 1944, 033.1151R/12–3144 RG 59, NARA.
[34] Ibid.

vital region, reinforcing Culbertson's decision to press for the rapid dissolution of MESC.[35]

The Culbertson Mission visited the Middle East at a critical moment in the development of U.S. interest in the region's vast oil reserves. In early 1944, a congressional committee headed by Senator Harry S. Truman had warned that with domestic reserves dwindling, Middle Eastern oil would become increasingly central to U.S. economic and strategic interests. Acting on this argument, Harold Ickes, head of the Petroleum Reserves Corporation (PRC) and a veteran New Dealer, proposed building a government-owned pipeline running for more than one thousand miles from the newly discovered oilfields of Saudi Arabia to the Mediterranean at Alexandria. Ickes's plan troubled U.S. oil companies, who saw it as an unwarranted governmental intrusion in private business. Even more importantly, it alarmed the British government, which recognized it as a threat to their control of Middle Eastern oil. Ickes dropped the plan in June 1944, but not before a testy exchange between London and Washington that concluded with Churchill accepting Roosevelt's assurance that he was not "making sheep's eyes" at British oilfields in Iraq and Iran in exchange for a British promise not to "horn in" on U.S. interests in Saudi Arabia.[36]

These mutual platitudes paved the way for the signing of the Anglo-American Oil Agreement in August 1944. The agreement was an anodyne compromise, simultaneously and contradictorily recognizing Britain's preeminent position in the Middle East *and* the "open door" right of U.S. oil companies seeking to operate in the region to be accorded "equal opportunity."[37] In effect the agreement was simply another way-marker registering the shifting balance of Anglo-American relations in the Middle East oilfields, and as such it failed to satisfy Congress, which refused to ratify it. The Oil Agreement's importance in terms of the Mediterranean – and particularly in terms of the work of the Culbertson Mission – was that it signified the growing interconnection between U.S. interest in Middle Eastern oil on the one hand, and the development of U.S. economic engagement with the Eastern Mediterranean on the other. Typically, these interests encompassed both the geopolitical concerns of policy makers, who increasingly saw the Middle East as a pivotal region in world politics, and the aspirations of the U.S. oil executives, who wanted to ship Middle East oil via the Mediterranean to the fuel-starved markets of Europe. In 1947, these intersecting interests resulted in the construction of the privately funded Trans-Arabian Pipeline, or "Tapline," running from Saudi Arabia to the port of Sidon in Lebanon. This important postwar development was prepared during the

---

[35] Leavell to State, November 2, 1944, 033.1151R/11-244 RG 59, NARA.

[36] Roosevelt to Churchill, March 3, 1944; Churchill to Roosevelt, March 4, 1944, Warren F. Kimball (ed.), *Churchill and Roosevelt: The Complete Correspondence* (London: Collins, 1984), 3: 14, 17.

[37] See Douglas Little, *American Orientalism: The United States and the Middle East Since 1945* (Chapel Hill: University of North Carolina Press, 2004), 50–51.

war by Washington's August 1944 recognition of Syria and Lebanon as independent nations, a decision designed to limit French influence in the Levant and to wedge open the route into the local economy opened by war and the work of the Middle East Supply Center.

Anglo-American tension over the postwar development of civil aviation unfolded along similar lines. British policy makers found themselves torn between welcoming U.S. supplies delivered to Egypt via the Takoradi Route, an aerial highway across Africa pioneered by Pan American Airways executives acting on Roosevelt's instructions, and fearing that U.S. operators would use their wartime experience as a springboard to postwar commercial domination.[38] As early as April 1942, Secretary of War Henry Stimson pointed to deepening problems in the operation of the Takoradi air route arising from a "lack of whole-hearted cooperation between the British and Americans, in part arising out of fear of post-war commercial designs."[39] Stimson dispatched C. R. Smith of American Airlines, then a colonel in the Air Transport Command and "the ablest airline operator in the country," to sort out the problem. It was hardly an appointment designed to calm British fears of commercial competition. Washington's subsequent insistence on unrestricted landing rights – referred to as the "Fifth Freedom" – culminated in a bitter fight with the British at the International Civil Aviation Conference in 1945. Here, too, the dispute ended in British acceptance of the open door, and in helpless acknowledgment of the fact that America's wartime operational experience, backed by its production of transport aircraft, would inexorably lead to postwar commercial hegemony.[40]

Having completed their business in the Middle East, Culbertson and his associates flew to Italy, visiting AFHQ Caserta on November 15, 1944 before establishing a temporary office in Rome.[41] In a series of meetings over the next two weeks, Culbertson's team met with Allied officers at AFHQ, U.S. members of the Advisory Council and of the Allied Commission, and Italian government officials and businessmen, before drafting a detailed fifty-page report on their findings. The speed with which the mission drew its conclusions suggests that Culbertson's brief in Italy was to oversee, approve, and if possible accelerate, a process that was already underway as the economic consequences of the "New Deal" announced at Hyde Park in September began to unfold. Supplemental instructions to Culbertson from the State Department pointed in precisely this direction, ordering the mission to examine the steps necessary to secure a rapid "resumption of trade to and from the United States through commercial channels."[42]

---

[38] See Deborah Wing Ray, "The Takoradi Route: Roosevelt's Prewar Venture beyond the Western Hemisphere," *Journal of American History* 62, no.2 (1975).

[39] Memorandum, Stimson to Roosevelt, April 4, 1942, PSF, Safe File, Box 6, FDRL.

[40] See Emily Rosenberg, *Spreading the American Dream: American Economic and Cultural Expansion, 1890–1945* (New York: Hill & Wang, 1982), 199–200.

[41] Culbertson, "Report on Italy," November 30, 1944, 033.1151R/12–1944, RG 59, NARA.

[42] Supplemental Instructions, State Department to Culbertson, October 18, 1944; Ibid., 1.

As prompted by the State Department, the Culbertson Mission favored shifting economic decision making out of the hands of the Allied Commission and into those of the Italian government and, more importantly, of businessmen from both countries. Drawing an explicit parallel with MESC, Culbertson argued that the AC's Economic Section had served as a "useful agency in a war economy," but concluded that it would inevitably "develop difficulties upon the resumption of commercial trade" and become an obstacle to the open door.[43] Culbertson concluded that the AC's Economic Section should be dissolved as soon as political conditions permitted, and that in the meantime the civilianization of the Allied Commission should be accelerated. Observing that "other governments, and especially the British" were also taking an "affirmative interest in the economic activities of their nationals" in Italy, Culbertson urged that civilian specialists should be recruited to strengthen the economic aspects of the embassy's work and to ensure that U.S. economic interests were not shouldered aside.[44] Culbertson had also been asked to investigate whether or not the U.S. Commercial Corporation should function in Italy in an interim capacity before the concluding of a final peace agreement brought a full resumption of free trade, but the mission, wary of introducing yet another layer of bureaucracy, rejected this suggestion.

With typical American brio, Culbertson's report pictured postwar Italy as country stripped of the Fascist-era "pretension" that it was a great industrial power and ready to be integrated into an U.S.-dominated international economy on the strength of its "agriculture and handicrafts."[45] While lacking the punitive dimensions of Treasury Secretary Henry Morgenthau's contemporary plan for the deindustrialization of Germany, the familial similarity between it and the vision of an Italy producing handicrafts and agricultural produce and dependent on the United States for industrial goods, is not hard to discern. This view also conformed to broader U.S. narratives of Italian incapacity that imagined a nation more at home with opera and ice cream than with war and industrial work.[46] Acting on these lines, by December 1944 the State Department was contemplating a temporary commercial agreement between the United States and Italy that would provide for "non-discriminating trade" between the two countries and pave the way for the full restitution of "normal" commercial channels. For Washington, at least, the postwar world was advancing apace.

Not everyone in the Allied command structure was enthusiastic about the work of the Culbertson Mission. After attending a reception for mission members hosted by Ambassador Kirk in Rome, the ever-acerbic Harold Macmillan simply recorded meeting a "rather dreary old man on some vague mission

[43] Ibid., 4.
[44] Ibid., 50–51.
[45] Ibid., 6.
[46] See Andrew Buchanan, "'Good Morning Pupil!' American Representations of Italianness and the Occupation of Italy, 1943–1945," *Journal of Contemporary History* 43, no. 2 (2008).

here."[47] For once Macmillan's normally perceptive grasp of U.S. policy making failed him; while Culbertson proposed no dramatic new initiatives, his mission nevertheless signaled a broad turn in U.S. economic policy throughout the Mediterranean, and one with far-reaching political consequences. From North Africa, to the Middle East, to France and Italy, U.S. policy makers were now ready to move away from the highly regulated mechanisms of wartime trade and toward a forceful reassertion of the open door. Despite their differences over whether to approach the countries of the Middle East on a regional or on a bilateral basis, U.S. policy makers agreed on the necessity of integrating the entire area into the newly-emerging circuits of U.S.-dominated world trade.

Given the new realities of power created in the Mediterranean by U.S. arms, this effort would necessarily unfold under highly favorable conditions; as Culbertson recognized, his assertion that his mission had left a "deep and favorable impression" that would help "substantially to build America's economic future in this region" rested directly on Washington's military, diplomatic, and political accomplishments.[48] Significantly, the mission also signaled Washington's growing interest in integrating the penetration of the Middle Eastern oilfields by U.S. companies directly into U.S.-dominated trade networks in the Mediterranean. In this light, it is hardly surprising that Culbertson's report was well received in both government and business circles, and that it marked a major turning point in U.S. policy.

The results of this shift soon became evident. In all the countries of the Mediterranean basin, the last years of the war and the first years of the postwar were marked by a significant expansion in economic relations with the United States. U.S. exports to Italy, for example, rose from an average of $141 million in the years between 1926 and 1930 (the last half-decade before the onset of depression and war) to $456 million in 1951.[49] Trade with French North Africa registered significant increases over the same period, with exports to Algeria and Tunisia rising from $8 million to nearly $29 million, while those to Morocco jumped from $3.6 million to $31.7 million. Similar patterns could be traced in relation to Greece, Turkey, and, as we have already seen, Egypt. And in Yugoslavia, where Tito's relative independence from Russian control permitted continued trade with the west, U.S. exports leapt from an average of around $1 million in 1926–1930 to $119.6 million in 1951.

Throughout the Mediterranean, as elsewhere in Western Europe, the "soft power" of American goods and American culture followed closely behind the "hard power" of tanks, warships, and aircraft. U.S. aid provided the initial articulating link between them, as packages of food and barrels of fuel – all with "U.S.A." clearly emblazoned on them – spread from the Alps to the Atlas.

---

[47] Macmillan, diary entry November 19, 1944, Harold Macmillan, *War Diaries: Politics and War in the Mediterranean, January 1943–May 1945* (New York: St. Martin's Press, 1984), 588.

[48] Culbertson to Stettinius, November 15, 1944, *FRUS 1944*, 5: 40.

[49] *Statistical Yearbook* (Washington, DC: U.S. Department of Commerce, 1939, 1948, 1952).

Throughout much of the region, many saw the United States as standing not only for a break with old-style European imperialism, but also for modernity itself; in Italy, as historian Stephen Gundle notes, U.S. soldiers appeared as representatives of a "more advanced and prosperous world that in its tangible aspects was immensely attractive."[50] For a while even the Italian Communist Party welcomed the "DDT, chocolate, chewing gum, and nylon stockings" of Moscow's U.S. ally, and by the time it recognized the necessity of contesting U.S. influence in the "cultural sphere," it faced an uphill battle against visions of capitalist progress and modernity driven by Hollywood and reinforced by the daily presence of American commodities.

In retrospect America's economic penetration of the Mediterranean in the late-war and early postwar seems straightforward, even inevitable. U.S. armies crushed the Axis powers and then, with its enemies devastated and its allies weakened, U.S. business helped, as Nelson Rockefeller put it, to "raise the living standards" of hard-hit local populations while earning "substantial profits" in the process.[51] With the help of U.S. diplomats, and benefiting from the broad range of commercial contacts developed through the wartime regulation of aid and trade, U.S. business could now unleash a torrent of commodities and cultural values that together offered an alluring vision of Americanism and modernity. Historian Victoria de Grazia draws particular attention to the efforts of Rockefeller's International Basic Economic Corporation, backed by new U.S. ambassador to Rome Clare Boothe Luce, to establish a chain of supermarkets in Italy. Rockefeller's bold and commercially successful project challenged long-established traditions of food purchase and preparation, and signaled the interlinked advance of U.S. economic interests and American culture. But without the sustained deployment of U.S. arms and the diplomatic and economic efforts that accompanied them – that is to say, without a grand strategic approach to the Mediterranean – none of this would have been possible.

---

[50] Stephen Gundle, *Between Hollywood and Moscow: The Italian Communists and the Challenge of Mass Culture, 1943–1991* (Durham, NC: Duke University Press, 2000), 32.

[51] Rockefeller, quoted in Victoria de Grazia, *Irresistible Empire: America's Advance through 20th-Century Europe* (Cambridge, MA: Belknap, 2005), 377.

13

"Balkan-phobia"?

The United States, Yugoslavia, and Greece, 1940–1945

Washington's wartime engagement with the Balkans began in early 1941, when future Office of Strategic Services head William Donovan visited the region on his swing through the Mediterranean as President Roosevelt's unofficial personal emissary. In a series of meetings with top officials in Bulgaria, Greece, and Yugoslavia, Donovan encouraged them to resist the impending German invasion, arguing that the United States intended to exert "all her enormous force [to] insure (sic) ultimate victory for England."[1] Beyond encouraging words, however, Washington had little to offer in terms of immediate aid. A message of support from Roosevelt to the Yugoslav government concluded feebly "our type of civilization ... will definitely be helped by resistance on the part of the nations which suffer from aggression."[2] These words, and Roosevelt's choice of the valiant but doomed "rear guard action" in Norway in 1940 as an exemplar of resistance to aggression, can hardly have inspired confidence in the face of the German forces then preparing their descent on the Balkans.

In Athens and Belgrade, Donovan promised to urge Washington to send military supplies, including uniforms and trucks, and to provide broad economic aid under the terms of the Lend-Lease bill then under discussion.[3] One thousand American-made military trucks were dispatched to Belgrade in early 1941, but at the time of the German invasion in April, the great bulk of Yugoslav military supplies and heavy equipment were still being moved by draft animals.[4]

---

[1] Earle to State, January 23, 1941, *FRUS 1941*, 1: 282; MacVeagh to State, January 17 1941, and Lane to State, January 25, 1941, *FRUS 1941*, 2: 637, 938. See also Douglas Waller, *Wild Bill Donovan: The Spymaster Who Created the OSS and Modern American Espionage* (New York: Free Press, 2011), 64–65.

[2] Roosevelt to the Yugoslav government, in Hull to Lane, February 22, 1941, *FRUS 1941*, 2: 947.

[3] See MacVeagh to State, January 17, 1941, and Adolf Berle, memorandum of conversation with Greek Minister, February 13, 1941, *FRUS 1941*, 2: 637, 691.

[4] Jozo Tomasevich, *The Chetniks: War and Revolution in Yugoslavia, 1941–1945* (Stanford: Stanford University Press, 1975), 61.

At the end of March, Washington welcomed a new Yugoslav government, led by King Peter II and established after the overthrow a short-lived pro-Axis regime, with Roosevelt sending the king a personal message of support and a promise of Lend-Lease supplies.[5] Washington also played an important, if indirect, part in another key effort to stiffen Balkan resistance to the Axis by supporting London's February 5 decision to halt its offensive in North Africa and to send a substantial force to Greece instead. This decision was reviewed at a meeting in Cairo in late February attended by Foreign Secretary Anthony Eden, senior generals John Dill and Archibald Wavell, and presidential envoy William Donovan – a remarkable assembly given that the United States was still formally a neutral country.[6] Donovan agreed to support the British initiative by seeking additional American shipping to provide critical logistical support, and U.S. diplomats were in no doubt that his presence had "played an important part in the decisions which the British have taken."[7]

In the event, Bulgaria's accession to the Tripartite Pact on March 1, 1941, and the subsequent German invasion of Balkans in early April, overwhelmed Yugoslav and Greek resistance before U.S. supplies could arrive in significant quantities. Washington's first foray into the tangled politics of the wartime Balkans therefore culminated in a rather inglorious failure. For the British, however, Washington's support for their belated effort to construct an anti-Axis front in the Balkans was deeply appreciated and, more importantly, seen as a harbinger of direct U.S. involvement in the war. Churchill thanked Roosevelt warmly for Donovan's "magnificent work" in carrying an "animating heart-warming flame" in the Balkans and the Middle East.[8] Churchill's gratitude was no doubt reinforced by the sense, encouraged by Donovan and underscored by the successful completion of the ABC-1 talks, that the putative allies were in broad agreement both on the importance of the Balkans and on the necessity of pursuing an "indirect" or "Mediterranean" strategy.

From the point of view of this early wartime engagement with the Balkans, later images of a "Balkan-phobic" United States recoiling from the region with something akin to "superstitious dread" seem somewhat out of place.[9] Yet the story of Washington's aversion to involvement in the Balkans has long furnished the predominant narrative, paralleling and reinforcing the regnant story

---

[5] See Welles to Lane, March 27, 1941, *FRUS 1941*, 2: 969; see also Walter R. Roberts, *Tito, Mihailović, and the Allies, 1941–1945* (New Brunswick, NJ: Rutgers University Press, 1973), 12–17.

[6] See Peter Ewer, "The British Campaign in Greece 1941: Assumptions about the Operational Art and Their Influence on Strategy," *Journal of Military History* 76, no. 3 (July 2012), 730.

[7] Fish to State, February 22, 1941, *FRUS 1941*, 2: 648–649.

[8] Churchill to Roosevelt, March 10 1941, Warren F. Kimball (ed.), *Churchill and Roosevelt: The Complete Correspondence* (London: Collins, 1984), I: 145.

[9] See Sir Henry Maitland Wilson, *Eight Years Overseas, 1939–1947* (London: Hutchinson & Co., 1950), 218; Richard M. Leighton, "Overlord Revisited: an Interpretation of American Strategy in the European War, 1942–1944," *The American Historical Review* 68, no. 4 (1963), 930.

of America's lack of interest in the Mediterranean as a whole. The story of American Balkan-phobia rests in part on the simple fact that, with the exception of attacks by U.S. aircraft on Rumanian oil facilities, the great bulk of Washington's military activity in the Mediterranean was concentrated in the western basin. A very different picture emerges, however, when the political, diplomatic, and economic aspects of U.S. grand strategy are considered. From this point of view, Washington's wartime involvement in the Balkans, if low-key and largely covert, was a persistent and significant element of its overall approach to the Mediterranean.

It is also useful to bear in mind the degree to which actual outcomes shape perceptions of possible outcomes, and that prior to the Tehran conference it was by no means clear that there would be no major U.S. military intervention in the Balkans. In line with his overall interest in the Mediterranean, in November 1942 Roosevelt urged the Joint Chiefs to consider exploiting the success of *Torch* with a "forward movement" into the Balkans; later, when the collapse of Italy opened new strategic opportunities, he endorsed Jan Smuts's advocacy of "offensives ... eastward to the Balkans and the Black Sea."[10] While the *Iowa* discussions seemed to resolve the issue of large-scale U.S. intervention – George Marshall insisted firmly "we must see this Balkan matter as settled" – Roosevelt nevertheless returned to it at Tehran.[11] Here, after Harry Hopkins had scribbled a despairing note to Admiral King asking "who is promoting this Adriatic business that the President continually returns to," Stalin finally squashed any suggestion of major U.S. operations in the Balkans.[12]

If the Tehran conference signaled the final abandonment of schemes for U.S. military action in the Balkans, it did not mark the end of U.S. interest in the region. Washington's approach was wrapped in ambiguity, with Roosevelt himself presenting a façade of studied indifference to Balkan affairs. Fighting between political factions in Greece, Roosevelt told Harold Ickes, could easily be solved by "giving every Greek a rifle and letting them fight it out," while he joked with Robert Murphy that Yugoslavia should be sealed off until the competing factions settled their differences, after which the United States could "do business with the winner."[13] Beneath this cynicism, however, Roosevelt and senior U.S. policy makers were keenly interested in the Balkans, and in the shape of the postwar balance of power there in particular. Their problem was

[10] See Maurice Matloff and Edwin M. Snell, *Strategic Planning for Coalition Warfare, 1941–1942* (Washington, DC: U.S. Government Printing Office, 1953), 363; Churchill to Roosevelt July 17, 1943; Roosevelt to Churchill July 19, 1943, *Correspondence*, 2: 331–332.

[11] Roosevelt meeting with JCS, November 19, 1943, *FRUS 1943*, Cairo and Tehran: 259.

[12] Robert E. Sherwood, *Roosevelt and Hopkins, an Intimate History* (New York: Harper & Bros., 1948), 780.

[13] Robert Dallek, *Franklin D. Roosevelt and American Foreign Policy, 1932–1945* (New York: Oxford University Press, 1979), 505; Murphy, *Diplomat among Warriors* (Garden City, NY: Doubleday & Co, 1964), 220.

not a lack of interest, but was rather the lack of an effective instrument of U.S. intervention. Having abandoned the idea of using military force, Washington was forced to advance its interests by using diplomatic, covert, logistical, and economic levers.

After the Tehran Conference, the broad outlines of Washington's Balkan policy were determined by the advancing division of Europe into spheres of influence. In May 1944, Churchill informed Roosevelt that "as a practical matter" he had proposed to Stalin that London should "take the lead" in Greece, while Moscow did likewise in Rumania.[14] Noting that this division corresponded to the existing military situation, Churchill insisted disingenuously that there was no intent to "carve up the Balkans into spheres of influence." State Department fears that Churchill was doing just that forced him to propose that these "arrangements" be adopted initially only for a "trial of three months," and on this basis Roosevelt approved the plan.[15] Despite Cordell Hull's warning that this thinly disguised spheres of influence agreement violated the "fixed rules ... of policy, principle, and practice," Washington's agreement to the implausible three-month trial inevitably pointed toward the long-term acceptance of such a division.[16] Roosevelt himself was more concerned with the language – "spheres of influence" seemed tainted with the old Great Power politics – than with actuality of a division not so far removed from his own notion of a postwar order structured around the "Four Policemen," each assuming responsibility for a specific geographical area.[17] Typically, Roosevelt took his distance from the language of power politics while embracing the actuality.[18]

After Tehran, the major problem faced by U.S. policy makers in the Balkans was not the establishment of spheres of influence – even if they did not like to use those words – but was making the broad lines of divide adopted by the great powers effective on the ground. Here, and in common with Moscow, Washington faced the uncomfortable fact that the increasingly powerful and well-organized resistance movements fighting the Axis occupations of Greece and Yugoslavia seemed bent on establishing postwar polities that, through their political radicalism and anti-capitalist dynamic, would challenge the putative divisions imposed on them from above. The emergence of radical socialist regimes, operating beyond the control of either Moscow or Washington and

---

[14] Churchill to Roosevelt, May 31, 1944, *Correspondence*, 3: 153.

[15] Churchill to Roosevelt, June 11, 1944; Roosevelt to Churchill, June 12 1944, *Correspondence*, 3: 180, 182.

[16] Hull, memorandum, May 30, 1944, *FRUS 1944*, 5: 113.

[17] Warren Kimball notes the similarity between Roosevelt's notion of the "four policemen" and traditional spheres of influence in his editorial comments in Kimball, *Correspondence*, 3: 200–201.

[18] In contrast, see the argument that the division was a "puzzling" product of presidential "weariness" in Lloyd Gardner, *Spheres of Influence: The Great Powers and the Partition of Europe, from Munich to Yalta* (Chicago: Ivan R. Dee, 1993), 194; see also Hugh de Santis, "In Search of Yugoslavia: Anglo-American Policy and Policy-Making, 1943–45," *Journal of Contemporary History* 16, no. 3 (1981), 554.

potentially offering an example to working people across the continent, could upend the carefully crafted structure of the postwar order. From this point of view, two interlinked imperatives aimed at consolidating the spheres of influence sketched out at Tehran and at containing (in Yugoslavia) or at crushing (in Greece) radical social movements emerging from the anti-fascist resistance, would dominate U.S. policy in the Balkans until the end of the war.

YUGOSLAVIA: TRYING TO CONTAIN THE PARTISANS

Resistance to the Axis occupation of Yugoslavia initially took shape under the leadership of Colonel (later General) Draza Mihailović. Mihailović's Četnik fighters were recruited largely from Serbia, and his movement operated under the aegis of the Yugoslav government-in-exile, based in London and led by King Peter II. Washington continued to recognize the government-in-exile as the legitimate government of Yugoslavia, welcoming the Četnik resistance and planning to supply it with arms. The situation on the ground in Yugoslavia, however, was not as clear-cut as it appeared in Washington. After early military reverses, Mihailović decided against waging a generalized war of resistance, opting instead to prepare a force that could operate in support an Allied landing in Yugoslavia at some later date. Until the landing materialized, the Četniks would carefully avoid large-scale conflict with Axis forces.[19]

The situation in Yugoslavia was further complicated by the emergence of a second resistance movement, formed by the Yugoslav Communist Party under the leadership of Josip Broz, better known as Tito. Tito's Partisans, based on all the main ethnic groups in Yugoslavia and recruited largely from the peasantry, advocated national equality in a federal Yugoslavia. This approach stood in sharp contrast to that of the Četniks, whose movement rallied, as Churchill put it, the "surviving elite of Yugoslavia" and championed Great Serbian nationalism. With these conflicting forces in the field, resistance to the Axis occupation quickly became intertwined with local social and regional conflicts.[20] From this matrix, and although the Partisans were admonished by Moscow to eschew revolutionary plans, the social-revolutionary dynamic of armed resistance to occupation, unfolding in the context of an old order shattered by war, emerged with full force in Yugoslavia.

These developments inevitably complicated Allied policy toward Yugoslavia. In May 1943, the British dispatched a fact-finding mission to the Partisans headed by Oxford don and Churchill confidant William Deakin.[21] The mission was later expanded under the leadership of the swashbuckling Brigadier Fitzroy Maclean, whose glowing assessment of the Partisans was reinforced by

[19] Roberts, *Tito, Mihailović, and the Allies*, 26–27.
[20] Churchill, *The Second World War*, 5: 461.
[21] See Simon Ball, *Bitter Sea: The Brutal World War II Fight for the Mediterranean* (New York: Harper, 2009), 199.

Ultra intelligence demonstrating collaboration between the Četniks and Axis forces. In the summer of 1943, London responded by ending arms shipments to Mihailović and throwing its support behind Tito instead.[22] These developments left Washington struggling to form a clear assessment of the situation. Despite an agreement in June 1942 recognizing the British Special Operations Executive (SOE) and the newly formed OSS as partners in intelligence gathering, the assignment of the Balkans to British operational control had allowed them to marginalize, obstruct, and exclude U.S. agents.[23] Clearly, despite the shifts in intra-Allied relations unfolding elsewhere in the Mediterranean, London was unwilling to relinquish senior partner status in the Balkans.

State Department officials recognized that, if the Washington hoped to "exert an American influence in the region," they had to establish a presence on the ground, but they feared being drawn into the rapidly deepening divide between London and Mihailović.[24] William Donovan had no such qualms, and a new agreement with the SOE negotiated in July 1943 allowed the OSS to begin operating in Yugoslavia. OSS leaders in Cairo regarded the new arrangement as a "declaration of independence," and agents soon began providing Washington with "our own intelligence, originated with Americans, communicated through our own channels, and processed through our people."[25] OSS prestige grew as its operations expanded, with an agency report noting smugly "the White House often consults General Donovan on the situation in Yugoslavia."[26] In October 1943, Roosevelt proposed sending Donovan himself back to Yugoslavia to help heal the factional divisions there, but Churchill rebuffed the offer, arguing that British military missions had matters under control and that the OSS head would be unable to "grip the situation."[27]

U.S. agents sent into Yugoslavia often came to share Britain's enthusiasm for the Partisans. OSS Major Linn Farish, who spent six weeks with Tito's forces in September and October 1943, submitted a glowing report that combined respect for the guerillas' military capability with praise for the social revolution unfolding in the wake of Partisan advances. Farish reported that, despite constant attacks by Axis forces backed by the Četniks and the fascistic Croatian Ustace, the Partisans had been able to carve out a "free community" within which "Mohammedans, Christians, Serbs, Croats, Slovenes, Communist Party

[22] See Winston S. Churchill, *The Second World War*, in 6 vols. (Boston: Houghton Mifflin, 1948–1954), 5: 463, 464.
[23] See Kirk Ford, Jr., *The OSS and the Yugoslav Resistance, 1943–1945* (College Station: Texas A&M University Press, 1992), especially chapter 2.
[24] Cannon, memorandum, May 17, 1943, *FRUS 1943*, 2: 1010.
[25] Lada-Mocarski to Sherpardson, December 22, 1943, Cairo SI Box 72, RG 226, NARA; OSS memorandum on Yugoslavia, December 24, 1943, Cairo SI Box 72, RG 226, NARA; see also Amy Schmidt, draft paper, "Croatia and the Western Allies," (NARA, 1995), author's collection, 14.
[26] Schmidt, "Croatia and the Western Allies," 14.
[27] Roosevelt to Churchill, October 22, 1943 and Churchill to Roosevelt, October 23, 1943, *Correspondence*, 2: 549, 554.

members, [and] any person of any religion or political belief" could engage in "free and enlightened discussion" on the character of the new state-in-becoming.[28] Farish was particularly impressed by the enthusiastic reception accorded to the U.S. mission and by the Partisan's "implicit faith" that the "United States would come to their aid."

Farish's report reached Roosevelt on the eve of the Tehran Conference, and its conclusion that the United States should abandon Mihailović and back Tito fed the general enthusiasm for the Partisans evident there. With an eye toward America's postwar influence, Farish pointed out that "cold, hungry, and inadequately armed men ... will surely remember from whence aid came," an argument that must have appealed to Roosevelt's overriding interest in the expansion of U.S. influence.[29] The president signaled his support for the new policy by presenting Stalin with a copy of Farish's report. One can only wonder what the Russian dictator made of this remarkable document, whose vision of an unfolding popular and democratic revolution was as far from his plans for the postwar Balkans as it was from those of the Allies.

At Tehran the Combined Chiefs ratified London's proposal to back Tito, agreeing to give "all possible help" to the Partisans and embedding this approach in their instructions to the new supreme commander in the Mediterranean, General Henry Wilson.[30] Churchill wrote to Tito informing his "heroic ... partisan army" of the decision "only to give help to you."[31] The convergence of great power interests at Tehran allowed the Partisans temporarily to command the combined support of London, Moscow, and Washington, and the fruits of this conjunctural alliance soon began to arrive in Yugoslavia. New special operations bases on Italy's Adriatic coast enabled the Allies to move 500 tons of supplies per month into Yugoslavia by air and a further 2,000 tons by sea.[32] Between October 1943 and January 1944, even before the full consequence of the Tehran decisions was felt, Tito's forces received more than 5,600 tons of supplies; in the same period, the Četniks received a mere 27 tons.[33]

In May, U.S. and Russian aircrews rescued Tito and his headquarters from German attack, relocating them on the Adriatic island of Vis. The following month, AFHQ established the Balkan Air Force (BAF), placing commando and naval forces under its command along with twenty-four squadrons of cargo, bomber, and fighter aircraft. Aided by air force liaison officers at Partisan

---

[28] Farish, "Preliminary Report on a visit to the National Army of Liberation, Yugoslavia," October 29, 1943, *FRUS 1943*, Cairo and Tehran: 606, 607.

[29] Ibid., 614.

[30] CCS#132, November 30, 1943, *FRUS 1943*, Cairo and Tehran: 556; see Fitzroy Maclean, *Eastern Approaches*, 1949 (reprint London: Penguin, 1991), 402.

[31] Churchill, *Second World War*, 5: 470–471.

[32] See Paul Freeman, "The Cinderella Front: Allied Special Air Operations in Yugoslavia during World War II," Research Dept., Air Command and Staff College (1997).

[33] CCS 489, February 17, 1944, RG 218, NARA.

FIGURE 13.1. Partisan snipers Vera Krizman and Vlasta Kertika, of Ljubljana, receive training from Allied forces in Bari, Italy. The OWI caption noted approvingly that "Vera is a commander of women partisans." (Courtesy of Franklin D. Roosevelt Library.)

headquarters, Allied airpower was integrated into resistance operations, and in September 1944 the BAF joined the Partisans in Operation *Ratweek*, a coordinated series of attacks on road and rail lines that disrupted the withdrawal of German forces.

After Tehran, Washington upgraded its relations with Tito. Noting that Fitzroy Maclean enjoyed "direct access to Prime Minister Churchill on political matters," William Donovan argued that OSS officers assigned to Tito's headquarters should constitute an independent U.S. mission and not, as London proposed, function as part of a British-led delegation.[34] Adolf Berle endorsed this conclusion, arguing that because "McLain [sic]" was "nominally a soldier but actually a foreign office man in uniform," Americans should not serve as "juniors" in what was in fact a "British political mission."[35] In February 1944,

---

[34] JCS 603/2, January 1944, Box 220, RG 218, NARA.
[35] Berle, memorandum, January 26, 1944, *FRUS 1944*, 4: 1339–1340.

OSS Colonel Richard Weil was assigned to head an independent U.S. mission. Tito welcomed Weil's arrival, writing to Roosevelt to thank him and his "great democratic country" for their efforts on behalf of the "striving of the people of Yugoslavia."[36] Despite this positive start, however, plans for a mission lead by a general officer did not come to fruition.[37]

As the prospect of a Partisan victory came into sharper focus in the summer of 1944, Washington's enthusiasm for the Communist-led resistance began to wane. Even Linn Farish, whose glowing report had helped secure U.S. support for Tito, had second thoughts. In a maudlin discussion with *New York Times* reporter Cyrus Sulzberger in July, Farish expressed his dismay over the anti-Četnik offensive then being waged by Partisans armed with U.S. weapons. "At one time," Farish sighed, "I worried because America was not getting proper recognition for her participation in supply operations. Now I wonder – do we want it?"[38]

Former OSS agent Franklin Lindsay concluded that Farish's early enthusiasm for the Partisans was a product of his exposure to Tito's rhetoric and the propaganda of his "skillful Agitprop section."[39] It is not necessary, however, to doubt the sincerity of the enthusiasm Farish and other Allied agents felt for the military and social revolution unfolding in Yugoslavia to understand how that sentiment wilted when exposed to the more conservative concerns of U.S. policy makers. In early 1944, only weeks after the decision to back Tito, senior analysts were expressing their concern about the potential consequences of a Partisan victory. State Department analyst Carl Norden spelled out the danger, arguing that the "old ruling cliques" in Yugoslavia had been so "thoroughly discredited" that the Yugoslav people were unwilling to return "to the *status quo ante*."[40] It is "unlikely," he concluded, that the Yugoslav revolution "can be stopped." Drawing a parallel between Yugoslavia and Russia during the early years of the revolution, Lincoln MacVeagh, Washington's ambassador to the Yugoslav government-in-exile, noted that Moscow was neither "directing nor funding" the Partisans, whose actions embodied the "international Communism of 1917" rather than that of the "present-day Moscow."[41]

This analysis pointed to dangerous conclusions. While Moscow might abide by the spheres of influence agreements – and the accumulating evidence in Italy, France, and Greece, indicated that it would – it seemed likely that the Partisans would follow the path of social revolution irrespective of

---

[36] Tito to Roosevelt, March 15, 1944, *FRUS 1944*, 4: 1356–1357.
[37] See JCS memorandum, March 22, 1944, RG 218, Box 220, NARA.
[38] C. L. Sulzberger, *A Long Row of Candles: Memoirs and Diaries, 1934–1954* (New York: Macmillan, 1969), 244–245.
[39] Franklin Lindsay, *Beacons in the Night: With the OSS and Tito's Partisans in Wartime Yugoslavia* (Stanford, CA: Stanford University Press, 1993), 25–27.
[40] Norden, OEA memorandum, January 19, 1944, *FRUS 1944*, 4: 1339.
[41] MacVeagh to Roosevelt, August 28, 1944, Lincoln MacVeagh papers, Box 3, Seely G. Mudd Manuscript Library, Princeton.

Stalin's wishes. Uniquely, and in de facto confirmation of the independence of the Partisans, Yugoslavia did not fall squarely into either of the emerging spheres of influence. This situation was codified when Churchill and Stalin met in Moscow in October 1944 to clarify the division of the Balkans, and agreed to split "predominance" in Yugoslavia between them 50–50. In contrast to Rumania and Bulgaria, which were clearly in the Russian sphere, and to Greece, where London would exercise control, neither side could plausibly claim Yugoslavia.[42]

The radicalism of the Yugoslav Partisans caused as much concern in Moscow as it did in Washington. Although Soviet leaders planned to include Yugoslavia in the defensive *glacis* separating Russia from Germany and the west, they viewed the stubborn independence and revolutionary dynamism of Tito's fighters with apprehension. A popular revolution in Yugoslav might, they feared, inspire emulation throughout the Balkans and Eastern Europe, with detrimental consequences for Russian control.[43] Given the problems of wartime communication, Moscow had little direct contact with the Partisans, and was forced to use radio broadcasts in an effort to persuade them to follow a "national" rather than a "socialist" course by joining forces with the royal government-in-exile in London. Stalin pressed this course on Tito when communications improved in late 1944, warning that the "bourgeoisie in Serbia is very strong" and urging him to abandon the path of social revolution.[44] Stalin's advice carried little weight with Tito who replied that, on the contrary, the Serbian bourgeoisie – and hence Serbian capitalism – was in fact extraordinarily weak.

To U.S. policy makers, London's hope that Tito might, as Ambassador Lincoln MacVeagh cynically put it, be "hitched ... to the car of British policy," seemed dangerously naïve.[45] To them, Churchill's policy combined cavalier disdain for the outcome – he told Maclean that because neither planned to live in Yugoslavia they need not worry "about the form of government they set up" – with the forlorn hope that the exiled government of King Peter might be used as a lever with which to control Tito.[46] As State Department analyst Carl Norden pointed out, this all rested on the increasingly unlikely assumption that "moderate and national elements in the Tito camp will ultimately prevail."[47] These hopes were reflected in wildly unrealistic plans for a "representative government" in Yugoslavia drafted by the State Department's Country and Area Committee in June 1944. A new government, policy makers hoped, could be

---

[42] Churchill, *Second World War*, 4: 198.
[43] Russian hostility to Tito gave rise to a plot to "liquidate" him, see Ford, *OSS and the Yugoslav Resistance*, 167–168.
[44] See Geoffrey Roberts, *Stalin's Wars: From World War to Cold War, 1939–1953* (New Haven, CT: Yale University Press, 2006), 211.
[45] MacVeagh to Roosevelt, August 28, 1944, MacVeagh papers, Box 3.
[46] Maclean, *Eastern Approaches*, 402–403.
[47] Norden, memorandum, January 19, 1944, *FRUS 1944*, 4: 1339.

based on the "trend towards decentralization" evident in the "Serb-Croat compromise of 1939," and composed – somewhat ambiguously – of "representatives of all the groups which have opposed the Axis."[48]

This approach embodied the hope that Washington could offset Partisan
influence by promoting moderate Serbian and Croatian leaders. Washington
pursued this line, often in opposition to British support for the Partisans, for
the remainder of the war. Given the Joint Chiefs' unwavering opposition to
military intervention, however, policy makers had few levers with which to
influence Yugoslav politics, and conducted an increasingly desperate search for
Yugoslav allies capable of containing Tito. In the first instance, this search led
back to King Peter's Serb-dominated government in London and to Mihailović's
Četniks.

In early 1944, London tried to square its own "chivalrous and honorable"
commitment to King Peter with its actual support for Tito by brokering an
accord between the two.[49] This problematic process was complicated by Tito's
formation in November 1943 of a provisional government, the Anti-Fascist
Liberation Council of Yugoslavia (AVNOJ), and by the evident fact that support for Peter and his Serbian-dominated government within the country was
waning rapidly. For his part, Tito was buoyed by military success and in a position to spin out the process of reconciliation while continuing to receive Allied
arms. In February 1944, he acknowledged that Peter "might be of value to the
Partisan movement," but stated that for talks to move forward the King had
to break all ties with Mihailović, dismiss his cabinet, and recognize the authority of AVNOJ.[50] London's willingness to force these terms on Peter alarmed
Washington, with Ambassador MacVeagh noting that the "talking to" given to
Prime Minister Bozidar Purić by Churchill was "not unreminiscent of Hitlerite
procedure with Satellite leaders."[51]

In this context, U.S. policy makers concluded that while it was necessary to
maintain "unity of purpose with the British and Russians," Washington could
not be bound to "specific British plans."[52] OSS reports that the Četniks continued to enjoy a "strong hold over the Serbian peasants" now encouraged
Washington to rebuild its relationship with Mihailović.[53] Following London's
lead, the OSS had withdrawn its mission to Mihailović in March, but Roosevelt
now insisted that because they now had no "source of intelligence ... in part
of the Balkans which may become important at some stage in the war," a new
mission should be dispatched forthwith.[54] This effort alarmed the British, who,
as Macmillan put it, feared that the Americans would no longer "follow the

[48] CAC 218, June 8, 1944, microfilm T1221, NARA.
[49] Churchill, *Second World War*, 5: 471.
[50] MacVeagh to Hull, February 15, 1944, *FRUS 1944*, 4: 1347.
[51] MacVeagh to State Department, February 29, 1944, *FRUS 1944*, 4: 1351.
[52] Norden, memorandum, January 19, 1944, *FRUS 1944*, 4: 1338.
[53] OSS memo, March 4, 1944, RG 218, Box 220, NARA.
[54] Roosevelt to Donovan, March 22, 1944, JCS #214, RG 218, Box 220, NARA.

P.M.'s pro-Tito policy."[55] Churchill warned Roosevelt that the new mission to Mihailović would "show throughout the Balkans a complete contrariety of action between Britain and the United States" at a time when London and Moscow were "throw[ing] all their weight on Tito's side."[56] Undeterred, Washington dispatched two missions to Mihailović, the first a rescue unit designed to evacuate downed fliers, and the second an OSS Secret Intelligence unit led by Colonel Robert McDowell.[57] A man of "violently pro-Četnik prejudices," McDowell arrived at Mihailović's headquarters in September 1944, just as a renewed Partisan offensive against the Germans and their Četnik allies was getting underway.[58]

Not surprisingly, both Tito and Churchill were outraged by the arrival of the McDowell Mission. It came at a time when the central contradiction in British policy appeared to be approaching resolution, with King Peter succumbing to British pressure and issuing a statement calling on Yugoslavs to rally to the Partisans. Washington's actions now threatened the whole delicate balancing act, and Churchill cabled Roosevelt to warn that "complete chaos" would follow if the Americans continued to "back Mihailović."[59] Wary of provoking a breach with London, Washington backed down. Roosevelt informed Donovan "in view of British objection ... it seems best to withdraw the mission to Mihailović," and McDowell's OSS team was ordered out of Yugoslavia.[60] The danger in the situation was quickly becoming evident: by the time he was evacuated in November, McDowell had already held two meetings with German officers who wanted to surrender to the Americans rather than to the Partisans or the Russians.[61] These negotiations threatened U.S. relations with the Russians and, moreover, left Tito wondering why Washington wanted to maintain relations with Mihailović after his collaboration with the Germans had been so "generally accepted [that] even King Peter had denounced him."[62]

Tito had a point: in terms of relations with Britain, Russia, and the Partisans, Washington's pursuit of contact with Mihailović was so far out of step with the unfolding reality of Yugoslav politics as to court disaster. U.S. policy was not accidental, however, and while doubtless driven in part by General Donovan's desire to make the OSS an indispensable instrument of U.S. policy, Roosevelt himself sanctioned every critical step in the process. This policy is therefore best understood as an effort to utilize whatever levers might be available to fashion a policy capable of avoiding a Partisan-dominated Yugoslavia. By the

[55] Macmillan, *War Dairies*, 526.
[56] Churchill to Roosevelt, April 6, 1944, *Correspondence*, 3: 80.
[57] JCS memo, September 16, 1944, RG 218, Box 220, NARA.
[58] See Harris R. Smith, *OSS: The Secret History of America's First Central Intelligence Agency* (Berkeley: University of California Press, 1972), 150.
[59] Churchill to Roosevelt, September 1, 1944, *Correspondence*, 3: 306.
[60] JCS Memo 307, September 16, 1944, RG 218, Box 220, NARA.
[61] See Smith, *OSS*, 150–151.
[62] Kirk to State, October 31, 1944, *FRUS 1944*, 4: 1415–1416.

time Washington embarked on this course, however, Mihailović was a very weak reed, and while not entirely abandoning the Četnik leader, the Americans were forced to retreat to avoid the potentially disastrous consequences of being tied too closely to him. In fact, even as U.S. officials were attempting to cultivate Mihailović, Washington was developing a more promising lever in the form of Croatian politician Ivan Šubašić.

Exiled after the Axis occupation, in 1942 Šubašić was working at the royal government-in-exile's Yugoslav Information Center in New York. This was a lowly posting for a former leader of the Croatian Peasant Party (HSS) and the head (or Ban) of the Banovia of Croatia, and one that reflected the Great Serb orientation of the exiled government. Šubašić's outspoken defense of a united and federal Yugoslavia, his advocacy of an alliance with the Partisans, and his claim to be the leader of numerous and well-organized peasant militia within the country, quickly brought him to the attention of officers in the Foreign Nationals branch of the OSS. By the end of the year he had been introduced to Allen Dulles, head of OSS Strategic Intelligence, and was rated "among those who can always be relied upon to act in close contact with us."[63] Šubašić worked closely with the OSS for the next two years, at times receiving per diem expenses for his services and giving Washington direct access to critical developments at the heart of Yugoslav exile politics.

Šubašić hoped to be included in the reorganized royal cabinet formed under British pressure in August 1943, but the premiership went instead to Serb politician Bozidar Purić. Continued Serbian domination of the government-in-exile emboldened Constantin Fotić, its ambassador to the United States, to close the "dissident" Information Center in New York.[64] Unemployed and disillusioned, Šubašić was soon drawn into closer collaboration with the OSS. After meeting with William Donovan, Šubašić and his OSS case officer Bernard Yarrow drew up an ambitious plan for the "penetration" of Yugoslavia. The resulting "Shepherd Project" called for Šubašić to return to Yugoslavia with the goal of "uniting all the resistance and fighting forces," winning over the army of the Croatian puppet government, and swinging the Nedić regime in Serbia "into line."[65] This implausible project rested largely on wishful thinking, with OSS officers arguing that an "overwhelming majority" of Croats revered Šubašić both "as their champion and leader" and as the commander of the "exceedingly well organized" forces of the Peasant Party.[66]

It is difficult to see how this wildly implausible scheme could ever have commanded serious consideration, let alone received top-level backing in Washington. The fact that it was approved by Adolf Berle at the State

---

[63] See Schmidt, "Croatia and the Western Allies," 15.

[64] Ibid., 16.

[65] "Penetration of Yugoslavia Project," September 21, 1943, RG 226, E160, NY-SI-PRO-17, Box 26, NARA.

[66] Ibid.

Department, by the Joint Chiefs of Staff, and finally by Roosevelt himself, however, speaks both to their concern over the course of events in Yugoslavia and, in the absence of U.S. military forces on the ground, to their lack an effective instrument for policy execution. Donovan touched on this question in memorandum to Roosevelt arguing that Šubašić would go into Yugoslavia "for the OSS," and that his efforts to "persuade the military leaders of the Croatian Puppet Army to join us," would give Washington a proxy army in the region.[67]

After the Tehran Conference, the Shepherd Project assumed new importance, with the decision to support the Partisans highlighting the urgency of finding a counter-balance to Tito within the putative new political order Yugoslavia. Acting in accordance with the emerging spheres of influence in the Balkans, Adolf Berle agreed to clear Šubašić's mission with both Tito and the Russians, and officials discussed the matter with Andrei Vyshinsky, Moscow's representative at AFHQ.[68] Vyshinsky raised no objections. Communications with Tito took a little longer, but by mid-February Linn Farish reported that Tito "will be glad to see the Ban at his headquarters."[69] Even the British, who like the Russians were in the dark about Šubašić's OSS connections, and who had delayed approval pending a response from Tito, now gave it the go-ahead. On February 19, 1944, Donovan issued orders "to push the Shepherd Project without delay."[70]

Despite having secured all the necessary approvals, however, the plan to send Šubašić into Yugoslavia was abruptly abandoned. The reasons for the cancellation are not clear, but in March 1944, Partisan attacks on the HSS leadership as collaborators increased sharply, leading U.S. officials to fear that Šubašić would be "completely at Tito's mercy."[71] Linn Farish also expressed concerns that Šubašić was "too well along in years" to withstand the rigors of parachute drops and guerrilla warfare.[72] The overriding reason for the cancellation of the mission, however, may have been that State Department and OSS officials were developing a new plan for utilizing Šubašić's talents. Now, instead of inserting "the Ban" directly into a combat zone, Šubašić would go to London to help lash together the royal government and the Partisans; U.S. officials also hoped that, as Šubašić pursued this critical task, he also would give them purchase on Yugoslav politics at the highest level.

This ambitious new project was presented at an April 1944 meeting between State Department official Cavendish Cannon and Šubašić's OSS

[67] Donovan to Roosevelt, October 21, 1943, E160, NY-SI-PRO-17, Box 26, RG 226, NARA.
[68] Yarrow report, December 21, 1943, E160, NY-SI-PRO-17, Box 26, RG 226, NARA.
[69] Toulmin to OSS, February 15, 1944, E160, NY-SI-PRO-17, Box 26, RG 226, NARA.
[70] See Yarrow, "Chronology of Shepherd Project," June 24, 1944, E160, NY-SI-PRO-17, Box 26, RG 226, NARA.
[71] Yarrow report, June 26, 1944, E160, NY-SI-PRO-17, Box 26, RG 226, NARA.
[72] Toulmin to OSS, February 15, 1944, E160, NY-SI-PRO-17, Box 26, RG 226, NARA.

case officer, Bernard Yarrow. Cannon stressed that London had failed to win Tito to a "more moderate position," succeeding instead only in bolstering the Communist leader by propagating "inflated" estimates of Partisan strength.[73] Despite its stated opposition to interference in Balkan affairs, Cannon argued that the United States had a strong interest in ensuring that the region did not become a "disturbing political factor," a goal that it could help to secure by promoting a "stable, democratic regime" in Yugoslavia. Instead of sending Šubašić into Yugoslavia, and thereby allowing Tito to claim him "as his supporter," Cannon proposed that he go to London for "consultations" with the king. Šubašić himself was unenthusiastic about the new turn in the Shepherd Project – he felt that the king had slighted him in the cabinet reshuffle the previous year – but once the OSS secured a personal invitation from Peter II he felt that it was his "duty to proceed at once."

Meeting with Donovan before leaving for London, Šubašić outlined his plans for the establishment of a provisional government in Yugoslavia based on an alliance between the royal government-in-exile, the Partisans, the Croatian Peasants Party, and the Četniks. This unlikely mélange would govern until conditions permitted the Yugoslav people to make a democratic decision on the "system under which they would prefer to live."[74] To begin assembling the provisional government, Šubašić proposed to urge the king to select "loyal and outstanding party leaders" who "enjoyed a high reputation among the people of Yugoslavia:" the outstanding leader both he and his American handlers had in mind was, of course, no other than the Ban himself. Donovan agreed to the plan, and proposed that Bernard Yarrow travel to London under diplomatic accreditation to be "on hand" for "the formation of the new Yugoslav government."[75]

This revamped version of the Shepherd Project was approved by both the Joint Chiefs and the president in early May. Roosevelt was already well aware of Šubašić's importance to the reorganization of the royal government, having received a telegram from Churchill informing him that "the Ban" was "essential" to the formation of a "broad-based government not obnoxious to the Partisans," and asking the Americans to "find the gentleman and put him on an aeroplane as early as possible."[76] Given Šubašić's relationship with the OSS, the Americans did not have to look far to find him. The precise chain of events remains unclear, but King Peter recalled Churchill telling him that "President Roosevelt had suggested, through General Bill Donovan, that I should choose Mr. Šubašić for my prime minister," a choice approved by the British leader in place of his own candidate, General Mirković.[77] In this light, it is entirely

[73] Yarrow report, June 26, 1944, E160, NY-SI-PRO-17, Box 26, RG 226, NARA.
[74] Ibid.
[75] Ibid.
[76] Churchill to Roosevelt, April 26, *Correspondence*, 3: 116.
[77] King Peter II of Yugoslavia, *A King's Heritage: Memoirs of King Peter II of Yugoslavia* (London: Cassell and Company, 1955), 147.

possible that Churchill's request to Roosevelt to find Šubašić might itself have begun life in Washington.

The developments in Yugoslav politics that unfolded in London in May 1944 were the product of a conjunctural convergence of British and U.S. interests. The British, concerned by Tito's growing strength, were eager to replace the Great Serbian cabinet of Bozidar Purić with one that would have more appeal to the Partisans, and they saw Šubašić as ideal prime ministerial material. And so, of course, did the Americans. Under British pressure, King Peter dismissed Purić on May 24, appointing Šubašić as prime minister in his place on June 1. Throughout the tortuous negotiations leading to his appointment, Šubašić worked closely with Bernard Yarrow who, in turn, kept the OSS and the State Department abreast of developments. The British, while helping to promote Šubašić's cause, were entirely ignorant of the fact that he was effectively on the OSS payroll.[78]

With Šubašić's appointment as prime minister, U.S. policy makers believed that they had finally gained significant influence at the center of Yugoslav politics. As was so often the case in Yugoslavia, however, nothing was quite what it seemed. With Šubašić in place, London and Washington set out to bring Tito under control. Believing the Partisan leader to have been "chastened" by recent military reverses and thereby rendered open to Allied influence, London arranged for a meeting between Tito and Šubašić at Partisan headquarters on the island of Vis.[79] On June 17, the two leaders signed an agreement promising a democratic federal Yugoslavia, a plebiscite on the monarchy, and an merger between the royal government and the Partisan-led AVNOJ. The new government would be formally constituted once Belgrade had been liberated, and Šubašić agreed to serve as foreign minister in a cabinet headed by Tito. London welcomed the Treaty of Vis, with Churchill participating directly in subsequent talks between Šubašić and Tito in Italy and informing Roosevelt that the agreement would "enable us with more confidence to increase our supplies of war material to the Yugoslav Forces."[80]

Washington took a more jaundiced view, with Cordell Hull suggesting that Tito and the British had forced the agreement on Šubašić, and that it reflected an "almost unconditional acceptance of Partisan demands."[81] The harsh reality, as U.S. policy makers began to realize, was that Šubašić – and his American boosters – had been brought face to face with the real relationship of forces in Yugoslavia: while Tito was the head of a powerful revolutionary army,

---

[78] Other accounts of the Shepherd Project, for example that in Ford, *OSS and the Yugoslav Resistance*, 165–166, emphasize that Šubašić and Yarrow were spying on the British during the complex negotiation leading to the formation of the new government. There was undoubtedly an espionage element to the Shepherd Project, but focusing on this aspect overlooks Washington's primary interest in the affair, which lay in the promotion of Šubašić's candidacy.

[79] Murphy to State Department, June 11, 1944, *FRUS 1944*, 4: 1378.

[80] Churchill to Roosevelt, August 14, 1944, *Correspondence*, 3: 275.

[81] Hull to Murphy, July 8, 1944, *FRUS 1944*, 4: 1387.

Šubašić's story of Croatian Peasant Party fighters ready to do battle under his command evaporated like the mirage it was. In this situation, Šubašić's secret ties to Washington counted for little. Tito, meanwhile, regaled Robert Murphy with his "enthusiasm" for the United States, his anticipation of American funding for postwar reconstruction, and his support for "democracy and the Four Freedoms."[82] Although Murphy was favorably impressed, policy makers believed that the Partisan leader was acting in "bad faith," and concluded that his forces were readying U.S.-supplied arms for use against "the Serbs."[83] To Washington, Šubašić appeared to have been politically entrapped by Tito, a fact that London seemed not only to accept, but to be complicit in.

In mid-September, Tito abruptly vanished from his British-sponsored stronghold on Vis, turning up in Moscow to discuss the Red Army's entry into Yugoslavia with Stalin. Stalin agreed that Russian troops would operate in Yugoslavia in support of the Partisans but – in a unique concession to the independence of Tito's forces – promised that they would not occupy the country.[84] In mid-October, Russian and Partisan troops joined forces to capture Belgrade, creating the preconditions for the establishment of the new government and, on November 1, the Democratic Federal Yugoslavia envisioned in the Treaty of Vis was established. The new government consisted of twelve members drawn from the Partisan movement and six from the royal government-in-exile. The king, in an agreement made without his approval, was to be represented by a three-member council of regents; he would not be allowed to return to the country before a plebiscite determined the future of the monarchy.

Reporting from Belgrade in early November, the American Military Mission noted gloomily that the Vis agreement had simply laid the basis for a "firm government under his [Tito's] command," with OSS officers adding that Šubašić now held only "weak cards."[85] With Mihailović "virtually eliminated as a military and political force," the only Yugoslav counterweight to Tito had been effectively neutralized, leaving Šubašić open to being "forced into a union on Tito's terms and in a regime dominated by him."[86] From AFHQ Caserta, Alexander Kirk reported that Šubašić had been shocked to find that the "whole of the country including Serbia" was "behind Tito," and he recognized that his own appointment as foreign secretary would simply make him a "subservient link [between Tito and] the outside world."[87] By mid-December, even

---

[82] Murphy to Hull, August 16, 1944, *FRUS 1944*, 3: 1396–1397.

[83] Matthews to Hull, August 18, 1944, *FRUS 1944*, 3: 1397–1399.

[84] See J. R. Whitman, "Drawing the Line: Britain and the Emergence of the Trieste Question, January 1941–May 1945" *The English Historical Review* 106, no. 419 (1991).

[85] Thayer to State Department, November 4, 1944, *FRUS 1944*, 4: 1420; OSS memo, November 3, 1944, Box 220, RG 218, NARA.

[86] OSS memo, November 3, 1944, Box 220, RG 218, NARA.

[87] Kirk to State Department, November 29, 1944, *FRUS 1944*, 4: 1425; Kirk to State Department, November 7, 1944, *FRUS 1944*, 4: 1421.

Bernard Yarrow had reluctantly been forced to conclude that the "Shepherd" was "completely under the domination of Tito."[88]

With the Red Army now in direct contact with Tito's forces for the first time, Russian tanks and other heavy weapons were soon flowing into Partisan hands, breaking the resistance movement's dependence on Allied supplies. Tito began to prepare for this new relationship of forces in late September by placing restrictions on the movement of Allied liaison officers. In Washington, the Joint Chiefs quickly concluded that with the "civil war all but in the bag," Tito did not want Allied officers observing the consolidation of his victory "in the political and economic fields."[89] Tito remained on friendly terms with individual Allied officers, but relations between Belgrade and the Allies cooled rapidly, particularly once the new government spelled out its intention to secure control of the formerly Italian Julian March at the head of the Adriatic. "The switch" in attitude, one OSS officer noted, "was a bit abrupt."[90]

By the end of 1944, the complete failure of the effort to "hitch" the Partisans to "the car of British policy" was apparent even to Churchill, whose "enthusiasm for Tito," Ambassador Kirk noted, had finally "diminished" amidst a welter of complaints about the Yugoslav leader's "unsatisfactory and rude attitude."[91] With typical sarcasm, Foreign Officer official Alexander Cadogan likened King Peter's efforts to resist being swept away by the Partisan triumph to a "twig defying an avalanche, and a rather rotten twig, too."[92] The only bright spot in this otherwise gloomy picture was Fitzroy Maclean's prescient observation that Tito did not intend to be anyone's "puppet," predicting future conflict between the Yugoslavs and their imperious allies in Moscow.[93]

From the standpoint of the Allies, the immediate danger in Yugoslavia was that, precisely as Lincoln MacVeagh had predicted, the victorious Partisans might turn out to be much more revolutionary than the Russians. Analyzing the situation from AFHQ Caserta, Alexander Kirk concluded that the "revolutionary and authoritarian" regime in Belgrade was the natural product of "one of the most dynamic and courageous of European resistance movements," a force led by battle-hardened veterans whose "asceticism" made them "dangerous men."[94] The new government, he argued, had the capacity to destabilize the "equilibrium of political and moral forces" throughout the entire region, and in neighboring Italy and the Eastern Mediterranean in particular.[95] Moreover, while happy to receive America's "proffered assistance"

[88] Yarrow, quoted in Donovan, memorandum to JCS, December 19, 1944, RG 218, Box 220, NARA.
[89] JCS Memo, September 25, 1944, Box 220, RG 218, NARA.
[90] Smith, *OSS*, 156.
[91] Kirk to State Department, December 9, 1944, *FRUS 1944*, 4: 1429.
[92] Cadogan, diary entry, January 15, 1945, David Dilks (ed.), *The Diaries of Sir Alexander Cadogan, 1938–1945* (New York: G. P. Putnam's Sons, 1972), 695.
[93] Kirk to State Department, November 2, 1944, *FRUS 1944*, 4: 1417.
[94] Kirk to State, November 2, 1944, *FRUS 1944*, 4: 1432.
[95] Ibid.

during the fighting, Partisan leaders did not seem eager to be "counted among our friends." Economic and military aid, it seemed, had not secured political deference. Driven by these worrisome conclusions, Washington declined to follow London's lead in recognizing the new government, refusing to establish diplomatic relations with Belgrade until March 1946.

In early 1945, Washington's opposition to Yugoslav territorial demands in the Julian March put it on a collision course with Belgrade. By the time the crisis came to a head in May, two critical elements in the relationship of forces had shifted to Yugoslavia's detriment. First, advance elements of the British Eighth Army had arrived in the city of Trieste, establishing an uneasy joint occupation with Partisan forces and for the first time giving the Allies the capacity to back their efforts to control Tito with military force. Second, Moscow declined to risk a military confrontation with the Allies by backing Yugoslav territorial claims. Motivated by a desire to perpetuate the wartime Grand Alliance, Stalin was also eager to curb the potentially destabilizing influence of a confident and independent-minded regime in the Balkans. This confluence of factors forced Belgrade to back down, dropping its claims in the Julian March and handing the Allies their first victory in the rapidly emerging Cold War.

Despite this success, it was clear that both London's effort to co-opt Tito, and Washington's attempt to utilize its relationship with Šubašić to gain leverage in Yugoslav politics, had ended in failure. Ivan Šubašić, it turned out, had fed his OSS handlers what they wanted to hear, securing U.S. backing for his own political ambitions by peddling vastly exaggerated claims about the forces at his disposal in Croatia. In this sense – and in confirmation of the ease with which intelligence services can be led to buy into schemes that conform to their own preexisting desires – Šubašić takes his place in a lineup stretching from the Group of Five in Algeria to Ahmed Chalabi and his Iraqi National Congress. If Šubašić turned out to be a weak reed, however, the Shepherd Project nevertheless demonstrates both the importance U.S. policy makers attached to Yugoslavia and their willingness to utilize whatever levers came to hand in an attempt to gain influence there. In this effort, and for the first time in U.S. history, Washington used strategic intelligence operations as a major instrument of policy. The close – if not always harmonious – relationship between President Roosevelt, the OSS, the State Department, and the Joint Chiefs forged in this process prefigured the postwar establishment of a national security apparatus with an integral intelligence and covert operations arm.

GREECE: CRUSHING THE RESISTANCE

In Greece, as in Yugoslavia, popular resistance to the occupation began to develop shortly after Axis forces completed their conquest of the country.[96]

---

[96] See Lawrence S. Wittner, *American Intervention in Greece, 1943–1949* (New York: Columbia University Press, 1982).

In the summer of 1941, the Greek Communist Party (KKE) initiated the formation of the National Liberation Front (EAM), a broadly based alliance that commanded the support of broad layers of the population, including former government officials and army officers. The following year, EAM signaled the beginning of a guerrilla campaign against the occupiers with the formation of the Greek People's Liberation Army (ELAS). By late 1943, OSS analysts were describing EAM as a "dynamic, imaginative, and fighting organization" that had the support of "good people all over Greece," and they estimated that ELAS could field some 30,000 guerrilla fighters.[97]

British policy makers regarded Greece as a key element in the putative postwar order in the eastern Mediterranean, and they were determined to exercise significant political influence in the country. As in Yugoslavia, London nurtured a monarchic government-in-exile, this one based in Cairo and led by King George II. However, in contrast to Yugoslavia – where a sober assessment of the balance of forces on the ground led the British to give political and material support to Tito's Partisans – in Greece, London made strenuous efforts to promote the National Republican Greek League (EDES) as a promonarchical counterweight to the communist-led EAM. This was an uphill task. George II's close association with the prewar dictatorship of Ioannis Metaxas undermined popular support for the government-in-exile within the country, and the military capacities of the forces commanded by EDES remained far inferior to those of ELAS. Nevertheless, as OSS analysts noted, London resolved this "clash" between "military" imperatives – which would have led them to back EAM/ELAS – and "political" necessity – which argued for backing the monarchical government-in-exile – firmly and unwaveringly in favor of the latter.[98]

Washington broadly endorsed London's approach to Greek politics, but U.S. policy makers were happy to let the British take the lead, as it allowed them to take their distance from an unpopular promonarchical policy. Anglo-American plans for postwar Greece were effectively underwritten by Moscow. The Russians did not view Greece as being critical to their postwar security, and in May 1944, following the general lines of divide established at Tehran, they signaled their willingness to consign the country to the Western sphere of influence by assigning the leading role in Greek affairs to London. British and U.S. policy makers could now bank on operating in Greece without Russian interference, and London prepared plans to dispatch troops to Athens lest a "tyrannical Communist government" emerge from the anti-fascist resistance in the aftermath of the anticipated German withdrawal.[99] In October, these steps were further reinforced by the division of the Balkans negotiated by Churchill and Stalin in Moscow: by according the Allies "the say" in Greece,

[97] OSS Report, November 26, 1943, Box 220, RG 218, NARA.
[98] Ibid.
[99] Churchill to Roosevelt, August 17, 1944, *Collected Correspondence*, 3: 278–279.

this agreement gave London the green light to use military force to secure a favorable post-occupation political outcome.[100]

Washington's backing for this approach was based on its long-standing view that the monarchy would provide the firmest political foundation for a post-war Greece that was firmly oriented toward the West. This was not an uncontroversial stance. In early 1943, State Department official Wallace Murray warned that because many Greeks viewed George II as a willing partner in the Metaxas dictatorship, his return to the country "under the wing of an Allied military occupation" might provoke "serious internal disorders."[101] Adolf Berle concurred, arguing that organizing to return George II to Greece before a popular referendum had determined the future of the monarchy could create significant "political and military problems."[102] Despite these warnings, however, Washington endorsed the monarchy as the foundation of a pro-western government in Greece, and at the *Quadrant* conference in August 1943 Allied leaders agreed to "continue to support the governments and regimes now recognized," thereby reaffirming George II as the legitimate head of state.[103] The conditions of the king's return were left deliberately vague. Where Murray had cautioned against his return *before* a plebiscite on the monarchy, Churchill's friend and adviser General Jan Smuts argued that "fair play" required that George II quickly resume his "former position," subject only to "later" approval by the Greek people.[104]

Given the balance of forces on the ground between EAM/ELAS and the pro-monarchical EDES, by the time of the *Quadrant* conference British leaders had concluded that the King would have to be returned to Greece courtesy of a "substantial" British force that was capable of establishing the "proper conditions of public tranquility."[105] The Americans agreed, with Roosevelt writing to George II expressing his support and explaining that, while the Greek people would have "full opportunity freely to express their political will" at the "earliest practicable moment," they should in the meantime rally behind the king.[106]

Roosevelt would in fact turn out to be even more promonarchical in Greece than the British. In the fall of 1943, British policy makers, doubting their ability to mount a successful invasion of Greece in the immediate future, reversed their earlier position and urged the king to delay his return until such time as a plebiscite on the monarchy could be held. After meeting privately with King George in Cairo while traveling to the Tehran Conference, Roosevelt forced

---

[100] Churchill, *Second World War*, 6: 198.
[101] Murray, "Greece," memorandum, March 16, 1943, *FRUS 1943*, 4: 126.
[102] Berle, memorandum, August 31, 1943, *FRUS 1943*, 4: 149.
[103] Conference minutes, August 22, 1943, *FRUS 1943*, Washington and Quebec: 932.
[104] Conference minutes, August 22. 1943, *FRUS 1943*, Washington and Quebec: 933.
[105] Churchill to Eden, August 19, 1943, Churchill, *Second World War*, 5: 536; Smuts to Churchill, August 20, 1943, *Second World War*, 5: 537.
[106] Roosevelt to King George II, September 6, 1943, *FRUS 1943*, Washington and Quebec: 1046.

the British to abandon their new plan and to agree that the king himself should decide when and how he should return to Greece. Pressing his case, Roosevelt launched a sharp attack on Foreign Secretary Anthony Eden, accusing him of "trying to deprive the King of his crown."[107] Noting that Lincoln MacVeagh, U.S. ambassador to the Greek government-in-exile, had joined the British in arguing for a plebiscite, Roosevelt administered a verbal "spanking" that caused the ambassador to pen a long exculpatory letter in an effort to regain the president's good graces.[108]

Roosevelt's display of anger – King George told American journalist Cyrus Sulzberger that the president had been "so furious that he rose out of his chair and walked a few steps" – underscored his insistence on maintaining Greece within the Allied sphere of influence, even if it meant backing an unpopular, undemocratic, and deeply conservative monarchy.[109] He had not, of course, been converted to monarchism per se; even as he reinforced the Greek monarchy, Roosevelt concluded that the situation in Italy necessitated abandoning Washington's earlier attachment to the monarch there and forcing the abdication of Victor Emanuel. The big difference was that there were substantial U.S. forces on the ground in Italy and none in Greece, and in their absence a plebiscite on the future of the Greek monarchy would be a dangerous and unpredictable gamble.

In early 1944 the Allies curtailed even the limited arms shipments that they had been making to the Communist-led Greek resistance, now described by Churchill as a "gang of bandits."[110] When Greek troops based in Egypt demonstrated in favor of a republic in April, Churchill concluded that they had been "contaminated by revolutionary and Communist elements" and ordered the use of force against them.[111] Surrounded by heavily armed British troops, the rebellious Greeks surrendered; as punishment for advocating a republic, more than 20,000 soldiers spent the rest of the war in British prisoner of war cages. Approving the forcible suppression of the rebellion, Roosevelt expressed the pious hope that the rebels might "retain a sense of proportion and … set aside pettiness."[112] Moscow did not protest the British action, and when the Russians did intervene in Greek affairs in August 1944, it was to instruct the KKE to join the new Government of National Unity formed under British supervision by Democratic Socialist Party leader Georgios Papandreou. This move broadened the Royal government, but the outcome of the army rebellion demonstrated graphically that real power in the exile movement lay with the king and his Allied backers, and EAM was justifiably wary of entering a government in which it could exert no real influence. Russian intervention forced the issue,

[107] Quoted in Wittner, *American Intervention*, 12.
[108] MacVeagh to Roosevelt, December 13, 1943, Box 3, MacVeagh papers,.
[109] Sulzberger, *Long Row of Candles*, 335.
[110] Churchill, *Second World War*, 6: 257.
[111] Churchill, *Second World War*, 5: 541.
[112] Roosevelt to Churchill, April 17, 1944, *Correspondence*, 3: 98–99.

risking a split in EAM that left the Communists on the movement's moderate wing in order to push the resistance movement into the government.

With this political settlement – effectively a Greek version of the "Salerno switch" – in place, British leaders prepared to establish a pro-Allied government in Greece by force of arms. A 10,000-man expeditionary force was readied to rush into Athens as soon as German troops withdrew. Roosevelt approved Churchill's request for U.S. aircraft to transport the force to Greece, noting that he had "no objection" to London's plan to "preserve order" in Greece.[113] Under Russian pressure, EAM signaled its willingness to cooperate, placing its fighters under government control and promising not to allow ELAS units to enter Athens.

As the Red Army moved into the Balkans in May 1944, German troops began withdrawing from Greece to avoid being entrapped by the Russian advance, and on October 4, British troops launched Operation *Manna*, heading for Athens with the Papandreou government in tow. They were greeted there not by fire from armed revolutionaries but by cheering crowds organized by EAM. Communist leaders, following Moscow's instructions, ensured that the resistance fighters made no attempt to seize political power in the capital; but, as one British officer noted, "if the EAM had wished to seize control of Athens … nothing could have prevented them."[114]

Despite the warm welcome extended to British troops by EAM, London had no intention of allowing the resistance movement any significant voice in the new government. In particular, the British viewed an EAM proposal that ELAS fighters should be incorporated into a new national army as an unwarranted concession to communism, a view endorsed by Ambassador MacVeagh on the grounds that the former guerrillas intended to "bore from within."[115] A confrontation soon became inevitable, with Churchill arguing that having "paid the price" to the Russians, "we should not hesitate to use British troops to support the Royal Hellenic Government."[116] Stiffening Papandreou's resistance to EAM demands for greater inclusion, the British reinforced their garrison in Athens, bringing in Greek troops that were, as MacVeagh observed dispassionately, "notably rightist in sentiment."[117] Fighting finally broke out when Greek security forces and British troops opened fire on a mass demonstration, called after EAM ministers resigned from the government on December 1. Even as street fighting raged, several thousand EAM protestors thronged the streets outside the U.S. embassy hopefully cheering President Roosevelt and the United States.[118] The following day, amid a general strike and the arrival of ELAS fighters, a full-scale civil war unfolded in Athens. Churchill's orders to

---

[113] Roosevelt to Churchill, August 26, *Correspondence*, 3: 133–134.
[114] Quoted in Wittner, *American Intervention in Greece*, 9.
[115] MacVeagh to State, November 9, 1944, *FRUS 1944*, 5: 137.
[116] Churchill to Eden, November 7, 1944, Churchill *Second World War*, 6: 250.
[117] MacVeagh to State, November 17, 1944, *FRUS 1944*, 5: 140.
[118] MacVeagh to State, December 3, 1944, *FRUS 1944*, 5: 141.

General Harold Scobie instructed him to "act as if you were in a conquered city where a local rebellion is in progress," and he proceeded to do just that.[119]

After protracted fighting British forces finally gained control of Athens, and Churchill arrived at Christmas to preside over a new political settlement. Archbishop Damaskinos was appointed regent, representing King George pending a plebiscite on the future of the monarchy; in a modest concession to popular sentiment, Allied leaders had decided that bringing the king directly into Athens was likely to hinder rather than help the consolidation of the new regime. With ELAS fighters locked in battle with British troops within earshot of the meeting, EAM leaders struggled to maintain the framework of the war-time "grand alliance," shaking the prime minister's hand and hailing Britian as "our great ally."[120] Damaskinos moved quickly to consolidate a conservative regime, appointing the rightist General Nicholas Plastiras as prime minister in place of Papandreou in early January 1945. In February, EAM signaled its capitulation by formally disbanding ELAS.

These steps left major social and economic questions unresolved. After the long struggle against the Axis occupation, popular democratic sentiment remained strong, with economic dislocation fueling continued political unrest and reinforcing what ambassador MacVeagh called the "present popularity of Communism."[121] However, whereas in Yugoslavia the Partisans carried through a social revolution, in Greece the leadership of the EAM crumbled under the combined weight of the British army and Russian political pressure. Of these factors, the influence of Moscow, acting in defense of the division agreed at Tehran and in opposition to the political will of a substantial section of the Greek population, was the weightiest. Where Tito subverted Moscow's injunction to subordinate social issues in Yugoslavia to Russian wartime diplomacy, the KKE remained entrapped within the framework of the "anti-Fascist alliance," greeting Churchill as an ally even as British troops were shooting down its own supporters.

Washington stood squarely behind London during the Greek crisis. Following Roosevelt's approval of British plans for the dispatch of troops to Greece, Harry Hopkins squashed a suggestion from Admiral King that Washington refuse the British use of U.S. landing craft, arguing that such an act would be tantamount to "walking out on a member of your family who is in trouble."[122] As fighting engulfed Athens, Roosevelt assured Churchill of his support in the face of the "tragic difficulties ... encountered in Greece," offering "to be of any help possible in the circumstances."[123] As a political solution emerged over Christmas 1944, Roosevelt backed the British effort by urging King George to

[119] Churchill, Orders to General Scobie, December 5, 1944, Churchill, *Second World War*, 6: 252.
[120] Churchill, *Second World War*, 6: 276.
[121] MacVeagh to State, November 9, 1944, *FRUS 1944*, 5: 136.
[122] Hopkins quoted in Sherwood, *Roosevelt and Hopkins*, 841.
[123] Roosevelt to Churchill, December 13, 1944, *Correspondence*, 3: 455-456.

accept the Damaskinos regency as a step toward the establishment of a stable monarchical government.[124] Given Roosevelt's longstanding support for the Greek monarchy, his message persuaded the king to approve the new arrangement. As Roosevelt had suggested, the usefulness of the regency as a tool for the preservation of the monarchy was vindicated when a majority of Greeks voted for it in the plebiscite held, under very different political conditions, in September 1946.

Despite their unwavering support for British policy, the fact that there were no American troops in Greece gave U.S. policy makers the opportunity to take their distance in public from events there by making some limited criticisms of British policy. Too close an association with British policy, Lincoln MacVeagh warned, would ensure that the United States would incur the same "dislike, suspicion, and distrust" that the Greeks already felt toward "our cousins."[125] State Department policy makers looked beyond the immediate crisis to the postwar order in the Eastern Mediterranean, concluding in June 1944 that the United States should provide substantial economic aid to facilitate the integration of Greece into an U.S.-led "multilateral world."[126] The United States, planners added, had an interest in enhancing Greece's strategic position in the Eastern Mediterranean, and should therefore look favorably on Greek territorial claims in Macedonia, Thrace, Bulgaria, and the Dodecanese Islands.

These long-term considerations spoke to the importance of avoiding being tied too closely to British policy, at least in the public eye. The fruits of this bifurcated policy were clearly evident on the streets of Athens where, as British troops battled street protests, EAM-led crowds mobbed the U.S. embassy cheering for President Roosevelt. In early December, the KKE newspaper *Resospastis* carried a declaration by Secretary of State Edward Stettinius reasserting Washington's stated – if frequently ignored – opposition to "interference in the internal affairs of countries now being liberated."[127] While Stettinius's statement made no specific criticism of British actions, it allowed Washington to present itself as the champion of democracy even as the British were suppressing it.[128]

This dual approach was also reflected within the Allied military leadership. Here, the Civil Affairs Committee of the Combined Chiefs of Staff endorsed the establishment of British military rule in areas of Greece in which there was "a serious state of disorder" and authorized a substantial relief operation involving the distribution of U.S. supplies channeled through UNRRA.[129] In mid-December, however, and with British troops in Athens facing "much stronger opposition

[124] Roosevelt to King George II, December 28, 1944, *FRUS 1944*, 5: 177.
[125] MacVeagh to Roosevelt, August 1944, Box 3, MacVeagh papers.
[126] State Department Country and Area Committee, CAC 203, June 6, 1944, microfilm T1221, NARA.
[127] MacVeagh to State, December 3, 1944, *FRUS 1944*, 5: 141.
[128] Stettinius to MacVeagh, December 12, 1944, *FRUS 1944*, 5: 147–148.
[129] CCAC October 13, 1944, Box 220, RG 218, NARA.

than anticipated," U.S. military leaders argued that it was inappropriate for the Combined Chiefs to discuss reinforcing the occupation force on the grounds that the operation had been launched in a "purely British capacity."[130]

A similar dualism guided Roosevelt's thinking, with his note to Churchill proffering support during the crisis also making it abundantly clear that the "mounting adverse reaction of public opinion" in the United States made it impossible to "take a stand with you" in public.[131] Edward Stettinius had already warned Roosevelt that public opinion had been "stirred to an unprecedented degree by the Greek crisis." Given the degree of domestic criticism of U.S. policy in Spain, North Africa, and Italy, this was something of an overstatement, but it resonated in the context of the "liberal turn" in U.S. policy opened by the capture of Rome in June.[132] In this context, domestic criticism of Britain's actions was not simply "stirred" by news from Greece, but was actively encouraged by the State Department. Mainstream opinion-makers had initially expressed solidarity with London, with the *New York Times* arguing that British forces were "bound" to defend recognized governments against "violence or armed insurrection," however "distasteful" this task might be.[133] Three days later, however, Stettinius joined the discussion, endorsing Churchill's affirmation that the form of government established in Greece was "entirely a matter for them [the Greek people]," but implying that British actions violated this pledge.[134]

Echoing Stettinius's critical tone, columnist Walter Lippmann argued that it was better to recognize "bad governments" that were based on "some of the characteristics of self-government" than it was to back "unpopular governments" with "tanks and bayonets."[135] The *Washington Post* welcomed Stettinius's implied criticism as a "breath of fresh air" that demonstrated that the "Atlantic Charter continues to have meaning."[136] Drew Pearson fueled the fire by printing the text of Churchill's orders to General Scobie in his syndicated "Washington Merry-Go-Round" column.[137] The prime minister's blunt instructions needed little editorial elaboration. Pearson's text came from a copy of Churchill's order circulated to senior officers at AFHQ and forwarded to Washington by Ambassador Kirk.[138] "Only a few high-ranking U.S. officials" had seen the orders, Pearson pointed out, and some found them "harsh, almost brutal, in tone."[139] At least one senior State Department official clearly believed

---

[130] CCS 750/1, December 19, 1944, Box 220, RG 218, NARA.
[131] Roosevelt to Churchill, December 13, 1944, *Correspondence*, 3: 456.
[132] Stettinius to Roosevelt December 13, 1944, *FRUS 1944*, 5: 149.
[133] Editorial, *New York Times*, December 4, 1944, 22.
[134] Stettinius, statement, December 7, 1944, *Department of State Bulletin 1944*, 2: 713.
[135] Lippman, *Washington Post*, December 7, 1944, 9.
[136] Editorial, *Washington Post*, December 7, 1944, 8.
[137] Pearson, "Washington Merry-Go-Round," *Washington Post*, December 12, 1944, 14.
[138] Kirk to State Department, December 5, 1944, *FRUS 1944*, 5: 143–144.
[139] Pearson, "Washington Merry-Go-Round," *Washington Post*, December 12, 1944, 14.

that Washington's critical distance from the events in Athens could be enhanced by leaking them to Pearson.

Faced with mounting public criticism on both sides of the Atlantic, Churchill found the contradiction between Washington's public word and private deed particularly irksome. "The fact that you are supposed to be against us," he complained to Roosevelt, "has added to our difficulties and burdens."[140] In parliament, Churchill struck a typically maudlin note. "Poor old England!" the prime minister complained, "we have to assume the burden of the most thankless tasks, and in undertaking them to be scoffed at, criticized, and opposed from every quarter."[141] He had a point: with London doing the dirty work to prevent the establishment of a communist-led government in Greece, Washington had the luxury of criticizing Britain's egregiously undemocratic and heavy-handed policy while privately acting to facilitate it. In public acknowledgment of Moscow's efforts to uphold the spheres of influence, Churchill noted that there had not been "one word of reproach" for Britain's actions in the Russian press.[142]

Washington's modest public critique of Britain's actions in Greece was part of its broader preparation for a postwar world in which the United States would assert its hegemony in liberal language issued from its self-proclaimed occupation of the moral high ground. Not surprisingly, U.S. criticism was strictly limited and abated quickly. Churchill's dramatic visit to Athens and the establishment of the Damaskinos regency soon allowed opinion-makers to recast British policy in a more favorable light. Congratulating Churchill for "grasping the Greek nettle firmly," the *New York Times* argued that the only alternative to the Damaskinos regency was continued "chaos."[143] The *Washington Post* felt likewise, arguing that because "peace and order [could now be] restored to that unhappy land" a "word of praise" for Churchill was "very much in order."[144] Even the liberal *Nation* hoped that the "grotesque and provocative comedy" enacted by Churchill in Greece might yet give cause for "optimism."[145]

With the reliably right-wing Plastiras government in place, and with domestic criticism of British policy easing, Washington moved ahead with a program of economic aid administered through the Greek government. The Greek economy was in ruins, with disease and malnutrition rampant, but U.S. officials hoped that the inflow of aid could solve the most pressing social problems while building support for the Plastiras government and justifying its pro-Western orientation; as State Department officials noted in June 1945, an "active and benevolent interest in Greece at this time offers one of the most

[140] Churchill to Roosevelt, December 15, 1944, *Correspondence*, 3: 458.
[141] Churchill, *The Second World War*, VI: 257.
[142] Ibid., 255.
[143] Editorial, *New York Times*, January 2, 1945, 18.
[144] Editorial, *Washington Post*, January 2, 1945, 6.
[145] Editorial, *Nation*, January 6, 1945.

practical means of demonstrating this government's determination to play an international role commensurate with its strength and public commitments."[146] In December 1944, U.S. officials discussed using Lend-Lease funding to ship 35,000 tons of relief supplies per month; and in February 1945, MacVeagh assured the Greek government that U.S. assistance would be available for the rehabilitation of health services and public utilities, as well as for the provision of immediate relief for "displaced persons."[147]

As they moved to implement these plans, U.S. diplomats and aid officials found that the establishment of the Plastiras government had opened the door to corruption and profiteering on a massive scale. Substantial quantities of U.S. aid ended up directly on the black market where, with the connivance of government officials, it was sold at greatly inflated prices. As complaints from diplomats and aid workers about the chronic corruption and inefficiency of the government grew, U.S. aid efforts were increasingly channeled through UNRRA – itself, of course, virtually an arm of the U.S. government. UNRRA's Greek Mission was soon functioning as a kind of parallel government, organizing the import and distribution of more than 100,000 tons of food per month, together with a broad range of basic household goods.[148] Continued graft and black market profiteering ensured that inadequate supplies reached those in most need, rendering the aid effort ineffective as a tool with which to promote political stability and quell popular dissent. Despite Moscow's continued adherence to the spheres of influence agreement, many Greek Communists and other radicals resisted the new government, and by the summer of 1946 renewed civil war had broken out. The following year, and with British power ebbing, Washington stepped in directly to back the Greek government with military aid.

Although the efforts by U.S. policy makers to gain purchase on Greek and Yugoslav politics were deprived of the powerful military backing that they enjoyed in North Africa, Italy, and France, their results were not entirely unsuccessful. In Yugoslavia, U.S. policy makers took comfort from the fact that the Partisan's stubborn independence presented Moscow with at least as big a problem as it did Washington and, after Tito and Stalin parted company in 1948, the United States emerged as the leading economic underwriter of Yugoslav independence. In Greece, support for Britain's crushing of the Communist-led resistance laid the basis for increased U.S. intervention in the immediate postwar period in defense of a regime oriented firmly toward the United States. Even if it lacked the apparent moral clarity of its intervention elsewhere in the Mediterranean, U.S. policy was far from being the limp and "Balkan-phobic" creature of historical memory.

---

[146] Quoted in Gabriel Kolko, *The Politics of War: The World War and United States Foreign Policy* (New York: Pantheon Books, 1990), 435.

[147] *Department of State Bulletin*, December 7, 1944, 2: 300–305; JCS Memo #366, February 26, 1945, Box 84, RG 218, NARA.

[148] See William I. Hitchcock, *The Bitter Road To Freedom: A New History of the Liberation of Europe* (New York, Free Press, 2008), 228–230.

14

"We Have Become Mediterraneanites"

As the great intra-Allied fight over the proposed invasion of southern France was gathering momentum in early 1944, George Marshall observed wryly that, with the British stressing the centrality of the cross-Channel assault and the Americans arguing vigorously for *Anvil*, it seemed that "we have become Mediterraneanites."[1] Marshall was well placed to appreciate the irony in this turn of events. For the previous two years, he and his colleagues on the Joint Chiefs of Staff had battled both the British and their own president in a series of rearguard action against the large-scale commitment of U.S. forces to the Mediterranean. But now, and with its political and military leaders in close accord, Washington was waging a determined and protracted campaign to shape the last great strategic initiative of the Mediterranean war. It all amounted, the normally humorless Marshall quipped, to a "great reversal of form."[2]

There was rather more to this than Marshall himself might have cared to admit. Great reversals of form, especially those involving the establishment of hegemony over a substantial region of the world, do not happen without concentrated effort. They are not chance events, but are instead the products, if not of grand strategic *plans*, then at least of the grand strategic *impulses* out of which strategies and operational plans might be crafted. In fact – and this is surely the heart of Sir John Seeley's famous observation that Britain had "conquered and peopled half the world in a fit of absence of mind" – at the level of grand strategy it cannot all be planned beforehand.[3] Even in the compressed timeframe within which U.S. hegemony in the Mediterranean was established, there were simply too many complex variables, and too many unforeseen outcomes, for any a priori scheme to have had validity. One can search the National Archives, the

[1] Marshall to Eisenhower, February 7, 1944, Alfred D. Chandler (ed.), *The Papers of Dwight David Eisenhower: The War Years* (Baltimore: Johns Hopkins University Press, 1970), 3: 1708.
[2] Marshall, quoted in Dill to Chiefs of Staff (COS), February 4, 1944, PREM 3/271/4.
[3] John Seeley, *Expansion of England*, 1883 (Reprint, Hong Kong: Forgotten Books, 2012), 10.

Franklin D. Roosevelt Presidential Library, and other repositories of top-level government records in vain for any wartime plan or memorandum advocating the establishment of U.S. hegemony in the Mediterranean. Yet, while the exact manner in which that hegemony was put together, and precise date at which it was consolidated, might be matters of debate, the indisputable fact remains that *all* the fundamental elements of America's postwar power in the Mediterranean were assembled during the war itself. So the question remains: What drove the grand strategic impulse that led the United States into the Mediterranean so powerfully and so effectively?

America's wartime impulse toward the Mediterranean was rooted in the interplay between the epoch-making expansion of U.S. capital, unleashing a dynamic that could only be fully realized through war, and the efforts of the most far-sighted representatives of the U.S. ruling class to shape and guide that process. It grew, in an appropriately Mediterranean analogy, out of the interrelationship between what French historian Fernand Braudel has described as the profound underlying "tides of history," and the political events (or "crests of foam") that they "carry on their strong backs."[4] Anne O'Hare McCormick suggested something very similar when she noted that the "key to the Roosevelt policies [is that he] consciously rides the currents of time in the direction in which they are going."[5] Noting that Roosevelt's "sense of history is his sixth sense," McCormick might have added that he not only rode the waves, but also sought to steer the ship, shaping course not with grand gestures but by nudging the tiller and trimming the sails to take advantage of the prevailing wind.[6] As was often the case, McCormick's insight was in part the product of discussion with Roosevelt himself.[7] Commenting on this question from a somewhat different angle the following summer, McCormick noted approvingly that the "effective coordination ... of action [and] of mind" then being "hammered out" between America's military leaders – presumably as they finally accepted the president's insistence on *Gymnast* – would "free Mr. Roosevelt from a lot of time-consuming detail and enable him to concentrate on problems of high strategy."[8]

As the United States rose to global predominance in the half-century following the Spanish American War, Washington lacked any organized mechanism

---

[4] Fernand Braudel, *The Mediterranean and the Mediterranean World in the Age of Philip II* (New York: Harper and Row, 1976), 1: 21.

[5] McCormick, "At 60 He Is Still a Happy Warrior," *New York Times*, January 25, 1942, SM3.

[6] Roosevelt's enthusiasm for Henry Wadsworth Longfellow's "Building of the Ship," with its injunction to: "Sail on, O ship of State!
  Sail on, O Union strong and great!"
  surely takes on special meaning in this light. See Winston S. Churchill, *The Second World War*, 6 vols. (Boston: Houghton Mifflin, 1948–1954), 3, 24–25.

[7] McCormick spent more than two hours with Roosevelt on January 14, 1942. Her birthday tribute appeared eleven days later. See "FDR Day by Day," January 14, 1942, FDRL.

[8] McCormick, "Abroad: Behind the Critical Debate on the Second Front," *New York Times*, July 25, 1942. McCormick attended a White House lunch with the president two days before this column appeared. See FDR Day-By-Day, July 23, 1942, FDRL.

for grand-strategic policy making; hence the idea of an "impulse" rather than a codified plan. But the absence of bureaucratic structure, even during the tumultuous years of world war, was not a reflection of weakness. On the contrary, the Roosevelt administration's freewheeling, multi-institutional, apparently uncoordinated, and often mutually contradictory, approach to the war effectively maximized the possibilities of exploiting hitherto unanticipated openings and opportunities. Moreover, the threads of numerous military, diplomatic, covert, political, economic, and propaganda, initiatives were concentrated in the hands of Roosevelt and his immediate circle and, particularly in the early phases of the war before the engagement of U.S. military force began to build a logic and momentum of its own, grand strategic direction flowed very much from the president himself.

Historically, there was nothing particularly unusual in this setup. The determination and direction of grand strategy rests by definition in the hands of the narrow circles providing "leadership at the top."[9] It is not usually a public or a democratic process. In Washington in the early 1940s, this general tendency was compounded by the specific characteristics of the chief executive, in particular his penchant for secrecy and for "flying solo."[10] In turn, Roosevelt's character was itself the product of the concrete specificities of his upbringing and experiences, and his grand-strategic thinking was formed in response to given geopolitical circumstances. Talented individuals, as Russian Marxist Gregori Plekhanov explained, are the "product of social relations," and their talents, which might be overlooked under different historical circumstances, are recognized precisely because they equip them to serve the "great social needs of [the] time."[11] Far from being a traitor to his class, as one biographer asserts, Franklin Roosevelt was the authentic product of the American elite in its rise to hegemony, the articulator of its needs, and in a very direct sense its chief executive officer. Moreover, if Roosevelt best embodied the needs of his class at this critical conjuncture, he was not alone. Wendell Willkie, Roosevelt's Republican opponent in the 1940 election, shared the same "interventionist" worldview, and Roosevelt's cabinet, with the weighty addition of Republicans Frank Knox and Henry Stimson, was genuinely bipartisan and reflective of the majority of the American elite.

Roosevelt grasped the essentials of a grand strategy in which, as Paul Kennedy explains, "fighting power" is but "one of the instruments" available.[12]

---

[9] Williamson Murray, "Thoughts on Grand Strategy," in Williamson Murray, Richard Hart Sinnreich, and James Lacey (eds.), *The Shaping of Grand Strategy: Policy, Diplomacy, and War* (Cambridge: Cambridge University Press, 2011), 21.

[10] See Colin S. Gray, "Harry S. Truman and the forming of American grand strategy in the Cold War, 1945–1953," in Murray et al., *The Shaping of Grand Strategy*, 226.

[11] Gregori V. Plekhanov, *The Role of the Individual in History*, 1898 (Honolulu: University of Hawaii Press, 2003), 53, 60.

[12] Paul M. Kennedy, "Grand Strategy in War and Peace: Towards a Broader Definition," in Paul M. Kennedy, ed., *Grand Strategies in War and Peace* (New Haven, CT: Yale University Press 1991), 3.

For Clausewitz, strategy was the "art of using battles to win the war," but in grand strategy economic and political means complement the purely military, even if they tend to produce a more circumlocutious or "peripheral" approach. For Roosevelt, the defeat of the Axis powers and the advance of U.S. interests – or of "Americanism" – went hand in hand, while the war and the postwar were aspects of a continuum, integrated and simultaneous processes rather than separate and sequential events. Roosevelt's grand strategic approach to the Mediterranean took shape in the complex geopolitical situation that opened in the summer of 1940, characterized on the one hand by the collapse of France and the erosion of British power, and on the other by the relatively precarious position of wartime Italy. From this time on, as a great many commentators have noted but few have explained, Roosevelt responded to this crisis by steering the United States resolutely toward the Mediterranean.

Schooled in the writings of Alfred Thayer Mahan and the geopolitical practice of Theodore Roosevelt, Franklin D. Roosevelt approached grand strategy with a navalist's eye for the long game, looking to the accumulation of bases, positions, and zones of control, rather than simply for the shortest road to military victory. He was, as Anne O'Hare McCormick noted after meeting with him in June 1940, "a firm believer in Admiral Mahan's theory that in the long run land power cannot defeat sea power."[13] Made at the at height of the crisis in France, this was no random observation; on the same day that he talked to McCormick, Roosevelt penned a note to French premier Paul Reynaud, arguing encouragingly to a government on the verge of being evicted from its homeland that "naval power in world affairs still carries the lessons of history."[14] From the start of the European war, Roosevelt's background and inclinations gave his strategic thought a distinctly maritime – or "peripheral" bent. And if he lacked formal military training – despite his seven years as Under Secretary of the Navy – he was hardly the "amateur strategist" of Army imagination.[15] The real problem for Eisenhower and other Army leaders was not Roosevelt's lack of technical military training, but the fact that, on the basis of his own considerable experience and insight, he drew grand strategic conclusions that were at odds with their cherished, if simplistic, notions of mass and concentration.

The U.S.-led invasion of North Africa was rightly regarded by both Roosevelt's allies and his opponents as the "President's personal policy," and as he pursued it in the face of the opposition of his military leaders, it truly became a "magnet

---

[13] McCormick, "Europe," *New York Times,* June 15, 1940; The White House stenographer's diary records a 5:00 meeting between McCormick and President Roosevelt on June 13, 1940, "FDR Day-by-Day," FDRL.

[14] Roosevelt to Reynaud, quoted in Roosevelt to Churchill, June 13, 1940, Warren F. Kimball (ed.), *Churchill and Roosevelt: The Complete Correspondence* (London: Collins, 1984), 1: 46.

[15] Eisenhower, personal memorandum, January 4, 1942, *Eisenhower Papers,* 1: 39; also see previous discussion, 36.

whose attraction never failed."[16] For Roosevelt, however, North Africa was never an end in itself: it was the gateway into the Mediterranean. As early as summer 1942, Anne O'Hare McCormick, her own thinking perhaps shaped by further discussions with the president, was arguing that the Mediterranean *already* constituted a "second front" and an "open gate" into Europe, and whichever side dominated it would have the "best chance of military victory" in the war.[17] Another key related theme emerged in McCormick's writing the following spring. Reporting that Roosevelt was now "thinking and talking of post-war problems [and] of the structure of the post-war world," she asked bluntly whether "community" – read capitalism and a pro-American orientation – or "civil war and anarchy" would prevail in postwar Europe. Allied forces, she concluded, would arrive as "liberating armies," but they would have to function as "armies of occupation" while working to create the framework for the "long-predestined test of democracy."[18]

After playing an indispensable role in securing the commitment of U.S. forces to the Mediterranean through his unwavering advocacy of *Gymnast/Torch*, Roosevelt continued to be closely involved in the formulation of U.S. policy in the region, particularly as the postwar order began to emerge from the fighting. Most importantly, the evidence suggests that he was instrumental in urging Mark Clark to march directly on Rome, thereby setting the stage for the reform of Italian politics and the consequent deepening of U.S. economic and political influence. Roosevelt also played a critical role in the decision to press ahead with the *Anvil/Dragoon* landings in the South of France, in backing British efforts to uphold the Greek monarchy, in running the Shepherd Project in an effort to gain political leverage in Yugoslavia, and in the formulation of policy toward Franco's Spain. As the momentum of U.S. involvement in the Mediterranean built, however, and as U.S.-led governmental and quasi-governmental bureaucracies were constructed in the theater, so the role of direct presidential leadership tended to diminish. As early as the conference at Casablanca in January 1943, even George Marshall recognized the necessity of postponing the cross-Channel invasion and consequently of accepting, even if not wholeheartedly embracing, extended Mediterranean operations.[19]

[16] Robert Murphy, *Diplomat among Warriors*, (Garden City, NY: Doubleday & Co, 1964), 68; Arthur Layton Funk, *The Politics of Torch: The Allied Landings and the Algiers Putsch 1942* (Lawrence: University Press of Kansas: 1974), 72.

[17] McCormick, "Abroad," *New York Times*, June 12 and August 17, 1942; on visits to the White House see "FDR Day-by-Day," July 23 and August 7, 1942, FDRL, and McCormick to Roosevelt, August 6, 1942, McCormick papers, New York Public Library.

[18] McCormick, "Abroad," *New York Times*, March 29 and March 31, 1943; McCormick had lunch with Roosevelt at the White House on March 25, 1943, "FDR Day-by-Day," FDRL.

[19] See James Lacey, "Towards a Strategy: Creating an American Strategy for Global War, 1940–1943," in Murray, Williamson, Richard Hart Sinnreich, and James Lacey (eds.), *The Shaping of Grand Strategy: Policy, Diplomacy, and War* (Cambridge: Cambridge University Press, 2011), especially 187–191.

The result of Washington's wartime engagement with the Mediterranean, conducted initially under direct presidential leadership and then carried forward by its own building momentum, was that on every level – military, diplomatic, political, and economic – and in relation to every country in the region with the partial exception of Yugoslavia, the United States emerged from the war immeasurably stronger than it entered it. By the end of the war, U.S. policy makers were developing a conscious grand strategic vision of the Mediterranean as a unified entity in which, as analyst William Reitzel explained in 1948, "American security" was linked to a "larger complex of Mediterranean issues."[20] These notions were particularly influential with James Forrestal, President Truman's Secretary of the Navy, who conceptualized the Mediterranean as the "southern flank" of a U.S.-oriented Europe in a rapidly deepening confrontation with the Soviet Union, and who developed the naval element of Mediterranean force-projection by establishing a powerful and permanent U.S. fleet there.[21] Where British naval power in the Mediterranean had primarily sought to secure the "imperial lifeline" from Gibraltar to Suez, its U.S. successor was part of a much grander hegemonic project. In the vision of Nicholas Spykman, now reformulated in the language of "containment," it aimed to utilize U.S. power in the maritime "rimland" to control Russia's Asiatic "heartland."

This great transformation in America's position in the Mediterranean was the product of the consistent and massive application of force. From November 1942 to June 1944, the Mediterranean was the site of the largest overseas deployment of U.S. forces, and even as the tides of war flowed away from the region after D-Day, the combat troops left behind them a residue of military bases, ports, repair and assembly facilities, and airfields that continued to provide critical points of support for U.S. power. These bases, ostensibly maintained at the "invitation" of the government (or colonial power) on whose territory they sat, and justified by the notion that they existed to deliver collective security, actually provided the indispensable organizational framework for the consolidation of U.S. hegemony.[22] Through them, America's armies and "after-armies," as John Hersey described them, also established an intangible legacy in the form of the skeins of political influence, networks of business and patronage, and webs of covert operations that continued to underpin the exercise of U.S. power after the fighting men had moved on.[23] As the wartime regulation of trade organized through the Lend-Lease Administration, the

---

[20] William Reitzel, *The Mediterranean: Its Role in American Foreign Policy* (New York: Harcourt, Brace and Co., 1948), 56.

[21] See Simon Ball, *Bitter Sea: The Brutal World War II Fight for the Mediterranean* (New York: Harper, 2009), 296–314.

[22] See Mark L. Gillem, *America Town: Building Outposts of Empire* (Minneapolis: University of Minnesota Press, 2007), especially chapter 2; see also James R. Blaker, *United States Overseas Basing: An Anatomy of a Dilemma* (New York, Praeger, 1990), especially 28.

[23] John Hersey, *Bell for Adano*, 1944 (Reprint, New York: Vintage Books, 1988), vii.

North African Economic Board, and the Middle East Supply Center began to be eased, these networks of political and economic influence, formed with the willing collaboration of local elites, bound country after country into the new world-system of free trade dominated by the United States.

While Washington's accomplishments in the wartime Mediterranean were predicated on the massive application of military force, its grand strategic orientation was never a narrowly military question. On the contrary, it was a complex, multilayered and multi-headed affair organized through the combined – and sometimes contradictory – efforts of the State Department, the Foreign Economic Administration, the Lend-Lease Administration, the Treasury, the Office of Strategic Services, and the United Nations Relief and Rehabilitation Agency, together with numerous special ambassadors and presidential representatives, all working uneasily together and in collaboration with the military bureaucracy in Washington and throughout the Mediterranean theater. Albert Wedemeyer, senior U.S. planner and incorrigible opponent of involvement in the Mediterranean, famously contrasted anarchic U.S. decision-making with London's sophisticated political/military integration, and this judgment has become an accepted historiographical truism.[24] What is easily overlooked here is an appreciation of just how *effective* U.S. policy making actually was. There was no manual – no *Global Hegemony for Dummies* – to guide U.S. policy makers toward becoming the predominant power in the capitalist world. What Washington had, however, was the ever-increasing economic and military muscle that allowed it to run numerous parallel projects, determining their relative efficacy in practice. From this point of view, sophisticated British committee work was the organizational expression of a declining power forced to marshal limited and waning resources in a fundamentally defensive effort. In contrast, and for all its apparent dysfunctionality, Washington's grand strategy in the Mediterranean successfully advanced "Americanism" throughout the region, laying the basis for the postwar consolidation of hegemony as it did so.

Even before the end of the war, it was evident that the freewheeling methods that had facilitated the acquisition of hegemony would be inadequate to the complex task of its maintenance and defense. As historian Melvyn Leffler points out, the experience of war impelled a "fusion" of "geopolitical, economic, ideological and strategic considerations" that transformed foreign policy goals into "national security imperatives."[25] By 1943, George Marshall was already floating the integration of the Navy and War departments, and two years later a committee headed by Admiral James Richardson proposed establishing of a unified department of defense.[26] Richardson's report, delivered the day before

[24] See Albert C. Wedemeyer, *Wedemeyer Reports!* (New York: Henry Holt, 1958), 174–180.
[25] Melvyn P. Leffler, *A Preponderance of Power: National Security, the Truman Administration, and the Cold War* (Stanford, CA: Stanford University Press, 1992), 24.
[26] See Arnold A. Offner, *Another Such Victory: President Truman and the Cold War, 1945–1947* (Stanford, CA: Stanford University Press, 2002), 186–187.

Roosevelt's death, initiated the process that culminated in the passage of the National Security Act in July 1947. With this act, the United States acquired an executive body capable of exercising genuine grand strategic leadership. When the National Security Council met, senior civilian and military policy makers would be in a position to integrate all aspects of grand strategy in a systematic manner. There was an element of personal leadership style here: It is hard to see Roosevelt, the consummate political juggler, being bound by the NSC's closely argued policy statements and precisely minuted decisions. But in this, as in much else, it fell to Truman and then to Eisenhower – the archetypal military "manager" – to consolidate America's wartime gains.

A critical aspect of America's accession to hegemony was the shifting relationship between London and Washington as the mantle of "senior partner" passed from one to the other. This, too, was a protracted and multilayered process. As historian B. J. C. McKercher argues, Britain's "relative decline in manufacturing, accumulating capital, and investment" from the turn of the century onward was not directly paralleled by a "concurrent political and strategic decline."[27] While systems of global hegemony must ultimately be rooted in economic strength, their acquisition requires a willingness to deploy the instrumentalities of military force and diplomatic persuasion. Rather than being characterized primarily by sudden cataclysmic disjunction and the direct passage from one world system to another, the emergence of a new hegemonic power is generally the product of a long chain of partly overlapping stages in which the development of economic influence facilitates the advance of political and military power and vice versa. In this case, the process began with the supersession of the formerly predominant British regime of capital accumulation by Germany and the United States during the "Great Depression" of the late nineteenth century, and it finally concluded with the global assertion of American military power during World War II.[28] Washington's wartime engagement with the Mediterranean was a critical piece of this broader process, demonstrating an increasing willingness to deploy military, diplomatic, and economic, instruments not only to win the war but also, and in the very course of the fighting, to structure the peace. And in the Mediterranean, a region long central to Britain's global position, this could only be done at the expense of British influence.

For the British, this outcome was the unwanted and largely unanticipated consequence of U.S. involvement in the Mediterranean. When British leaders presented their "peripheral" strategy to their American counterparts at the *Arcadia* conference in Washington over Christmas 1941, their plan for the Mediterranean was to secure U.S. support for British-led operations in what would remain a British-controlled theater. Similarly, while Churchill wrapped

---

[27] B. J. C McKercher, *Transition of Power: Britain's Loss of Global Pre-eminence to the United States 1930–1945* (Cambridge: Cambridge University Press, 1995), 5.

[28] See Giovanni Arrighi, *The Long Twentieth Century: Money, Power, and the Origins of Our Time* (London: Verso, 2010), 219–220.

his correspondence with Roosevelt in great conviviality, during the critical discussions on *Gymnast* he cast himself as the sage mentor to a president inexperienced in matters of grand strategy. Roosevelt's obvious enthusiasm for the Mediterranean in the face of persistent opposition from his own chief military advisers reinforced this notion: when General Dill reported from Washington that "a good number of people in authority here ... feel that we have led them down the Mediterranean garden path," there were surely those in London who took pride in this apparent accomplishment.[29]

This sense of British leadership was reinforced at the Casablanca Conference by a series of decisions that have been widely viewed by both contemporaries and historians as marking the triumph of London's "Mediterranean Strategy." In fact, by opening the way for Allied advances into Sicily and mainland Italy, Casablanca achieved exactly what Roosevelt wanted. There is no evidence that he shared his military advisers' anguished sense of being outmaneuvered by the wily and well-prepared British, and plenty that he embraced the conference's Mediterraneanist conclusions. Moreover, as the war in the Mediterranean unfolded following Casablanca, and as the commitment of American men and material to the theater increased, so the balance of power within the Anglo-American relationship began to shift. Within months of Casablanca, Roosevelt challenged London's claim to be the "senior partner" in the military government of Sicily, and by the early stages of the invasion of mainland Italy senior British officials in the region were broadly in agreement with the Americans on the critical question of the liberalization of the Italian government. The Mediterranean was not destined to remain a British bailiwick.

The decisive turning point in Anglo-American relations came in the summer of 1944, and it was marked by two interlinked developments. First, Washington utilized its military power to facilitate the establishment of a new liberal government in Italy, paving the way for the further extension and consolidation of U.S. political and economic influence there. Second, the Americans insisted, in the face of dogged British opposition, on mounting an invasion of southern France, a decision that effectively signaled their assumption of control over the direction of Anglo-American strategy in the Mediterranean.[30] Given the importance of political developments in southern France to the consolidation the new French government, the decision for *Dragoon* also demonstrated the underlying importance of Washington's relationship with de Gaulle's CFLN, despite its often tortured and tempestuous course. The point – and it was not lost on London – was that the Mediterranean was quickly becoming America's *Mare Nostrum*.

---

[29] Quoted in Andrew Roberts, *Masters and Commanders: How Four Titans Won the War in the West, 1941–1945* (New York: Harper, 2009), 300.

[30] The irony was not lost on historian Trumbull Higgins, who noted that the British "opposed to the end the only fully successful military operation in the Mediterranean between the fall of Tunis and the final collapse of Germany." Trumbull Higgins, *Soft Underbelly: The Anglo-American Controversy over the Italian Campaign, 1939–1945* (New York: Macmillan, 1968), 220.

By the end of 1944, U.S. influence was supplanting that of Britain throughout the western Mediterranean, and even in Greece the demonstrative exercise of British military power would have been impossible without American logistical support. At the same time, and as the Culbertson Mission signposted, the United States began to dismantle the bureaucratic Anglo-American planning boards that had regulated commercial activity throughout the region in the earlier part of the war in preparation for a rapid return to bilateral free trade and the open door. In the broader context of the wartime expansion of the American economy, this shift allowed U.S. business to exercise enormous competitive advantages, even in longstanding bastions of British power like Egypt. Not surprisingly, British policy makers found it hard to reconcile themselves to the new dispensation. Some, like Harold Macmillan, clung to the illusion that as worldly-wise "Greeks" they could steer their unschooled "Roman" cousins by a combination of sophisticated guile and good advice. Others, like Generals Noel Mason-MacFarlane and Henry Wilson, accommodated themselves to the new reality by collaborating closely with U.S. officials and following their lead on several critical questions, braving Churchill's wrath in the process. Meanwhile Churchill himself, one of the primary architects of the trans-Atlantic axis, continued to rail against its deleterious consequences for British power, causing some of his closest colleagues to doubt his mental stability.

The transition of power in the Mediterranean was not completed during the war, and London retained significant influence in the region into the early postwar period, particularly in the eastern basin. Here Washington's support for Turkey in 1946, the promulgation of the Truman Doctrine and the intervention into the Greek Civil War in 1947, and U.S. support for the creation of the state of Israel in 1948, would be emblematic both of the deepening Cold War and of the further strengthening of America's predominance in the Mediterranean. Yet here, too, the substantive steps had already been taken during the war, signified by the critical support extended by Washington to British operations in Greece, by the strengthening of U.S. diplomatic and economic influence in Egypt, and by Washington's participation in, and subsequent dissolution of, the Middle East Supply Center. Moreover, as U.S. influence extended throughout the eastern basin in the late 1940s, it rested securely on the bases of power secured in the western basin during the war. When the 6th Fleet was established in 1948 to give U.S. power genuinely pan-Mediterranean scope, it was headquartered in Naples before being supported by postwar bases established in Greece and Turkey.[31]

As Washington's wartime engagement with the Mediterranean unfolded, it increasingly did so within the framework of the division of Europe into spheres of influence first registered at the Tehran Conference in late 1943. The Washington-Moscow axis that emerged fully at Tehran is rightly credited with

---

[31] See C. T. Sandars, *America's Overseas Garrisons: the Leasehold Empire* (New York: Oxford University Press, 2000), 242.

finally forcing the British to accept a firm commitment to the cross-Channel invasion; at the same time, the conference was also critical to the success of Washington's Mediterranean strategy, with the spheres of influence sketched out there allowing the consolidation of pro-American governments, and relatively stable capitalist economies, in countries where potentially revolutionary social crises had been taking shape. Without Moscow's active support, exercised through its guiding influence over all the Communist parties in the region except that in Yugoslavia, Washington would have had considerable difficulty in defusing the revolutionary dynamism of the anti-Axis liberation movements. The potentially far-reaching challenge to capitalism posed by these movements should not be under-estimated. To U.S. policy makers, beginning with William Bullitt's 1940 plea for automatic weapons for use against new Paris Communards, the possibility that wartime social dislocation might unleash popular radicalism was viewed as a decidedly clear and present danger. In the event, and with Moscow's help, the radical challenge was contained and defused throughout the region, from French North Africa, where Washington feared a "premature" push toward independence, to Italy, France, and Greece.

Washington's ability to secure a relatively seamless transition from war to postwar rested not only on the large scale deployment of Allied troops but also, and equally importantly, on the political accord with Moscow that assigned Western Europe to the Americans in exchange for Allied acceptance of a Russian-dominated Eastern Europe. In Italy this arrangement, signaled by Palmiro Togliatti's return from Moscow and the ensuing reversal of PCI policy toward Badoglio and the monarchy, directly facilitated the establishment of the liberal Bonomi government and the subsequent containment of the "wind from the North." Without this agreement with Moscow and the resulting cooperation of local Communist parties, U.S. troops would in all likelihood have ended up fighting Italian and French partisans. As it was, an armed clash between Allied troops and Tito's Partisans in Trieste was only averted when Stalin refused to back Yugoslav territorial claims in the Julian March. Any major armed confrontations between Allied troops and partisan fighters would have had substantial and unpredictable consequences both for the postwar political settlement in Europe and for the development of domestic politics within the United States. Whatever the outcome, such a clash would, to say the least, have dented the image of the "Good War" and disrupted the formation of the Cold War liberalism that rested on it.

Moscow undoubtedly sought to exercise influence over the postwar settlement in Western Europe, urging the participation of local Communist parties in coalition governments and pressing direct Russian involvement in bodies such as the Advisory Council in Italy. But Stalin neither expected nor sought a decisive say in Western European affairs. The radical aspirations of local resistance fighters and of the peasants and urban workers who supported them counted for nothing in Moscow's worldview. The ability of the Russian leadership to impose its views on Communist parties throughout Western Europe bears witness to their internal party discipline and to the tremendous political authority enjoyed by the Soviet Union at the end of the war. U.S. commanders in both Italy and France, while far from embracing the politics of local Communist parties and the partisan fighters under their direction, quickly appreciated that they acted as a stabilizing influence and as a force for the preservation and rehabilitation of capitalist social relations. The ultimate wartime test of the spheres of influence agreement came in Greece, where Moscow stood aside as British troops, with critical U.S. backing, broke the National Liberation Front's bid for inclusion in the post-occupation settlement. Wisely, Washington left the dirty work to London, leaving Churchill to complain that British suppression of the Communist-led resistance in Athens received more criticism from the United States than it did from Russia.

From the standpoint of the American ruling class, the blunting of the radical political dynamic of anti-fascist liberation movements in southern Europe must surely be rated as one of the great-unsung accomplishments of Washington's Mediterranean strategy. It is difficult to see London, with its impulsive reliance on the most conservative social forces and its bitter resistance to political liberalization, being able to craft political settlements capable of accommodating and absorbing this popular political dynamism. It is also worth noting that the Allies faced no equivalent partisan challenge in Germany, where years of Nazi repression had taken its toll of the German Communist Party, and long months of Allied bombing had "dehoused" – in Churchill's euphemistic neologism – and demoralized the German working class. As a consequence, Allied troops advancing into Germany encountered a profoundly dislocated economy, desperate food shortages, and millions of "displaced persons," but no anti-Fascist fighters intent on "auto-liberation." In contrast, without the collaboration of Moscow and without the presence of large numbers of Allied troops in the Mediterranean – including the reequipped French army returned to the metropole via *Dragoon* – the war could have ended quite differently in countries where Communist organizations had not been smashed during the occupation and where workers and peasants had not been demoralized by sustained Allied bombing.

The Yugoslav Revolution offers a glimpse of the alternative possibilities latent throughout southern Europe. For much of the war, Tito's Partisans operated in relative isolation from Moscow, allowing them to enjoy greater freedom from Stalin's control than was possible in either France or Italy. As a result, the radical social dynamic of the Yugoslav resistance struggle unfolded unchecked by either Moscow or the Allies: the 50–50 division of Yugoslavia agreed by Churchill and Stalin in October 1944 gave mathematical expression to the fact that the troublesome Partisans were under no one's control. Under different circumstances, Stalin might have countenanced either a "Polish" or a "Greek" solution in Yugoslavia, incorporating the country into Russia's defensive glacis or else standing aside while the Allies crushed the Partisans. As it was, the independent-minded Yugoslavs pursued their own course, becoming a constant source of irritation to Moscow and a potentially inspiring model of a revolutionary "third way" that avoided subservience to either superpower.

In many ways, the Americans understood the unfolding situation in wartime Yugoslavia better than the British, who hoped to woo Tito with a combination of arms shipments and political blandishments. But despite their skepticism of British policy, U.S. policy makers lacked a viable lever with which to exercise political influence in Yugoslavia, a failing highlighted by Washington's protracted dalliance with Mihailović and then by its quixotic attempt to promote Ivan Šubašić as a counterweight to Tito in a unified Yugoslav government. This effort demonstrated Washington's new willingness to utilize covert operations to achieve political influence when more conventional levers were unavailable. But the "Shepherd Project" rested on unverifiable premises and exaggerated claims, promised much more than it could deliver, and gave early indication of the weaknesses of all such covert projects. Above all, the revolutionary turmoil in Yugoslavia offers striking back-handed confirmation that elsewhere in the Mediterranean the division agreed with Moscow *did* hold, sparing Washington the necessity of bloody confrontation with radical forces emerging from the anti-fascist resistance, and laying the basis for a postwar Mediterranean that was capitalist in economic structure and pro-American in political orientation.

Washington's ability to exercise political leverage in the wartime Mediterranean was reinforced by its deployment of an extraordinarily flexible range of notions concerning the construction and recognition of political legitimacy. Throughout Europe, the prevailing norms of national sovereignty and autonomy were repeatedly breached during World War II, as first the Axis powers and then United States and the Soviet Union sought to shape both the social foundations and political structures of states within their respective spheres of influence.[32] In this process, U.S. policy makers were unconstrained by abstractions, strenuously upholding the principle of nonintervention in the internal affairs of other states in some cases while openly violating them in others, and effectively "decoupling" their practice from the norms of Westphalian sovereignty that had been held to govern relations between nation states.[33] In the course of its war in the Mediterranean, the United States pursued an entirely pragmatic and – from the standpoint of idealist principle – highly erratic course on questions of governmental legitimacy and national sovereignty. So, for example, it recognized the legitimacy of the Franco and Pétain governments (one by dint of military victory over the elected government, the other as the putative continuator of the fallen Third Republic); upheld French colonial rule in North Africa (despite the promises of self-determination proffered in the Atlantic Charter); recognized first King Victor Emmanuel and Marshal

---

[32] See Stephen D. Krasner, *Sovereignty: Organized Hypocrisy* (Princeton, NJ: Princeton University Press, 1999), 184.

[33] Ibid., 200.

Badoglio, and then the "Six" anti-Fascist parties, as the basis of sovereign government in Italy (despite the lack of electoral confirmation); long refused to recognize the CFLN as the basis of a sovereign government in France (citing the lack of electoral confirmation); and backed the exiled monarchies of Peter II and George II (avoiding electoral confirmation and ignoring substantial evidence that both regimes lacked popular support).

In one sense there was nothing new here: fluid and conditional notions of sovereignty had long underpinned repeated U.S. interventions in the Americas, as justified by the Roosevelt Corollary to the Monroe Doctrine. But what was new was the projection, beginning in the Mediterranean, of this pragmatic modus operandi into Europe, the center of the old world order. Established during the war, this approach was manifest in the postwar period in ongoing interventions in the internal affairs of ostensibly sovereign states, ranging from the decisive support given to the Christian Democrats in the critical 1948 Italian general election, to military intervention in the Greek Civil War. In every case, from occupations that did not disturb existing structures of colonial rule (North Africa), to regimes of military governance (Italy), to armed backing for regrouped and rearmed sections of the old ruling classes (France), Washington utilized its extraordinary military power to establish – with the willing collaboration of local elites whose own legitimacy had often been radically undermined by fascism, collaboration, and war – new relations of dominance and subordination.[34]

U.S. liberalism accommodated itself to this process with surprising ease. In the early days of America's wartime engagement with the Mediterranean, liberals were outraged by the administration's pragmatic dealings with the rightist governments of Franco, Pétain, Darlan, and Badoglio. U.S. practice everywhere seemed to contradict the principles proclaimed in the Atlantic Charter, and liberals feared that it would discredit the ideological foundations of a war ostensibly being fought for freedom and justice, thereby undermining the possibility of constructing a democratic new world order under U.S. leadership. Yet as the "liberal turn" unfolded in the summer of 1944 – with U.S. arms facilitating the establishment of the Bonomi government in Rome and the provisional government in Paris, and with Washington adopting a more critical stance toward Franco – American liberals fell into line. By the end of the war, and despite the fact that the underlying pragmatism at the heart of U.S. policy remained unchanged, American liberalism – and American public opinion in general – was broadly supportive of the emerging U.S.-sponsored order in Mediterranean and throughout Western Europe.

The paternalist discourse that simultaneously shaped and justified U.S. intervention in the Caribbean and the Philippines was now projected into the Mediterranean, furnishing the essential master narrative for "rehabilitation" in

[34] See Paul A. Kramer, "Power and Connection: Imperial Histories of the United States in the World," *American Historical Review* 116, no. 5 (December 2011), especially 1356–1357.

Italy and beyond.[35] A clear ideological voice for Washington's Mediterranean grand strategy was provided by John Hersey, whose popular novel, stage play, and movie *Bell for Adano* used the experience of Allied military government in Sicily to urge Americans to embrace the burdens of leadership in Europe. Major Joppolo's "wonderful zeal for spreading democracy" would, Hersey concluded, provide the basis of America's "future in the world," normalizing military occupation and military government as vehicles for remaking the old order and helping to establish a new world-system with the United States at its head.[36]

If, as I have argued here, Washington not only had a multilayered grand strategic approach to the Mediterranean during World War II, but pursued it with determination to a highly successful conclusion, one obvious question remains: How could this achievement have been so thoroughly erased from both popular memory and scholarly historiography? Or, to put it another way, how is it that the wartime Mediterranean is almost universally viewed as a preeminently British theater into which the United States lurched more or less unwillingly, played an important but secondary military role, and then got out as quickly as possible? Hopefully, this study has begun to reverse this erasure. But the question remains: Why did such a lacunae exist in the first place? Writing on U.S. policy for the influential Institute of International Studies at Yale in 1948, William Reitzel argued for the development of a *regional* approach to the countries of the Mediterranean in the face of alleged Russian expansionism. Reitzel argued that Americans, encouraged by official policy statements, tended to view the deployment of the U.S. military force in the Mediterranean solely in terms of "completing the defeat of Germany." In reality, he suggested, "American power" had not gone away at the end of the war, remaining instead as a "present reality" shaping military, political and economic conditions throughout the region.[37] There was, Reitzel concluded, "no general appreciation in the United States of the extent to which the actual basis of power in the Mediterranean had shifted during the war from British to American shoulders."[38]

The popular misperceptions of Washington's continuing presence in the Mediterranean identified by Reitzel conformed to the widespread – and officially encouraged – notion that America's task in the war had been simply to get the job done and go home, eschewing any long-term engagement, military

[35] See, for example, Mary Renda, *Taking Haiti: Military Occupation and the Culture of U.S. Imperialism, 1915–1940* (Chapel Hill: University of North Carolina Press, 2001); Michael Adas, *Dominance by Design: Technological Imperatives and America's Civilizing Mission* (Cambridge, MA: Belknap, 2006); Andrew Buchanan, "'Good Morning Pupil!' American Representations of Italianness and the Occupation of Italy, 1943–1945," *Journal of Contemporary History* 43, no. 2 (2008).
[36] *New York Times*, February 6, 1944; Hersey, *Bell for Adano*, 2.
[37] See Reitzel, *The Mediterranean*, 50.
[38] Ibid.

occupation, or involvement in what would today be called "nation-building." To a striking degree, this popular conception, rooted in the decoupling of U.S. military action from broader political and economic concerns, paralleled the notions advanced by George Marshall and the Joint Chiefs of Staff in the early months of the war. The division between the Joint Chiefs and the president that reached its height in the fight over *Gymnast* pitted a strategy based on abstract military principles against a grand strategic approach that privileged strengthening America's *postwar* position over simply following the line that military leaders believed to offer the shortest route to victory. In a democracy, however, where the capacity for the all-out mobilization of human and material resources necessary to wage modern total war rests to a significant degree on popular consent, it is much harder to suggest that war is being waged to secure postwar standing and economic advantage than it is to argue that everything is being done to secure victory by the quickest and most painless route possible. It is possible, as Henry Luce demonstrated his advocacy for U.S. global leadership in the "American Century," to make the former case in a popular and persuasive manner. But, with an eye to maintaining morale in difficult and unpredictable circumstances, the Roosevelt administration consistently declined to do so.

In the absence of a forceful countervailing argument from Washington, the convergence between apparent military common sense and the popular desire to get the war over as quickly as possible inevitably shaped public understanding of strategic decision making. Buttressed by a substantial media campaign, the Normandy landings and the subsequent drive into Germany quickly took pride of place over the apparently endless and politically confusing efforts in the Mediterranean. As Douglas Porch points out, it was not difficult for opinion-formers to draw a clear distinction between the "pure" and fast-moving campaigns in northern Europe on the one hand, and the often-unsavory political complexities which burdened operations in the Mediterranean on the other.[39] This popular perception was reinforced by the political arrangements made with such self-evidently undemocratic figures as Franco, Pétain, Darlan, Badoglio, and the kings of Yugoslavia and Greece. Whatever their military justifications, the series of appeasements, deals, and compromises that marked the opening phases of America's war in the Mediterranean could not easily be reconciled with the bright shining banner of a global struggle between freedom and slavery under which the war was being fought. The "liberal turn" began to resolve this discontinuity between practice and ideological justification, but it was soon subsumed into the politically clear and militarily decisive campaign unfolding in northern Europe. By the end of 1944, the advancing erasure of America's war in the

---

[39] Douglas Porch, *The Path to Victory: The Mediterranean Theater in World War II.* (New York: Farrar, Straus and Giroux, 2004), 681.

Mediterranean was already reflected in the bitterly sarcastic self-description of Allied soldiers in Italy as "D-Day Dodgers."[40]

If these factors help account for the eclipse of the Mediterranean in popular memory, why have so few academic historians sought to set the record straight? First, it is worth noting that academics are by no means immune to the forces that shape popular perception. For much of the Cold War it was extremely difficult to step outside of the self-justifying discourse of U.S. triumphalism that pictured other countries – and particularly Britain – as pursuing tainted "political" motives, while the United States thought only of winning quickly and then going home. According to this narrative, Washington had had no interest in any long-term involvement in European affairs, and the postwar engagement that did develop was therefore *not* a continuation of wartime policy, but rather a radical break from it motivated by the necessity of responding to the new challenges of the Cold War. In this context, the extensive discussion on Anglo-American strategy in the Mediterranean that unfolded after 1945 – described by Trumbull Higgins as the "historians war" – assumed a narrowly military character and, insofar as politics intruded on the debate at all, they were the politics of the contemporary Cold War and not of the wartime Mediterranean.

The postwar debate over Allied strategy in Europe, structured around a binary opposition between *Overlord* and the Mediterranean, thus separated military strategy from its political and economic underpinnings. No substantial alternative narrative was advanced to challenge this bifurcation; even as they campaigned to build public support for a sustained global commitment to the "containment" of Russian "totalitarianism," it suited U.S. policy makers and opinion-formers to present the "Good War" as a noble and politically disinterested crusade. Since the 1960s, many historians have chipped away at pieces of this over-arching U.S. war-myth, but military affairs have remained largely disconnected from the broader narrative of the advance of U.S. political and economic power, thereby blurring an understanding of the actual grand strategic integration of these elements.

I hope that this study has gone some way toward reestablishing the essential military, political, and economic unity of U.S. grand strategy in a way that permits a reevaluation of the place of the Mediterranean in America's war. Given the free-wheeling and often chaotic character of Washington's grand-strategic decision making – itself a product of the rising arc of America's march to hegemony – this has not been a straightforward task. Washington would only, and in fact could only, rise to clear and integrated grand-strategic planning *after* assuming

---

[40] Often attributed to British soldiers, the phrase "D-Day dodgers" and the song of the same name were equally popular in the ranks of the American Fifth Army. This point was underscored for me by the inclusion of the song in the personal papers of Captain James MacDevitt, who served in the 85th Division from the Garigliano to the Apennines. MacDevitt papers, authors' collection.

the undisputed leadership of the "free world," leaving its wartime grand-strategic impulses to be judged by results, not by plans. The deed, it turns out, preceded the word: but as this study demonstrates, the full spectrum of U.S. grand-strategic engagement in the Mediterranean was decisive, not only for winning the war, but also for structuring the peace

Bibliography

Primary Materials

Unpublished Archival Sources

United States

Franklin D. Roosevelt Library, Hyde Park, NY
    Franklin D. Roosevelt Day-by-Day, http://www.fdrlibrary.marist.edu/daybyday/
    Map Room File
    Official File
    President's Secretary's File (PSF)
National Archive and Record Administration, College Park, MD
    RG 59, Records of the State Department
    RG 84, State Department Records of Foreign Posts
    RG 169, Records of the Foreign Economic Administration
    RG 218, Records of the Joint Chiefs of Staff
    RG 226, Records of the OSS
    RG 331, Records of Allied Operational and Occupational Headquarters
    RG 389, Records of the Provost Marshal General, Military Government
Records of the Joint Chiefs of Staff, European Theater, microfilm collection, accessed at Alexander Library, Rutgers University, New Brunswick, NJ
Records of State Department's Advisory Committee on Postwar Foreign Policy (Notter Files, microfiche), accessed at Alexander Library, Rutgers University, New Brunswick, NJ

United Kingdom

National Archives, Kew
    Foreign Office Political Papers, FO 371
    War Office, WO 214
Papers of the Prime Minister's Office
    PREM 3, Operational Papers (Microfilm) accessed at Alexander Library, Rutgers University, New Brunswick, NJ.

Unpublished Private Papers

Alexander, Harold, Field Marshal. WO 214, National Archives, Kew
Berle, Adolf A. Sterling Memorial Library, Yale University, CT
Bullitt, William. Sterling Memorial Library, Yale University, CT
Eddy, William A. Seely G. Mudd Manuscript Library, Princeton, NJ
Goodfellow, Millard Preston. Hoover Institution, Stanford University, CA
Greenfield, Major I. G. Imperial War Museum, London
Hayes, Carlton. Columbia University Library, NY
Harriman, Averell. Library of Congress, Washington, DC
Hopkins, Harry. Franklin D. Roosevelt Library, Hyde Park, NY
Hull, Cordell. Library of Congress, Washington, DC
MacDevitt, James C. Author's collection
MacVeagh, Lincoln. Seely G. Mudd Manuscript Library, Princeton, NJ
Mason-Macfarlane, General Sir Noel. Imperial War Museum, London
McCormick, Anne O'Hare. New York Public Library, New York, NY
Morgenthau, Henry. Franklin D. Roosevelt Library, Hyde Park, NY
Murphy, Robert. Hoover Institution, Stanford University, CA
Stimson, Henry L. Sterling Memorial Library, Yale University, CT
Taylor, Myron. Franklin D. Roosevelt Library, Hyde Park, NY
Welles, Sumner. Franklin D. Roosevelt Library, Hyde Park, NY

Published Official Documents and Correspondence

Daniels, Jonathan (intro.). *The Complete Press Conferences of Franklin D. Roosevelt.*
    New York: DaCapo Press, 1972.
Department of State Bulletin. Washington, DC: Department of State, 1940–1945.
Foreign Relations of the United States. Relevant vols. 1940–1945. Washington, DC:
    U.S. Government Printing Office, 1955–1970.
Kimball, Warren F. (ed.) *Churchill and Roosevelt: The Complete Correspondence.*
    Princeton, NJ: Princeton University Press, 1984.
Ross, Stephen T (ed.). *U. S. War Plans: 1938–1945.* Boulder, CO: Lynne Rienner
    Publishers, 2002.
U. S. Department of Commerce. *Statistical Abstract of the United States.* Relevant vol-
    umes, 1939, 1946, 1952. Washington, DC: U.S. Department of Commerce, 1940,
    1947, 1953.

Published Diaries, Memoirs and Autobiographies

Alexander, Field Marshal Earl. *The Alexander Memoirs.* New York: McGraw-Hill,
    1962.
Badoglio, Pietro. *Italy in the Second World War.* London: Oxford University Press,
    1948.
Beaulac, Willard L. *Franco: Silent Ally in World War II.* Carbondale and Edwardsville:
    Southern Illinois University Press, 1986.
Blum, John Morton (ed.). *The Prince of Vision: The Diary of Henry A. Wallace, 1942–
    1946.* Boston: Houghton Mifflin, 1973.

Blumenson, Martin (ed.). *The Patton Papers, 1940–1945.* Boston: Houghton Mifflin, 1974.

Bullitt, Orville H. (ed.). *For the President Personal and Secret: Correspondence between Franklin D. Roosevelt and William C. Bullitt.* Boston: Houghton Mifflin, 1972.

Bundy, McGeorge, and Henry L. Stimson. *On Active Service in Peace and War.* New York: Harper & Bros, 1947.

Butcher, Harry C. *My Three Years with Eisenhower: The Personal Diary of Captain Harry C. Butcher, USNR, Naval Aide to General Eisenhower, 1942 to 1945.* New York: Simon and Schuster, 1946.

Cantril, Hadley. "Evaluating the Probable Reactions to the Landing in North Africa in 1942: A Case Study," *The Public Opinion Quarterly* 29, no. 3 (1965).

Chandler, Alfred D. (ed.). *The Papers of Dwight David Eisenhower: The War Years.* Baltimore: Johns Hopkins, 1970.

Childs, J. Rives. *Foreign Service Farewell: My Years in the Near East.* Charlottesville: The University Press of Virginia, 1969.

Churchill, Winston S. *The Second World War.* 6 vols. Boston: Houghton Mifflin, 1948–1954.

Clark, Mark W. *Calculated Risk.* New York: Harper and Brothers, 1950.

Dalton, Hugh. *The Second World War Diary of Hugh Dalton, 1940–45.* London: Jonathan Cape, 1986.

Danchev, Alex and Daniel Todman (eds.). *Field Marshal Lord Alanbrooke, War Diaries, 1939–1945.* London: Phoenix Press, 2002.

De Gaulle, Charles. *The War Memoirs of Charles de Gaulle: Unity, 1942–1944.* Trans. Richard Howard. New York: Simon and Schuster, 1959.

Dilks, David. *The Diaries of Sir Alexander Cadogan, 1938–1945.* New York: G. P. Putnam's Sons, 1971.

Djilas, Milovan. *Conversations with Stalin.* New York: Harcourt, Brace & World, 1962.

Eisenhower, Dwight D. *Crusade in Europe.* New York: Doubleday, 1948.

Feis, Herbert . *The Spanish Story: Franco and the Nations at War.* New York: W. W. Norton, 1948.

Ferrell, Robert H. (ed.). *The Eisenhower Diaries.* New York: W. W. Norton, 1981.

Hayes, Carlton J. H. *Wartime Mission to Spain, 1942 – 1945.* New York: Macmillan, 1945.

Hoare, Sir Samuel. *Complacent Dictator.* New York: Alfred A. Knopf, 1947.

Hull, Cordell. *The Memoirs of Cordell Hull.* New York: Macmillan, 1948.

Ickes, Harold. *The Secret Diary of Harold Ickes.* New York: Simon and Schuster, 1954.

de Lattre de Tassigny, Jean. *History of the French First Army.* London: George Allen and Unwin, 1952.

Leahy, Admiral William D. *I Was There: The Personal Story of the Chief of Staff to Presidents Roosevelt and Truman Based on His Notes and Diaries Made at the Time.* New York: McGraw Hill, 1950.

Lindsay, Franklin. *Beacons in the Night: With the OSS and Tito's Partisans in Wartime Yugoslavia.* Stanford, CA: Stanford University Press, 1993.

Luce, Henry R. "The American Century." 1941. Reprint, Diplomatic History 23, no. 2 (1999).

Maclean, Fitzroy. *Eastern Approaches*. 1949. Reprint, London: Penguin, 1991.

Macmillan, Harold. *War Diaries: Politics and War in the Mediterranean, January 1943– May 1945*. New York: St. Martin's Press, 1984.

Murphy, Robert. *Diplomat among Warriors*. Garden City, NY: Doubleday & Co, 1964.

Pendar, Kenneth. *Adventures in Diplomacy: Our French Dilemma*. 1945. Reprint, New York: Da Capo Press, 1976.

Peter II, King of Yugoslavia. *A King's Heritage: Memoirs of King Peter II of Yugoslavia*. London: Cassell and Company, 1955.

Plenn, Abel. *Wind in the Olive Trees*. New York: Bonni and Gaer, 1946.

Pogue, Forrest. *George C. Marshall, Interviews and Reminiscences*. Lexington, VA: George C. Marshall Research Foundation, 1991.

Roosevelt, Elliott. *As He Saw It*. New York: Duell, Sloan and Pearce, 1946.

Sherwood, Robert E. *Roosevelt and Hopkins, an Intimate History*. New York: Harper & Bros, 1948.

Stimson, Henry R. *On Active Service in Peace and War*. New York: Harper & Bros., 1948.

Sulzberger, C. L. *A Long Row of Candles: Memoirs and Diaries, 1934–1954*. New York: Macmillan, 1969.

Tompkins, Peter. *Italy Betrayed*. New York: Simon and Schuster, 1966.

Truscott, Lt. General L. K. *Command Missions*. New York: E. P. Dutton, 1954.

Wedemeyer, Albert C. *Wedemeyer Reports!* New York: Henry Holt, 1958.

Weygand, Maxime. *Recalled to Service: The Memoirs of General Maxime Weygand*. Trans. E. W. Dickes. Garden City, NY: Doubleday and Company, 1952.

White, Theodore H. (ed.). *The Stilwell Papers*. New York: William Sloane, 1948.

Wilson, Field Marshal Sir Henry Maitland. *Eight Years Overseas, 1939–1947*. London: Hutchinson & Co., 1950.

Newspapers and Magazines

Atlantic Monthly
Chicago Tribune
Christian Science Monitor
Fourth International
Harper's Magazine
Life Magazine
The Militant
The Nation
The New Republic
New York Times
PM
Saturday Evening Post
Time Magazine
Washington Post

Films

At the Front in North Africa, (dir. Darryl Zanuck and John Ford, Twentieth Century Fox, 1943).

Casablanca, (dir. Michael Curtiz, Warner Bros., 1942).
Sahara, (dir. Zoltan Korda, Columbia, 1943).
A Bell for Adano, (dir. Henry King, Twentieth Century Fox, 1945).

Novels

Burns, John Horne. *The Gallery*. 1947. Reprint, New York: New York Review Books, 2004.
Hersey, John. *Bell For Adano*. New York: Alfred A. Knopf, 1944.
Lewis, Norman. *Naples '44*. 1987. Reprint, New York: Carroll & Graf, 2004.

Secondary Works

Books and Monographs

Abramson, Rudy. *Spanning the Century: The Life of W. Averell Harriman, 1891–1986*. New York: William Morrow, 1992.
Adas, Michael. *Dominance By Design: Technological Imperatives and America's Civilizing Mission*. Cambridge, MA: Belknap, 2006.
Agarossi, Elena. *A Nation Collapses: The Italian Surrender of September 1943*. Trans. Harvey Fergusson II. Cambridge: Cambridge University Press, 2006.
Arrighi, Giovanni. *The Long Twentieth Century: Money, Power, and the Origins of Our Time*. London: Verso, 2010.
Atkinson, Rick. *An Army at Dawn: The War in North Africa, 1942–1943*. New York: Henry Holt, 2002.
———. *The Day of Battle: The War in Sicily and Italy, 1943–1944*. New York: Henry Holt, 2007.
———. *The Guns at Last Light: The War in Western Europe, 1944–1945*. New York: Henry Holt, 2013.
Baldwin, Hanson Weightman. *Great Mistakes of the War*. New York: Harper, 1950.
Ball, Simon. *Bitter Sea: The Brutal World War II Fight for the Mediterranean*. New York, Harper, 2009.
Baram, Phillip J. *The Department of State in the Middle East 1919–1945*. Philadelphia: University of Pennsylvania Press, 1978.
Behan, Tom. *The Long Awaited Moment: The Working Class and the Italian Communist Party in Milan, 1943–1948*. New York: Peter Lang, 1997.
Bidwell, Shelford, and Dominick Graham. *Tug of War; The Battle for Italy, 1943–45*. London: Hodder and Stoughton, 1986.
Birkhimer, William E. *Military Government and Marshal Law*. Kansas City, MO: Franklin Hudson Publishing Company, 1914.
Black, Conrad. *Franklin Delano Roosevelt: Champion of Freedom*. London: Public Affairs, 2005.
Black, Jeremy. *The Age of Total War, 1860–1945*. Lanham, MD: Rowman and Littlefield, 2010.
Blair, Leon Borden. *Western Window in the Arab World*. Austin: University of Texas Press, 1970.
Blaker, James R. *United States Overseas Basing: An Anatomy of a Dilemma*. New York: Praeger, 1990.
Brewer, Susan. *Why America Fights*. New York: Oxford University Press, 2010.

Brinkley, Alan. *The Publisher: Henry Luce and his American Century*. New York: Alfred
    A. Knopf, 2010
Brogi, Allesandro. *Confronting America: The Cold War between the United States and
    Communists in France and Spain*. Chapel Hill: University of North Carolina Press,
    2011.
Brownell, Will, and Richard N. Billings. *So Close To Greatness: A Biography of William
    C. Bullitt*. New York: Macmillan, 1987.
Bryant, Sir Arthur. *Triumph in the West; a History of the War Years Based on the Diaries
    of Field-Marshal Lord Alanbrooke, Chief of the Imperial General Staff*. New York:
    Doubleday, 1959.
Burdick, Charles B. *Germany's Military Strategy and Spain in World War II*. Syracuse,
    NY: Syracuse University Press. 1968.
Butler, Ewan. *Mason-Mac: The Life of Lieutenant General Sir Noel Mason-Macfarlane*.
    London: Macmillan, 1972.
Bykovsky, Joseph, and Harold Larson. *The Transportation Corps: Operations Overseas*.
    Washington, DC: U.S. Government Printing Office, 1957.
Casey, Steven. *Cautious Crusade: Franklin D. Roosevelt, American Public Opinion, and
    the War against Nazi Germany*. Oxford: Oxford University Press, 2001.
Chubarian, A.O., Warren F. Kimball, and David Reynolds, (eds.). *Allies At War: The
    Soviet, British, and American Experience, 1939–1945*. New York: St. Martin's
    Press, 1994.
Clarke, Jeffrey J. *Riviera to the Rhine: The European Theater of Operations*. Washington,
    DC: Center for Military History, United States Army, 1993.
Clausewitz, Carl von. *On War*. 1832. Reprint, Princeton, NJ: Princeton University
    Press, 1976.
Coakley, Robert W, and Richard Leighton. *Global Logistics and Strategy*. 2 vols.
    Washington, DC: U.S. War Department, 1955–68.
Cogan, Norman. *Italy and the Allies*. Cambridge, MA: Harvard University Press,
    1956.
Coles, H. L. and A. K. Weinberg. *Civil Affairs: Soldiers Become Governors*. Washington,
    DC: U.S. War Department, 1964.
Cortada, James W. *United States-Spanish Relations, Wolfram, and World War II*.
    Barcelona: Manuel Pareja, 1971.
Dallek, Robert . *Franklin D. Roosevelt and American Foreign Policy, 1932–1945*. New
    York: Oxford University Press, 1979.
D'Este, Carlo. *Fatal Decision: Anzio and the Battle for Rome*. New York: Harper
    Collins, 1986.
————. *Eisenhower: A Soldier's Life*. New York: Owl Books, 2002.
de Grazia, Victoria. *Irresistible Empire: America's Advance through 20th-Century
    Europe*. Cambridge, MA: Belknap, 2005.
de Kay, James Tertius. *Roosevelt's Navy: The Education of a Warrior President, 1882–
    1920*. New York: Pegasus Books, 2012.
Diggins, John P. *Mussolini and Fascism: The View from America*. Princeton, NJ:
    Princeton University Press, 1972.
Dinan, Desmond. *The Politics of Persuasion: British Policy and French African Neutrality,
    1940–42*. Lanham, MD: University Press of America, 1988.

Dougherty, James J. *The Politics of Wartime Aid: American Economic Assistance to France and French Northwest Africa, 1940–1946.* Westport, CT: Greenwood Press, 1978.

Edwards, Brian T. *Morocco Bound: Disorienting America's Maghreb, from Casablanca to the Marrakech Express.* Durham, NC: Duke University Press, 2005.

Ellwood, David W. *Italy 1943–1945.* New York: Holmes & Meier, 1985.

Eubank, Keith. *Summit at Teheran.* New York: William Morrow & Co, 1985.

Feis, Herbert. *Churchill, Roosevelt, Stalin: The War They Waged and the Peace They Sought.* Princeton, NJ: Princeton University Press, 1967.

Filippelli. Ronald L. *American Labor and Postwar Italy, 1943–1953.* Stanford: Stanford University Press, 1989.

Footitt, Hilary. *War and Liberation in France: Living with the Liberators.* New York: Palgrave Macmillan, 2004.

Footitt, Hilary, and John Simmonds. *France 1943–1945.* New York: Holmes & Meier, 1988.

Ford Jr., Kirk. *OSS and the Yugoslav Resistance, 1943–1945.* College Station: Texas A&M University Press,1992.

Forgacs, David (ed.). *The Antonio Gramsci Reader.* New York: NYU Press, 2000.

Funk, Arthur Layton. *The Politics of Torch: The Allied Landings and the Algiers Putsch 1942.* Lawrence: University Press of Kansas, 1974.

———. *Hidden Ally: The French Resistance, Special Operations, and the Landings in Southern France, 1944.* Westport, CT: Greenwood Press, 1974.

Gardner, Lloyd. *Economic Aspects of New Deal Diplomacy.* Madison: University of Wisconsin Press, 1964.

———. *Spheres of Influence: the Great Powers and the Partition of Europe, from Munich to Yalta.* Chicago: Ivan R. Dee, 1993.

Gat, Moshe. *Britain and Italy, 1943–1949: The Decline of British Influence.* Brighton: Sussex Academic Press, 1996.

Gillem, Mark L. *America Town: Building Outposts of Empire.* Minneapolis: University of Minnesota Press, 2007

Ginsborg, Paul. *A History of Contemporary Italy.* New York: Palgrave, 2003.

Glantz, David M. and Jonathan M. House. *When Titans Clashed: How the Red Army Stopped Hitler.* Lawrence: University of Kansas Press, 1995.

Glantz, Mary E. *FDR and the Soviet Union; The President's Battles over Foreign Policy.* Lawrence: University of Kansas Press, 2005.

Gundle, Stephen. *Between Hollywood and Moscow: The Italian Communists and the Challenge of Mass Culture, 1943–1991.* Durham, NC: Duke University Press, 2000.

Harris, C. R. S. *Allied Military Administration of Italy, 1943–1945.* London: HMSO, 1957.

Higgins, Trumbull. *Soft Underbelly: The Anglo-American Controversy over the Italian Campaign, 1943–1945.* New York: Macmillan, 1968.

Hitchcock, William I. *The Bitter Road to Freedom: A New History of the Liberation of Europe.* New York, Free Press, 2008.

Hogan, Michael J. *A Cross of Iron: Harry S. Truman and the Origins of the National Security State, 1945–1954.* Cambridge: Cambridge University Press, 1998.

Holzman, Michael. *James Jesus Angelton, the CIA, and the Craft of Counterintelligence.* Amherst: University of Massachusetts Press, 2008.

Horne, Alistair. *To Lose a Battle: France 1940.* London: Penguin, 1969.

———. *A Savage War of Peace: Algeria 1954–1962.* New York: NYRB, (1977) 2006.

Howard, Michael. *The Mediterranean Strategy in the Second World War.* New York: Frederick A. Praeger, 1968.

Hurstfield, Julian G. *America and the French Nation, 1939–1945.* Chapel Hill: University of North Carolina Press, 1986.

Jackson, Julian. *France: The Dark Years, 1940–1944.* Oxford: Oxford University Press, 2001.

Johnson, Chalmers A. *Peasant Nationalism and Communist Power: The Emergence of Revolutionary China, 1937–1945.* Stanford, CA: Stanford University Press, 1962.

Jones, Matthew. *Britain, the United States, and the Mediterranean War 1942–1944.* New York: St. Martin's Press, 1996.

Katz, Robert. *The Battle for Rome.* New York: Simon and Schuster, 2003.

Keegan, John. *Six Armies in Normandy: From D-Day to the Liberation of Paris, June 6–August 25, 1944.* New York: The Viking Press, 1982.

Kennedy, Paul M., ed., *Grand Strategies in War and Peace.* New Haven, CT: Yale University Press, 1991.

Kimball, Warren F. *The Juggler: Franklin Roosevelt as Wartime Statesman.* Princeton, NJ: Princeton University Press, 1991.

———. *Forged in War: Roosevelt, Churchill, and the Second World War.* New York: William Morrow, 1997.

Kleinfeld, Gerald R. and Lewis A. Tambs. *Hitler's Spanish Legion: The Blue Division in Russia.* Carbondale: University of Southern Illinois Press, 1979.

Kogan, Norman. *Italy and the Allies.* Cambridge, MA: Harvard University Press, 1956.

Kolko, Gabriel. *The Politics of War: The World War and United States Foreign Policy, 1943–1945.* New York: Pantheon Books, 1990.

Krasner, Stephen D. *Sovereignty: Organized Hypocrisy.* Princeton, NJ: Princeton University Press, 1999.

Lacoutre, Jean. *De Gaulle: The Rebel, 1890–1944.* Trans. Patrick O'Brian. New York: W.W. Norton, 1993.

Lambert, Frank. *The Barbary Wars: American Independence in the Atlantic World.* New York: Hill and Wang, 2007.

Langer, William L. *Our Vichy Gamble.* New York: Alfred Knopf, 1947.

Leffler, Melvyn P. *A Preponderance of Power: National Security, the Truman Administration, and the Cold War.* Stanford, CA: Stanford University Press, 1992.

Leitz, Christian. *Sympathy for the Devil: Neutral Europe and Nazi Germany in World War II.* New York: NYU Press, 2001.

Linn, Brian McAllister. *The Echo of Battle: The Army's Way of War.* Cambridge, MA: Harvard University Press, 2007.

Lippmann, Thomas W. *Arabian Knight: Colonel Bill Eddy USMC and the Rise of American Power in the Middle East.* Vista, CA: Selwa Press, 2008.

Little, Douglas. *Malevolent Neutrality; The United States, Great Britain, and the Origins of the Spanish Civil War.* Ithaca, NY: Cornell University Press, 1985.

———. *American Orientalism: The United States and the Middle East, Since 1945.* Chapel Hill: University of North Carolina Press, 2004.

Maguire, G. E. *Anglo-American Policy towards the Free French*. New York: Palgrave Macmillan, 1995.

Mandel, Ernest. *The Meaning of the Second World War*. London: Verso, 1986.

Matloff, Maurice. *Strategic Planning for Coalition Warfare, 1943–1944*. Washington, DC: U.S. Government Printing Office, 1959.

Matloff, Maurice, and Edwin M. Snell. *Strategic Planning for Coalition Warfare, 1941–1942*. Washington: U.S. Government Printing Office, 1953.

Mayers, David. *FDR's Ambassadors and the Diplomacy of Crisis: From the Rise of Hitler to the End of World War II*. Cambridge: Cambridge University Press, 2013.

McKercher, B. J. C. *Transition of Power: Britain's Loss of Global Pre-eminence to the United States 1930–1945*. Cambridge: Cambridge University Press, 1999.

Middlebrook, Martin, and Chris Evertitt. *The Bomber Command War Diaries*. Leicester: Midland Publishing, 1990.

Miller, James Edward. *The United States and Italy, 1940 – 1950*. Chapel Hill: University of North Carolina Press, 1986.

Murray, Williamson, and Allan R. Millett. *A War to Be Won: Fighting the Second World War*. Cambridge, MA: Belknap Press, 2001.

Murray, Williamson, Richard Hart Sinnreich, and James Lacey (eds.). *The Shaping of Grand Strategy: Policy, Diplomacy, and War*. Cambridge: Cambridge University Press, 2011.

Offner, Arnold A. *Another Such Victory: President Truman and the Cold War, 1945–1947*. Stanford, CA: Stanford University Press, 2002.

O'Sullivan, Christopher. *Sumner Welles, Postwar Planning, and the Quest for a New World Order, 1937–1943*. New York: Columbia University Press, 2007.

Paret, Peter, ed. *Makers of Modern Strategy: From Machiavelli to the Nuclear Age*. Princeton, NJ: Princeton University Press, 1986.

Paxton, Robert O. *Vichy France: Old Guard and New Order, 1940–1944*. New York: Columbia University Press, 2001.

Pogue, Forrest C. *George C. Marshall: Ordeal and Hope*. New York: Viking Press, 1965

Porch, Douglas. *The Path to Victory: The Mediterranean Theater in World War II*. New York: Farrar, Straus and Giroux, 2004.

Preston, Paul. *Franco: A Biography*. New York: Basic Books, 1994.

Puzzo, Dante A. *Spain and the Great Powers, 1936 – 1941*. New York: Columbia University Press, 1962.

Reynolds, David. *From Munich to Pearl Harbor: Roosevelt's America and the Origins of the Second World War*, Chicago: Ivan R. Dee, 2001.

———. *In Command of History: Churchill Fighting and Writing the Second World War*. New York: Basic Books, 2005.

———. (ed.). *The Origins of the Cold War in Europe: International perspectives*. New Haven, CT: Yale University Press (1994).

Reitzel, William. *The Mediterranean: Its Role in America's Foreign Policy*. New York: Harcourt, Brace & Co., 1948.

Renda, Mary A. *Taking Haiti: Military Occupation and the Culture of U.S. Imperialism, 1915–1940*. Chapel Hill: University of North Carolina Press, 2001.

Roberts, Andrew. *Masters and Commanders: How Four Titans Won the War in the West, 1941–1945*. New York: Harper, 2009.

Roberts, Geoffrey. *Stalin's Wars: From World War to Cold War, 1939–1953*. New Haven, CT: Yale University Press, 2006.

Roberts, Walter R. *Tito, Mihailovic, and the Allies, 1941–1945*. New Brunswick, NJ: Rutgers University Press, 1973.

Robertson, Charles L. *When Roosevelt Planned to Govern France*. Amherst, MA: University of Massachusetts Press, 2011.

Rosenberg, Emily S. *Spreading the American Dream: American Economic and Cultural Expansion, 1890–1945*. New York: Hill & Wang, 1982.

Sallager, F. M. *Operation 'Strangle': A Case Study of Tactical Air Interdiction*. Santa Monica, CA: Rand Publications, 1972.

Sandars, C. T. *America's Overseas Garrisons: the Leasehold Empire*. New York: Oxford University Press, 2000.

Schmitz, David F. *The United States and Fascist Italy, 1922–1940*. Chapel Hill: University of North Carolina Press, 1988.

Sheehy, Edward J. *The U.S. Navy, the Mediterranean, and the Cold War, 1945–1947*. Westport, CT: Greenwood Press, 1992.

Smith, R. Harris. *OSS: The Secret History of America's First Central Intelligence Agency*. Berkley: University of California Press, 1972.

Spykman, Nicholas John. *America's Strategy in World Politics: the United States and the Balance of Power*. New York: Harcourt Brace, 1942.

———. *The Geography of the Peace*. New York: Harcourt Brace, 1944.

Stoff, Michael B. *Oil, War, and American Security*. New Haven, CT: Yale University Press, 1980.

Stoler, Mark. *Politics of the Second Front*. Westport, CT: Greenwood Press, 1977.

———. *George C. Marshall: Soldier-Statesman of the American Century*. New York: Twayne Publishers, 1987.

———. *Allies and Adversaries: The Joint Chiefs of Staff, the Grand Alliance, and U.S. Strategy in World War II*. Chapel Hill: University of North Carolina Press, 2000.

———. *Allies in War: Britain and America against the Axis Powers, 1940–1945*. London: Hodder Arnold, 2007.

Thorne, Christopher G. *Allies of a Kind: The United States, Britain, and the War against Japan, 1941–1945*. New York: Oxford University Press, 1978.

Tierney, Dominic. *FDR and the Spanish Civil War: Neutrality and Commitment in the Struggle that Divided America*. Durham, NC: Duke University Press, 2007.

Tomasevich, Jozo. *The Chetniks: War and Revolution in Yugoslavia, 1941–1945*. Stanford, CA: Stanford University Press, 1975.

Tomblin, Barbara Brooks. *With Utmost Spirit: Naval Operations in the Mediterranean, 1942–1945*. Lexington: University of Kentucky Press, 2004.

Tuchman, Barbara W. *Stilwell and the American Experience in China, 1911–45*. New York: Grove Press, 1970.

Tucker-Jones, Anthony. *Operation Dragoon: The Liberation of Southern France, 1944*. Barnsley, S. Yorkshire: Pen and Sword Books, 2009.

Vaughan, Hal. *FDR's 12 Apostles: The Spies Who Paved the Way for the Invasion of North Africa*. Guilford, CT: The Lyons Press, 2006.

Vigneras, Marcel. *Rearming the French*. Washington, DC: Center for Military History, United States Army, 1989.

Wall, Irwin. *The United States and the Making of Postwar France*. Cambridge: Cambridge University Press, 1991.

Waller, Douglas. *Wild Bill Donovan: The Spymaster Who Created the OSS and Modern American Espionage*. New York: Free Press, 2011.

Weigley, Russell. *The American Way of War*. New York: Macmillan, 1977.

Weinberg, Gerhard. *A World at Arms*. Cambridge: Cambridge University Press, 1994.

Wilmington, Martin W. *The Middle East Supply Center*. Albany: State University of New York Press, 1971.

Wilmot, Chester. *The Struggle for Europe*. New York: Harper, 1952.

Winfield, Betty Houchin. *FDR and the News Media*. Urbana: University of Illinois Press, 1990.

Winks, Robin W. *Cloak and Gown: Scholars in the Secret War, 1939–1961*. 2nd ed. New Haven, CT: Yale University Press, 1987.

Wittner, Lawrence S. *American Intervention in Greece, 1943–1949*. New York: Columbia University Press, 1982.

Woodbridge, George. *UNRRA: The History of the United Nations Relief and Rehabilitation Administration*. 3 vols. New York, Columbia University Press, 1950.

Woodward, Sir Llewellyn. *British Foreign Policy in the Second World War*. London: HMSO, 1962.

Woolner, David B. and Richard G. Kurial (eds.). *FDR, the Vatican, and the Roman Catholic Church in America, 1939 – 1945*. New York: Palgrave Macmillan, 2003.

Journal Articles and Book Chapters

Barker, Thomas M. "The Ljubljana Gap Strategy: Alternative to Anvil/Dragoon or Fantasy." *The Journal of Military History* 56, no. 1 (1992).

Borden Blair, Leon. "Amateurs in Diplomacy: The American Vice-Consuls in North Africa 1941–1943." *Historian* 35, no. 4 (1973).

Buchanan, Andrew. "A Friend Indeed? From Tobruk to El Alamein: The American Contribution to Victory in the Desert." *Diplomacy and Statecraft* 15, no. 2 (2004).

———. "'Good Morning Pupil!' American Representations of Italianness and the Occupation of Italy, 1943–1945." *Journal of Contemporary History* 43, no. 2 (2008).

———. "Washington's Silent Ally in World War II? United States Policy Towards Spain, 1939–1945." *Journal of Transatlantic Studies* 7, no. 2 (2009).

Byrnes, Mark. "Unfinished Business: The United States and Franco's Spain, 1944–1947." *Diplomacy and Statecraft* 11, no. 1 (2000).

Bywater, Hector C. "The Changing Balance of Forces in the Mediterranean." *International Affairs* 16, no. 3 (1937).

DeNovo, John A. "The Culbertson Economic Mission and Anglo-American Tensions in the Middle East, 1944–1945." *The Journal of American History* 63, no. 4 (1977).

de Santis, Hugh. "In Search of Yugoslavia: Anglo-American Policy and Policy-Making, 1943–45." *Journal of Contemporary History* 16, no. 3 (1981).

Eckes, Alfred E. Jr. "Open Door Expansionism Reconsidered: The World War II Experience." *The Journal of American History* 59, no. 4 (1973).

Ewer, Peter. "The British Campaign in Greece 1941: Assumptions about the Operational Art and Their Influence on Strategy," *The Journal of Military History* 76, no. 3 (July 2012).

Fenwick, C. G. "The International Status of Tangier," *The American Journal of International Law* 23, no. 1 (1929).

Fisher, Thomas R. "Allied Military Government in Italy." *Annals of the American Academy*, (January 1950).

Freeman, Major Paul J. "The Cinderella Front: Allied Special Air Operations in Yugoslavia During World War II," Research Dept., Air Command and Staff College (1997).

Funk, Arthur. "Negotiating the 'Deal with Darlan.'" *Journal of Contemporary History* 8, no. 2 (1973).

Godfried, Nathan. "Economic Development and Regionalism: United States Foreign Relations in the Middle East, 1942–5." *Journal of Contemporary History* 22 (1987).

Haglund, David G. "George C. Marshall and the Question of Military Aid to England, May–June 1940." *Journal of Contemporary History* 15, no. 4 (1980).

Halstead, Charles R. "Historians in Politics: Carlton J. H. Hayes as American Ambassador to Spain, 1942–45." *Journal of Contemporary History* 10, no. 3 (1975).

Harrison, Mark. "Resource Mobilization for World War II: The USA, UK, USSR, and Germany, 1938–1945." *The Economic History Review* n.s., 41 (1988).

Higgins, Trumbull. "The Anglo-American Historians' War in the Mediterranean, 1942–1945." *Military Affairs* 34, no. 3 (1970).

Kanet, Roger E. "The Soviet Union, the French Communist Party, and Africa, 1945–1960." *Survey* 22 (Winter 1976).

Kennedy, Emmet. "Carlton J. H. Hayes's Wartime Diplomacy: Making Spain a Haven from Hitler." *Diplomatic History* 36, no. 2 (April 2012).

Kramer, Paul A. "Power and Connection: Imperial Histories of the United States in the World." *American Historical Review* 116, no. 5 (December 2011).

Lasterle, Philippe. "Could Admiral Gensoul Have Averted the Tragedy of Mers el-Kébir?" *Journal of Military History* 67, no. 3 (2003).

Leighton, Richard M. "Overlord Revisited: An Interpretation of American Strategy in the European War, 1942–1944." *The American Historical Review* 68, no. 4 (July 1963).

Linsenmeyer, William S. "Italian Peace Feelers before the Fall of Mussolini." *Journal of Contemporary History* 16, no. 4 (1981).

Livermore, Seward W. "The American Navy as a Factor in World Politics, 1903–1913." *The American Historical Review* 63, no. 4 (1958).

Maza, Herbert. "Turkish-Arab Economic Relations with the United States." *World Affairs* 143, no. 3 (1979).

Pike, David Wingate. "Franco and the Axis Stigma." *Journal of Contemporary History* 17, no. 3 (1982).

Pons, Silvio. "Stalin, Togliatti, and the Origins of the Cold War in Europe," *Journal of Cold War Studies* 3, no. 2 (2001).

Resis, Albert. "Spheres of Influence in Soviet Wartime Diplomacy." *The Journal of Modern History* 53, no. 2 (1981).

Reynolds, David. "1940: Fulcrum of the Twentieth Century?" *International Affairs* 66, no. 2 (1990).

Roucek, Joseph S. "The Geopolitics of the Mediterranean. I." *American Journal of Economics and Sociology* 12, no. 4 (July 1953).

———. "The Geopolitics of the Mediterranean. II." *American Journal of Economics and Sociology* 13, no. 1 (Oct. 1953).

Sadkovich, James J. "Understanding Defeat: Reappraising Italy's Role in World War II," *Journal of Contemporary History* 24, no. 1 (1989).

Stoler, Mark. "From Continentalism to Globalism: General Stanley D. Embick, the Joint Strategic Survey Committee, and the Military View of American National policy during the Second World War." *Diplomatic History* 6 (Summer 1982).

Sullivan, Brian R. "Review of Raimondo Luraghi, *Eravamo partigiani: Ricordi del tempo di Guerra.*" *Journal of Military History* 69, no. 3 (2005).

Thomas, Martin. "Colonial Violence and the Distorted Logic of State Retribution: the Sétif Uprising of 1945," *Journal of Military History* 75 (January 2011).

Tierney, Dominic. "Franklin D. Roosevelt and Covert Aid to the Loyalists in the Spanish Civil War, 1936–39." *Journal of Contemporary History* 39, no. 3 (2004).

Vitalis, Robert. "The 'New Deal' in Egypt: The Rise of Anglo-American Commercial Competition in World War II and the Fall of Neocolonialism." *Diplomatic History* 20, no. 2 (1996).

Walker, David A. "OSS and Operation Torch." *Journal of Contemporary History* 22, no. 4 (1987).

White, Donald W. "The 'American Century' in World History." *Journal of World History* 3, no. 1, (1992).

Whittam, J. R. "Drawing the Line: Britain and the Emergence of the Trieste Question, January 1941–May 1945." *The English Historical Review* 106, no. 419 (1991).

Wilmington, Martin W. "The Middle East Supply Center: A Reappraisal." *Middle East Journal* 6, no. 2 (1952).

Wilt, Alan F. "The Significance of the Casablanca Decisions, January 1943." *Journal of Military History* 55, no. 4 (1991).

Wing Ray, Deborah. "The Takoradi Route: Roosevelt's Prewar Venture beyond the Western Hemisphere." *Journal of American History* 62, no.2 (1975).

Zahniser, Marvin R. "Rethinking the Significance of Disaster: The United States and the Fall of France in 1940." *The International History Review* 14, no. 2 (1992).

Zartman, William. "The Moroccan-American Base Negotiations." *Middle East Journal* 18 (1964).

Theses, Unpublished Manuscripts, and Web Sources

Brinkley, Alan. "The Idea of an American Century." www.lse.ac.uk/collections/LSEPublicLecturesAndEvents/pdf/20060207-Brinkley.pdf. (2006).

Hunter, Yvonne L. "Cold Columns: Anne O'Hare McCormick and the Origins of the Cold War in the *New York Times*, (1920–1954)," MA Thesis, Nipissing University, 2009.

Schmidt, Amy. "Croatia and the Western Allies." (n. p., n. d.) Published in Croatia, English transcript made available by author. (1995).

Steury, Donald P. "Tracking Nazi Gold: the OSS and Project *Safehaven*." Center for the Study of Intelligence, CIA website, https://www.cia.gov/library/center-for-the-study-of-intelligence/kent-csi/docs/v44i3a04p.html

Index

Lightning Source UK Ltd.
Milton Keynes UK
UKHW011230310719
347151UK00003B/612/P